D1083244

A Lion Looks Back

A Lion
Looks Back

Jim Craig

JOHN DONALD PUBLISHERS LTD
EDINBURGH

© Jim Craig 1998

All rights reserved.
No part of this publication may be reproduced
in any form or by any means without
the prior permission of the publishers
John Donald Publishers Limited,
73 Logie Green Road, Edinburgh, EH7 5HF.

ISBN 0 85976 501 6

British Library Cataloguing in Publication Data.

A catalogue record for this book is available
from the British Library.

Typesetting and origination by Brinnoven, Livingston.
Printed & bound in Great Britain by The Cromwell Press, Trowbridge, Wiltshire.

MBN Promotions

are delighted to support

A Lion Looks Back by Jim Craig

Should you wish to book

Jim Craig or a range of speakers from

the world of sport

contact

MIKE NEWLIN

at

MBN Promotions

MBN Promotions, Builder House, 2 Mayors Road, Altrincham, WA15 9RP

Telephone: 0161 926 9569   Fax 0161 929 1437

E-Mail: sales@mbnpromotions.co.uk   Internet: http://www.mbnpromotions.co.uk

Acknowledgements

I am indebted to many friends, former players and colleagues, including Malcolm MacDonald, Willie Miller, John McPhail, Paddy Crerand, and all the 'Lisbon Lions'. My thanks also to Mike Newlin of MBN Promotions and Jack Murray.

Jim Craig

Contents

Introduction

JUST WHEN I THOUGHT the writing was all finished, the phone rang. It was Donald Morrison, from John Donald Publishers Ltd. 'Jim', says he in very cheerful fashion, 'would you please write an introductory chapter, telling us why you wanted to do the book in the first place and that sort of thing?'.

Now that seems a reasonable question, particularly as several histories of Celtic FC have already been published. In fact, the question was posed fairly frequently during the spring and summer months of 1998 by my wife Elisabeth, who would rather belittle the issue by adding 'when you could be doing something useful like gardening or cleaning the windows!'.

The truth is that I have been fascinated by the story of Celtic Football Club ever since I was a kid. Teasing remarks by my paternal grandfather in Leith, very much a supporter of the other green and white team in Scotland, pushed me further towards Celtic and I voraciously read everything ever written about the club. Years later, of course, I was very privileged to pull on the hooped jersey at a very successful time in Celtic's history. My seven-year Parkhead career – from 1965 to 1972 – was a wonderful time in my footballing life, when I met and worked with many talented players and coaches. The result, in my case, was seven league championship medals, four for the Scottish Cup, three League cup and one European cup medal!

Frankly, this book should have been written many years ago but whenever I started, something else always arose to deflect my intention. That, perhaps, has been no bad thing, as it allowed me to continue my research into the club's past and clarify just what I wanted to achieve.

The various histories of Celtic FC already written and published have been well researched and presented, the authors fully deserving of our thanks for their efforts. However, they have all been written by either historians or supporters – sometimes both in the same person – with the photographs and, where provided, the results, inserted at set areas of the book.

I set out to tell Celtic's story in chronological order, incorporating the results on a year by year basis, having any photographs matching the specific year or month of their relevance. In each season, I have provided a performance analysis based on the league tables plus a review of the Scottish and, later, League Cup campaigns. The Glasgow and Charity Cup results are also included, together with reports of the various successful finals.

Throughout the book I have tried to assess the incidents, personnel and tactics from a footballer's viewpoint. The basis of any football club is obviously the game itself but this does not take place in a soulless environment.

Players, managers, coaches and fans all play a specific role which, throughout the years at Celtic Park, has embraced moments of inspiration, invention, cooperation, disappointment, tragedy, humour and triumph.

Even its conception was unusual, if not unique. Some hard-working people of Irish extraction in the East End of Glasgow were so moved by the plight of their poor fellow citizens that they organised various events to raise money for them, and particularly for their children. In time, they realised that the new football matches were becoming a popular spectator sport, so they started to organise those and charge for admission.

Then a team from Edinburgh, also founded and supported by Irish immigrants, won the Scottish Cup. The Irish in Glasgow hosted a dinner that night to honour the winners and the latter's secretary, in his speech of thanks, suggested that the Glasgow folk start up a similar team of their own.

This idea gained credence very quickly and nine months later, a team was born, to be named Celtic. The men involved began to build a new stadium, which was ready in a further seven months. Within the following three months, players arrived from near and far and the club made its debut in the Scottish Cup the following season. Who could fail to be stimulated by a story like that?

In terms of success on the field, Celtic's history can be roughly summed up as follows. Thirty years of success (1889–1919) followed by 20 years of disappointment (1920–1940); then 25 years of drought (1940–1965) before the years of plenty (1965–). Even in the poorish times, though, Celtic could rise to the occasion. The Scottish Cup triumphs regularly made up for the disappointments in the league, while, in the 'one-off' trophies, the success rate was high e.g. Exhibition Cup, St Mungo Cup, Victory in Europe Cup and the Coronation Cup. Almost from its earliest days, Celtic's name became synonymous with football success. In the period up to the turn of the century, four League Championships and three Scottish Cups was a better record than any other team in the country. Obviously, the presence of good players makes such an achievement possible but other facets of the club deserve praise as well.

Once the stadium was built, in 1888, the committee men appointed to the task had only three short months to assemble a team. That they did this effectively, was beyond dispute, although the methods used, almost certainly the promise of financial rewards, were quite against the amateur rules then in operation.

Many personalities worked hard to establish Celtic at this period but several names stand out. Brother Walfrid was an early influence, not only in forming the club but in monitoring its charitable aims. After he was posted to London in 1892, John Glass tried to continue his work, but gradually men came in who wished to see a more business-like approach. These were led by John H. McLaughlin, appointed Celtic's first Chairman of the Board in 1897, the same year Willie Maley was appointed secretary/manager, a post he was to hold for the next 43 years.

Even in the early successful years, however, various problems surfaced. In 1892, an avaricious landlord prompted a move to a new ground. Coming only four years after the voluntary workforce had helped to build the first Celtic Park, another move was probably unwanted. However, in the long run, it proved the right decision. A fine stadium was eventually completed, quite suitable to host internationals in the 1890s and early 1900s. From then on, it enjoyed a chequered career.

In 1897, it hosted the World Cycling Championships. In 1904, fire destroyed the stand and damaged the pavilion on the Janefield St. side. The latter was totally destroyed by another fire in 1929, the same year a new South Stand replaced the Grant Stand.

Events outside football have occasionally been staged at Celtic Park. An exhibition baseball match between teams representing the US Forces took place in 1918; Scotland met Ireland at hurling in 1913; in 1937, Benny Lynch was beaten by Ulsterman Jim Warnock over 15 rounds in a non title bout; a speedway meeting drew a crowd of 5'000 in 1918; several open air masses were celebrated at different times; the stadium hosted the opening ceremony of the Special Olympics in 1990 ; and the following year, in the month of June, while Rod Stewart and Status Quo attracted 40,000 in one night, the American evangelist Billy Graham brought in 150,000 over five nights. Now, completely rebuilt, it hosts the largest weekly attendance of any club in Britain.

Two other notable landmarks in the first decade occurred in 1897, first in January when Celtic suffered probably their most surprising defeat in any competition, and then in December when the first Board of Directors was appointed. All in all, it had been an enterprising and successful first decade.

Not surprisingly, it was followed by something of a slump as Willie Maley created and moulded a new team. After a historic Scottish Cup win in 1904, however, when Jimmy Quinn scored the first final hat-trick, this fine side took the League Championship for the following six years, even though a fairly small pool of players was involved.

More than any other achievement, it was this run of success which stamped Celtic's name, not only on the fans in Britain, but on the Continent as well. The club made its first visit there in 1904 and this soon became a fairly regular event.

Two other Scottish Cup wins accompanied this six year run, the one in 1906–07 making Celtic the first Scottish team to achieve the 'Double' of League and Cup. This feat was repeated the following year, but a third consecutive 'double' was prevented when the cup was withheld in 1909 after the Hampden Riot. In the history of the club, only 11 such momentous seasons have occurred, with yours truly fortunate enough to play a part in four, 1966–67, 1968–69, 1970–71 and 1971–72.

By the early 1900s, fans were becoming more interested in the cult of the 'star' than ever before. From its earliest days, Celtic had its share of those, like the extrovert full-back Dan Doyle, the future 'Father of Czech football' Johnny Madden or the prolific goalscorer Sandy 'Duke' McMahon, at 6ft 1in. and 12 stone 7lbs, almost a giant among the smallish forwards of the day.

The six-in-a-row team of 1905-10 was always recognised as an effective unit, but even then, the 'Iron man' Jimmy Quinn at centre forward and 'Napoleon', Jimmy McMenemy at inside-right, had star quality.

As the league form dipped, two successive Scottish Cup successes boosted the support, before a new team went on a four-in-a-row sequence through the war years, including Celtic's third league and cup 'double' in 1913–14. The 'Mighty Atom', Patsy Gallagher kept all the sports correspondents busy at this period thinking of new adjectives to describe his dazzling performances.

The final League Championship of the decade – 1918–19 – was the climax to an astonishing first 31 years during which, if we include the two local competitions, the Glasgow and Charity Cups as well as the League Cup, there were only three trophyless seasons (1896–97; 1901–02; 1902–03) to disappoint the support. It was a heady time; unfortunately, one not destined to last.

The following decade was disappointing, not just for the players but for the fans as well. They were there for match after match and knew that the squad was as good as any in the country. Unfortunately, the end products – trophies – were few and far between. The twenties may have been roaring in many areas but Parkhead was not one of them.

I was unable to find any insider from that era to ask the obvious question. Was the Celtic team of the 1920s a non-achieving outfit or had the opposition raised their game? From my own research, I would suggest one-third the former, two-thirds the latter. Certainly, Celtic were slow to alter their style like most other teams after the offside law change in 1925. In winning their 17th championship that year, the defence conceded only 40 goals in 38 matches. That had risen the following season to 55. This was fairly symptomatic of the roller-coaster run during these years. Yet, all through the decade, the stars continued to shine. The incomparable Patsy Gallagher, although now a veteran, still showed his class; Tommy McInally, wayward and awkward, but with an excellent goal scoring rate; and the wonderful

McGrory, whose goal-a-game tally made him the subject of a tranfer bid by Arsenal.

As the club entered the equally disappointing 1930s, he was still scoring freely, in spite of a complete change of personnel around him. Once again, in terms of collecting trophies, Celtic usually failed to deliver. As in the previous decade, two league championships and three Scottish cups might have appeased the fans of many other teams, but not those at Celtic Park. They were casting envious glances over to Ibrox where Rangers had had a renaissance since the war and were now firmly in the driving seat.

Fortunately, I was able to interview that fine player and good Celtic servant Malcolm MacDonald – regarded by many judges as among the finest pure footballers ever to pull on the hooped jersey – about this period. Malky signed in 1932 and was at Parkhead for almost 13 years. His interview, which I just run in full, gives us a fascinating insight into the personalities of the 1930s, from the manager Willie Maley to the Exhibition Cup team of 1938 and then into the war years. What comes across quite clearly is that the players themselves seemed to be quite well aware of the problems present yet little was done to correct them. For instance, at a time when the Celtic defence was leaking badly, it is surprising to discover that a pure two-footed footballer like Malcolm MacDonald was often played at centre half! Most clubs by that time had an out and out stopper in that position.

The 1930s, of course, had begun well for Celtic. A Scottish Cup victory over a fine Motherwell team was followed by the first ever tour of North America. Unfortunately, disaster soon struck. John Thomson's death at Ibrox in September 1931 cast a pall over the activities of the whole club and it was quickly followed by the premature retirement and death from TB of Peter Scarff. We will never know the psychological damage which these tragedies caused in the minds of the Celtic players, but surely it was considerable.

Malcolm MacDonald was still present for one of the major changes in Celtic's history, when Willie Maley, albeit reluctantly, gave up (or was he pushed?) the reins in 1940, to be replaced by Jimmy McStay. However, as can be gleaned from Malcolm's interview this made little difference behind the scenes. Indeed, this may have been the moment when the Board decided to have a more positive input into team selection, an accusation regularly held against the Directorate throughout the tenures of Jimmy McStay and his successor, Jimmy McGrory.

The War Years were abysmal for the Celtic fans. Rangers were more dominant in those six years than at any other period of Scottish football history. The reasons for this are quite clear and are covered in the relevant chapter, as well as the latter half of Malcolm MacDonald's interview.

For a further viewpoint, I have included a statement from another major Celtic star of the time. Willie Miller joined Celtic from Maryhill Harp in

May 1942 and made the goalkeeping berth his own the following season. The newspaper reports of the time highlight his value to the club. Behind a poor defence, he rescued Celtic time and again, often at great expense to his own body, particularly around the head, where he reckons he must have had around 100 stiches put in. Willie was present when Jimmy McStay lost his job, in rather distasteful circumstances, to be replaced by Jimmy McGrory. The goalscoring hero's return was greeted with joy by the fans, but they were soon to be disillusioned, as little improvement was forthcoming, the rumours about the influence of the Board re-surfacing – and continuing – for the next 20 years! The post-war years of the late 1940s were merely a continuation of the disappointments during the war. The league form was uncertain, there were some early exits in the Scottish Cup, while in four successive seasons, Celtic failed to qualify from its section in the new league cup competition. The worst ever league season occurred in 1947–48, when Celtic travelled to Dundee, knowing a win might be required to avoid relegation. In the end, they finished 12th in a 16-team division. Ironically, they also reached the semi-final stage of the Scottish Cup that season, going out to Morton after extra time.

One man present through all those years – and into the mid 1950s – was John McPhail. John was only 17 when he arrived at Celtic Park in 1941 and soon made the first team, playing anywhere in the half-back or forward line. His interview is a revealing insight into the Parkhead of this period. Among the topics covered are the quality of the players present; who picked the team?; the tactics used; his relationships with the players at Ibrox and the 1951 Scottish Cup success.

In addition, he explains how he was involved in bringing to Celtic another of those magical names in their history – Charlie Tully. The man from Northern Ireland was a shining light at a depressing time in the Celtic story and the tales of his exploits, as much off the field as on it, have persisted to this day.

The cup win of 1951 was a great start to a new decade, the first victory in this competition since 1937. In a fascinating re-run of the scenario of twenty years before, the beaten finalists were Motherwell and the success was followed by a tour of North America. Ninth and 8th places in the league in consecutive seasons, however, were clear indications that problems were still around, yet, within a further year, Celtic not only became Champions of Britain by winning the Coronation Cup but went on to do the league/cup 'double' of 1953–54, the 4th in the club's history.

The arrival of Jock Stein at Parkhead in December 1951 was much unheralded but after a surprising elevation to the first team, he was the anchor at centre half in these competitions, helping to solidify a hitherto leaking defence. I interviewed him several times on my own behalf during the 70s and early 80s and have used these insights during both the chapter on the Coronation Cup and the section devoted entirely to Jock Stein.

After this successful season of 1953–54 the remainder of the 1950s was a disappointing period for players and supporters. Never quite consistent enough to challenge for the league title, they looked to the cups for success and even here, second or third best was the usual story. There were two exceptions, of course, in 1956 and 1957, when the League Cup was picked up, the first victory a rather stuttering win after a replay against Partick Thistle, the second the result of a wonderful display against Rangers, the 7-1 thrashing still kept alive in song, verse and story.

These were two good moments, though, in a deeply unsatisfying period. Even in these two years of league cup success, the league placings of 5th and 3rd were no more than respectable. In fact, during the following seven years, two other 3rd places were the best Celtic achieved, with two 9th place finishes in there as well. Rangers quickly recovered from that League Cup humiliation and became a fine, dominant side, whose only flaw was an under achievement in Europe. Along the way, they gave Celtic some serious wounds, like the 4-1 defeat in the Scottish Cup semi-final replay in 1960, the 3-0 reverse in the replayed Final of 1963 or the 2-0 loss in the quarter-final of 1964. Perhaps even more disconcerting were the defeats by the so-called 'provincial' teams. In the Scottish Cup, for instance, 0-4 to St Mirren (SF 1959), 0-2 to Dunfermline (Final 1961) and 1-3 to St Mirren again (SF 1962).

My fourth interviewee was at Celtic Park from 1957–63. Pat Crerand has always worn his Celtic heart on his sleeve and was no less devoted when I spoke to him in the summer of 1998. He gives a most illuminating insight into the behind-the-scenes activities of the time, explains the reasons for his leaving the club and names the man whom Manchester Utd might have signed in preference to him.

As the 1960s began, the first change to the strip since 1903 occurred, when numbers were put on the shorts. This period also saw the advent of European competition, firstly through the Anglo-Franco Scottish Friendship Cup in 1960–61, in which Celtic played poorly against Sedan of France and then the Fair Cities Cup the following season, when Valencia proved too strong over two legs.

Celtic seemed to learn quickly though, because one year later, in the Cup Winners Cup, they had an unbelievable run, disposing of Basle, Dinamo Zagreb and Slovan Bratislava before dreadful naivete, in the second leg of the semi-final against MTK Budapest lost their 3-goal lead from the home tie.

Shortly after this point, this history becomes more autobiographical as I joined Celtic in 1965. From that date on, I give a fairly brief account of my career there, explore the highs and lows, attempt to give an insight into the dressing room atmosphere and assess both the back room staff and my fellow players.

This was also the beginning of a remarkably successful period for Celtic FC. Many of the factors involved in the make-up of a winning team were already in place but there is no doubt in my mind that without Jock Stein, we would never have achieved our potential.

He was the driving force behind our success, the human catalyst who fused the various personalities, the perfectionist who raised our standards. In many ways, the chapter which I devoted to him was the most difficult to write in the whole book. It was hard to portray in words the charisma, his impatience, his laughter, his confidence, his ruthlessness and his single-mindedness.

The final chapter is about Lisbon. The winning of the European Cup in 1967 was, without doubt, the most definitive achievement of any Celtic team in the entire history of the club. Granted, some memorable moments have occurred in these 100 odd years, not only in domestic competition but British contests like the Exhibition or Coronation Cup. The win in Lisbon, though, surpassed all these. Not only was it a triumph for Scottish and British football over the rest of Europe but it enhanced the image of soccer by the style of the performance. For a few years, the Catenaccio system of Inter-Milan was swept away and teams like Manchester United, Ajax, Bayern Munich, Liverpool, Nottingham Forest and Aston Villa combined success with entertainment in this competition. This period has been covered in many biographies and autobiographies already, so I have refrained from a detailed analysis. I have merely covered what I remember most about the day and my feelings at that time. The reader may be surprised at my decision to conclude this history of the club in 1967 but this was quite deliberate.

Any classic story should have a good beginning, a strong middle and an innovative ending. The first two factors are certainly present in the Celtic story, so the obvious choice for the finale was 25 May 1967. That's not to say, if asked, I would not want to bring the story through to the present day. But that's for another time – and a very different type of tale?

From a footballing point of view, the day when Celtic beat Inter-Milan was undoubtedly the most important day in my career. However, the more perceptive reader may notice that I finish this story on the day after Lisbon, which turned out to be the best day of my life!

Jim Craig

CHAPTER ONE

A Dream Comes True

'You know, Jimmy, without the old Hibees there would never have been a Celtic!' I often heard those words when I was a boy. In fact, if I close my eyes, I can quickly conjure up a picture of my paternal grandfather saying them in his flat at the bottom of Great Junction Street in Leith. Frankly, as a Celtic-daft laddie from Glasgow, I did not want to know about Hibs, especially at that period of the early fifties, when they always seemed to beat my team. So, like most young people when confronted by the wisdom of their elders, I treated Pop Craig's utterances with a large pinch of salt. Unfortunately, years later, when I began to review the history of Scottish football and realised that my grandfather was quite correct, he had passed on and I was unable to express my apologies for doubting him!

THE STORY OF the founding and development of Celtic Football Club has an almost dream-like quality about it. It is a fascinating tale, and all those involved, not only the management and players, but also the unsung heroes behind the scenes, deserve the utmost praise. However, to get the full extent of their achievement, we must consider the club's story as part of the overall history of Scottish football. Throughout the 1870s and 1880s, teams had been forming throughout the Central Belt, in response to the public demand for 'entertainment'. By that time, ordinary working men 'knocked off' about one o'clock on a Saturday and were so fascinated by this novel game of soccer that they were prepared to pay for the privilege of watching these teams play.

YEARS OF TEAM'S FORMATION

Queen's Park	1867	Kilmarnock	1869
1870s		**1880s**	
Airdrie	1878	Albion Rovers	1882
Arbroath	1878	Alloa	1883
Clyde	1878	Berwick	1881
Dumbarton	1872	Cowdenbeath	1881
Falkirk	1876	Dunfermline	1885
Hamilton	1875	East Stirlingshire	1881
Hearts	1874	Forfar	1884
Hibernian	1875	Motherwell	1886
Montrose	1879	Raith Rovers	1883
Morton	1874	St Johnstone	1884
Partick Thistle	1876	Stenhousemuir	1884
Rangers	1873		
St Mirren	1876		
Stranraer	1870		

The Scottish Cup had begun in 1873, with 16 entries. By 1887, an early pivotal year for Scottish football, the number of contesting teams had risen to 141. For the first 13 years of the Scottish Cup, it had become the preserve of teams from the West of Scotland, of which Queen's Park and Vale of Leven were the most prominent.

SCOTTISH CUP FINALS

YEAR	FINALISTS		ATTENDANCE
1874	Queen's Park 2	Clydesdale 0	2,500
1875	Queen's Park 3	Renton 0	7,000
1876	Queen's Park 2	Third Lanark 0	6,000 after 1-1 draw
1877	Vale of Leven 3	Rangers 2	12,000 after two 1-1 draws
1878	Vale of Leven 1	Third Lanark 0	5,000
1879	Vale of Leven 1	Rangers 1	9,000 Rangers refused replay
1880	Queen's Park 3	Thornliebank 0	4,000
1881	Queen's Park 3	Dumbarton 1	10,000
1882	Queen's Park 4	Dumbarton 1	14,000 after 2-2 draw
1883	Dumbarton 2	Vale of Leven 1	12,000 after 2-2 draw
1884	Queen's Park	w.o. Vale of Leven	
1885	Renton 3	Vale of Leven 1	5,500
1886	Queen's Park 3	Renton 1	7,000

Attendances at finals varied, depending on the teams involved. The local derbies of 1874 (Queen's Park *v.* Clydesdale), 1880 (Queen's Park *v.* Thornliebank) and 1885 (Renton *v.* Vale of Leven) were poorly attended, whereas those involving Dumbarton, Third Lanark and Rangers always attracted good crowds.

Then in 1887, a new name appeared in the final line-up. Hibernian had been founded in 1875 by Canon Edward Hannan of St Patrick's in the Cowgate in Edinburgh and Michael Whelehan of the CYMS attached to that parish. This part of Edinburgh was called Little Ireland, where many immigrants had arrived after the Irish Rebellion of 1798 to join the 1,000 Scots Catholics already there. By 1875, this figure had risen to over 40,000 so there was plenty of support for the new team. In spite of initial difficulties with both the Edinburgh Association and the Scottish Football Association over its 'Irishness', Hibs persevered and their fine play brought them semi-final places in the Scottish Cup in 1884, 1885 and 1886. Their moment of glory came the following year when, on 12 February 1887 (note the early date for the finale of the season at that time), Hibernian overcame Dumbarton by 2 goals to 1 in front of a crowd estimated at between 12,000 and 15,000 to take the cup east for the first time.

However, the team, plus its directors and officials, did not go straight back to Edinburgh. Their many Irish supporters in the west had arranged for them to attend a celebratory dinner in St Mary's Hall in the Calton district of Glasgow, where their admirers fussed over the victorious players

Note the early date for the final match of the season and the late starting time, which would have meant a very dark finish to the contest. Clocks going forward and back only began during the First World War.

and joined in their festivities. During the evening, the Hibs Secretary John McFadden, full of the joys of victory and probably pumped up with the Irishness and Catholicity of the occasion, made a suggestion that the football-minded people present should perhaps form a similar club for the Irish Catholics of the west.

Fortunately, among the euphoria, there were several men in the crowd that night who realised that such a venture might well pay off. Between them, Dr John Conway, a local GP, John Glass, a local builder and Brother Walfrid, the headmaster of St Andrew's school in the city centre, had often discussed the plight of the less fortunate members of the Irish community in Glasgow, a number increasing constantly.

Brother Walfrid was an amazing character. As well as a hard working headmaster, he was also Brother Superior of the Marist Teaching Order in Glasgow, yet he seemed to have access to all levels of the newly-formed football teams all over Scotland, regularly using them to play matches for charity.

MATCHES ORGANISED BY BROTHER WALFRID		
1886	St Peter's (Partick) Select *v.* Hibs	
	Glengarry Park, Bridgeton	1,000 present
April 1887	Clyde *v.* Dundee Harp	
	Barrowfield Park	4,000 present
May 1887	East End Charity Cup	
	Renton *v.* Hibs	
	Barrowfield Park	12,000 present

He must have been particularly pleased by the attendance at the Renton-Hibs match, the holders of the Glasgow Charity Cup against the Scottish Cup holders. The teams competed for a 'one-off' trophy, the East End Charity Cup, and, as the match ended in a draw, a replay was organised in August which Renton won comfortably in front of another large crowd. By the autumn of 1887, the three men, plus many other Catholics in the East

End, were convinced that John McFadden's suggestion could be implemented and that a club similar to Hibs in that area would be very successful. After the deduction of the necessary expenses in running such a team, any remaining monies could be directed towards the East End Conferences of the St Vincent De Paul Society and thus the Poor Children's Dinner Tables in the parishes of St Mary's, St Michael's and the Sacred Heart.

So, the meeting to formally constitute the new club was held in St Mary's Hall in East Rose Street on Sunday 6 November 1887, chaired by John Glass. There was some discussion concerning the name of the new club, Glasgow Hibernian being much favoured, but at the specific behest of Brother Walfrid, it was named Celtic Football Club. Unlike many other clubs of Irish extraction formed at this time which complained that the Press ignored their fixtures and activities, Celtic's beginnings were noted in a popular journal of the time, the *Scottish Umpire*.

We learn that the efforts which have lately been made to organise in Glasgow a first-class Catholic football club, have been successfully consummated by the formation of the "Glasgow Celtic Football and Athletic Club," under influential auspices. They have secured a six-acre ground in the east-end, which they mean to put in fine order. We wish the "Celts" all success.

Almost immediately, a circular was put out, explaining the aims and objectives of the new club. His Grace the Archbishop of Glasgow, Archbishop Eyre agreed to be patron and his name topped a fairly substantial list of subscribers:

His Grace the Archbishop	20 shillings
The Very Rev. Canon Carmichael	20 shillings
The Rev. F.J. Hughes	20 shillings
Rev. A. Bayaert	20 shillings
Rev. A. Vanderhyde	20 shillings

Archbishop Eyre had family links with the Continent so note the foreign influence in the subscription list with Father Arthur Bayaert from Belgium and Father Adrian Vanderhyde from Holland. From that first meeting in St Mary's Hall, everything seemed to slide into place, what I called the 'dream-like' quality of Celtic's development, although obviously much work was done behind the scenes. The committee which had been formed to oversee the rise of the club was certainly one of vision. While the other half of the Old Firm led an early nomadic existence to find a suitable playing surface, from Glasgow Green to Burnbank on Great Western Road to Kinning Park, the Celtic committee decided to build a new ground from scratch. Half-a-dozen acres of ground running east of Janefield Cemetery were secured on 13 November 1887 for an annual rental of £50, and a whole host of unskilled helpers assisted a handful of skilled craftsmen to prepare it.

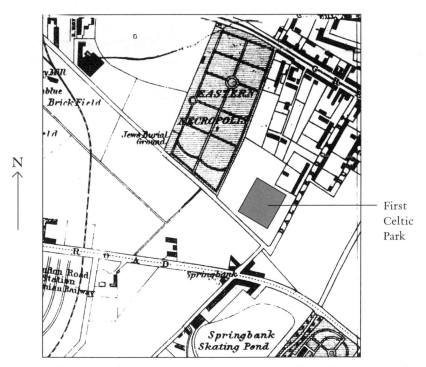

The site chosen for the first Celtic Park, just to the east of the Eastern Necropolis. Entrance was from Dalmarnock Road.

Work progressed astonishingly quickly and within 6 months a level pitch was ready. Its dimensions of 110 yards x 66 yards were in line with the new regulations recently laid down by the International Board; there was a track surrounding the pitch intended for cycling events and beyond that, on the east side there was an open air stand which held nearly 1,000 people. Under the stand was the pavilion, consisting of a committee room and two dressing rooms with baths and toilet facilities. There were nine gates for spectators, for whom entrance was sixpence (2½p), with ladies, and later, soldiers in uniform allowed free admittance.

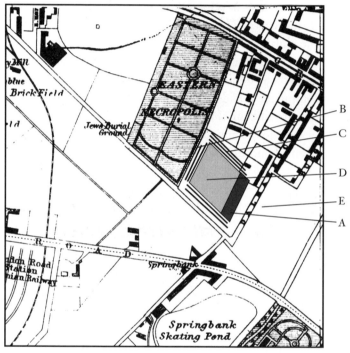

This is my impression of what the first Celtic Park would have looked like: A – open air stand; B – wall of the cemetary which many spectators sat on to watch the play; C – rough, earthen 'terracing' around the other three sides; D – the pitch; E – entrance gates.

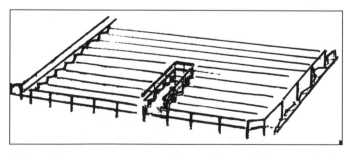

The inside of the stand as I picture it. It was very basic, so the tunnel-like entrance for the players may be too fanciful.

Tuesday 8 May 1888 was an important day in the history of Glasgow. For most citizens, the main event was the opening of the First Glasgow International Exhibition, held over 60 acres at Kelvingrove Park. The Prince and Princess of Wales, the future Edward VII and his Queen, did the honour and admission was gained by the payment of 1 shilling.

The front page of the programme for the International Exhibition of 1888, which ran from 8 May until 10 November. It attracted an attendance of 5,748,379 and made a profit of £41,700.

For Glasgow's Irish Community, though, particularly in the East End, the bigger event was the first match on Celtic's new ground when Hibs and Cowlairs fought out a 0-0 draw, in front of 3,000 spectators.

Opening of Celtic Football and Athletic Park,
Dalmarnock Street, Parkhead.
Grand Opening Match—Exhibition Day, May 8

HIBERNIANS
versus
COWLAIRS

Kick-off at 6 p.m. prompt.   Admission 6d., Ladies Free.
Grand Stand Sixpence extra each person.
The Park is two minutes' walk from the Parkhead and
London Road Tramcar and Railway Stations.

This advert from Scottish Umpire *is very informative and shows iniative on the part of the committee. Note that the day of the match was designated 'Exhibition Day' for reasons explained above.*

Almost three weeks later, Celtic took the field for the first time, in shirts gifted by a Bridgeton sports outfitter, Penman Brothers, consisting of a white shirt with a green collar and a Celtic cross in red on the breast. The team for this first match was very much a scratch eleven, players from various sides receiving an invitation to take part. Rangers, perhaps apprehensive about all the publicity regarding the new club and its ground, put out their second eleven – the Swifts – which was duly dispatched by five goals to two. If the result was good, the overall achievement was even better. For a club founded on 6 November 1887 to play its first match in a newly-built stadium on 28 May 1888 was little short of miraculous.

> It would appear as if the newly-formed Glasgow club, the Celtic F.C., has a bright future before it. At any rate, if the committee can place the same eleven in the field as opposed the Rangers last Monday evening, or an equally strong one, the Celtic will not lack for patronage and support. A good team is essential to success, and this fact the committee have not lost sight of. It will be interesting to many of our readers to know the composition of the team which represented the new organisation in its first club match. Here it is :—Goal, Dolon (Drumpellier) ; backs, Pearson (Carfin Shamrock) and M'Lachlan (Whitefield) ; half-backs, Maley (3rd Lanark), Kelly (Renton), and Murray (Cambuslang Hibs.) ; forwards, M'Callum (Renton), Maley (3rd Lanark), Madden (Dumbarton), Dunbar (Hibs.), and Gorevin (Whitefield)—a pretty good eleven. The Rangers were without D. Gow, J. R. Gow, Hotson, Peacock, Allan, and Aird ; but had Suter (Partick Thistle) doing duty—the remainder being drawn from the Swifts. The match was a capital one, fast and friendly—the home organisation playing with a combination which could scarcely have been expected for an opening display. The Celtic retired victors by 5 goals to 2—a result which must be indeed gratifying to their supporters. After the match, over 70 gentlemen sat down to supper in the Hall, East Rose Street, where a pleasant evening was spent. Dr. Conway occupied the chair, and on the platform were also Messrs. M'Fadden (Hibs.), M'Culloch (Our Boys), Grant (Rangers), and the Rev. Brother Walfrid. The latter gentleman, who took a deep interest in the origin of the club, has every reason to flatter himself as to the success of the Celtic. Long may it flourish in our midst.

A review of Celtic's first match and subsequent events, written in the chatty prose of the period. Of the team named, the two Maleys, Kelly, McCallum, Madden and Dunbar later joined up at Celtic Park.

Unfortunately, it must be stated that the football of those days bore little relation to that of today in all aspects: pitches and their markings, rules and regulations, equipment for players and tactics.

Pitches and their Markings

By 1888, the International Board, which had been founded to oversee the laws of the game in 1886 and consisted of one member from each of the Home Countries, had begun to standardise the field of play. Pitch markings were very basic as shown; the goal posts now had a bar across the top but the dimensions of the playing area were still very large compared to today. A maximum length of 200 yards, minimum 100 yards; a maximum width of 100 yards, minimum 50 yards.

Fig 1.1. By 1875, a bar had replaced tape across the goalposts. These basic outlines continued until the early 1890.

By the late 1890s more markings had been added and the dimensions reduced as shown in Fig 1.2. There were two concentric six yard circles around the goal, a twelve yard line from which the penalty kick, introduced in 1891, was taken, and an optional 18 yard line. The length and width of

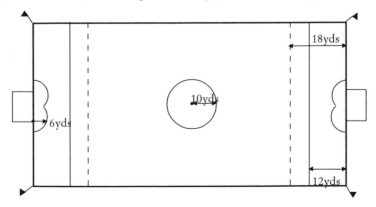

Fig 1.2. These changes followed the introduction of the penalty kick in 1891.

the pitch were reduced to those of today. Matches were now to last 90 minutes, unless otherwise mutually agreed, while goalkeepers, who were distinguished from their team mates by a cap, could handle the ball only in their own half of the field. In the early days, officialdom consisted of one umpire appointed to each side (decisions given by waving a white handkerchief) and a neutral referee called on in cases of dispute. By 1891, a neutral referee was in charge assisted by two linesmen.

Tactics

Tactics were primitive but improving. In the early days, everybody wanted to get hold of the ball and rush or dribble it towards the opposing goal, so systems reflected this.

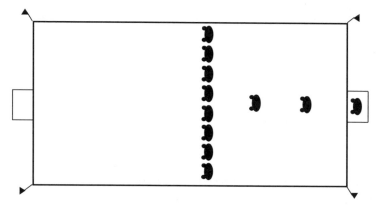

Fig 1.3. One goalkeeper, one full-back, one half-back with eight forwards. This would have been the way football was played in the 1860s and early 1870s.

By the late 1870s Queen's Park had developed a style of play which became known as the Scottish game. In contrast to the English teams of the time which were very reliant on the dribble, Queen's Park developed a passing

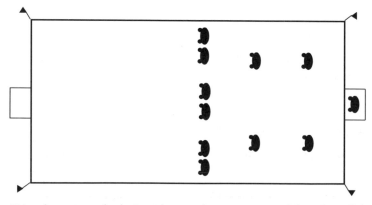

Fig 1.4. Using the passing style, the Scottish national team won nine and drew three of the first 14 matches against England.

game and to do this, became a more balanced formation with two full backs, two half backs and six forwards.

This meant that triangles of movement were easily produced, with space available for the wingers to come in towards goal.

Not to be out done, the great Preston North End team of the 1880s developed this even further, deciding on a 2-3-5 system.

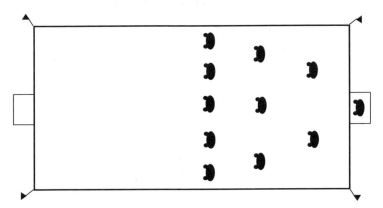

Fig 1.5. This system, with slight variations, lasted until the late 1920s, although a few teams, notably Uruguay, still used it until the early 1950s.

This was a fairly rigid system, the wingers for instance seldom leaving the touch line. The most important player was the centre half who was really an attacking player, seldom involved in defence. This would be the style adopted by Celtic's early teams. Cynics would already note that all these changes have been towards stopping the opposition and reducing the number of attackers, a feature followed right through the following century.

The Players

The player's equipment was fairly substantial. Strips would have been heavy, boots were over-the-ankle for protection and shin guards were worn over the stockings.

The game itself, even under the guidance of the new neutral referees would have been tough. Hacking and tripping had only been banned some 10 years before and a few enthusiasts were still around. Goalkeepers in particular received little protection and few went through a career at this time without serious injury.

In 1887, the SFA ordered that the following notice be posted in all grounds:

> Rough play, as specified in Rule 10, is tripping, ducking, hacking, jumping at a player, pushing and charging.

Various incidents in the matches of both this season and the one before obviously annoyed those in charge. It is easy to imagine the amusement of many players when they read this particular missive.

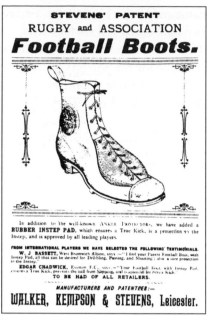

Note the knockerbocker-style shorts of thoses early days, and the efforts by this company to make 'their' boot slightly different, with padding over the ankle-bone and instep.

So, in the mid summer of 1888, Celtic Football Club had a fine stadium and a healthy core of supporters. Now to find the players.

In the December of the previous year, only days after the inaugural meeting, three Celtic representatives including Brother Walfrid, had travelled to the Maley home in Cathcart to speak to Tom Maley, a young man training to be a teacher and a noted player who had turned out for Hibs, Third Lanark and Partick Thistle. He was not at home but brother Willie was, and the Celtic men were so impressed by his views that he was invited along to a meeting with the Club's founders. From that point on, the fairytale developed. Soon the Maley brothers formed the backbone of the team; within six months, thanks to Tom, several players had defected from Hibs to the new club; and, in the biggest capture of them all, they were joined by attacking centre-half James Kelly from Renton.

It is puzzling to consider, though, why experienced players should want to come to a brand new club with no guarantee of success. After all, this was ostensibly the age of the amateur, the only payments allowed being money paid for loss of wages in their regular work when playing football or training. The obvious conclusion, therefore, is that Celtic paid their players long before professionalism was legalised in Scotland in 1895. This was why a joiner like James Kelly was able to buy a public house costing £650; or why one of the first Celtic heroes, full-back Dan Doyle, should forsake professional Everton for amateur Celtic. Whatever the reason, a strong team

MATCHES PLAYED IN CELTIC'S FIRST SEASON

1888		OPPONENTS		VENUE	SCORE
August	1	Abercorn	Exhibition Cup	Exhibition	1-1
	4	Hibs		Home	3-2
	11	Airdrie		Away	6-0
	18	Clyde		Away	5-1
	21	Dumbarton	Exhibition Cup	Exhibition	3-1
	22	Third Lanark		Away	3-4
	23	Abercorn		Away	4-2
	27	Northern		Away	3-0
	29	Partick Thistle	Exhibition Cup	Exhibition	1-0
September	1	Shettleston	Scottish Cup	Home	5-1
	3	Whitefield		Away	5-1
	6	Cowlairs	Exhibition Cup	Exhibition	0-2
	8	Dumbarton		Home	3-0
	15	Dumbarton		Away	2-1
	22	Cowlairs	Scottish Cup	Home	8-0
	29	Airdrie		Home	4-1
October	6	Shettleston	Glasgow Cup	Home	11-2
	13	Albion Rovers	Scottish Cup	Home	4-1
	15	Dundee Harp		Away	7-1
	20	Hibs		Away	3-0
	27	Rangers	Glasgow Cup	Away	6-1
November	3	St Bernard	Scottish Cup	Away	4-1
	10	Renton		Home	1-0
	17	Queen's Park	Glasgow Cup	Home	0-2
	24	Clyde		Home	0-1
December	1	Port Glasgow		Away	4-2
	8	Clyde	Scottish Cup	Home	9-2
	15	East Stirlingshire	Scottish Cup	Away	2-1
	22	Vale of Leven		Away	2-1
	29	Clydesdale	North-Eastern Cup	Away	5-1
	31	Mitchell's St George		Home	7-1
1889					
January	3	Corinthians		Home	6-2
	5	Thistle		Away	2-3
	12	Dumbarton	Scottish Cup	Away	4-1
	19	Morton		Away	5-4
	26	Airdrie		Home	1-1
February	2	Third Lanark	Scottish Cup	Hampden	0-3
	9	Third Lanark	Scottish Cup	Hampden	1-2
	16	Corinthians		Away	1-3
	23	Clydesdale		Home	0-3
March	2	Abercorn		Home	4-4
	9	Hibs		Home	5-4
	16	Northern	North-Eastern Cup	Home	4-1
	23	Newcastle West End		Away	4-3
	30	Third Lanark		Home	4-1
April	6	Motherwell		Away	8-3
	13	Cowlairs		Away	1-0
	19	Bolton Wanderers		Away	0-2
	20	Burnley		Away	3-1
	22	Distillery		Away	1-0
	23	United Belfast		Away	5-2
May	4	Renton	Charity Cup	Hampden	2-5
	11	Cowlairs	North-Eastern Cup	Barrowfield	6-1
	18	Thistle		Away	2-0
	23	Bolton Wanderers		Home	5-1
	25	Preston North End		Home	2-1

Do not tear the Coupon from the Paper.

SPECIALLY GUARANTEED BY THE
GENERAL ACCIDENT AND EMPLOYERS' LIABILITY
ASSURANCE ASSOCIATION (LIMITED),
157 WEST GEORGE STREET, GLASGOW,
TAY STREET, PERTH,
To whom notice of Claims under the following conditions must be sent
within 14 days.

£100.   SCOTTISH
ATHLETIC JOURNAL
INSURANCE COUPON.

ONE HUNDRED POUNDS will be paid by the above Insurance Company to the
legal representatives of any person killed or fatally injured by an accident received
while playing in a Football Match should death result within three
months after such accident.   Provided that at the time of such accident the
Person so killed or fatally injured was the owner of this INSURANCE COUPON
for the Current Week, with their usual signature written in ink underneath.

Signature... ....

This Insurance is limited to One Coupon for each holder, and is not invalidated
by any other Insurance effected with the General Accident and Employers
Liability Assurance Association (Limited), or any other Insurance Company, but
is in addition thereto.—November 23, 1887.

The 1880s was a tough time and the football reflected this. I wonder, though, just how many players had the initiative — and the money — to take advantage of this opportunity.

was quickly put together for the first full season of 1888/1889. There was no Scottish League at this time but a full list of fixtures was organised and of course there was the Scottish Cup. However, in August 1888, the new club made a competitive debut in the Exhibition Cup, a tournament staged on a pitch close to the towers of Glasgow University, as part of the 1888 International Exhibition.

There were some heady moments during this season. After having lost to Cowlairs in the Exhibition Cup, there was great satisfaction in defeating them 8-0 in the Scottish Cup. A report in the *Scottish Umpire* of the Glasgow Cup tie on the 27 October 1888, which finished Celtic 6 Rangers 1, stated:

> The Celtic came away with a brilliance which has seldom, if ever, been equalled on Ibrox Park. The dodging and dribbling of the whole forward quintet was a caution, while the shooting was dead on.

When Celtic beat Dumbarton 4-1 on a crisp, dry, winter's day on 12 January 1889, their play much impressed the reporter from the *Scottish Referee*:

> There was no cohesion in Dumbarton's front. Their rushing one-man game contrasted strongly with the machine-like work of their opponents.

Scottish Sport was even more complimentary: 'The Celts played a game as few can nowadays'.

In their Scottish Cup run, after convincing victories over Shettleston (5-1), Cowlairs (8-0), Albion Rovers (4-1) and at St Bernards (4-1), Celtic

SCOTTISH CUP TIE — Saturday, 3rd Nov.

CELTIC v. ST. BERNARDS.
POWDERHALL, EDINBURGH.

The Committee have made arrangements with N.B.R. Company to run a Special Train to Edinburgh, on Saturday, 3rd November, 1888. Train leaves Bellgrove 1.30 p.m., and Parkhead 1.35, returning from Edinburgh (Waverley) at 7.30 p.m. prompt. Return Tickets, 2s. 6d., available by this Train only. Tickets may be had (8 to 9 p.m.) from Tuesday till Friday at the League of the Cross Hall, St. Mary's, 67 East Rose Street, St. Michael's, Great Eastern Road, and Sacred Heart, Howard Street, or from any member of the Committee.

Another piece of innovative thinking by the Celtic committee of the day. It undoubtedly helped towards the crowd of 6,000, by far the biggest of the 4th-round ties.

found themselves accused of unsportsmanlike behaviour in their fourth round tie against Clyde. After losing 1-0, Willie Maley, at that point Match Secretary as well as player, immediately lodged a protest with the SFA.

Protests were quite common in the early days of the Scottish Cup. In season 1888/1889, when a record 161 teams entered the competition, 35 protests were lodged. In years gone by, some reasons for protests were bizarre, to say the least. In 1882, Arthurlie were ordered to replay Thornliebank because an oval ball had been used! In 1886 Lugar Boswell beat Dalry 3-2, but the latter claimed that the referee was inebriated! With a fully sober official in charge of the rematch, Lugar Boswell again won, this time by 6 goals to 1. Celtic's protest was based on three factors. Firstly, that Clyde had arrived late for the kick-off; secondly, that the start had further been delayed when three Clyde players had been ordered to remove illegal bars from their boots; and thirdly, that due to the late start, the match had finished in semi-darkness and stormy conditions.

Much to Clyde's disgust, the protest was upheld and the match was replayed. The Clyde players turned up all ready in strip for the fray but refused to enter the pavilion. Celtic won 9-2. In the quarter-final at Falkirk, a late rally enabled Celtic to scrape home 2-1 against East Stirling; while the semi-final against Dumbarton at Boghead (note that there were no neutral venues for semi-finals) turned into a romp with Celtic displaying real class. After that display of brilliance, both matches of the final turned out to be something of a disappointment. Towards kick-off time on 2 February 1889, the weather deteriorated, heavy snow covering both the pitch and terraces of second Hampden. The supporters still turned up though, some 18,000 of them, to see how Celtic, in their new strip of green and white vertical stripes would cope with the stiff opposition of Third Lanark, finalists on two previous occasions. Such was the interest that the SFA raised the entrance fee from sixpence (2½p) to one shilling (5p).

Unfortunately, due to some discussions between the two clubs behind the scenes, this crowd, having paid £920 6s 8d (£920.35p) in total, (the largest gate ever taken at a Scottish ground), was unknowingly watching a friendly, which Third Lanark won 3-0. Then the SFA stepped in and ordered a replay, to be played one week later at the same venue. A crowd of 16,000 attended this game on a wet day. Controversy slightly reared its head before the match when Third Lanark protested that the playing conditions were difficult and three of their players were reluctant to compete for a trophy they felt they had already won. Any chance of further problems was avoided when after a closely-fought encounter, Third Lanark won 2-1. Any disappointment that the club and its supporters felt over defeat in what should have been the climax of the season had to be tempered, as the club still had some 18 fixtures left to play. In most of these they were successful. Matches were played in London, Newcastle, Bolton, Burnley and Belfast. In May, they picked up their first trophy, when they beat Cowlairs 6-1 in the final of the North-Eastern Cup. So, the first season drew to a close with a good record of 56 played, 42 won, 11 lost, 3 drawn, 197 goals for, 85 goals against.

Nor was the charitable aspect of the Club's aims ignored. During that first season, £421 16s 9d (£421.35p) was given to charity. In addition, it was estimated that a further £150 was raised in matches played throughout the country. Principal recipients were the SVDP Conferences, given £164; £50 to the Whitevale Refuge and £50 to the Little Sisters of the Poor; and £5 a week was its regular contribution to the Poor Children's Dinner Table of the three East End parishes.

1888–1889 SCOTTISH CUP

01/09/88	Shettleston	(H)	5-1		
22/09/88	Cowlairs	(H)	8-0	6,500	
13/10/88	Albion Rovers	(H)	4-1	600	
03/11/88	St Bernard's	(A)	4-1	6,000	
24/11/88	Clyde	(H)	0-1	7,000	Celtic Protested: Upheld
08/12/88 R	Clyde	(H)	9-2	9,000	
15/12/88 QF	East Stirlingshire	(A)	2-1	3,000	
12/01/89 SF	Dumbarton	(A)	4-1	5,000	
02/02/89 F	Third Lanark		0-3	17,000	Hampden
Replay	Third Lanark		1-2	13,000	Hampden

Team: John Kelly; Gallagher, McKeon; W Maley, James Kelly, McLaren; McCallum, Dunbar; Groves; Coleman, T Maley – Scorer McCallum

1888–1889 CHARITY CUP

Renton	(Hampden)	2-5

1888–1889 GLASGOW CUP

Shettleston	(H)	11-2
Rangers	(A)	6-1
Queen's Park	(H)	0-2

Back row, left to right: Joe Anderson (Trainer), J. Quillan, D. Malloy, J. Glass, J. McDonald (Committeemen). 2nd row: J. O'Hara, W. McKillop (Committeemen). 3rd row: W. Groves, T. Maley, P. Gallacher, W. Dunning, W. Maley, H. Dunbar. Font row: J. Coleman, J. McLaren, J. Kelly, N. McCallum, M. McKeown.

An early team wearing the first strip. Note that the keeper is wearing a cap to mark him out from the others. This team played only two matches together, the Scottish Cup 2nd round tie at Celtic Park against Cowlairs on 22 September 1888, where this photograph was probably taken, and the 4th round tie against St Bernard's in Edinburgh on 3 November 1888.

1889–1890 Scottish Cup				
	Queen's Park	(H)	0-0	16,000
Replay	Queen's Park	(A)	1-2	11,000

Celtic versus Queen's Park was the tie of the first round, although top scorers were Cowlairs, winning their away tie against Victoria 21-1. The first match, at Celtic Park, in front of 16,000 was abandoned at 0-0 due to crowd disturbance. There would appear to have been some difference of opinion as to the attendance in this first match. All ten entrances at Celtic Park were opened well before the game but the huge crowd still took ages to come in. Several times during the match, crowds encroached on to the playing surface and in the second half, they just could not be contained behind the lines and the referee had no option but to abandon the tie. Some observers said the crowd was nearer 25,000.

One week later the teams met again at Hampden. The weather was favourable this time but the price of admission was doubled and this kept the numbers down. This match was often a case of the Queens' defence holding out against the good play of the Celtic forwards. All the goals came in the second half, Peter Dowds scoring Celtic's only goal and the Queens' winner came just when another draw beckoned.

The Amateurs (although technically all players were amateurs at this time) went all the way to the final.

1889–1890 GLASGOW CUP			
	United Abstainers	(H) 5-1	
	Cambuslang	(H) 4-1	
Final	Queen's Park	2-3	12,000 Cathkin Park 14/12/89

1889–1890 Charity Cup			
3R	L.R.V.	0-2	Hampden

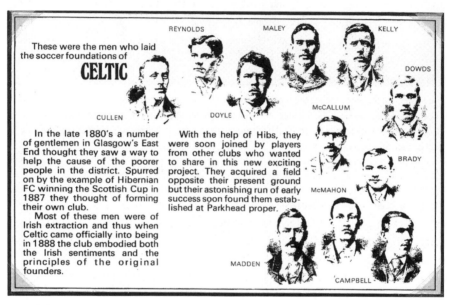

These were the men who laid the soccer foundations of

CELTIC

In the late 1880's a number of gentlemen in Glasgow's East End thought they saw a way to help the cause of the poorer people in the district. Spurred on by the example of Hibernian FC winning the Scottish Cup in 1887 they thought of forming their own club.

Most of these men were of Irish extraction and thus when Celtic came officially into being in 1888 the club embodied both the Irish sentiments and the principles of the original founders.

With the help of Hibs, they were soon joined by players from other clubs who wanted to share in this new exciting project. They acquired a field opposite their present ground but their astonishing run of early success soon found them established at Parkhead proper.

REYNOLDS — MALEY — KELLY — DOWDS — McCALLUM — BRADY — McMAHON — CULLEN — DOYLE — MADDEN — CAMPBELL

A card illustrating the story of Celtic's early years. The players shown played in the first match of the 1892 Scottish Cup final against Queen's Park. This was won 1-0 by Celtic, but a replay was ordered which Celtic won 5-1. For the second game, Paddy Gallacher replaced Johnny Madden.

CHAPTER TWO

Glasgow — And the Irish

IN THOSE EARLY DAYS, Celtic's support would have been of Irish extraction and very confined to the east end of the City. The three parishes which supplied the men to make the dream come true were St Mary's in Abercrombie Street; St Andrews' and St Alphonsus in London Road, all of which were established to meet the needs of the increasing number of Catholic families in those areas.

Where Did They Live?

Before the Industrial Revolution, in the late 18th century, Glasgow's prosperity was engendered by its maritime trade, although the population peaked at a modest 40,000. By 1830, however, this had increased to 200,000, accompanied by an equally rapid growth of new streets and buildings. As that 200,000 rose to the 550,000 of the 1870s, housing became a priority and the working-class tenement was born, bought or built by an absentee, sometimes foreign landlord and managed by a factor. These were sub-divided to accommodate several families, but overcrowding became so intense that a 'ticket' system was introduced. The 'ticket' was a metal plate fixed to the side of the building showing the number of adults and children allowed to sleep there. The authorities had the power to make spot raids to check these figures, and the cry of: 'It's the Night Men' in the early hours would have caused many a rumpus as bodies moved up and down the stairs and into the back court.

The worst slum areas in Glasgow were not, as often thought, in the Gorbals, but in the alleys and wynds just off the High Street and Saltmarket in the centre of the city. These were not only ramshackle but vermin-ridden, and were eventually demolished by the City Improvement Trust in the 1860s and early 1870s. The people were moved. The wealthy moved westward, to Park Circus, Woodside and Great Western Road; those who could afford to buy – the lower middle classes of professional people, salesmen and clerks – moved to the new suburbs in a ring around the city, Maryhill, Pollokshields, Bellahouston, Crosshill, Cathcart, Mount Florida and so on. As for the mass of relatively poor, they overflowed from the city centre into the neighbouring areas; Anderston to the west, Bridgeton and Calton to the east and the Gorbals to the south, creating even more zones of overcrowding.

The Irish

There had always been immigrants arriving from Ireland into Scotland. Indeed, during past centuries, this was very much a reciprocal thing, with many Scots also going over there. However, after the Irish Rebellion of 1898, the numbers arriving here increased. The men were mainly labourers, meeting the demands of the expansion of industrial Scotland at that time, although some were still employed in agriculture.

Most came to Glasgow and its environs, but Edinburgh and Dundee were other destinations. By 1821 for instance, there were 12,000 Irish in the Cowgate area of Edinburgh and 800 in Leith. This had risen to 16,000 by 1841 and 25,000 by 1855. The disastrous Irish famines of 1845–1848 increased the numbers. It must be kept in mind that this 'famine' was not due to a lack of food in the country. A census produced in 1847 showed that the value of agricultural produce in Ireland amounted to almost £45 million and was quite sufficient to feed more than twice the population. This 'famine' was politically inspired, the landlords wanting the small farmers off their land.

My maternal grandfather's antecedents lived in Westport in County Mayo and a few of these came to Glasgow shortly after this time. Just east from Westport in Castlebar, one landlord was noted for his particular brand of cruelty to those who could not pay his rent, tearing down their miserable shacks and even closing down the workhouse. I wonder if many of these poor creatures were still alive six years later to take some comfort when that same landlord, the 3rd Lord Lucan, took the blame for one of the worst disasters in British Military History, the Charge of the Light Brigade.

It was estimated that over 100,000 immigrants arrived between 1841 and 1851, the majority during the latter years. The table below shows a report from 1847 highlighting the problem:

DRAFT OF A RETURN TO THE BOARD OF SUPERVISION SHOWING THE NUMBER OF DESTITUTE IRISH LANDED IN GLASGOW FROM 1 JANUARY 1847 TO 30 NOVEMBER 1847.

Number of destitute Irish landed	49,993
Amount of expense incurred by The Parish of Glasgow on account of the Influx	
Infirmary charges	£3,713
Grant to the Infirmary	300
Temporary Relief	6,000
Interments	564
Wine, Rice, etc	576
Clothing	170
Transmission of Paupers	760
Inspecting Irish Steamboats	500
Cost of erecting New Poorhouse & Fever Hospital	8,000
Extra Officers salaries	350
Extra pay to District Surgeons	170
Medicine	200
TOTAL	£21,303

The authorities were particularly concerned, not only at the overcrowding in areas like the Calton, which inevitably led to disease, but over the Irish custom of the 'wake'. These all-night drinking parties were particularly condemned by health officers alarmed at the possibility of plague spreading from the corpses, often cholera or typhus.

1866 – 68 deaths from cholera
1869 – 970 deaths from typhus

By the time Celtic was playing its first League matches, Glasgow's population had risen to around 750,000, most of whom lived clustered around the city centre. Table 2.2 shows how crowded most of these areas were. The stinking wynds of the High Street and Saltmarket may have been demolished some years before, but overcrowding was obviously an issue there again.

Table 2.2. POPULATION DENSITY IN GLASGOW IN 1891

District	Population	Persons per Acre
High St. and Closes W.	9,223	223 (33 per cent)
St Rollox	16,545	350 (37 percent)
Barrowfield	26,944	219 (38 per cent)
Calton	21,747	343 (38 per cent)
Brownfield	3,451	345 (40 per cent)
Cowcaddens	16,235	266 (43 per cent)
Anderston	29,251	234 (38 per cent)
Gorbals	13,199	282 (38 per cent)
Pollockshields W. and Bellahouston	3,538	4 (12 per cent)

Note, by contrast, the relative freedom for the middle classes in areas like Pollokshields West, and Bellahouston. By this time, thankfully, plagues like cholera and typhus were being kept under control, although levels of hygiene were primitive by the standards of today. Even so, epidemics regularly broke out with the infectious fevers the notable cause of mortality, particularly among the young.

CAUSES OF DEATH – 1884

Whooping Cough	767
Scarlet Fever	421
Measles	353
Small Pox	12
Diphtheria	174

Like most immigrants in a growing city, the Irish initially took over the worst housing and gained employment in the lowest paid jobs. At that time, though, there was plenty of work, not only in the heavy industries like iron and steel, railways and shipbuilding, but on the many building works throughout the area. Wages at this period varied considerably and workers were expected to do a six day week. The wages of the time were approximately 12/- for a labourer, 21/- for a joiner, for a skilled shipyard worker between 25/- and 30/- and for a top man in the iron-works about 60/- a week. That does not sound very much but then the costs were lower. Three shillings would cover the rent for a one-room house; sugar was 2p a pound; while a large loaf was from 8p–10p.

What Did the People Do?

Until the 1870s leisure for a Glaswegian was almost non-existent, as most were too busy working! The wealthy, naturally, had their clubs in which to wine, dine and play cards, and their large houses for songs round the piano, quadrilles and polkas. For the remainder there was not much to do. Some early theatres had gone on fire, the average house was too small and too overcrowded to offer scope for gracious entertainment. Standing at street corners or other selected places for a chat was the remit of the poor; the better-off 'promenaded' along Great Western Road or Sauchiehall Street. For many, though, pay-day meant a session in one of Glasgow's hundreds of drinking shops, characterised by incoherent shouting and brawling, people being sick or just collapsing. The cheapness and strength of the national drink, whisky, or in Irish pubs, whiskey, was a major problem.

In 1853, for a population of around 350,000, there were 2,053 licensed premises in Glasgow. High Street, in Glasgow, had four adjoining spirit-shops at one site. In another part of the street, only a baker's shop broke a line of six of them. In a small area of the Gallowgate, there were 79 while the short streets of Saltmarket and Broomielaw had 56 and 65 respectively. Gradually, the numbers decreased, only 2,000 for a population of 800,000 in 1898. But drunkenness was still a major problem and led directly to most of the crimes in Glasgow. The figures in this table show a very high number of drunk and incapable convictions for that year, working out at one for every 50 of the population.

Offences Committed in Glasgow in 1888		
	Number	Acquitted
Drunk and Incapable	14,944	155
Begging and Destitute	404	—
Reckless Driving	293	93
Obstructing the Police	148	24
Throwing Stones to the Annoyance of Passers-By	220	31
Offering Indecent Books for Sale	6	6
Prostitutes Importuning	2,631	143
Deserters	59	—
Falsely Impersonating the Chief Constable	1	—
Lunatics	36	—

There would appear to be have been little doubt about the guilt of the vast majority of those drunk and incapable or of the ladies offering their services. Reckless driving during this period would surely have involved horses, and one wonders just what the purpose was for impersonating the Chief Constable? The number of desertions indicates that army life was undesirable, and it is horrifying to note that mental deficiency was regarded as an offence.

Slowly, a Temperance movement grew, culminating in the Scottish Temperance League (1844) and the Band of Hope (1870). These did little though to stem the national crime rate and eventually Gladstone's Government took action in 1871, bringing in simple controls. These seem

'Whitebait's Concert Rooms' sounds quite grand, but it was more like a saloon than a proper theatre. Note the Irish influence on the programme.

remarkably moderate today – no one under 16 was to be served and pubs were to be shut at 12 midnight – yet Gladstone lost the next election. In the same decade, the Bank Holiday Acts (1871–1875) originated the idea of a regular annual paid holiday. The 1870s and 1880s also saw a rise in the working man's standard of living and a reduction in his working hours, the cessation of work at lunchtime on Saturday having a dramatic effect on the rise of football as a public spectacle.

The 'Glasgow Fair' also changed its meaning. Originally a huge fair on Glasgow Green – dancing bears, merry-go-rounds, shooting booths, showmen etc – the term was now transferred to the week's holiday, in July, usually spent 'doon the watter' via one of the new steamers.

The Britannia Theatre of Varieties was in the Trongate.

In the second half of the 19th century, the Glaswegian could visit some of the new 'music halls' opening across the city. For the Irish, there was an abundance of melodrama across Scotland, in Glasgow, Edinburgh, Dundee, Paisley, Greenock and Coatbridge. Plays and shows depicting Irish life and themes were very popular, even the larger theatres in Glasgow catering specifically for their Irish 'patrons' with special week-long 'attractions'. In addition to purely Irish entertainment, the Glasgwegian could seek relaxation in theatres like the Britannia; or visit a saloon music hall like Whitebaits in St Enoch's Wynd and Lane.

No doubt the Celtic support of this time had their own songs to sing, many reflecting on the life and times they had left behind. But they were also used to hearing these popular songs of the day, some in Music Halls, pubs and by ubiquitous street entertainers.

SONGS OF THE DAY	
1874	Silver Threads Among the Gold
1876	Grandfather's Clock
1877	The Lost Chord
1884	Love's Own Sweet Song
1890	Passing By
1892	Daddy Wouldn't Buy Me a Bow-Wow
1894	I Don't Want to Play in Your Yard
1896	Sweet Rosie O'Grady
1898	When You Were Sweet Sixteen
1900	Goodbye Dolly Gray
1092	Won't You Come Home Bill Bailey
1904	Stop Your Tickling Jock
1906	Waiting at the Church

Some of these songs were made popular in later years by well-known artistes, e.g. *Stop Your Tickling Jock* (Harry Lauder), *I Don't Want to Play in Your Yard* (Ertha Kitt), and *When You Were Sweet Sixteen* (Foster & Allan).

Travel

Access into and out of Glasgow was made much easier in the second half of the 19th century by the expansion of the railways, with stations in the city initially at St Enoch Bridge Street and Queen Street. Many workers were employed in the great locomotive building works at St Rollox and Springburn. In the city, though, until 1870, little had changed in the way of transport. One either walked or took a cab. By then, there were five cabs to choose from; the first-class Noddy, Clarence or Harrington at one shilling and sixpence per mile; or the second-class Cab or Minibus at one shilling per mile. However, in 1870 came the horse-drawn trams onto the streets, so providing easy and cheap transport for all. By agreement, working men going to work were charged half price by the private company which started the service, although Glasgow Corporation owned the track. By 1894 the

```
GLASGOW & SOUTH-WESTERN RAILWAY.
———
FOOTBALL  MATCH,
"ENGLAND  V,  SCOTLAND."
———
CHEAP  EXCURSION
TO
BLACKBURN
ON  FRIDAY, 18TH  MARCH.
———
                         Pullman Train.
      RETURN FARES      p.m.           FROM
GLASGOW, St Enoch, ...      ...  9.15     1ST CLASS.  3RD CLASS.
PAISLEY, Gilmour Street,    ...  8.17
GREENOCK, Princes Pr.,      ...  7.40
JOHNSTONE,    ...    ...    ...  8.25        16/       8/
AYR ...        ...    ...    ...  9.15
KILMARNOCK, ...     ..   ...  9.55
  Passengers return on SUNDAY, 20th March, by Train leaving
BLACKBURN at 1.52 a.m. (Saturday Midnight).
  Through Carriages are run to and from ST. ENOCH and BLACK-
BURN.
             JOHN MORTON, Secretary and General Manager.
  Glasgow. March. 1887.
```

The Glasgow and South-Western Railway was one of three companies offering this service in 1887. Significantly, all three charged the same prices. The match was won by Scotland by three goals to one.

Corporation went into business on its own account, improved the range of services and by 1901 introduced electrified overhead cables.

Glasgow changed in other ways in these latter years of the century. The large stores opened. Copland and Lyles (1878), Pettigrews (1888) and Trerons (1890) joined Frasers (opened in 1849). In 1852, Kelvingrove Park was laid out; to be joined for leisure in 1857 by Queen's Park. For the improvement of the mind, the Mitchell Library opened in 1877 and the Kelvingrove Art Galleries in 1902, both free.

The amazing rise of popularity of football during the 1870s and 1880s was dependent on several factors. The first was that the standard of living of many workers rose sufficiently so that a full six-day working week was no longer necessary. The growth in demand for a Saturday half-day holiday was an important factor in the development of football as a spectator sport. Once this was achieved, it became part of the British way of life and was unknown on the continent. Secondly, regular and cheap transport was necessary not only to bring spectators into the city but to allow movement between grounds. The expansion of the railways provided this. Thirdly, particularly so in Scotland, the teams themselves formed in places which were never far away from each other, so, in the beginning, competition was local and lively.

Fourthly, the advent of Cup competitions and later the Scottish League, added much more interest to the game. People in an area or town started to identify with their team and rivalry grew.

At the beginning of the first season of the Scottish League, 1890–1891, 28 of the teams playing today were involved in the campaign. Most of these were spread across the Central Belt, with some surprising off-shoots, like Arbroath (established 1878), Montrose (1879), Stranraer (1870), or Berwick (1881).

Those following were late developers: Aberdeen (1903), Clydebank (1965), East Fife (1903), Ayr United (1910), Dundee (1893), Queen of the South (1919), Brechin City (1903), Dundee United (1923), and Stirling Albion (1945).

Then, of course, there are the more recent additions: Livingston Thistle (1974), Ross County (established in 1929, but brought into the Scottish League in 1994), and Inverness Caledonian Thistle (1994).

CHAPTER THREE (1890–1900)
New Ground: First Board

THE LAST DECADE of the 19th century was very productive and successful for Celtic Football Club, not least in terms of trophies won. At this period, both the Charity Cup and Glasgow Cup were regarded as important competitions and must be included beside the League Championship and the Scottish Cup in any list of statistics. So, in these ten years, from the possible list of 40 trophies, Celtic won 17. In addition, they were in a cup final on another six occasions and finished runners up in the league three times.

CELTIC RECORD IN COMPETITIONS 1890–1900

	LEAGUE	CUP	GLASGOW CUP	CHARITY CUP
1890–91			Celtic	
1891–92		Celtic	Celtic	Celtic
1892–93	Celtic			Celtic
1893–94	Celtic			Celtic
1894–95			Celtic	Celtic
1895–96	Celtic		Celtic	Celtic
1896–97				
1897–98	Celtic			
1898–99		Celtic		Celtic
1899–1900		Celtic		

Unlike Celtic, many other clubs had been unable to arrange enough friendly matches to fill a season and these had lobbied the authorities to set up some form of League competition as England had done in 1888. Eventually these pleas were answered and the Scottish League First Division commenced in season 1890/1891, with these 11 teams:

Abercorn	Hearts
Cambuslang	Rangers
Celtic	Renton
Cowlairs	St Mirren
Dumbarton	Third Lanark
Vale of Leven	

Almost immediately, though, there was a problem. Celtic's first league match was against Renton at First Celtic Park, where they were on the receiving end of a 4-1 defeat. However, Renton was soon suspended from the competition for playing a friendly match against St Bernards from Edinburgh, a team already banned by the SFA for dabbling with

The original strip of white shirt with green collar and celtic cross on the breast plate (see page 25) was worn only during the first season of 1888–89. This striped shirt in emerald green and white was brought in for the following season.

professionalism. So, Celtic's first official league match was therefore a 5-0 victory over Hearts at Tynecastle on the 23 August 1890. Renton was not the only club to transgress the rules, as Celtic themselves had four points deducted for fielding an ineligible player-goalkeeper, Jim Bell.

❧

1890–1891 League Championship							
	P	W	D	L	F	A	Points	Position
Dumbarton	18	13	3	2	61	21	29	1st
Rangers	18	13	3	2	58	25	29	1st
Celtic	18	11	3	4	48	21	21	3rd

Fixtures		
	H	A
Abercorn	2-0	5-1
Cambuslang	5-2	1-3
Cowlairs	2-0	5-0
Dumbarton	1-0	2-2
Hearts	1-0	5-0
Rangers	2-2	2-1
St Mirren	3-2	0-1
Third Lanark	1-1	1-2
Vale of Leven	9-1	1-3

Celtic had four points deducted for playing James Bell in their first official league match against Hearts on 23 August 1890. A fortnight had to pass between a player playing for one club and then another, and Bell was within this time. Jim Bell was goalkeeper for almost the whole of the first season, but was replaced by Tom Duff for the following year.

The first title was shared between Dumbarton and Rangers. The loss of the four points would not have made much difference to Celtic's challenge, as generally, a lack of consistent goal scoring was their problem. Although the team hit five on four separate occasions and they crushed Vale of Leven in the penultimate match of the season ('Duke' McMahon scoring four and Jimmy McGhee notching a hat-trick) chances were made but not taken on too many other occasions. Throughout this new league campaign, one big name was missing. Queen's Park refused to take part. The match against Renton, later expunged from the records, was an unfortunate moment for Willie Naughton, signed from Carfin Shamrock. He only played one game for Celtic's first team and this was it, at inside-right between Neilly McCallum and Willie Groves. Renton fought their case through the courts and eventually came back into the league the following season. As for 'Chippy' Naughton, he went on to Wishaw Thistle, Stoke and Southampton.

1890–1891 Scottish Cup				
06/09/90	Rangers	(H)	1-0	15,000
27/09/90	Carfin Shamrock	(H)	2-2	
04/10/90	Replay	(A)	3-1	5,000
18/10/90	Wishaw Thistle	(A)	6-2	4,000
08/11/90	Our Boys	(A)	3-1	6,000
29/11/90	Royal Albert	(A)	2-2	
06/12/90	Replay Royal Albert	(A)	4-0	5,000
13/12/90	2nd Replay Royal Albert		2-0	2,000 Ibrox Park
20/12/90	QF Dumbarton	(A)	0-3	

This was one of only two occasions when the Old Firm have met in the first round of the Scottish Cup. A crowd of 15,000 saw the ex-Hibs star, Willie Groves, score the winner in the first half. The first match against Royal Albert was deemed a friendly, as the pitch was unplayable. The second, also at Larkhall, was abandoned with Celtic leading 4-0, after a pitch invasion. League winners Dumbarton were just too strong in the quarter-final, although the Sons, after beating Abercorn comfortably in the semi-final, played poorly against Hearts in the final, losing 1-0 and thus missing the chance to do a League and Cup 'double'.

1890–1891 Charity Cup		
3rd L.RV	8-1	(A) Protested Tie
Replay 3rd L.RV	6-1	(H)
Dumbarton	0-3	(Cathkin Park)

1890–1891 Glasgow Cup			
	Battlefield	7-0	(H)
	Northern	2-1	(A)
	Clyde	5-0	(H)
	Partick Thistle	5-1	(H)
Final	Third Lanark	4-0	(Hampden) 10,000

Team: Bell; Reynolds, McKeown; Gallacher, Kelly, W. Maley; Madden, Boyle; Dowds; Campbell, Dunbar.

Celtic chose to face the wind after winning the toss. Both teams opened adventurously and the goalkeepers were soon in action. Celtic, though, looked the stronger attack and opened the scoring after 20 minutes. This was a rather fortuitous affair, a cross by John Campbell coming off the post, and Third's left-half, Lochhead, knocking it into his own net. From then to the interval, although both sides had chances, there was no further scoring. In the second half, with the wind behind them, Celtic took control, allowing Third Lanark only sporadic opportunities. Dowds scored the second from a corner by Johnny Madden, Campbell got a disputed third and then fired home his second, and Celtic's fourth, direct from a free-kick.

During the same season, Sunderland, Everton, Bolton Wanderers, Burnley, Preston North End, Wolves, Notts County, Aston Villa and Blackburn all came to First Celtic Park and return visits were paid. In all, 49 matches were played, of which 34 were won, 8 were lost and 7 drawn, 148 goals for and 62 against. In the same period the reserve team played 36 matches, won 30, lost none and drew six, with 187 goals for and 32 against. They also won the 2nd eleven cup.

Willie Maley (right) and Tom E. Maley (left). The Maley brothers were two of the main instigators of Celtic's early success. Willie eventually became secretary/manager in 1897, a post he held until 1940. Tom was a member of the provisional board in 1897, but he left Celtic shortly afterwards. He went on to manage Manchester City whom he led to an FA Cup win in 1904, and then Bradford City.

1891–1892 SCOTTISH LEAGUE DIVISION I

	P	W	D	L	F	A	Points	Position
Dumbarton	22	18	1	3	79	28	37	1st
Celtic	22	16	3	3	62	21	35	2nd

FIXTURES

	H	A		H	A
Abercorn	3-1	5-2	Leith Athletic	2-0	1-2
Cambuslang	3-1	4-0	Rangers	3-0	1-1
Clyde	0-0	7-2	Renton	3-0	4-0
Dumbarton	2-0	0-1	St Mirren	2-1	2-1
Hearts	3-1	1-3	Third Lanark	5-1	3-1
			Vale of Leven	6-1	2-2

Cowlairs had dropped down to the Second Division after the first season, Renton were re-instated, and both Clyde and Leith Athletic brought in. So 12 teams contested the Championship. Celtic were unbeaten at home, the defence in particular being very miserly, only conceding six goals in 11 matches. Away from home, though, it was a different story. Fifteen goals were lost and three defeats left them just two points off the first place team. One of these defeats came against Hearts in the opening match; the other two, against Leith Athletic and Dumbarton, came in April on successive Saturdays, with the latter game almost a League decider. The goals were shared between Sandy McMahon (19), Neil McCallum (12), Johnny Madden, John Campbell and Alec Brady. In a friendly at Celtic Park against Dumbarton on New Year's Day 1892, goal nets were used for the first time. Celtic lost 8-0. Goalkeeper Tom Duff got the blame and Joe Cullen was brought in from Benburb.

1891–1892 SCOTTISH CUP

	28/11/91	St Mirren	(A)	4-2	4,000	
	11/12/91	Kilmarnock Ath	(H)	3-0	200	
	23/01/92	Cowlairs	(H)	4-1	4,000	
SF	06/02/92	Rangers	(H)	5-3	11,000	
Final	12/03/92	Queen's Park		1-0	40,000	Hampden
Replay	09/04/92	Queen's Park		5-1	22,000	Hampden

Celtic had a fairly uneventful run to the Finals, with some varying crowds. The Rangers tie was eagerly anticipated as a re-run of the year before. Celtic was four up at the interval but Rangers pulled three back in the second half before Alec Brady scored the all-important winner late on.

The first match of the final attracted a 40,000 gate, by far the biggest up to then, and was won by Celtic, although due to crowd encroachment, it was classified as a friendly. In the re-match, Celtic were at their dazzling best in the second half, with goals by Sandy McMahon (2), John Campbell (2), and an own goal, taking the Scottish Cup to Parkhead for the first time. The team: Cullen; Reynolds, Doyle; Maley, Kelly, Dowds; McCallum, Brady; Madden; Campbell, McMahon.

	1891–1892 Glasgow Cup		
	Kelvinside Athletic	11-1	(H)
	Partick Thistle	3-1	(A)
	Northern	6-0	(H) Protested Tie
	Replay Northern	3-2	(H)
	Linthouse	9-2	(H)
Final	Clyde	7-1	(Cathkin Park) 12/12/91 6,000

Clyde kicked off in a downpour at 2.15 pm and started aggressively but Celtic soon began to wear them down, missing a good many chances by dallying in front of goal. McCallum scored the first goal in 20 minutes, followed by Brady on the half-hour mark. The rain continued to come down in sheets but shortly after half-time it changed to snow just as Clyde pulled one back.

Celtic, however, were unstoppable, and quickly made it 6-1 through McMahon, Kelly, Madden and Campbell. Near the end, with interest in the match all gone and spectators leaving to avoid the appalling weather, Celtic scored their seventh. The team: Duff; Reynolds, Doyle; Dowds, Kelly, Maley; Brady, McCallum; Madden; Campbell and McMahon.

	1891–1892 Charity Cup		
	Dumbarton	3-1	(Ibrox)
Final	Rangers	2-0	(Celtic Park) 01/06/92 16,000

Rangers were not at full strength. Two players were ill – Mitchell and Scott – while another, Frank Watt, failed to turn up at all. The Celtic team was Cullen; Reynolds, and Doyle; Maley, Kelly, and Gallagher; McCallum, Brady; Madden; McMahon and Campbell. After heavy rain, the ground was not in good condition, pools of water lying on the surface. Rangers kicked off with the breeze in their favour but Celtic had the better of the early play. Their forward line was much superior to Rangers' attack and kept a lot of the action in the Light Blue's half. However, chances constantly went a-begging and by the interval, it was still all square.

Celtic opened the scoring on the hour mark, a fine run and cross by Sandy McMahon, giving, John Campbell the chance to head home. Rangers continued to press but Celtic always looked the more likely side to score and got their second a few minutes from time, another Campbell header, this time from a Johnny Madden cross, sealing victory by two goals to nil.

The Players

The crowds which poured into Celtic Park in those early days did not have their heroes to seek. Playing the 2-3-5 formation mentioned in the previous chapter, successive teams brought smiles to their lips and joy to their hearts.

The team which won the Charity Cup in 1892. Most of the players in this side also collected the Scottish and Glasgow cups in the same season. Joe Cullen was the first 'regular' Celtic goalkeeper. His 20 shut-outs in 73 appearances (27 per cent) ranks him alongside many other good Celtic custodians, although a severe kicking which left him unconscious at Sunderland in September 1892 severely dented his confidence. Later, he moved to Spurs, and then to Lincoln. He returned to Glasgow on retirement from the game in 1900 and died from pneumonia in 1905.

In the earliest team, James Kelly starred as centre-half, his pace, skill and reading of a game allowing him to both cover and attack when necessary. Kelly had been a member of the Renton team which beat both West Bromwich Albion (FA Cup Holders 1888) and Preston North End (FA Cup runners-up) in 1888 and was often regarded as the best team in the world. He got eight caps for his country and was the first Celtic player to captain the national side. At full-back, was the first well-known full-back partnership of Jerry Reynolds and Dan Doyle. Reynolds was stocky, his headers as powerful as other peoples shots, with a furious all-action style; Doyle was one of the first 'characters', sure in the tackle and able to punt the ball a long way. He had been a star at Everton, and Celtic were regarded as being very 'lucky' to get his services (i.e. Celtic, to be blunt, must have influenced his return by proffering cash in the amateur age!). He also captained Scotland against England on 7 April 1894.

In goal, the dangerous position of the time, the great Dan McArthur came to the fore. 36 shut-outs in 120 appearances (30 per cent) in an attack-minded era is a superb achievement. There was Sandy 'Duke' McMahon, at inside forward, six feet in height, a superb dribbler and supposedly the best header of a ball in Scotland; Willie Groves at centre-forward, sometimes greedy but with great ball control and looks to please the ladies. (Interestingly it was once reported that Willie Groves' grandfather was a London policemen sent north to help the Edinburgh force with their enquiries into the Burke and Hare body-snatching case!)

At inside left, Johnny Madden, the ball artist of his day with all the tricks; the feint, the back-heel, the dummy, the spurt. His 49 goals in 118 games is excellent; even more so was his career after leaving Celtic, when he moved to Prague to become the 'father of Czech football'. Madden was replaced by Jimmy Blessington, whose 58 goals in 99 matches is also impressive. Approaching the turn of the century, Barney Battles returned to the club. Battles was an aggressive, rather one-paced player, but was an inspiring leader on the field. He had had some problems with press coverage in his first stint at Parkhead and left for Dundee and Liverpool but he was brought back to Celtic Park in 1898 to give another six years of good service. His tragic death from influenza in 1905 affected the whole club. The first of three Divers to wear a Celtic strip also starred at this time. John Divers had been in the same bother with the press as Barney Battles (see season 1896–1897) but from 1898 played his part, with 40 goals in 87 appearances well worthy of respect.

We can gain some insight as to formation and system by listing an early team, with the heights and weights (where known) and their goal-scoring record in their Celtic career.

CELTIC FC SCOTTISH CUP WINNERS 1893

1.	Joe Cullen	73 appearances	20 shut-outs	5 ft 7 in	11 st 7 lbs
2.	Jerry Reynolds	74 appearances	0 goals	5 ft 8 in	12 stone
3.	Dan Doyle	133 appearances	6 goals	5 ft 11 in	12 stone
4.	Willie Maley	96 appearances	2 goals	5 ft 10 in	11 st 10 lbs
5.	James Kelly	139 appearances	11 goals	5 ft 8 in	11 st 7 lbs
6.	John Curren	26 appearances	0 goals	5 ft 7 in	11.st 7 lbs
7.	Jim Blessington	99 appearances	38 goals	5 ft 8 in	11 st 6 lbs
8.	John Madden	118 appearances	49 goals	5 ft 8 in	11 st 7 lbs
9.	Joe Cassidy	36 appearances	17 goals	5 ft 8 in	11 st 7 lbs
10.	Sandy McMahon	217 appearances	171 goals	6 ft	12 st 4 lbs
11.	John Campbell	215 appearances	109 goals	5 ft 9in	11 st 10 lbs

If we put these statistics, even if some are approximate, into a team pattern, then the way the team played would be roughly as shown in Fig 3.1.

The two full-backs were essentially defensive and with the goalkeeper formed the solid platform at the back. Reynolds never scored at all in his career and would rarely have left his own half; Doyle scored six, mostly from free kicks. Willie Maley and John Curren, at wing-half, would also have had

Football tactics were slowly developing from the 8-man forward line of the earlier years. In this Celtic team, James Kelly, at centre-half, was the playmaker from the back. All the forwards had good goalscoring records, but I suspect that Johnny Madden played slightly deeper in order to spray passes around, aided by Jim Blessington at outside-right. Sandy McMahon's scoring rate – 171 goals in 217 appearances – was particularly impressive.

a defensive attitude 80 per cent of the time, leaving Jimmy Kelly the freedom to move up and down the field. All five forwards were goal scorers, Madden, Campbell and Cassidy all averaging one goal every two matches, Blessington a slightly lower rate, while McMahon, (obviously using his extra height and weight compared to the others) was an undoubted star; his goal tally per game is second only to Jimmy McGrory in the overall Celtic record.

SEASON 1892–1893 SCOTTISH LEAGUE DIVISION I

	P	W	D	L	F	A	Points	Position
Celtic	18	14	1	3	54	25	29	1st

FIXTURES

	H	A		H	A
Abercorn	3-2	2-4	Rangers	3-0	2-2
Clyde	3-1	2-1	Renton	4-3	2-0
Dumbarton	5-1	3-0	St Mirren	4-1	3-1
Hearts	5-0	1-3	Third Lanark	2-5	6-0
Leith Ath.	3-1	1-0			

This was a fine performance by Celtic, although bad defeats by Aberdeen in the second match and Third Lanark on the last day of the season almost cost them dear. As it was, they finished only one point ahead of the chasing pack, with Rangers at the head, to take the Club's first ever Championship. Top scorers were McMahon (10), Madden (6), Campbell (16), Blessington (5) and Davidson (7).

1892–1893 Scottish Cup					
26/11/92		Linthouse	(H)	3-1	3,000
17/12/92		Sth KRV	(H)	7-0	
21/01/93	QF	Third Lanark	(H)	5-1	8,000
04/02/93	SF	St Bernard's	(H)	5-0	11,500
25/02/93	F	Queen's Park		1-0	18,771 Ibrox
11/03/93		Replay Queen's Park		1-2	13,329 Ibrox

Celtic had a fairly comfortable passage into the final, Johnny Madden scoring five against Sth Kirkcudbright RV and Sandy McMahon notching three in the quarter-final against Third Lanark.

Queen's Park were once again the opponents in the final, but due to a hard pitch, the clubs agreed to play the first match as a friendly. Celtic won 1-0 but this only whetted the appetite of the crowd for the second meeting, held on 11 March 1893. Queens were two up before the interval, the second goal somewhat controversial as the Celtic team were sure that Dan Doyle had knocked the ball past the post. The referee, however, gave a goal and although Celtic pulled one back through Jimmy Blessington, the Cup went

The squad which won Celtic's first two League Championships, in 1892–93 and 1893–94. Back row, left to right: J. Curran, D McArthur, J. Blessington, J. Cullen, T. Bonnar (Trainer), T. Dunbar, J. Campbell, J. Reynolds, Mr P. Gallacher (Linesman). Middle row: J. Cassidy, J. Madden, J. Kelly, D. Doyle, W. Maley. Front row: J. Divers, A. McMahon C. McEleney.

Note the below-knee-length trousers, the shinguards worn outside the socks and the obvious strength of the full-backs, Reynolds and Doyle.

to Queen's Park. The team in the cup final: Cullen; Reynolds, Doyle; Maley, Kelly, Dunbar; Towie, Blessington; Madden; McMahon and Campbell.

1892–1893 GLASGOW CUP FINAL

	Pollokshaws	(A)	7-2
	Partick Thistle	(A)	2-1 Protest
Replay	Partick Thistle	(A)	1-1
Replay	Partick Thistle	(H)	8-0
	Third Lanark	(H)	5-2
Final	Rangers	(Cathkin)	1-3 18/02/93 9,000

1892–1893 CHARITY CUP FINAL

	Dumbarton	(A)	1-1
	Reply Dumbarton	(A)	3-1
Final	Rangers	(Celtic Park)	5-0 27/05/93

This match was played in very warm weather on a very firm pitch.

Team: Cullen; Doyle and Dunbar; Curran, Kelly and W Maley; Madden, Blessington; Dowds (Aston Villa); Campbell and Cassidy (Newton Heath).

This match was never less than interesting, but as a contest was quite one-sided. Rangers could play some nice football; Celtic could also do that – and score too! The goal scoring started in 25 minutes through John Campbell and before half-time another four had arrived through Blessington, Campbell (2) and Dowds. Celtic opened the second half in dashing style but could not find the net again. As the match progressed they seemed quite content to hold Rangers who, on the day, were very disappointing opponents. Of the two trialists in this match, Peter Dowds had already been with Celtic from 1889 to 1892, then had one season with Aston Villa and another with Stoke, before rejoining Celtic in May 1894. Joe Cassidy, a strong and burly player, signed for Celtic one month after this Charity Cup Final but made only 28 appearances in two years before returning to Newton Heath in Manchester.

1893–1894 SCOTTISH LEAGUE RESULTS

	P	W	D	L	F	A	Points	Position
Celtic	18	14	1	3	53	32	29	1st

FIXTURES

	H	A		H	A
Dumbarton	0-0	5-4	Renton	3-2	3-0
Dundee	3-1	4-1	St Bernards	5-2	2-1
Hearts	2-3	4-2	St Mirren	5-1	2-1
Leith Ath.	4-1	0-5	Third Lanark	5-0	3-1
Rangers	3-2	0-5			

Another publicity card of the team which won Celtic's first Scottish Cup, beating Queen's Park 5-1.
Cullen, Reynolds, Doyle; Maley, Kelly, Dowds; McCallum, Brady; Madden, McMahon, Campbell.
Peter Dowds scored 21 goals in 49 appearances during his two spells with Celtic, but that scourge of the
time – consumption – caused his death in 1895 at 24 years of age.

Obviously not a vintage season for football if the winners, admittedly
scoring just under three a game, can afford to lose about two per match at
the other end. Note how heavy two of the defeats were at Leith and Ibrox.
Surprisingly, Celtic finished three points clear of the rest. The first of the
Joe Cassidys to star for the club, had a good season, scoring seven, but 'Duke'
McMahon was the star, with 18, a goal a game, with contributions from
Jimmy Blessington (6), John Campbell (5), John Divers (4), John Madden
(6) and a rare effort from Dan Doyle.

1893–1894 SCOTTISH CUP

25/11/93		Hurlford	(H)	6-0	2,000
16/12/93		Albion Rovers	(H)	7-0	1,500
13/01/93	QF	St Bernard's	(H)	8-1	2,500
03/02/93	SF	Third Lanark	(A)	5-3	12,000
17/02/93	F	Rangers		1-3	17,000 Hampden

Celtic had a real goal-scoring run on the way to the final, Sandy McMahon
scoring twelve in the four matches. After two defeats by Celtic in recent

years, though, Rangers were ready for this first Old Firm final. The pitch was very wet but Rangers adapted much better to the conditions and Celtic were well beaten. There was no scoring in the first half, but Rangers got their first in 55 minutes, their second in 65 minutes and their third shortly after. With a quarter of an hour to go Willie Maley pulled one back but to no avail. It was Rangers' day. Although founded 14 years before Celtic, this was their first cup win. Unfortunately, their name does not appear on the Scottish Cup as the last space had been taken up by Celtic. Rangers' name for their first one is on the plinth.

1893–1894 GLASGOW CUP

Linthouse	(A)	2-1
Northern	(A)	3-2
Thistle	(A)	7-0
Rangers	(A)	0-1

1893–1894 CHARITY CUP

	3rd L.R.V.	(Hampden)	3-3		
Replay	3rd L.R.V.	(Hampden)	3-2		
Final	Queen's Park	(Ibrox)	2-1	12/05/94	18,000

Team: McArthur; Reynolds and Doyle; Maley, Kelly and McEleny; Blessington, Madden; Cuddihy; Campbell and Divers.

Queen's Park opened the stronger, the Celtic forwards finding the strong

An early photograph of a 'Brake Club'. This one was from St Mary's League of the Cross, in Abercrombie Street. The player incorporated in the banner is Tom Maley. By the dates shown at the front, the years when the club won five charity cups on the trot, Celtic were playing in green-and-white stripes, so the hooped jersey worn by the boy in the middle is something of a puzzle.

wind against them impeding their close-passing game. The game was tough, the tackling very physical but by half-time, neither side had broken the deadlock. A few minutes into the second half, Queen's Park opened the scoring; almost immediately, though, the Celtic forward line raced down-field, Jim Blessington crossed and Johnny Madden poked it in. That was the signal for both sides to attack with renewed vigour but the superior strength of Celtic soon began to show. Six minutes from time, a free-kick by Dan Doyle was deflected away, only as far as Jim Blessington, who blasted the ball into the net for what proved to be the winning goal. The following day, most newspaper reports agreed that it was a hard, but not brilliant game.

1894–1895 SCOTTISH LEAGUE DIVISION I

	P	W	D	L	F	A	Points	Position
Hearts	18	15	1	2	50	18	31	1st
Celtic	18	11	4	3	50	29	26	2nd

FIXTURES

	H	A		H	A
Clyde	2-0	4-2	Rangers	5-3	1-1
Dumbarton	6-0	2-0	St Bernard's	5-2	2-0
Dundee	2-1	1-1	St Mirren	2-2	3-0
Hearts	0-2	0-4	Third Lanark	4-4	1-2
Leith Ath.	4-0	6-5			

Celtic's poor results against Third Lanark (one home draw; one defeat) contributed to their downfall but they were well beaten by the eventual champions, both home and away. A miserly Hearts defence helped their cause greatly. Celtic's defence, on the other hand, was occasionally wide open (at Tynecastle, and Leith) and the attack certainly preferred the home matches. There would appear to have been off-field problems surrounding the away defeat by Hearts. In spite of sterling work by goalkeeper Dan McArthur, more than one observer noted that some players – and officials – seemed less than interested in the match. In the following week's match against Third Lanark, there were changes in defence at right-back, right-half, centre-half and left-half, the famous Walter Arnott, Scottish International full-back, playing his one and only match for Celtic.

1894–1895 SCOTTISH CUP

24/11/93		Queen's Park	(H)	4-1	15,000
15/12/93		Hibs	(A)	0-2	12,000 Protest
29/12/93		Replay Hibs	(A)	2-0	3,000
19/01/94	QF	Dundee	(A)	0-1	12,000

The Cup campaign opened with a big local derby watched by 15,000 spectators. Goals by Campbell, Cassidy and and T. Dunbar took Celtic through. In the second round, Hibs won the first match 2-0 but Celtic protested that Hibs had fielded an ineligible player and this was upheld. The rematch, also in Edinburgh, was won thanks to goals by Campbell and Divers. In the quarter-final 12,000 were present at Dundee to see Celtic give a very poor performance, a first half goal by Sawers enough to take Dundee through to the semi-final where they were beaten by Renton.

		1894–1895 Glasgow Cup			
	Battlefield	(H)	2-2		
Replay	Battlefield	(H)	4-1		
	Clyde	(H)	4-1		
	Cowlairs	(A)	2-0		
Final	Rangers	(Cathkin)	2-0	20,000	17/11/94

The weather was uncertain for this match, the pitch wet and slippy.

Team: McArthur; Dunbar and Doyle, McEleny, Kelly and Maley; Campbell, Madden; Cassidy; McMahon and Divers.

Celtic won the toss and chose to kick with the wind behind them in the first half. It proved to be a good decision. Although both teams rose to the occasion, Celtic just had that little edge and went two up by the interval. The first came in 30 minutes from a free-kick by Dan Doyle; the second, just on the whistle, by John Divers after a fine move by the whole forward line. Shortly in the second half, the crowd broke onto the field at some points of the perimeter but the police were quickly to the fore and play was only briefly held up. The sides were down to ten men each in this half – Smith for Rangers and McMahon for Celtic not re-appearing due to injury. Rangers bombarded the Celtic goal but Dan McArthur was in top form and held them out. At the end, the Celtic fans' relief was evident, as they raced onto the pitch and carried several players in triumph to the pavilion.

		1894–1895 CHARITY CUP			
	Queen's Park	(A)	1-0		
Final	Rangers	(Cathkin)	4-0	25/05/95	

Team: McArthur; Meechan and Doyle; O'Rourke, Kelly, McEleny; Morrison, Madden; McMahon; Divers and Ferguson.

As appeared to be the norm in matches around these early days, Celtic started slowly allowing Rangers an initial flurry, which they failed to take advantage of. Celtic soon raised their game, though, and scored two before the interval, the first a header by Sandy McMahon from a Peter O'Rourke throw-in, and the second from a free-kick by James Kelly after Tom Morrison had been fouled. Celtic kept up the pressure in the second half against a rather ragged Rangers who only attacked sporadically. Two further goals by McMahon late in the match made the final score 4-0, a true reflection of the difference in standard on the day.

Professionalism

The biggest change for every player in that first decade was, of course, the advent of professionalism. It seems quite obvious that Celtic had paid their players from the very beginning. It is unlikely that they could have attracted the services of players like Kelly from Renton, Groves, McMahon and McLaren from Hibs or Doyle from Everton purely on charm! Soon Kelly and Doyle were running public houses and the arrival of the latter made the so-called 'amateurs' in the team threaten to strike unless their status was equally improved. The committee agreed to a regular wage of £2 per week plus bonuses for important matches. For winning the Scottish Cup in 1892, the players received a £3 bonus plus a new suit! In 1893–1894, it was agreed that no player's bonus should exceed £5. The following year the bonus was fixed at 10 shillings (50p) for a win and 5 shillings (25p) for a draw for all league matches. Bonuses were to be decided by the committee. For season 1895–1896, it was agreed that the team should receive a £10 bonus if they won the league and £5 for every Cup win. The League Championship was duly won so Kelly, McMahon, Meechan, Madden, Martin, Blessington, Ferguson, Battles, Doyle and McArthur all received £10 each while £4 went to O'Rourke, Crossan, Dunbar, Morrison, Divers and King. What was eventually to prove the most significant occurrence of this decade for the future of Celtic occurred in 1897. Three years before that Willie Maley had informed the committee of an offer for him to go to Sheffield, although he would have preferred to stay with Celtic. After several meetings, it was decided to offer him a special contract as manager of the Club in addition to that of a player. He had received £100 for past services in 1894 and an honorarium of £75 in 1896, before becoming Secretary/Manager in 1897 with a salary of £150. For the next 50 years he was the man at Celtic's helm.

1895–1896 Scottish League Division 1

	P	W	D	L	F	A	Points	Position
Celtic	18	15	0	3	64	25	30	1st

FIXTURE

	H	A		H	A
Clyde	3-0	5-1	Rangers	6-2	4-2
Dumbarton	3-0	3-2	St Bernard's	2-1	0-3
Dundee	11-0	2-1	St Mirren	4-0	3-1
Hearts	0-5	4-1	Third Lanark	7-0	2 1
Hibs	3-1	2-4			

Celtic's third Championship was a good performance with some surprising inconsistencies – no draws but three heavy defeats all to Edinburgh teams early in the season. Celtic lost their third match to Hibs at Easter Road 4-2 and made two good recoveries in beating St Mirren 4-0 and Rangers 4-2 before losing heavily first to Hearts at home 5-0 and then St Bernard's away 3-0. From that point on they won their last 11 matches including their biggest ever victory, against Dundee at Celtic Park on October 26 when the rather bewildered visitors lost one player before the interval and one at half time, so having only nine men for the second half. It should be said, however, that Celtic were six up at that point! Most unusually for those days, the two full-backs Peter Meechan and Dan Doyle both scored.

1895–1896 SCOTTISH CUP					
18/01/96	Celtic	2	Queen's Park	4	26,000

The pitch was very heavy for this local derby and Queen's Park's long-ball cross-field, passing game was more suited to it than Celtic's close-passing style, especially near goal. Celtic were 2-1 up at half time through a Jim Blessington shot and a Dan Doyle penalty. Early in the second half, Queens equalised from a penalty and from that point Celtic crumbled, the amateurs scoring twice more. R.S. McColl got two for Queen's Park and was reckoned to be the finest forward on the field. Celtic were strong at the back, full-backs Peter Meechan and Dan Doyle particularly solid, but the forwards had a poor day, Willie Maley commenting afterwards that it was 'the worst our forwards had been all season'. Two penalties in one match was quite uncommon at this time. It was reported that both custodians had come out to the six-yard line – obviously to no avail! Gate takings came to £843 15s 6d (£843.77p).

1895–1896 GLASGOW CUP					
	Linthouse	(A)	7-1		
	Cambuslang	(H)	6-1		
	Partick Thistle	(H)	5-1		
Final	Queen's Park	(Ibrox)	6-3	24,000	16/11/95

There were so many packed into Ibrox for this match that the crowd encroached on to the pitch at both the Copland Road end and the North Stand. The ground was very soft after continuous rainfall and initially Queen's Park coped better, going in at the interval leading by 3-1. However, in the second half, Celtic's superior fitness told. Queen's Park played too open a game, allowing Celtic, with James Kelly superb at centre-half, to take control and win comfortably. The Celtic team: McArthur; Meechan, Doyle; Maley, Kelly, Battles; Madden, Blessington; Martin; McMahon and Ferguson.

The Celtic team which won both the Charity and Glasgow Cups in 1895–96, pictured here with the Glasgow Cup. Back row, left to right: T. Maguire (Trainer), J. Kelly, A. Martin, D. Doyle, B. Battles, D. Ferguson. Middle row: J. Madden, A. McMahon, P. Meechan, W. Maley,. Front row: J. Blessinton, D. McArthur.

No distinguishing feature at all in this picture for for the goalkeeper, Dan McArthur. Alan Martin only played this one season at centre-forward before joining Hibs, but he played in most of the league matches thus gaining a Championship medal, as well as winner's medals for the Charity and Glasgow Cups. In 18 games, he scored 18 goals.

1895 1896 Charity Cup					
	Rangers	(A)	6-1		
Final	Queen's Park	(Ibrox)	2-1	11,000	16/05/96

Team: McArthur; Meechan and Doyle; McEleny, Kelly and Battles; Madden, Blessington; Martin; McMahon and Ferguson.

This match was played on a scorching, hot, May day at Ibrox – the third time that season that the two teams had met in a cup tie. The score was tied 1-1 after normal time, so the match went to extra time, with Celtic scoring the winner in the 104th minute. They owed their victory mainly to their very sound defence, the forward line having some injury problems – Jim Blessington lame for most of the match and Johnny Madden playing with an injured shoulder.

1896–1897 Scottish League

	P	W	D	L	F	A	Points	Position
Hearts	18	13	2	3	47	22	28	1st
Celtic	18	10	4	4	42	18	24	4th

Fixtures

	H	A		H	A
Abercorn	5-0	6-0	Rangers	1-1	0-2
Clyde	4-1	7-2	St Bernard's	2-0	2-1
Dundee	0-1	2-2	St Mirren	2-1	0-2
Hearts	3-0	1-1	Third Lanark	2-0	3-0
Hibs	1-1	1-3			

A poor season for Celtic, with much off-field discussion and argument, resulting in numerous team changes. The goal-scoring rate was way down on the previous season, although the defence held firm, only losing a goal a game. The games lost were the first of the season against Hibs and the last three against Rangers, Dundee and St Mirren. It was to prove James Kelly's last season and there was a debut match for his successor Davie Russell on 15 August 1896.

1896–1897 Scottish Cup

09/01/97	Arthurlie	(A)	2-4

This was probably the biggest upset in Scottish Cup history. At least when Rangers lost to Berwick in 1967, the latter were in the Second Division. Arthurlie were non League; and in the second round were beaten 5-1 by Second Division Morton in front of 4,000 (for full story – see text below).

1896–1897 Glasgow Cup

	Clyde	(H)	5-1		
	'Queen's Park	(A)	4-2		
Final	Rangers	(Cathkin)	1-1		
Replay	Rangers	(Cathkin)	1-2	15,000	21/11/96

1896–1897 Charity Cup

Rangers	(Hampden)	1-4

The Arthurlie Disaster

In the latter half of this decade, there were times when relationships behind the scenes seemed to affect performances on the field. The players brought in by Celtic's officials during the early years had, of course, been reared by others clubs, and joining this new club must have seemed a real boost, not only to their status, but also to their bank balance. Good players they may have been, but quite a few were essentially mercenaries, willing to ply their trade wherever the remuneration was highest. This would hardly have

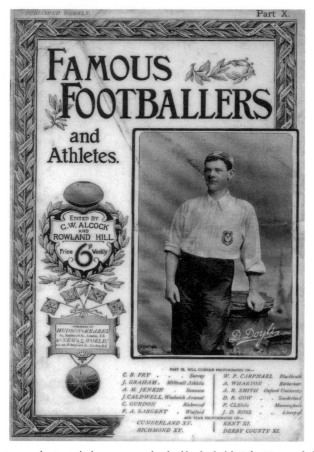

Dan Doyle in very distinguished company in this booklet backed by The News of the World.

endeared them to the Celtic officials of the time, for whom the Club came first. At the same time, these very same officials were locked into discussions behind the scenes over the future direction of the club and its financial matters. Many alliances would have been joined and promises made, with each grouping no doubt having relationships with its own favourite player or players. Unfortunately the Secretary/Manager, Willie Maley, would have been heavily involved in all these discussions, as well as trying to pick, adjust and cajole the players.

However, the league championship was won in 1895–1896 and the following season, after a bad reverse in the first match to Hibs (1-3) in Edinburgh, Celtic then went twelve matches unbeaten. The play, however, was not admired by all, particularly the *Scottish Umpire*. On 16 November 1896 it quoted 'some of Celtic's players are often guilty of unnecessary charging and the stupidity of their conduct is highlighted by the fact that...they have no need to adopt such tactics'.

On 25 November 1896, at Cathkin Park, 15,000 watched the Glasgow Cup

Final, when Rangers won 2-1 in a surprisingly easy fashion. Two days later, several periodicals were harsh in their verdict. 'As much as we regret the fact, we are forced to the conclusion that Doyle as a left back is not the Doyle of old. However much past experience stood him in good stead on Saturday, one could not fail to perceive that his tackling ability has sadly deteriorated…We have also to remember that Battles did not enhance his reputation as a left back…a little less pugilism and a little more football would be much more effective…' (*Scottish Umpire*, 23/11/96). Whether the report was accurate or not, it was certainly wounding. The *Scottish Referee* had also written reports of a similar nature in recent weeks, right-back Peter Meechan and inside-right John Divers being mentioned disparagingly.

Five days later, just before the home match with Hibs, three players, Meechan, Divers and Battles, refused to play unless the press box was cleared of reporters from these papers. Their ultimatum was delivered just minutes before the match but the Celtic officials refused to back down. Twelfth man Barney Crossan was pressed into service as was Willie Maley, who had officially retired the previous season. Even so, the team had only ten men until 15 minutes into the second half, when Tom Dunbar took the field at left-back, having been recalled from the reserve team match at Hampden. A 1-1 draw was the result but then the Club exacted retribution, suspending all three players indefinitely and cutting their wages. Rather surprisingly, the revamped team won its next two matches, against Third Lanark (3-0) and Clyde (4-1) before going down to Rangers (0-2) in the last match before Christmas.

The next official match was three weeks later against Arthurlie in a first round Scottish Cup tie. One can only wonder at the behind-the-scenes discussions and arguments which would have gone on over this period, a time which players would have regarded as something of a holiday, even though some friendlies were played. Christmas was not celebrated at that time in the same way as today. The New Year was 'the' festival time, with drink a-plenty and as you would imagine, the players then were no more abstemious than the general public. The players would also have regarded Arthurlie as easy victims. The Barrhead club was a non-league outfit, having had to fight its way through the Qualifying Cup to get entry to the Scottish Cup. They had gained this place by beating Kilmarnock Athletic 2-1 in the quarter-final but were then trounced 8-2 by Falkirk in the semi-final. What did favour them though, was a pitch at Dunterlie Park known locally as 'The Humph', not only narrow but very uneven, quite unsuitable for the close-passing Celtic style of the time. The troubles behind the scenes had escalated during the holiday period with several players showing a less than enthusiastic endeavour for the task. Some players were injured and one, Dan Doyle, failed to turn up at all.

Reports of the match suggest that Celtic started with only seven men and were two down before Barney Crossan was again thrust onto the field, still wearing his normal trousers! Arthurlie were 2-1 up at half-time and eventually won 4-2, the Celtic defence being regarded in the press 'as wide open as a barn door'. It was a humiliating defeat, one of the biggest shocks ever in the Scottish Cup and the Celtic officials again applied swift punishment. Dan Doyle was fined £5 and a week's wages; John Madden and Tom Morrison had their wages reduced. At the end of the season, came a purge, when outside-right Tom Morrison was transferred to Burnley for £20, full-back John King went to East Stirling, Harry McIlvenny centre-forward to New Brighton, right-back Peter Meechan to Everton for £100, wing half Barry Battles to Dundee and inside-forward John Divers to Everton.

Six weeks later, on the 20th February Celtic lost 0-1 to Dundee at Celtic Park in their penultimate league match and in the final game at Paisley went down 0-2 to St Mirren on the 13 March. It was a dreadful end to the season and not unnoticed by the Press. The *Scottish Sport* at the end of January 1897 said 'there is a pretty widespread feeling that all is not well at Parkhead...a super abundance of unpatriotic apathy which is doing even more to degrade the club than any multiplicity of structure'. Six points had been lost in the last three matches of the season yet Celtic finished only four points behind Hearts in fourth place; and of course they had an embarrassing exit to the Scottish Cup at the hands of a non-league team. There were certainly problems behind the scenes not only between manager and players but among officials – problems which had to be addressed – and quickly!

------------ ❁ ------------

1897–1898 Scottish League Division I

	P	W	D	L	F	A	Points	Position
Celtic	18	15	3	0	56	13	33	1st

FIXTURES

	H	A		H	A
Clyde	6-1	9-1	Rangers	0-0	4-0
Dundee	2-1	2-1	St Brnard's	5-1	2-0
Hearts	3-2	0-0	St Mirren	3-0	0-0
Hibs	4-1	2-1	Third Lanark	4-0	1-0
Partick Thistle	3-1	6-3			

A fourth Championship gained by Celtic, who finished four points clear of Rangers and never lost a match. All the ingredients for a league win were there; an average of three plus goals per game and a miserly defence. The three draws (Rangers home, St Mirren away, Hearts away) were all 0-0; while the back three of goalkeeper Dan McArthur and full-backs Dan Doyle and Jimmy Welford, were together for 13 of the 18 matches. Top scorer was

George 'Dod' Allan, signed from Liverpool in May 1897. He scored 14 in 17 matches, including 5 in the 9-1 defeat of Clyde on Christmas Day. He left again for Liverpool at the end of the season but was struck down by TB and died in October 1899.

1897–1898 SCOTTISH CUP				
08/01/98	Arthurlie	(A)	7-0	3,000
22/01/98	Third Lanark	(A)	2-3	13,000

Ironically, Arthurlie were again the first round opponents and 3,000 turned up at Dunterlie Park in Barrhead to see if they could repeat their success of the previous year. Celtic, however, were not to be caught out this time, the goals coming from Sandy McMahon (2), George Allan, Hugh Goldie (his only goal ever for the Club), John Campbell and a brace by Adam Henderson, playing his first and only Scottish Cup tie. It was a different matter against Third Lanark at Cathkin though, where 13,000 were present. The match was finely balanced 2-2 at the interval – goals by John Campbell and Alec King – but Thirds were the better side in the second half and deserved to go through. They were eventually beaten by Rangers in the semi-final, after two replays.

1897–1898 GLASGOW CUP					
	Clyde	(H)	2-1		
	Rangers	(H)	2-2		
Replay	Rangers	(A)	1-1	30,000	
Replay	Rangers	(A)	1-3	25,000	20.11.97

1897–1898 CHARITY CUP		
Rangers	(Cathkin)	0-2

The Ground

Off the field, this decade is noticeable for two important events in Celtic's history. Firstly, the move to a new ground and secondly the registration of the Club as a Limited Company.

The first ground had been built on land leased on a yearly basis, the sum of £50 per annum having been agreed. Since most of the club's committee men at this time were of Irish extraction, it would have come as no surprise when the landlord, after three years at this figure, wanted an increase. Frankly, in commercial terms, an increase was probably justified. The crowds which attended Celtic's matches were way in excess of any other club in Scotland. In that first Scottish Cup run of 1888–1889 for instance 6,500 were present at the Cowlairs game, a total of 16,000 watched the two matches against Clyde, while well over 30,000 witnessed the final and the subsequent replay.

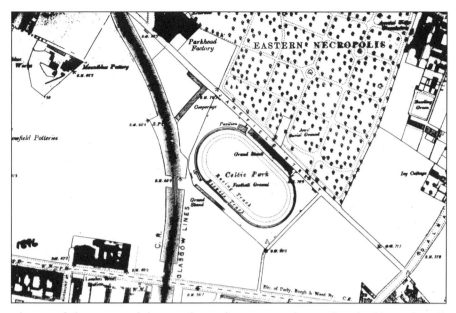

This map of the area around the new Celtic Park – c. 1895 – does not show the old ground at all. Notice how stark the surroundings are, and the lack of a stand on the south side while the ground there settled.

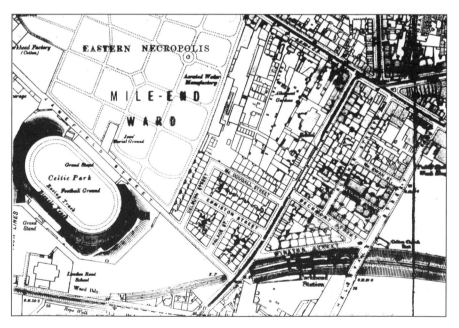

By 1912, the date of this map, houses now occupied the site of the first ground. The Grant Stand was up, the terracing was more organised and the school had been built on London Road.

The Celtic Pavilion, with the selected ones on both the verandah and the area in front. From the strips that the Celtic players are wearing, this photograph was taken in season 1903.

Three years later, in the cup run of 1891–1892, the attendances were 4,000 for St Mirren, 4,000 for Cowlairs, 11,000 for Rangers in the semi-final, 40,000 for the first match in the final and 26,000 for the second. On the basis of these figures, perhaps the landlord had some justification for a rent increase, but the rise suggested, from £50 to £450 was just plain greed and the Celtic committee said no!

Various new sites were suggested, particularly in Possilpark and Springburn, but Cowlairs were already established in that area so the idea was abandoned. Instead, the committee took a ten-year lease on a piece of ground between their then stadium and London Road. It was an unprepossessing choice – a quarry hole in fact half-filled with water and many enthusiasts were required to fill it with materials to raise it level with the surrounding surface.

Eventually, a very fine stadium arose on this unlikely site. The pitch was surrounded by two tracks, one for running and one for cycling, the latter

A drawing of Celtic Park from the London Road side. In the foreground is the Grant Stand; to the north is the stand and pavilion. The drawing was completed in April 1904. One month later, both the stand and pavilion were damaged by fire.

banked at the corner. A barrier surrounded the tracks and beyond that stretched the terracing. This was constructed of wood with steps three feet broad ascending gradually to twelve feet in height.

On the north side the pitch and two tracks were adjoined by a covered stand 320ft long to protect spectators from bad weather. To the west of this, was a two-storey pavilion complete with verandah overlooking the whole playing, running and cycling area. Inside were separate changing areas for the two teams – toilets, hot and cold baths and an office. The area at the front of the covered stand was terraced and enclosed, to be used by those who paid slightly higher prices than spectators elsewhere in the ground. On the south or London Road side, where most of the infill work had taken place, the ground had been left to settle before a stand could be built. In the meantime, uncovered seating accommodation was provided there with a press box alongside. All in all it was the most impressive stadium with a 50,000 capacity.

At a very emotional ceremony on the 20th March 1892, the centre sod of the new pitch, a shamrock-covered piece of turf brought over from Donegal that very morning, was placed in position by Michael Davitt, the Irish patriot, to great acclaim. The first event held there was the Annual Sports, which Willie Maley, a former runner himself, eventually raised to an international event. The first match there took place on the 20 August 1892 when Celtic beat Renton by 4-3.

In 1895, Celtic installed turnstiles at Celtic Park. These were installed by a Lancashire engineering firm (W.T. Ellison & Co) at a cost of £445. Before this time, Celtic had used rolls of admission tickets, numbered in sequence and stamped with the Club's crest.

Three years later, James Grant, a director originally from Northern Ireland, used his initiative and financial acumen to build a palatial stand on the London Road side of Celtic Park. Grant came to an agreement with the Club and took a percentage of the admission money as a way of recouping his investment.

The stand was two-tiered and had tip-up seats as well as a glass front designed to protect the paying customer. Unfortunately the stand was not popular, partly because the spectators felt that the stairs were too steep and partly because the architect had not allowed for condensation, so the glass steamed up, making vision impossible. Eventually, the glass was removed but the stand's unpopularity remained.

1898–1899 SCOTTISH LEAGUE DIVISION I

	P	W	D	L	F	A	Points	Position
Rangers	18	18	0	0	79	18	36	1st
Celtic	18	11	2	5	51	33	24	3rd

FIXTURES

	H	A		H	A
Clyde	9-2	0-0	Rangers	0-4	1-4
Dundee	4-1	4-1	St Bernard's	1-0	3-2
Hearts	3-2	2-2	St Mirren	4-1	0-4
Hibs	1-2	1-2	Third Lanark	2-1	4-2
Partick Thistle	4-0	8-3			

The perfect season for Rangers, the first and only time this occurred in Scottish Football. Celtic slipped badly from the heights of the year before, inconsistency being their downfall. High scoring in some matches (9 *v.* Clyde, 8 *v.* Partick Thistle, 4 *v.* Dundee (twice) Partick Thistle, St Mirren and Third Lanark) was countered by poor defending in others, leading to heavy defeats (0-4 and 1-4 to Rangers; 0-4 to St Mirren). Predictably, a glance at the team selections showed many changes during the eighteen matches, for example two goalkeepers, three right-backs, three left-backs, five centre-halves with even more in the forward line.

1898–1899 SCOTTISH CUP

14/01/98		6th GRV Dalbeattie	(A)	8-1	300	
04/02/98		St Bernards	(H)	3-0	3,000	
18/02/98	QF	Queen's Park	(H)	2-4	12,000	Abandoned
25/02/98	QF	Replay Queen's Park	(H)	2-1	9,000	
11/03/98	SF	Port Glasgow Ath	(H)	4-2	9,000	
22/04/98	F	Rangers	(Hampden)	2-0	25,000	

The elusive 'double' escaped again. League champions Celtic had failed in the finals of 1892–1893 and 1893–1894, and now it was Rangers' turn to fall at the final hurdle. While the men from Ibrox powered their way past Hearts, Ayr Parkhouse, Clyde and St Mirren, Celtic received two frights on their way to the final. In the quarter-final against Queen's Park, the tie was abandoned mid-way through the second half, when fading light, plus a touch of what we now know as smog, made play impossible. Queens were leading 4-2 at the time and protested – unofficially – that they should be awarded the tie. The SFA disagreed, however, and Celtic, through goals by Sandy McMahon, made no mistake in the rematch.

Celtic also received an unwelcome fright in the semi-final when Port Glasgow Athletic, from the Second Division, showed the form which had taken them past Partick Thistle 7-3 in the previous round. After the huge attendance for the Queen's Park rematch in the quarter-final, many fans obviously thought that this tie would prove to be a walkover but Port Glasgow proved to be doughty opponents, held Celtic to 2-2 at half-time before goals by Sandy McMahon and John Divers took Celtic through.

For the final, Rangers prepared at the coast, Celtic at home. By the kick-off time of 3.30 pm 25,000 were inside, a good attendance considering that the admission prices had been doubled for this match, which eventually took in £1,234 8s 6d (£1,234.42). The weather was good, the football rather disappointing. The first half was goalless with Celtic having a slight edge and this was continued in the second half, the wind now in their favour. In 47 minutes, 'Duke' McMahon scored with a header and then the Celtic rearguard took over, never faltering as Rangers stepped up the pressure. With fifteen minutes to go, outside-right Johnny Hodge scored the clincher in only his fifth game for the Club.

1898–1899 Glasgow Cup			
	Clyde	(H)	7-0
	Rangers	(A)	1-1
Replay	Rangers	(H)	1-2

1898–1899 Charity Cup			
	Queen's Park	(Cathkin)	4-0
Final	Rangers	(Ibrox)	2-0

This match was played on 27 May 1899 in front of 20,000 spectators. Even though five of their cup-winning team were missing – Storrier, Marshall, King, Campbell and Bell – Celtic won easily, goals by Sandy McMahon in the first half and Peter Somers in the second taking the cup back to Parkhead. £568 14s 6d (£568.72p) was taken at the various gates which when added to the income from previous grounds, left £1,136 for distribution to the various charities.

Behind the Scenes

Behind the scenes, there was much wrangling during these formative years about the future direction of the Club. Almost from its inception, the men involved were split into two camps; those who saw Celtic FC merely as a vehicle for the raising of money for charitable purposes and those who wished to put the Club on a more structured – and business-like – footing. The initial aim of course, proclaimed in the first circular, was to help the needy of the east end. For many early enthusiasts however, there was another political influence to their thinking. Many of Celtic's early committee men – John Glass, James Quillan, Arthur Murphy, William McKillop – were equally devoted members of the Irish National League or more specifically one of its Glasgow off-shoots, the Home Government Branch!

The Irish National League was the dominant voice of Irish politics in Scotland and its devotees raised large amounts of money for the cause of Home Rule. In the mid-1870s, the organisation had been beset by divisions, one group wishing to maintain the non-sectarian view prevalent since its inception, another faction proposing a more Catholic outlook. Eventually, the former group held sway, the one which comprised many of the Celtic committee men. So, when the Club itself was involved in discussions regarding their future, it came as no surprise when these same people again opted for a more open, practical dimension.

There were early casualties. At the AGM of 1891, held in the Mechanics Hall in Bridgeton, Dr John Conway, the Honorary President of the Club since its inception, was deposed. During the same evening, he lost another vote to become President and was almost ostracised until his death in 1894. A review of the elected officials of the Club in the early- and mid-1890s shown in Tables 3.3 and 3.4 (see page 66) shows the same names occupying the senior positions with a plethora of 'would-bes' jockeying for the places on the committee. AGMs were long and lively; that of 1891 began at 8 pm and finished at 3 am in the following morning. In that season, income totalled £4,427 11s 2d (£4,427.61p). The twenty two league matches raised £1,100, the thirteen friendlies nearly £1,400, while £1,140 came from Cup ties. The sum of £969 5s 4d (£969.27p) went to visitors and guarantees; while £445 was apportioned to charity, the Poor Children's Dinner Table receiving £220.

One year later, 1892, that figure for charity was cut to £230. In 1893, £63 in donations to charities with nothing going to the Poor Children's Dinner Table. And so it continued. Almost as soon as Dr Conway had been deposed and Brother Walfrid transferred to London in 1892, the charitable aims had been replaced by practicalities.

FROM THE FINANCIAL REPORT	
1894	1895
£1,000 Ground Improvements.	James McKay and Willie Maley both
£236 Reduction of Debt.	awarded £100 for turning professional .
£100 Honorarium to Treasurer.	£91 – Charity.
	Poor children's dinner tables – nil.

The idea of a limited company was originally proposed by Joseph Shaughnessey, the Club's Honourable President and a Glasgow lawyer but was initially defeated in 1893. At a fairly bitter half-yearly meeting in December 1895, it was raised again, with Tom Maley the chief critic, using his experience as the Superintendent of a School for Destitute Children in Slatefield to push for more money to charity. But the businessmen continued to pressurise others and got their way in March 1897, using the pretext of structural changes to the ground to hold the World Cycling Championships there in July 1897. It was argued that the money required to make these changes would be more effectively raised as a limited liability company.

Eventually, the protagonists carried the day and 'Celtic Football and Athletic Company Limited' came into existence in April 1897 and a provisional board was appointed. Very quickly though, both sides would have sound reasons for prolonging the original argument. Advocates of the new set-up could point to the Club's enhanced capacity to raise capital, which resulted in Celtic becoming the first football club to own its ground outright by the payment of £10,000 to the landlord – Lord Newlands – in December 1897. Opponents of the new set up though, could point with scorn to the distribution of funds in the Club's first year of operation. An income of £16,267 meant a 20 per cent dividend for shareholders and directors. Unfortunately, for charity, there was nothing!

TABLE 3.3. CELTIC OFFICE-HOLDERS 1890–97

	1890–91	1891–92	1892–93	1893–94	1894–95	1895–96	1896–97
Honorary President	D. John Conway	J. Shaughnessey	J. Shaughnessey	W. McKillop	W. McKillop	W. Mckillop	
President	John Glass	John Glass	John Glass	John Glass	John Glass	John Glass	John Glass
Vice-President	James Quillan	Tom Maley	Tom Maley	J.H. McLaughlin	J.H. McLaughlin	J.H. McLaughlin	J.H. McLaughlin
Treasurer	Hugh Darroch	James McKay	James McKay	James McKay	James McKay	James McKay	James McKay
Secretary	John O'Hara	J.H. McLaughlin	J.H. McLaughlin	Willie Maley	Willie Maley	Willie Maley	Willie Maley
Match Secretary	Willie Maley	Willie Maley	Willie Maley	—	—	—	—
Committee	J.M. Nelis H. Cairns W. McKillop D. Malloy J. McGrory P. Walsh J. Shaughnessey J.H. McLaughlin T. Maley J. McDonald D. Meikleham	S. Henry A. Murphy J. Kelly J. O'Hara T. Walls J. McQuade J. Moore J. Cairns	S. Henry J. Kelly T. Walls J. Cairns A. Murphy J. O'Hara J. McQuade J. Cairns	A. Murphy J. Henry T. Maley J. Kelly J. O'Hara J. McQuade J. Cairns J. Moore P. Gallacher T. Walls	A. Murphy H. Dunbar J. McCann J. Kelly F. McErlean J. O'Hara J. Curtis P. Gallacher T. Walls J. Moore	H. Dunbar J. McCann A. Murphy J. McCreadie J. McQuade J. Curtis P. Gallacher F. McErlean J. McGrory C. Docherty J.H. McBride	H. Dunbar J. McCann A. Murphy J. McCreadie J. McQuade J. Curtis P. Gallacher F. McErlean P. McMorrow F. Havelin J. Warnock
Leaseholders		J.H. Nellis D. Meikleham W. McKillop G. Bradley	J.H. Nellis D. Meikleham W. McKillop G. Bradley	J.H. Nellis D. Meikleham G. Bradley J. Shaughnessey	J.H. Nellis D. Meikleham G. Bradley J. Shaughnessey		

TABLE 3.4. PROVISIONAL BOARD 1897

J.H. McLaughlin	Michael Hughes
John O'Hara	Michael Dunbar
T. Maley	James McKay
John Glass	

FROM THE FINANCIAL REPORT	
1896	
£1,156	Ground Improvements.
£723	Reduction of Debt.
£75	Treasurer James McKay.
£75	Secretary Willie Maley.

An appeal from St Vincent De Paul Society for help for the Poor Chiuldren's Dinner Tables – Refused.

Of the provisional board appointed in April 1897, Tom Maley and Michael Hughes were originally very critical of the Executive Committee's move away from the original aims of the Club. By being members of this very Board, it would appear that both had bowed to the inevitable and thrown in their lot with their more business-like colleagues. Perhaps, though, memories were long, because when the first Board of Directors was appointed in the autumn of 1897, these two names were missing, replaced by John McKillop and James Grant.

1899–1900 SCOTTISH LEAGUE DIVISION I

	P	W	D	L	F	A	Points	Position
Rangers	18	15	2	1	69	27	32	1st
Celtic	18	9	7	2	46	27	25	2nd

FIXTURES

H	A		H	A	
Clyde	3-2	5-0	Rangers	3-2	3-3
Dundee	1-1	2-1	St Bernard's	5-0	1-1
Hearts	0-2	2-3	St Mirren	3-1	2-2
Hibs	2-1	1-1	Third Lanark	5-2	3-0
Kilmarnock	3-3	2-2			

The same chopping and changing of personnel as the previous year, the same inconsistency of results. The defence was solid enough, a reasonable number of goals were scored but not comparable to Rangers. Seven draws did not help the cause, particularly two at 3-3 and two at 2-2. Both League matches against Rangers were played at Celtic Park as ground alterations were being made at Ibrox.

1899–1900 SCOTTISH CUP

13/01/1900		Bo'ness	(H)	7-1	1,000
27/01/1900		Port Glasgow	(A)	5-1	4,000
17/02/1900	QF	Kilmarnock	(H)	4-0	8,000
24/02/1900	SF	Rangers	(A)	2-2	30,000
10/03/1900	Replay	Rangers	(H)	4-0	32,000
14/04/1900	Final	Queen's Park	(Ibrox)	4-3	15,000

This was a comfortable and high-scoring passage through the early rounds for Celtic. In the semi-final tie at Ibrox, all the goals came in the second half but in the replay, Celtic were two up at the interval and finished comfortable

4-0 victors, with goals from Sandy McMahon (2) John Hodge and John Bell. In the final, held at Ibrox, before a disappointing crown of just over 15,000, Celtic won the toss and chose to play with the wind at their back. Queen's Park opened well, though, and took the lead early in the match. This spurred Celtic into action to raise their game but the Queens' defence held out. Just before the interval, though, it was breached when Sandy McMahon scored with a header; within minutes it was pierced again when McMahon headed across goal for John Divers to tap in and in forty three minutes John Bell made it 3-1. That should have effectively finished the match as a contest. But although Divers scored again early in the second half to make it 4-1, Queen's Park came back well, with the strong Celtic defence undergoing various trials and tribulations and also losing two goals. But at the final whistle, the favourites were still ahead 4-3. The team: McArthur; Storrier, Battles; Russell, Marshall, Orr; Hodge, Campbell; Divers; McMahon and Bell.

	1899–1900 GLASGOW CUP				
	Partick Thistle	(H)	5-1		
	Linthouse	(H)	5-1		
Final	Rangers	(Cathkin)	1-1	10,000	11/11/99
Replay	Rangers	(Cathkin)	0-1	4,000	18/11/99

	1899–1900 CHARITY CUP				
	Queen's Park	(Cathkin)	3-2	Abandoned	
Replay	Queen's Park	(Cathkin)	6-1		
Final	Rangers	(Hampden)	1-5	15,000	12/05/1900

CHAPTER FOUR (1900–1910)
A Poor Start — Then Six-in-a-Row

AT THE BEGINNING of the 20th century, Celtic were in the middle of a difficult period. The management and supporters had become used to success during the 1890s and also accustomed to a style which was purely 'Celtic'.

Inconsistency had set in, however, not helped by off-field incidents amongst senior players which proved an embarrassment to the Club. As the years rolled by, for instance, Dan Doyle, by now 35, was becoming even less and less amenable to discipline. In a match at Stoke in aid of the Hanley Church Building Fund, his on-field conduct was much abhorred by the sports writers present. In August 1898, *Scottish Sport* reported a court case involving the seduction of a young girl by Jack Reynolds, recently signed from Aston Villa. That was bad enough but more worrying for the Club was the information given in evidence that Reynolds and 'other prominent Celtic players' had been betting on horses and losing heavily. Eventually, a string of poor performances provoked an outburst from Chairman J.H. McLaughlin, 'enough to make the directors inclined to clear the whole crowd of players out if they could and get an entirely fresh lot to represent the green and white'. (*The Glasgow Examiner*, 23 December 1899).

From 1900 to 1903, that is precisely what manager Willie Maley did. The transformation was uncomfortable and difficult. Within that three-year period, Celtic reached six Cup Finals – and lost all of them! In the Scottish Cup they lost to the Edinburgh duo in successive seasons (1901–1902); while in the League campaigns, they finished second, second and fifth. The tide began to turn at the end of season 1902–1903, when St Mirren were beaten 5-2 in the Charity Cup Final at Ibrox. In the following campaign, performances improved, more goals were scored and the team finished a respectable third in the table. The highlight for the fans was the return of the Scottish Cup to Parkhead, with new star Jimmy Quinn scoring the first ever Cup Final hat-trick as Rangers were beaten 3-2.

Willie Maley had achieved a remarkable job in these years, pushing out the old guard, bringing in younger players and moulding a team. A comparison of the cup winning sides of 1900 and 1904 clearly shows the transformation accomplished:

1900		1904	
1.	McArthur	1.	Adams
2.	Storrier	2.	McLeod
3.	Battles	3.	Orr
4.	Russell	4.	Young
5.	Marshall	5.	Loney
6.	Orr	6.	Hay
7.	Hodge	7.	Muir
8.	Campbell	8.	McMenemy
9.	Divers	9.	Quinn
10.	McMahon	10.	Somers
11.	Bell	11.	Hamilton

1900–1901 SCOTTISH LEAGUE DIVISION I

	P	W	D	L	F	A	Points	Position
Rangers	20	17	2	1	60	25	35	1st
Celtic	20	13	3	4	49	28	29	2nd

FIXTURES

	H	A		H	A
Dundee	1-2	1-1	Partick Thistle	3-3	6-2
Hearts	1-3	2-0	Queen's Park	2-0	2-0
Hibs	3-1	2-2	Rangers	2-1	1-2
Kilmarnock	1-0	1-2	St Mirren	3-0	4-3
Morton	4-2	3-2	Third Lanark	5-1	2-1

The years between 1897 and 1904 were very much transition years for Celtic, particularly in the League. A new team was evolving and teams take time to achieve their potential. One more team had been added to the League for this season making eleven in total. Celtic did not do too badly in terms of goals for and against, but lost some vital matches. Rangers were on a roll yet Celtic gave them their only defeat of the season. Unfortunately, home defeats by Hearts and Dundee and a more surprising one away to Kilmarnock, allowed Rangers to take a third Title. The final match of the season, on the 19 January against St Mirren, was to prove important. On that day, a young man from Croy made his debut at outside-left. Jimmy Quinn scored on that debut, the first of many for Celtic.

1900–1901 SCOTTISH CUP

12/01/01		Rangers	(H)	1-0	28,000
26/01/01		Kilmarnock	(H)	2-1	Friendly
09/02/01		Kilmarnock	(H)	6-0	12,000
16/02/01	QF	Dundee	(A)	1-0	7,000
23/03/01	SF	St Mirren	(H)	1-0	17,000
06/04/01	F	Hearts	(Ibrox)	3-4	16,000

The first-round tie between the two top teams in the League was eagerly anticipated, yet in the end, it was an own goal by left-back Drummond that broke the deadlock. The first match against Kilmarnock in the second round

Jimmy Quinn in his early days. Some idea of his strength can be gleaned from that bull-neck. Jimmy joined Celtic in 1901 and retired from the game in 1915. During that period, in 331 appearances for his one and only senior club, he scored 216 goals.

was played as a friendly because no referee turned up! Celtic really went to town in the second match with goals by John Campbell (2), Rab Findlay, John Divers, Sandy McMahon and Willie McOustra.

In the final, Celtic were always struggling to catch up, with keeper Dan McArthur normally so secure, having a bad day. 2-1 down at half-time they pulled back to 3-3 before Dan McArthur fumbled a Bobby Walker shot and outside-left Bell scored the winner for Hearts.

1900–1901 Glasgow Cup

Rangers	(A)	3-4

1900–1901 Charity Cup

	Rangers	0-0		
Replay	Rangers	1-0		
Final	Third Lanark	0-0	8,000	
Replay	Third Lanark	0-3	23/05/01	7,000

All matches for the Charity Cup took place at the Exhibition Ground in Kelvingrove Park. This was the worst Celtic season so far with no trophies to show for their efforts.

Celtic were beaten by Rangers in the final of the Exhibition Cup, held to commemorate the 2nd Glasgow International Exhibition in 1901. Ironically, the same trophy did eventually arrive at Celtic Park in unusual circumstances (see page 79). This photograph of the Russian section at that exhibition.

1901–1902 SCOTTISH LEAGUE DIVISION I

	P	W	D	L	F	A	Points	Position
Rangers	18	13	2	3	43	29	28	1st
Celtic	18	11	4	3	38	28	26	2nd

FIXTURES

	H	A		H	A
Dundee	1-1	3-2	Queen's Park	1-0	2-3
Hearts	1-2	2-2	Rangers	2-4	2-2
Hibs	2-2	2-1	St Mirren	3-1	3-2
Kilmarnock	4-2	1-0	Third Lanark	3-2	2-0
Morton	2-1	2-1			

Rangers set a then record of four championships in a row, but their team, as can be seen from the results, was not the side of the previous three years. Goal scoring is down, defensive losses are up. Like them, Celtic lost three but the fact that they could not beat Rangers, plus a home defeat by Hearts and an away loss to Queen's Park blew their chances. In goal, Dan McArthur (30 per cent shut-out rate) had been replaced for the campaign by Robert McFarlane, whose 17 per cent score refers purely to this one season. McArthur played his last match on 16 September versus Hibs at Easter Road. During this season, Willie Loney's name appeared for the first time in the half-back line.

1901–1902 SCOTTISH CUP

11/01/02		Thornliebank	(H)	3-0		
25/01/02		Arbroath	(A)	3-2	5,000	
08/02/02	QF	Hearts	(A)	1-1	14,000	A friendly
			due to weather conditions			
15/02/02		Hearts	(A)	1-1	20,000	
22/02/02		Replay Hearts	(H)	2-1	30,000	
22/03/02	SF	St Mirren	(A)	3-2	35,000	
26/04/02	F	Hibs	(Celtic Park)	0-1	16,000	

The 1901 Exhibition Trophy.

The squad which beat Sunderland 5-1 and Rangers 3-2 to take the above trophy back to Parkhead. Back row, left to right: B. Battles, W. Loney, H. Marshall, J. Moir, A. McMahon, H. Watson, J. Campbell, W. Orr, A. McPherson, D. McLeod, P. Somers. Front row: J. Quinn, J. McMenemy, W. McCafferty, W. Maley (Manager), A. Crawford, T. McDermott, J. Hamilton.

The surprise here was in the final itself. Firstly that, considering the crowds in the earlier ties, only 16,000 turned up to see the event; and secondly, there was much astonishment when Celtic failed to take advantage of a home-tie and fell to a late goal caused by poor marking at a corner.

	1901–1902 GLASGOW CUP				
	Clyde	(H)	3-0		
	Third Lanark	(H)	5-1		
Final	Rangers	(Ibrox)	2-2	40,000	26/10/01
Replay	Celtic scratched				

After a ballot at a meeting of the Glasgow Association, Ibrox was awarded the final. Celtic claimed that in fairness, the replay should go to Parkhead. Rangers argued that the tie be continued at Ibrox. The Association sided with Rangers so Celtic scratched from the competition.

	1901–1902 CHARITY CUP				
	Hearts	(H)	3-1		
	Third Lanark	(A)	5-0		
Final	Hibs	(Hampden)	2-6	8,000	31/05/02

In 1901–1902 and the following season, clubs outside the city took part in the competition to raise funds for the Ibrox Disaster Fund.

1902–1903 SCOTTISH LEAGUE DIVISION I								
	P	W	D	L	F	A	Points	Position
Hibs	22	16	5	1	48	18	37	1st
Celtic	22	8	10	4	36	30	26	5th

FIXTURES					
	H	A		H	A
Dundee	2-2	0-2	Port Glasgow	3-0	1-1
Hearts	2-2	2-1	Queen's Park	1-1	1-2
Hibs	0-4	1-1	Rangers	1-1	3-3
Kilmarnock	3-1	3-1	St Mirren	2-2	1-3
Morton	1-1	2-0	Third Lanark	1-0	2-1
Partick Thistle	4-1	0-0			

Certainly Celtic's poorest ever League season in terms of games won. With 12 teams now in the League, Celtic fielded a new goalkeeper, Andy McPherson, who had an emerging defence and forward line in front of him, with the whole team not scoring enough and losing too many. Rangers slipped badly, losing the same number of goals as Celtic to finish third. Jimmy Quinn appeared as centre-forward in a few matches this season but was generally employed on the wing, partnered by another future star Jimmy McMenemy. Hibs fans were ecstatic. The Cup the year before and now the League! It would be 45 years before their name appeared on a major trophy again.

1902–1903 SCOTTISH CUP

	Date	Opponent		Score	Att.
	24/01/03	St Mirren	(H)	0-0	16,000
Replay	31/03/03	St Mirren	(A)	1-1	14,000
Replay	07/02/03	St Mirren	(A)	1-0	9,000 – At Ibrox
					abandoned due to bad weather
Replay	14/02/03	St Mirren	(H)	4-0	30,000
	21/02/03	Port Glasgow	(H)	2-0	2,000
QF	28/02/03	Rangers	(H)	0-3	40,000

A struggle most of the way for Celtic who needed four matches to get past St Mirren in the initial round and gave a poorish performance against Port Glasgow Athletic at home. In the quarter-final in front of 40,000, again at Celtic Park, Rangers were much the better team, Celtic picking this day to have one of their poorest displays of a rather dire season and went down heavily by 3-0.

1902–1903 GLAGOW CUP FINAL

	Queen's Park	(A)	2-1		
	Clyde	(A)	4-1		
Final	Third Lanark	(Ibrox)	0-3	20,000	25/10/02

1902–1903 CHARITY CUP FINAL

	Hibs	(Cathkin)	0-0			
Replay	Hibs	(A)	5-0			
Final	St Mirren		5-2	15,000	23/05/03	Ibrox

This match took place on a beautiful summer's day. St Mirren took an early lead but by half-time Celtic were 4–1 up. Alex Bennett got the fifth shortly after the interval. Team: McPherson; Watson, Battles; Moir, Young, Orr; Loney, Somers; Bennett; McMenemy and Quinn.

———— ✿ ————

1903 1904 SCOTTISH LEAGUE DIVISION 1

	P	W	D	L	F	A	Points	Position
Thirds	26	20	3	3	61	26	43	1st
Celtic	26	18	2	6	69	28	38	3rd

FIXTURES

	H	A		H	A
Airdrie	3-0	3-4	Partick Thistle	2-1	4-0
Dundee	4-2	1-2	Port Glasgow	4-1	3-2
Hearts	4-0	1-2	Queen's Park	3-0	0-1
Hibs	1-0	2-0	Rangers	2-2	0-0
Kilmarnock	6-1	6-1	St Mirren	3-1	1-0
Morton	5-1	1-0	Third Lanark	1-3	1-3
Motherwell	6-0	2-1			

Third Lanark's only title. In spite of being around for years, only this League Championship and two Scottish Cups went to Cathkin. In this season, they took their chance, Celtic and Rangers, (who finished on the same points) too interested in each other and letting Thirds sneak in. Celtic lost twice to the champions and were very inconsistent away from home, losing three matches in the final run-in to Airdrie, Dundee and Hearts. There was a definite improvement, though, over the previous four years. Davie Adams was now the regular goalkeeper, Loney and Hay were in the half-back line, Somers and Hamilton on one wing, Bennett, Quinn and McMenemy there for the goals. In a major change for the Club, Celtic changed their strip, the green and white stripes being replaced by hoops. This strip was first worn at Parkhead on 29 August 1903 and had an inauspicious start, Celtic losing 3-1 to Third Lanark.

The caption to this cartoon from 1903 is 'A Lucky Save', and it is intended to emphasise the change in Celtic's strip from stripes to hoops. At this time, the goalkeeper still wore the same strip as the others, only a cap marking out his specific role.

		1903–1904 SCOTTISH CUP			
	23/01/04	Stanley (Perthshire) scratched: Celtic WO			
	13/02/04	St Bernard's	(A)	0-4	5,000
QF	20/02/04	Dundee	(H)	1-1	18,000
Replay	27/02/04	Dundee	(A)	0-0	20,000
Replay	05/03/04	Dundee	(H)	5-0	30,000
SF	19/03/04	Third Lanark	(H)	2-1	36.000
Final	16/04/04	Rangers	Hampden	3-2	64,472

This match was played on a fine afternoon, with both teams having to make changes upfront. Alex Bennett had been indisposed all week so his place in the Celtic line-up went to Jimmy Quinn. Rangers had the wind in their favour in the first half and after 15 minutes of constant Celtic pressure broke away twice and scored twice. By half-time though, Quinn had levelled the scores. The second half was equally fast and furious, play swinging from end to end. Celtic were the younger and fresher team and their fine team-work began to tell, Quinn scoring the winner near the finish and failing to get more mainly through bad luck. This was the first-ever hat-trick in a Scottish Cup Final, a feat repeated 68 years later by another Celtic centre-forward, John 'Dixie' Deans.

	1903–1904 GLASGOW CUP				
	Queen's Park	(H)	1-1		
Replay	Queen's Park	(A)	1-0		
	Clyde	(A)	2-0		
Final	Third Lanark	(Ibrox)	1-1	23.000	
Replay	Third Lanark	(Ibrox)	0-1	17,000	28/11/03

	1903–1904 CHARITY CUP				
	Queen's Park	(Cathkin)	2-1		
Final	Rangers	(Hampden)	2-5	25,000	14/03/04

Disaster – and Triumph!

Soon after the Cup Final of 1904, Celtic set off for their first tour of the Continent, playing matches in Vienna and Prague. While they were abroad, a fire broke out at Parkhead which destroyed the North Stand and most of the Pavilion. The former, which had seating for 3,500, made of wood with a galvanised iron roof, was completely destroyed. The Pavilion suffered damage which could be repaired while the Grant Stand on the South Side, although torched, was saved. To replace the stand, a covered enclosure was built, 300 feet in length, 36 feet deep and 40 feet high, terraced to accommodate a few thousand spectators. In later years, this was to become immortalised as 'The Jungle'.

A few months later, Willie Maley brought in Alec McNair from Stenhousemuir to complete his squad which, comprising a remarkably small list of players, took the Scottish League Championship for the next six years. They also completed the first 'double' of League and Cup in 1906–1907 and repeated that achievement the following season. During 1907–1908, Celtic also won the Glasgow and Charity Cup thus winning every trophy open to them.

However, they say every good team needs to be a lucky one as well and Dame Fortune certainly smiled on Celtic during the first league championship of their six-in- a-row run. After 26 matches, Celtic and Rangers were tied on 41 points. At that time, neither goal-scoring nor goal-

The squad which set out for the Continent on the first tour in 1904. Back row, left to right: P. Bennett, A. McNair, D. McLeod, J. Young, D. Adams, W. Orr, R. Templeton, J. Hay, R. Davis (Trainer). Front row: D. Hamilton, J.McMenemy, P. Somers, R. Craig, J. Bauchop, W. Loney, J. Quinn, A. Wilson, E. Garry.

difference was an accepted method of deciding a tie, a fact very much to Celtic's benefit, as Rangers' goal record was much better (Rangers 83 F – 28 A; Celtic 68 F – 31 A). The deciding matter in use then was a play-off, held at Hampden Park on the 6 May 1905. Several times during that season and in a previous season there had been trouble at Old Firm matches, so the SFA decided to take no chances and sent for an English referee – Mr Kirkham from Preston – to handle this most important tie. In the end Celtic won the match 2-1, with goals from Davie Hamilton and Jimmy McMenemy to take the League Title, the first of a six-in-a-row run.

The Old Firm – Rivals

In the very early days, relationships between the Celtic and Rangers officials were always cordial. Indeed, the future Celtic Chairman, J.H. McLaughlin, a keen organist, accompanied the Rangers Glee Club for several years! By the beginning of the twentieth century though, that relationship had cooled as the rivalry deepened. Competition between them comprised not only football but extended to their stadia as well.

Ibrox had been chosen to host the lucrative Scotland-England fixture of 1892, but the new Celtic Park got the nod in 1894, 1896, 1898 and 1900. Ibrox by then, of course, had been restructured (in 1899) and was again awarded the 1902 contest. Unfortunately, a section of wooden planking on the West Terracing gave way under pressure from the huge crowd, many fans falling to the lower area. Twenty-five died and over 500 were injured in the disaster, which made the name of Ibrox Stadium known throughout British football for all the wrong reasons. Since there had been some bitterness among the Celtic camp over losing the income from this particular fixture, it is perhaps not surprising that one or two injudicious comments were made publicly – and no doubt instantly regretted. The atmosphere was soured even more when the *Glasgow Observer* columnist, unashamedly pro-Celtic, pointed out that Celtic's 'splendidly equipped ground, which had stood the test of previous record grounds – would have safely accommodated Saturday's mammoth muster'.

The new Ibrox stadium had already been an unwitting cause of dispute between the clubs. Ibrox was awarded, by ballot, the Glasgow Cup Final on 26 October 1901 when a crowd of 30,000 watched the Old Firm draw 2-2. Celtic's contention that the replay should be at Celtic Park was overruled by the Glasgow Association, so they scratched from the competition in protest. Another bone of contention soon loomed. Rangers had won the Exhibition Cup in 1901, a trophy presented to mark the 2nd Glasgow International Exhibition in Kelvingrove Park, ironically beating Celtic in a rather rough Final. They now decided to put the Trophy up for competition again, the proceeds going to the Disaster Fund, and invited Sunderland, Everton and Celtic to take part.

Both Scots teams beat their English opponents in the semi-final (Celtic crushing Sunderland 5-1) to reach the final held at Cathkin Park on 17 June 1902 before an estimated crowd of 7,000. Celtic won 3-2 and duly took the Glasgow Exhibition Trophy back to Parkhead. Unfortunately, Rangers appeared to think that the Cup would be returned to them the following season and made this request not once but several times. Celtic declined each time and this increased the bitterness.

The following table shows the honours won by the Old Firm during the early years.

THE OLD FIRM'S RECORD IN COMPETITIONS 1890–1900

	LEAGUE	CUP	GLASGOW CUP	CHARITY CUP
1890–91	Rangers*		Celtic	
1891–92		Celtic	Celtic	Celtic
1892–93	Celtic		Rangers	Celtic
1893–94	Celtic	Rangers	Rangers	Celtic
1894–95			Celtic	Celtic
1895–96	Celtic		Celtic	Celtic
1896–97		Rangers	Rangers	Rangers
1897–98	Celtic	Rangers	Rangers	
1898–99	Rangers	Celtic		Celtic
1899–1900	Rangers	Celtic	Rangers	Rangers
1900–01	Rangers		Rangers	
1901–02	Rangers			
1902–03		Rangers		Celtic

* shared with Dumbarton.

Honours were fairly even, 18 for Celtic, 17 for Rangers. What comes across quite clearly, even in these early years, is their domination in the League

Championship, a feature still prevalent today. Even in the Scottish Cup, with seven victories from thirteen possibles, their presence is very evident; while in the local competitions, Rangers seemed as keen to collect the Glasgow Cup as Celtic were to hold on to its Charity counterpart.

One must remember though, that Celtic were only founded in 1887, whereas Rangers had been around since 1873. So, were the men from Ibrox just late developers, or was Celtic's almost immediate success the spur to a quick improvement down Govan way? No matter the reason, a challenge had been issued and accepted; Scottish football would never be quite the same again!

1904–1905 SCOTTISH LEAGUE DIVISION 1

	P	W	D	L	F	A	Points	Position
Celtic	26	18	5	3	68	31	41	1st

FIXTURES

	H	A		H	A
Airdrie	2-3	3-1	Partick Thistle	2-2	5-0
Dundee	3-0	1-2	Port Glasgow	3-0	4-1
Hearts	1-1	0-2	Queen's Park	1-1	3-2
Hibs	2-0	2-2	Rangers	2-2	4-1
Kilmarnock	3-1	3-0	St Mirren	1-0	3-2
Morton	5-2	1-0	Third Lanark	2-1	2-1
Motherwell	4-2	6-2			

Celtic's fifth Championship. Both Celtic and Rangers finished level on points but at this time there was no method like goal average or goal difference used to decide the final positions. This was just as well for Celtic as Rangers were superior in both. The preferred method was the play-off, which took place at Hampden Park on 6 May 1905. Celtic won 2-1. Both Old Firm matches, on 15 October (2-2) and 25 February (4-1), were very troublesome both on and off the pitch.

1904–1905 SCOTTISH CUP

	28/01/04	Dumfries	(A)	2-1	3,000
	11/02/04	Lochgelly Utd	(H)	3-0	2,000
QF	25/02/04	Partick Thistle	(H)	3-0	25,000
SF	25/03/04	Rangers	(A)	2-0	36,000

There was a crowd invasion near the end of this semi-final at Ibrox which caused its abandonment but in spite of the matter being referred to the SFA, the result stood.

1904–1905 GLASGOW CUP

	Queen's Park	(H)	3-0	
	Partick Thistle	(H)	2-0	
Final	Rangers		2-1	50,000

Over 50,000 turned out at Hampden on 8 October 1904 to see this Final with both teams at full strength. The weather was fine but the play was disappointing, apart from ten minutes at the start and also at the end.

Rangers, playing with the wind, scored first but Celtic equalised before half-time. After the interval, they always had the upper hand, their defence in particular giving nothing away. Alex Bennett scored the winner late on for a thoroughly deserved victory.

Team: Adams; McLeod, Orr; Young, Loney, Hay; Bennett, McMenemy; Quinn; Somers and Hamilton

1904–1905 Charity Cup			
	Queen's Park	(Cathkin)	3-0
Final	Partick Thistle	Ibrox	2-0	27/05/05

Only 12,000 were present on a day not suitable for football and witnessed a tight game although Celtic were always the better side. The team: Adams; Watson, Orr; Young, Loney, Hay; McNair, McMenemy; Quin; Somers and Hamilton. Davie Hamilton opened the scoring and then a shot by Jimmy McMenemy was turned past his own keeper by right-back Howie. Two up at the interval, Celtic continued to be the better side in the second half, while Partick Thistle were never really dangerous.

———— ❖ ————

1905–1906 Scottish League Division 1								
	P	W	D	L	F	A	Points	Position
Celtic	30	24	1	5	76	19	49	1st

Fixtures						
	H	A		H	A
Aberdeen	1-0	0-1	Morton	4-0	4-0
Airdrie	2-1	5-2	Motherwell	3-1	4-0
Dundee	3-1	0-1	Partick Thistle	4-1	3-0
Falkirk	7-0	5-0	Port Glasgow	0-1	1-0
Hearts	1-0	1-1	Queen's Park	5-1	6-0
Hibs	1-0	1-0	Rangers	1-0	2-3
Kilmarnock	2-0	4-2	St Mirren	2-1	3-1
			Third Lanark	0-1	1-0

Note the increasing number of matches played. The League had been extended to 16 clubs and Celtic finished 6 points ahead of their nearest challengers. If one is being critical, five is a large number of games for a successful team to lose in one season. Two of these, surprisingly, were at home (Port Glasgow and Third Lanark) and three of them came in the last six matches of the season – Dundee, Aberdeen and Third Lanark. The goals were spread; Quinn (19), McMenemy (10), Bennett (13) and Hamilton (8). Alex McNair made his debut against Port Glasgow on 7 January 1906.

1905–1906 SCOTTISH CUP					
	27/01/06	Dundee	(A)	2-1	25,000
	10/02/06	Bo'ness	(H)	3-0	5,000
QF	24/02/06	Hearts	(H)	1-2	52,000

The largest attendance for the whole competition that season was at Celtic Park for the quarter-final tie against Hearts, who went on to beat Third Lanark in the Final.

1905–1906 GLASGOW CUP					
	Queen's Park	(H)	3-0		
	Partick Thistle	(H)	4-0		
Final	Third Lanark	Hampden	3-0	25,000	07/10/05

Bad weather contributed to the poor attendance of 25,000. The greasy surface was more suited to Celtic, whose forwards seemed very sure-footed in contrast to the cumbersome Third's defence. Jimmy Quinn scored the first early on and Peter Somers the second shortly after, so it was 2-0 at half time. For the first 15 minutes of the second half, Third Lanark came back into it, but Celtic soon took control again and Jimmy McMenemy got a third. The team: Adams; Campbell, Orr; Young, Loney, Hay; Bennett, McMenemy; Quinn; Somers and Hamilton.

1905–1906 CHARITY CUP		
Rangers	(A)	3-5

The pool of players used in 1905–06. Back row, left to right: R. Davis (Trainer); R. Campbell, D. McLeod, H. Watson, D. Hamilton, A. McNair, A. Wilson, E. Garry, J. McCourt, D. Adams. Front row: J. Young, J. Hay, A. Bennett, J. McMenemy, W. Loney, J. Quinn, P. Somers. W. McNair.

The Celtic team of this time was becoming a very settled formation, which meant few chances for those on the periphery. Of the squad, for instance, Robert Campbell (FB) made only 11 appearances, Willie McNair (OL) only one, Ned Garry (OR) six, and Jim McCourt none.

The Brake Clubs

The Brake Clubs were the first organised supporters groups and started, in Celtic's case, shortly after the Club was founded in 1887. A 'brake' was a large wagonette, drawn by four horses, capable of carrying twenty-five people. In the early days, they assembled at Carlton Place, on the south-bank of the Clyde and formed a colourful procession as they wound their way to matches. Naturally, their games were near at hand. For trips to Edinburgh or Dundee, the train was more suitable. The name of each club was embroidered on a cloth banner, often with a portrait of a favourite player incorporated. Originally the club's sprang from branches of the League of the Cross, a Catholic Temperance Society, in the central Glasgow parishes.

Unfortunately, although the Brake Clubs gave great support to the club and its original charitable ideals, they occasionally fell from grace. In 1897, for instance, they advocated on all-Catholic club; while in 1908, they organised a boycott of a Scottish Cup tie with Rangers after the admission price had been doubled. By the early 1920s, Brake Clubs had acquired — rather ironically, considering their Temperance Society association — a reputation for disreputable standards of behaviour and soon disappeared from the scene to be replaced by motor transport or the train.

1906–1907 SCOTTISH LEAGUE DIVISON I								
	P	W	D	L	F	A	Points	Position
Celtic	34	23	9	2	80	30	55	1st

FIXTURES					
	H	A		H	A
Aberdeen	2-1	2-2	Kilmarnock	5-0	2-2
Airdrie	2-1	2-0	Morton	2-1	2-0
Clyde	3-3	2-0	Motherwell	1-1	6-0
Dundee	0-0	0-0	Partick Thistle	4-1	2-0
Falkirk	3-2	3-2	Port Glasgow	4-0	1-1
Hamilton	2-0	5-2	Queen's Park	2-1	4-0
Hearts	3-0	3-3	Rangers	2-1	1-2
Hibs	2-1	1-0	St Mirren	1-1	3-0
			Third Lanark	2-0	1-2

Another two clubs had been added, making 18 in all, with Celtic comfortable winners, seven points ahead of the rest. The team by this time was fairly settled, except perhaps in the full-back position — Davie Adams in goal; Young, Loney and Hay at half-back; a forward line of Bennett, McMenemy, Quinn, Somers and Hamilton. The team seemed comfortable home and away — scoring 40 in each, losing 14 at home, 16 away — but drew a surprisingly high number of matches, six of which came in the last ten League games. Dundee seemed to be the bogey team with two 0-0 draws.

	02/02/07	Clyde	(H)	2-1	25,000	
	09/02/07	Morton	(A)	0-0	11,000	
Replay	16/02/07	Morton	(H)	1-1	25,000	
Replay	23/02/07	Morton	(H)	2-1	30,000	
QF	09/03/07	Rangers	(A)	3-0	60,000	
SF	30/03/07	Hibs	(H)	0-0	25,000	
Replay	06/04/07	Hibs	(A)	0-0	25,000	
Replay	13/04/07	Hibs	(H)	3-0	30.000	
Final	20/04/07	Hearts	Hampden	3-0	50,000	

1906–1907 Scottish Cup

This final was a good game on a rotten day. For the first hour, Hearts gave as good as they got, then their defence gave way in the last 30 minutes. From start to finish, Celtic were very aggressive, creating a few chances in the first half but not taking them. Celtic's left-wing duo in the first half was truly brilliant, as was their right-wing pair in the second.

At half-time the game was still scoreless but Celtic were awarded a disputed penalty ten minutes into the second half and Willie Orr scored. Hearts went to pieces in the last half-hour and Peter Somers added two more. This was the first 'double' in Celtic's and Scottish Football's history. The team: Adams; McLeod, Orr; Young, McNair, Hay; Bennett, McMenemy; Quinn; Somers and Hamilton.

1906–1907 Glasgow Cup

	Partick Thistle	(A)	2-0		
	Queen's Park	(H)	5-0		
Final	Third Lanark	Hampden	3-2	40,000	06/10/06

The team: Sinclair; McLeod, and Orr; Young, McNair and Hay; Templeton, McMenemy; Quinn; Somers and Hamilton.

Good conditions and an exciting game. Celtic started badly and were 2-1 down at half-time, their goal coming from a penalty by Willie Orr. In the second half, however, goals by Jim Young from a Bobby Templeton corner and a lovely drive from Peter Somers took the Cup back to Celtic Park. Goalkeeper Tom Sinclair was on loan from Rangers, as Davie Adams had an injured hand. He played six matches for Celtic, with six shut-outs, before going back to Ibrox complete with a Glasgow Cup-Winner's Medal.

1906–1907 Charity Cup

	Queen's Park	(Cathkin)	6-2
Final	Rangers	(Cathkin)	0-1

1907–1908 Scottish League Division I

	P	W	D	L	F	A	Points	Position
Celtic	34	24	7	3	86	27	55	1st

Fixtures

	H	A		H	A
Aberdeen	3-0	1-2	Morton	2-0	3-2
Airdrie	1-1	0-0	Motherwell	3-0	2-2
Clyde	5-1	2-0	Partick Thistle	4-1	3-0
Dundee	3-2	0-2	Port Glasgow	5-0	3-0
Falkirk	3-2	1-1	Queen's Park	4-1	2-0
Hamilton	3-0	4-2	Rangers	2-1	1-0
Hearts	6-0	0-1	St Mirren	4-0	2-2
Hibs	4-0	2-1	Third Lanark	1-1	3-1
Kilmarnock	4-1	0-0			

Four points clear in the championship race, this was the most impressive performance statistically of these good years. Eighty-six is a good number of goals to score and losing only 27 in 34 matches is a sign of a strong defence. Fifty-seven of these goals were scored at Celtic Park, where the team was unbeaten, winning 15 and drawing two. The team did not seem to like the East Coast, the three defeats being at Aberdeen, Dundee and Hearts.

Jimmy Quinn got 19 at one end; Davie Adams secured 15 shut-outs at the other. Falkirk were the main challengers with Rangers third. Celtic's 1-0 defeat of Rangers at Ibrox in the third last match was vitally important. Quinn and McMenemy picked up injuries in the first half, Quinn having to hobble on the right wing for most of the 90 minutes. Alex Bennett scored the vital goal just before the interval; one month later, he was a Rangers player.

1907–1908 Scottish Cup

	25/01/08	Peebles Rovers	(H)	4-0	4,000
	08/02/08	Rangers	(A)	2-1	40,000
QF	22/02/08	Raith Rovers	(A)	3-0	14,000
SF	21/03.08	Aberdeen	(A)	1-0	20,000
F	18/04/08	St Mirren	Hampden	5-1	58,000

The two goals against Rangers in the second round were scored by Willie Kivlichan, only signed recently from the same club. In the Final, Saints Captain McAvoy won the toss but elected to give Celtic advantage of the wind, a bonus on which the League Champions duly capitalised. They were aided by some doubtful refereeing decisions especially when Jimmy Quinn, looking clearly off-side, scored Celtic's second goal mid-way through the first half. Two down at half-time, St Mirren were never in it and crashed decisively in the second half. The other goals came from Alex Bennett (2), Peter Somers and Davie Hamilton, Celtic doing the 'double' for the second season running.

1907–1908 GLASGOW CUP					
	Queen's Park	(H)	2-0		
Final	Rangers	(Hampden)	2-2		
Replay	Rangers	(Hampden)	0-0		
Replay	Rangers	(Hampden)	2-1	56,000	26/10/07

The team: Adams; McNair, and Hay; Young, Loney, and Mitchell; Bennett, McMenemy; McLean; Somers and Hamilton

There was great interest in all three Old Firm matches of the final, 56,000 the biggest attendance of the three. Rangers started brightly and made several chances but Celtic's defence held out and in two quick raids, scored through Peter Somers and Davie McLean. With 15 minutes left, Rangers pulled one back and from then on, played very well but Davie Adams was in outstanding form for Celtic and kept them in front.

1907–1908 CHARITY CUP					
	Partick Thistle	(H)	3-2		
Final	Clyde	(H)	2-0	31,000	30/05/08

The team: Adams; McLeod and Weir; Young, Loney and Hay; Moran, McMenemy; Quinn; Somers and Hamilton.

Clyde had the better of the first half with the wind behind them, but at half-time there was no scoring. Celtic scored twice in the second half but

Winner of the Scottish, Glasgow and Charity Cups plus League Championship 1908. Back row, left to right: Directors; T. White, J. Kelly, T. Corcan, J. McKillop, J. Grant, M. Dunbar. Middle row: W. Maley (Manager), J. Young, P. Somers, J. McMenemy, D. Adams, J. Mitchell, J. Weir, R. Davis (Trainer). Front row: D. Hamilton, D. McLeod, W. Loney, J. Hay, J. Quinn, A. McNair.

Charity Cup Final

A publicity card to commemorate Celtic's very successful season in 1907-08, although the result of the Charity final is totally wrong. Celtic beat Clyde 2-0 to take the trophy on 30 May 1908.

the final score rather flattered them in this rather nasty game. Martin Moran, at outside-right, a very lightweight player, played only three League matches for Celtic after re-joining them from Chelsea but had the consolation of this Charity Cup win.

1908–1909 Scottish League Division 1

	P	W	D	L	F	A	Points	Position
Celtic	34	23	5	6	71	24	51	1st

Fixtures

	H	A		H	A
Aberdeen	2-0	2-0	Morton	5-1	5-0
Airdrie	0-0	2-1	Motherwell	4-0	2-1
Clyde	0-1	2-0	Partick Thistle	3-0	1-0
Dundee	2-0	1-2	Port Glasgow	2-1	4-1
Falkirk	2-0	1-1	Queen's Park	4-0	5-0
Hamilton	1-1	2-1	Rangers	2-3	3-1
Hearts	1-1	2-1	St Mirren	0-1	1-0
Hibs	2-0	0-1	Third Lanark	1-0	1-1
Kilmarnock	5-1	1-3			

As with any good run of success there is a peak, then a falling away and Celtic were, although winning on the slope in this season. They could thank a miserly defence for this Championship; Adams; McNair and Weir; Young, Loney and Hay the most consistent names. Davie Adams had 15 shut-outs yet there was a surprising number of defeats, including three at home (Clyde, Rangers and St Mirren). The lack of high scoring allied to a strong defence usually means drawn games, all of which were low scoring. At the end, Celtic finished only one point ahead and can thank both the 21 goals of Jimmy Quinn plus the 14 of Jimmy McMenemy for a successful conclusion. Both fixtures against Partick Thistle were played at Celtic Park as the Jags were without a ground during this season; while the Queen's Park *v.* Celtic match was played at Cathkin as Hampden was closed after the 'Riot'.

1908–1909 SCOTTISH CUP

	21/01/09	Leith Athletic	(A)	4-2	7,000
	06/02/09	Port Glasgow	(H)	4-0	7,000
QF	20/02/09	Airdrie	(H)	3-1	20,000
SF	20/03/09	Clyde	(H)	0-0	40,000
Replay	27/03/09	Clyde	(H)	2-0	35,000
Final	10/04/09	Rangers	(Hampden)	2-2	70,000
Replay	17/04/09	Rangers	(Hampden)	1-1	60,000

The cup was withheld after crowd trouble in the replay (see page 89).

1908–1909 GLASGOW CUP

	Queen's Park	(A)	4-4		
Replay	Queen's Park	(H)	2-1		
	Rangers	(H)	2-2		
Replay	Rangers	(A)	2-0		
Final	Third Lanark	(Hampden)	1-1	21,000	17/10/08
Replay	Third Lanark	(Hampden)	2-2	26,000	24/10/08
Replay	Third Lanark	(Hampden)	0-4	17,000	28/10/08

The second replay was played on a Wednesday afternoon, hence the reduced attendance.

1908–1909 CHARITY CUP FINAL

	Clyde	(H)	2-1		
Final	Rangers	(H)	2-4	25,000	15/05/09

Trouble at Hampden

This was a wonderful time to be a Celtic supporter, particularly during the 'double' years of 1906–1907 and 1907–1908. They could possibly have made it a hat-trick but after winning the Championship in 1908/09, they were deprived of a Scottish Cup success when the SFA withheld the trophy after the notorious Hampden riot.

The first match in this latest of Old Firm finals ended 2-2 before a crowd of 70,000, while another 60,000 were there for the replay, which again ended in a draw, this time 1-1. After the final whistle, though, several players lingered on the pitch, obviously unsure about the possibility of extra time. After some delay, they moved towards the Pavilion but the crowd, feeling that they were to be deprived of further action, erupted in anger. This ire soon turned into a rampant display of hooliganism, during which police and firemen were attacked, the stadium badly damaged and eventually, parts of it set alight.

The Football Authorities were not amused. Public opinion, not only in Glasgow but throughout Britain, was horrified – and wanted action! As usual though, little blame was accepted by anyone in authority. The Scottish Football Association abandoned the tie and contributed £500 to Queen's Park for damage to their ground; both clubs were ordered to pay £150 to Queen's Park; and in future, extra time was advised in Old Firm Finals. That would not be an immediate problem, as the next such Final would not occur until 1928.

The Players

Although the Celtic side of this time was very much a 'team' in terms of support and spirit, they were all good players in their own right. Davie Adams was a tallish, strong goalkeeper adept at keeping his concentration behind such a solid defence that for long periods he was redundant. At full-back, Donald McLeod was small but quick and strong; his partner, Willie Orr, an all-round footballer of sound judgement. Three other full-backs also played their part. Jim Weir at left-back was noted for his strong tackling, as was Hugh Watson, not subtle in any way but always giving of his best; while Alec McNair, the 'Icicle', calm and unflappable, was not very quick but a master at jockeying his opponent into a disadvantageous position.

At wing-half 'Sunny' Jim Young, (the nickname a touch of sarcasm for his ferocious play), was quick, his height a decided advantage; and Jimmy Hay, the captain, broad and strong, but not without a range of more subtle skills. In between them, Willie Loney, the attacking centre-half was strong and solid in the tackle but consistent in his play and capable of good runs. On the right wing, Alex Bennett had a great touch on the ball, was a fine crosser and also had a good scoring record himself; Jimmy McMenemy, 'Napoleon' was a brainy, classic inside-forward with good dribbling skills and vision. The left-wing comprised a similar combination. Peter Somers at inside-left was a perfectionist who could slide the ball to his wing or centre through any defence and in any conditions; and Davie Hamilton, whose speed and control, allied to a dangerous cross and shot, made him the perfect partner. For a time, Bobby Templeton came on to the wing, but for all his talents he was regarded as too much of an individualist to be part of such an unselfish team. More to the supporters' liking was Willie Kivlichan, even with his Ibrox background.

The apex of the team though, the man who drove all the moves towards the opposing goal was the 'Iron Man', Jimmy Quinn. Quinn was broad-shouldered, capable of taking on any defence in a very tough era. Regularly, he powered his way through the opposition, the very epitome of determination. As we would now say, he was the original 'Jersey Player'.

Jimmy Quinn was obviously a great player. Unfortunately, like all

A later photograph of Jimmy Quinn, without the moustache of his youth. He played in the following internationals: England – 1908, 1909, 1910, 1912; Wales – 1906, 1910, 1910; Ireland – 1905, 1906, 1908, 1910; Irish League – 1909, 1910; English League – 1904, 1905, 1906, 1909, 1910, 1912.

footballers, there comes a time when one's powers are not the force of former years. This was impressed upon me memorably shortly after we moved into our first house in 1969. An old Irishman, Charlie Dougherty, appeared one day looking for some gardening work and from then on became an invaluable help.

One lovely summer's day, we were having a chat over a cup of tea. 'When did you come over, Charlie?', I asked. 'In 1913', he replied, 'I started work at the Milngavie reservoir'. He paused for a moment, 'I used to go to Parkhead regularly'. 'Did they have some good players at that time' I wondered aloud. By now Charlie's mind was working overtime, 'Aye, they did, some great players. I even saw the great Quinn'. I was impressed and immediately asked him what he was like. His answer was not what I expected. 'Ah, he was a good player, but by the time I saw him, he was done!'

If we show the heights and weights of each player, we can get some idea of the physical attributes and from the appearance record and number of goals scored, we can also show – roughly – just how the team played.

Goalkeeper

Davie Adams	291 appearances	124 shut-outs	6ft	13st 7lbs

Full-Backs

Donald McLeod	155 appearances	0 goals	5ft 8in	12st 7lbs
Alec McNair	604 appearances	11 goals	5ft 8in	11st 10lbs
Willie Orr	212 appearances	23 goals	5ft 9in	12st
Jim Weir	96 appearances	1 goal	5ft 9in	12st 7lbs
Hugh Watson	58 appearances	1 goal	5ft 9in	12st

Half-Backs

Jim Young	443 appearances	13 goals	6ft	12st 7lbs
Willie Loney	305 appearances	29 goals	5ft 9in	11st 10lbs
Jim Hay	255 appearances	17 goals	5ft 8in	12st
Alex Bennett	152 appearances	53 goals	5ft 8in	11st 7lbs
Bobby Templeton	35 appearances	6 goals	5ft 9in	11st 3lbs
Willie Kivlichan	92 appearances	22 goals	5ft 8in	12st
Jimmy McMenemy	515 appearances	168 goals	5ft 7in	11st 7lbs
Jimmy Quinn	351 appearances	216 goals	5ft 9in	12st 10lb
Peters Somers	219 appearances	62 goals	5ft 9in	11st
Davie Hamilton	260 appearances	60 goals	5ft 6in	10st 4lbs

Adams

2
Hugh Watson
Alec McNair

3
Donald McLeod
Willie Orr
Jim Weir

4
Jim Young

5
Willie Loney

6
Jim Hay

7
Jimmy McMenemy

8
Peter Somers

9
Alex Bennett
Bobby Templeton
Willie Kivlichan

10
Jimmy Quinn

11
Davie
Hamilton

As was the style of the time, the team played a 2-3-5 formation, with the centre-half an attacking player, or to use the modern term, a goal-maker. In goal, Davie Adam's record ranks with any Celtic keeper and surpasses most. The full-backs – at (2) and (3) – played further in towards the middle than they did later mainly to cover the frequent absence of the centre-half. As can be seen from their goal tally, they did not come up the park very often, Donald McLeod never scoring at all and Jim Weir only getting one in 96 appearances. Alex McNair's 11 goals came from his frequent appearances at wing-half in the early days, while Willie Orr was the penalty and free-kick taker hence the 23 goals.

The wing-half's job of the time – (4) and (6) – was to cover early breaks by the winger and fill in, for the attacking surges of the centre-half. It was a very hard, demanding role, since they had also to feed their own forwards. Celtic were very well-served in this area by 'Sunny' Jim Young and Jim Hay, whose goals per game tally show their role to be more defensive than attacking.

Up front, the system becomes more complicated. Both Alex Bennett and Davie Hamilton must have been out and out raiding wingers, pushing forward all the time, ready to sweep crosses into the centre-forward but at the same time not averse to having a crack themselves. By contrast, both Bobby Templeton and Willie Kivlichan, would from their record, appear to have been mainly providers rather than finishers.

Quinn's record was excellent – two goals in every three matches – but both inside forwards, while their main role was supplying the passes must have played pretty far up the park and followed in most of the attacks, as McMenemy and Somers tally of one goal every three and a half games is also very good.

This team's record in the years from 1904–1910 is quite remarkable:

		TOTAL POINTS 1904–1910				
P	W	D	L	F	A	Points
192	136	33	23	444	133	305

This performance was achieved with a remarkably small group of players, without the benefit of a reserve team. Unfortunately, such consistency and its resultant success, had unusual effects, summed up very accurately by that Celtic sympathiser of the time, 'Man in the Know':

> As the Celtic team, unchanged season after season, marched on from victory to victory, the public actually became satiated with the never-ending chapter of Celtic's successes. The gates began to dwindle and we were presented with the astonishing spectacle of the worlds best football team playing their home games before a beggarly array of empty benches. (*Glasgow Observer*, 16 July 1927)

1909–1910 SCOTTISH LEAGUE DIVISION I

	P	W	D	L	F	A	Points	Position
Celtic	34	24	6	4	63	22	54	1st

FIXTURES

	H	A		H	A
Aberdeen	2-0	1-0	Morton	3-0	1-2
Airdrie	3-1	2-0	Motherwell	2-2	3-1
Clyde	2-1	1-0	Partick Thistle	3-1	3-1
Dundee	1-0	0-0	Port Glasgow	4-0	3-2
Falkirk	2-0	0-2	Queen's Park	6-0	1-0
Hamilton	3-1	5-1	Rangers	1-1	0-0
Hearts	1-0	2-1	St Mirren	1-1	1-2
Hibs	0-0	0-1	Third Lanark	2-0	1-0
Kilmarnock	2-1	1-0			

The tenth Championship for Celtic in total and their sixth in a row. That superb defence gave its finest ever performance in keeping the goals against down to 22, while between them Quinn (24) and McMenemy (10) contributed much towards the goals for tally. The 17 shut-outs by both Davie Adams and then Willie Duncan in his absence (Adams had pneumonia) was a particularly excellent area.

For those who wish to ask the obvious question, then a comparison with the first six years of Celtic's nine-in-a-row in the late 60s and early 70s is as follows:

POINTS TOTAL FOR THE SIX WINNING SEASONS 1904–10

P	W	D	L	F	A	Points
192	136	33	23	444	153	305

POINTS TOTAL FOR THE SIX WINNING SEASONS 1966–1971

P	W	D	L	F	A	Points
204	158	29	17	597	175	345

1909–1910 SCOTTISH CUP

	22/01/10	Dumbarton	(A)	2-1	10,000
	12/02/10	Third Lanark	(H)	3-1	50,000
QF	19/02/10	Aberdeen	(H)	2-1	21,000
SF	12/03/10	Clyde	(A)	1-3	40,000

A very high attendance for the local derby of the second round and the semi-final, where Celtic had an off-day against Clyde. The latter took three matches to dispose of Queen's Park in the third round and in the final there were two replays before Dundee took the Cup home for the first time.

1909–1910 GLASGOW CUP					
	Queen's Park	(A)	1-1		
Replay	Queen's Park	(H)	6-1		
Final	Rangers	(Hampden)	1-0	55,000	09/10/09

The final was played at Hampden on a fine day with the pitch in very good condition. The team: Adams; McNair and Weir; Young, Loney and Hay; Kivlichan, McMenemy; Quinn; Johnstone and Hamilton.

Celtic had the wind behind them in the first half and put the Rangers' defence under severe pressure which they withstood well to keep the game goalless at half-time.

The main feature of the match was the brilliance of the Celtic attack and the equally superb play of the Rangers rearguard. The Ibrox attack on the day was almost non-existent. Although limping from an injury, Jimmy Quinn scored the only goal.

1909–1910 CHARITY CUP		
Third Lanark	(1)	0-1

The Celtic squad at the beginning of season 1910–11, with some new faces. Back row, left to right: D. Hamilton, D. Munroe, J. McMenemy, J. Mitchell, W. Kivlichan. Middle row: P. Johnstone, Jim Young, J. Hay, P. Somers, J. Quinn, A. McNair, D. Adams, J. McKintosh, R. Davies(Trainer). Front row: W. Glover, John Young, D. McLean, L. McLean, I. Dodds, W. Loney, Jas Weir.

CHAPTER FIVE (1910–1920)
Four-in-a-Row — Then War!

THE FIRST DECADE of the 20th century had proved a most successful era for Celtic. Six Scottish league championships, three Scottish cups, five Glasgow cups plus three Charity cups was a wonderful haul in only ten years, unequalled by any other team in Britain. The success of any football team is dependent on many factors, some obvious, others less so. A good team embraces most of these facets; a great side has all of them. The Celtic team of this era certainly had them in abundance.

Firstly, and not surprisingly, there must be good players present. There were relatively few involved (around 18) consistently in these years at Celtic Park and their quality can easily be checked by a glance at any reference book. Eleven were internationalists, few with more than ten, but the only fixtures at that time were against England, Wales or Ireland.

Secondly, there must be a rapport between the various personnel. This seemed to be a most singular fixture of this Celtic team. The goalkeeper and two backs (Adams – McNair/Orr/Weir) worked well as a defensive unit. Both wing-halves (Young and Hay) provided strength and grit; the inside-forwards (McMenemy and Somers) were skilful and intelligent. The attacking centre-half (Loney) came forward with telling effect, while the wingers (Bennett, Hamilton, Kiulichen, Templeton) seized eagerly on their passes and, of course, at the apex was Quinn.

Thirdly, the team must be well-managed. At this time, Willie Maley was at the height of his powers and few managers have ever equalled his talent for creating and adjusting a team.

And fourthly, there must be a sense of harmony. Players perform better when untroubled by either outside events or internal squabbling. The period between the grandstand fire in 1904 and the Hampden riot of 1909 was a particularly calm one at Parkhead, success on the pitch over-riding all other issues.

Yet, in spite of all the success, the attendance figures did drop towards the end of the six-in-a-row run. This has happened to other teams in dominant periods and is not truly surprising. When victory can be assured, the idea of a contest becomes irrelevant, and crowds become satiated with success or perhaps bored. In either case, many cannot be bothered to attend. There was, though, one other factor which might have influenced the size of the crowds at Celtic Park towards the end of that era. From contemporary accounts it seems clear that the Celtic full-backs, and, occasionally the half-backs, became adept at the 'pass-back' to the keeper to avoid trouble. Safe this might have been, but most spectators do not like it and often vent their displeasure – by not turning up perhaps?

1910–1911 SCOTTISH LEAGUE DIVISION I

	P	W	D	L	F	A	Points	Position
Rangers	34	23	6	5	90	34	52	1st
Celtic	34	15	11	8	48	18	41	5st

FIXTURES

	H	A		H	A
Aberdeen	0-0	0-1	Morton	0-1	1-1
Airdrie	3-0	0-0	Motherwell	3-0	1-2
Clyde	2-0	2-0	Partick Thistle	2-0	1-1
Dundee	2-1	0-1	Queen's Park	2-0	1-0
Falkirk	0-0	1-2	Raith Rovers	5-0	1-2
Hamilton	3-0	1-0	Rangers	0-1	1-1
Hearts	0-0	1-1	St Mirren	5-0	1-1
Hibs	2-0	4-0	Third Lanark	0-0	1-1
Kilmarnock	2-0	0-1			

A real collapse by Celtic in their attempt to win a seventh consecutive title. Ironically, there was very little change in personnel and the defence gave its best ever performance, losing only 18 goals (19 shut-outs) but something was wrong somewhere and the attack managed only one and a half goals per match. The home record was not at all bad, with only two single-goal defeats (Morton and Rangers) but Oh! those away performances – 6 defeats, 7 draws, scoring 17, losing 15. That made the difference; even the great Quinn was held to 14 goals.

1910–1911 SCOTTISH CUP

	28/01/11	St Mirren	(H)	2-0	15,000
	11/02/11	Galston	(H)	1-0	5,000
QF	25/02/11	Clyde	(H)	1-0	5,000
SF	11/03/11	Aberdeen	(H)	1-0	48,000
Final		Hamilton	(Ibrox)	0-0	45,000
Replay		Hamilton	(Ibrox)	2-0	28,000

Team: Adams; McNair and Dodds; Young, McAteer and Hay; Kivlichan, McMenemy; Quinn; Hastie and Hamilton.

Team in replay: Adams; McNair and Hay; Young, McAteer and Dodds; McAtee, McMenemy; Quinn; Kivlichan and Hamilton.

After a low-scoring run to the Final, Celtic gave a poor performance in the first match, causing Willie Maley to re-shuffle his team for the replay.

Conditions on the Wednesday could not have been worse with heavy wind and rain making for a very slippy pitch. Losing the toss, Celtic started

A publicity card used by the Scottish entertainers Lindsay & Harte around 1912 in a football sketch called 'Oor Best Man'. The player in question was Patsy Gallacher, second from the left in the front row. Notice how the heads of the players on either side of him have 'turned' towards him.

against the elements and came under severe pressure from Hamilton, but the defence coped well and Davie Adams had only a couple of saves to make. In the second half, with the wind now behind them, Celtic began to take control, although the forwards, apart from Willie Kivlichan, were not at their best. However, with the defence coping well with Hamilton's occasional attack, pressure told, the goals coming from Jimmy Quinn with a shot from an acute angle and Andy McAtee, after a good run.

1910–1911 GLASGOW CUP					
	Partick Thistle	(A)	2-1		
	Third Lanark	(H)	1-0		
Final	Rangers	(Hampden)	1-3	65,000	08/10/10

1910–1911 CHARITY CUP					
	Third Lanark	(H)	5-2		
Final	Rangers	(Hampden)	1-2	22,000	10/05/11

1911–1912 SCOTTISH LEAGUE DIVISION I								
	P	W	D	L	F	A	Points	Position
Rangers	34	24	3	7	86	34	51	1st
Celtic	34	17	11	6	58	33	45	2nd

FIXTURES

	H	A		H	A
Aberdeen	1-0	1-1	Morton	1-1	1-1
Airdrie	3-0	0-0	Motherwell	2-0	2-3
Clyde	3-2	1-1	Partick Thistle	3-0	1-1
Dundee	2-0	1-3	Queen's Park	2-1	4-1
Falkirk	3-1	1-1	Raith Rovers	1-1	2-1
Hamilton	2-1	0-1	Rangers	3-0	1-3
Hearts	1-1	1-2	St Mirren	3-1	1-1
Hibs	3-1	1-1	Third Lanark	3-1	0-1
Kilmarnock	2-0	2-0			

Rangers stuttered but Celtic stumbled and lost the chance of another Championship. There were notable changes in the usual well-tried line-up during this season. Mulrooney in for Adams in goal; Johnstone for Dodds; McAtee in place of Kivlichan, and Brown for Hamilton. Celtic were unbeaten at home – 14 wins, 3 draws – but again the away form was poor – losing 6 and drawing 8. That made all the difference at the finish, when a not too convincing Rangers team took the title. Patsy Gallagher made his debut against St Mirren at Love Street on 2 December 1911.

1911–1912 SCOTTISH CUP

	27/01/12	Dunfermline Athletic	(H)	1-0	6,000
	10/02/12	East Stirlingshire	(H)	3-0	3,000
QF	24/02/12	Aberdeen	(A)	2-2	25,000
Replay	09/03/12	Aberdeen	(H)	2-0	30,000
SF	30/03/12	Hearts	(Ibrox)	3-0	40,000
Final	06/04/12	Clyde	(Ibrox)	2-0	45,000

The team: Mulrooney; McNair and Dodds; Young, Loney and Johnston; McAtee, Gallagher; Quinn; McMenemy and Brown.

The first season in which the cup semi-finals were played on neutral grounds. Celtic's play had not been convincing during the season and the management was hoping for a good performance in the Final to boost the support. Unfortunately, a high wind blew and spoiled much of the play. Celtic had this wind in their favour during the first half and pressed their attacks home constantly, eventually taking the lead through Jimmy McMenemy from close in. They played more cautiously in the second half against the wind, but the defence coped comfortably with what few attacks Clyde could muster and Celtic won easily in the end, the second goal coming from Patsy Gallagher.

1911–1912 GLASGOW CUP

	Partick Thistle	(H)	3-3
Replay	Partick Thistle	(A)	0-3

1911–1912 CHARITY CUP

	Partick Thistle	(A)		5 corners to 2 corners	
Final	Clyde	(Hampden)	25,000	11/05/12	
				7 corners to 0 corners	

Jimmy McMenemy (left) and Patsy Gallagher (right), two great stars of these years. McMenemy made 515 appearances for Celtic, scoring 168 goals. Gallagher played 464 matches, scoring 196 goals.

The team: Mulrooney; McNair and Dodds; Young, Johnstone and Mitchell; McAtee, Gallagher; Quinn; McMenemy and Brown.

This was a very hard competitive match. Celtic's superiority – although never reflected in goals – was evident in the number of corner kicks. Only once in the whole game did Clyde look likely to pierce a strong Celtic defence, so Celtic took the Cup on corner kicks, a feature of this particular trophy.

1912–1913 SCOTTISH LEAGUE DIVISION I

	P	W	D	L	F	A	Points	Position
Rangers	34	24	5	5	76	41	53	1st
Celtic	34	22	5	7	53	28	49	2nd

FIXTURES

	H	A		H	A
Aberdeen	2-0	0-3	Morton	1-0	2-1
Airdrie	1-1	4-1	Motherwell	1-2	0-1
Clyde	3-0	1-1	Partick Thistle	1-0	3-2
Dundee	2-0	1-3	Queen's Park	1-0	1-0
Falkirk	1-2	0-0	Raith Rovers	4-1	1-2
Hamilton	2-1	1-0	Rangers	3-2	1-0
Hearts	1-0	0-0	St Mirren	2-1	3-1
Hibs	1-1	0-1	Third Lanark	2-0	1-0
Kilmarnock	4-1	2-0			

Still a team in transition, Celtic finished four points behind Rangers and can point to that column of seven defeats as the reason. To beat Rangers twice in the campaign, yet lose at home to Falkirk and Motherwell was careless, if not disastrous. Unexpected away defeats on the East Coast – Aberdeen, Dundee and Raith Rovers – also helped tip the balance in Rangers' favour. The bad news was that Jimmy Quinn was now playing less often (26 league matches, 12 goals); the good that new boy Patsy Gallagher was getting among the goals (11 in total).

	1912–1913 SCOTTISH CUP				
	08/12/13	Arbroath	(H)	4-0	9,000
	22/02/13	Peebles	(H)	3-1	5,000
QF	08/03/13	Hearts	(H)	0-1	66,000

The quarter-final crowd was the biggest attendance at Parkhead so far for any visitors other than Rangers. Unfortunately, a Bobby Walker goal settled the tie in Hearts favour, but rather surprisingly the Tynecastle men went out in the semi-final to the eventual winners Falkirk.

	1912–1913 GLASGOW CUP				
	Clyde	(H)	0-0		
Replay	Clyde	(A)	4-0		
Final	Rangers	(Hampden)	1-3	90,000	12/10/12

	1912–1913 CHARITY CUP				
	Clyde	(H)	1-0		
	Third Lanark	(A)	2-1		
Final	Rangers	(Celtic Park)	3-2	30,000	10/05/13

Team: Shaw; McNair and Dodds; Young, Loney and McMaster; McAtee, Gallagher; Connolly; Browning and Hill.

A real difference in attendances for two Old Firm Finals but generally the Glasgow Cup Finals – played during the season – always had the higher figures. Rangers were two up within minutes of the start and played much the better football in the first half, although Patsy Gallagher pulled one back shortly before the interval. Due to injury, Rangers had to re-arrange their team just after the interval and Celtic came more into the game, equalising early in the second half and then snatching the winner near the end, the scorer on both occasions, centre-forward Barney Connolly.

Further Changes

After the glory of the six-in-a-row years, with two 'doubles' in that time as well, a relative drop in standards was almost to be expected. Certainly, in League terms, that did occur with positions of fifth in 1910–1911 and second in both 1911–1912 and 1912–1913. Even so, two Scottish Cup wins in these three years kept the supporters happy.

This match was played in May 1911 against Ferencsvaros. From the left: J. Young, J. Mitchell, W. Maley, J. Hastie, A. Donaldson, J. Grant, H. Simpson, J. Quinn, J. McMeneny, A. McAtee, J. Dodds, T. McGregor, W. Nicol, J. Davie, P. Johnstone, A. Donnelly.

An extensive Continental tour was also undertaken in 1911, visiting Dresden (6-1), Prague (3-0 and 1-1 against Deutsche FC), Budapest (Ferencsvaros 2-0 and 1-1), Vienna (2-1 *v.* Deutsche FC), Basle (5-1) and Paris (8-1 *v.* Red Star) before returning for the Epsom Derby. In Budapest, a local newspaper mentioned 'the new insight into Association Football provided by the Scots'; while in Prague, the team met up with former Celtic star Johnny Madden, then coach of SK Slavia.

New players came in at different times. The peerless Patsy Gallagher made his debut against St Mirren on 2 December 1911. Goalkeeper Charlie Shaw replaced Davie Adams and along with Alec McNair and Joe Dodds, formed the perfect defensive triangle, using the back-pass to great effect. Andy McAtee, a very strong-legged winger, replaced Willie Kivlichan and Peter Johnstone came in for Willie Loney after signing on as an inside-left. Willie Maley also came up trumps when he changed John McMaster from centre-half to left-half where McMaster grafted with consistency and strength. When the great Quinn's legs eventually gave out, Jimmy McColl was brought in from St Anthony's to fill the breach. Since the turn of the century, Willie Maley had been active in the transfer market to build his various teams but a consideration of the sums involved is almost laughable by today's standards; Jimmy Hay (Glossup) £100; Jim Young (Bristol City) £50, John Bell (Everton) £250; Dave Storrier (Everton) £400; Peter Somers (Hamilton) £120; Bobby Templeton (Arsenal) £250; and Charlie Shaw (QPR) £500.

By season 1913–1914, Celtic were back on top of the League once more, only conceding 14 goals in 38 matches, the lowest ever in Scottish Football. Three more consecutive Championships were to be gained, as well as the last Scottish Cup before the tournament was suspended during the war, Hibs being beaten 4-1 in the replay at Ibrox before 30,000 spectators, the Club's third League and Cup 'double'. Again Willie Maley had rung the right changes. The comparison of two Cup winning sides five years apart, shows the alterations in personnel:

1908–1909

Adams, McNair and Weir, Young, Dodds and Hay, Munro, McMenemy, Quinn, Somers and Hamilton.

1913–1914

Shaw, McNair and Dodds, Young, Johnstone and McMaster, McAtee, Gallagher, McColl, McMenemy and Browning.

There was much to admire about the two different eras. The team that won six-in-a-row scored an average of 2.31 goals a match, losing 0.79 at the other end. The four-in-a-row team's record of P – 152, W – 119, D – 23, L – 10, F – 367, F – 79, Points 304 – gives then an average of 2.41 for, 0.51 against. Not much in it in terms of goal-scoring but the four-in-a-row side definitely was more compact in defence.

Continental tours were very much in vogue then and Celtic went over once more in 1912, first to Copenhagen, where they beat Boldklubben B93 3-1 and then lost 4-1 to the Danish Olympic Squad. The team then travelled to Oslo where in the space of two days, they twice beat the Norwegian Olympic Team before crushing a Drammem XI 9-0.

Celtic FC 1912–13. New faces, new trainer. Back row, left to right: M. Quinn (Trainer), W. Loney, J. McMenemy, J. Dodds, J. Quinn, P. Johnstone, W. Maley (Manager). Front row: J. Brown, A McAtee, T. McGregor, J. Young, P. Gallagher, J. Mulrooney, A. McNair.

An action shot from the European tour of May 1914 in the match against Leipzig, which Celtic lost 1-0. The caption beneath the picture says 'Leipzig 1 Celtic — England 0'!

In the summer of 1914, Celtic returned to the Continent to Germany where after falling 1-0 to Leipzig, they comfortably beat Hertha Berlin 6-0. When they travelled on to Budapest, they discovered that some Hungarian officials had organised a match without letting them know in advance. It was not just any old match either, but a prestigious contest against the English Cup Winners Burnley! The Celtic party was not pleased but, as the proceeds were to go to charity and a local newspaper had provided a cup and medals, they felt they had no choice but to compete. After 90 minutes on a blazingly hot summer's day, the score was 1-1 and the referee asked for another ten minutes' extra time. The players, however, had had enough and started to come off the pitch. The spectators, on the other hand, wanted more action. Eventually, officials of both clubs reached an understanding. They tossed for the Cup, and Burnley won. The sponsors, though, would not agree to hand it over until the deciding game had been played, at Glasgow, Burnley or on neutral ground.

The match was eventually played on 1 September 1914 at Turf Moor four weeks into the First World War and Celtic won 2-1. No Budapest Cup was ever presented, though. It had apparently been won by a professional wrestler in a raffle run on behalf of the Austrian Red Cross Fund during the early days of the Great War! It was a frustrating incident in Celtic's history. Yet it showed that the Club was always in the vanguard of new ideas, quite ready to submit to complicated travel arrangements to pit their talents against good or emerging teams far from home. On this occasion, though, it nearly backfired on them. The matches in Germany took place in mid May; the Burnley match in Budapest on 27 May. Just a month later, Arch Duke Franz Ferdinand was assassinated at Sarajevo and Europe was plunged into a disastrous war.

1913–1914 Scottish League Division I

	P	W	D	L	F	A	Points	Position
Celtic	38	30	5	3	81	14	65	1st

Fixtures

	H	A		H	A
Aberdeen	2-1	1-0	Hibs	3-0	2-1
Airdrie	1-0	1-0	Kilmarnock	4-0	1-0
Ayr United	5-1	6-0	Morton	3-0	4-0
Clyde	2-0	1-0	Motherwell	0-0	1-1
Dumbarton	4-0	4-0	Partick Thistle	1-1	0-0
Dundee	1-0	1-0	Queen's Park	5-0	2-0
Falkirk	4-0	0-1	Raith Rovers	2-1	2-1
Hamilton	1-0	2-1	Rangers	4-0	2-0
Hearts	0-0	0-2	St Mirren	0-2	3-0
			Third Lanark	3-0	3-1

This was the first of a four-in-a-row for Celtic in an expanded League of 20 teams. It was an excellent performance, particularly defensively, where the 14 against is the best ever. With Charlie Shaw in goal, 26 of the 38 games were shut-outs. Goal-scoring, at just over two per match, was only average but being difficult to beat helps towards a title and Celtic eventually finished six points clear of Rangers.

Quinn was now being replaced more and more by Jimmy McColl, with Andy McAtee on one wing and John Browning on the other. Perhaps the highlights of the League season were the two comfortable victories over Rangers.

1913–1914 Scottish Cup

	07/02/14	Clyde	(A)	0-0	46,000
Replay	10/02/14	Clyde	(H)	2-0	40,000
	21/02/14	Forfar Ath	(A)	5-0	6,000
QF	07/03/14	Motherwell	(A)	3-1	18,000
SF	28/03/14	Third Lanark	(Ibrox)	2-0	50,000
Final	11/04/14	Hibs	(Ibrox)	0-0	56,000
Replay	16/04/14	Hibs	(Ibrox)	4-1	40,000

Team: Shaw; McNair and Dodds; Young, Johnstone and McMaster; McAtee, Gallagher; Owers; McMenemy and Browning. For the replay, McColl replaced Owers.

This replay was played on a Thursday evening with a troublesome setting sun which was into Celtic's face in the first half. Hibs started well, but from mid-way through the first half, Celtic took control and scored two in three minutes through Jimmy McColl, the first a close-range flick, the second a fine shot from an awkward angle. John Browning added a third before half-time. Hibs pressed strongly from the re-start but never looked like matching the League Champions. Browning added a fourth and although Hibs pulled

The Celtic team which won the last Scottish Cup before the tournament was suspended for the duration of the war. Notice that the goalkeeper, Charlie Shaw, is now in a yellow jersey.

one back 20 minutes from time, Celtic were always in control and won their ninth Scottish Cup also completing their third League and Cup 'double'.

1913–1914 GLASGOW CUP			
	Third Lanark	(H)	0-0
Replay	Third Lanark	(A)	0-1

1914–1915 CHARITY CUP				
	Queen's Park	(A)	3-0	
Final	Third Lanark	Hampden	6-0	22,000 12/05/14

Team: Shaw; McNair and Dodds; Young, Johnstone and McMaster; McAtee, Gallagher; McColl; McMenemy and Browning.

This was a brilliant victory on a fine Thursday evening. Celtic were superior in every way to their opponents. The combination play between the forwards was very good and the relationship between the backs and the goalkeeper excellent. In the first half, Celtic took advantage of the moderate breeze and scored three through Dodds, McColl and McMemeny. McMaster made it four before going off injured. Three minutes from time, Johnstone raced through to make it five and right on the final whistle Jimmy McMenemy got his second and Celtic's sixth for a comfortable win.

1914–1915 SCOTTISH LEAGUE DIVISION I								
	P	W	D	L	F	A	Points	Position
Celtic	38	30	5	3	91	25	65	1st

	H	A		H	A
			FIXTURES		
Aberdeen	1-0	1-0	Kilmarnock	2-0	3-1
Airdrie	3-0	1-0	Morton	6-2	2-0
Ayr United	4-0	0-1	Motherwell	1-0	1-1
Clyde	3-0	2-0	Partick Thistle	6-1	2-0
Dumbarton	1-0	4-1	Queen's Park	5-1	3-0
Dundee	6-0	3-1	Raith Rovers	3-1	2-2
Falkirk	1-0	1-0	Rangers	2-1	1-2
Hamilton	3-1	1-0	St Mirren	2-1	3-3
Hearts	1-1	0-2	Third Lanark	1-0	4-0
Hibs	5-1	1-1			

The defence could scarcely be expected to continue the miserliness of the previous season, but 25 against in 38 matches is still very presentable and the goals scored moved up considerably. Both McColl (26) and Gallagher (14) had excellent returns, but McAtee (8), McMenemy (14) and Browning (17) also showed their worth. The team was unbeaten at home, the three defeats coming at Ayr, Hearts and Rangers.

1914–1915 SCOTTISH CUP

The competition was suspended during wartime

1914–1915 GLASGOW CUP

Clyde	(A)	0-2

1914–1915 CHARITY CUP

	Queen's Park	(A)	2-1		
	Partick Thistle	(A)	1 goal 4 corners to 1 goal 3 corners		
Final	Rangers		3-2	25,000	08/05/15

Team: Shaw,; McNair, Dodds; Young, Johnstone, McMaster; McAtee, Gallagher; McColl; McMenemy, Browning.

There was plenty of enthusiasm in this match, certainly too much bad temper and some indifferent football. Rangers opened well with the wind behind them and although Dodds scored in 12 minutes much against the run-of-play, Rangers replied twice before the interval to go 2-1 up.

Celtic had played the tactical game in the opening session against the wind, slowing the game down, taking plenty of time with corners, free kicks and so on. Not unexpectedly, Rangers did the same in the second half but Celtic kept pressing, got the equaliser from Browning and the winner from McMenemy two minutes from the end. It was a deserved triumph. Rangers at their best were as good as Celtic, but the latter lasted better.

The Board

The Provisional Board had been agreed at a fateful meeting, on the 4th March 1897 in the same St Mary's Hall where the first gathering to establish the

> *The Original Board*
>
> NAMES, ADDRESSES, AND DESCRIPTION OF SHAREHOLDERS.
>
> *John Glass 597 Gallowgate Glasgow. Manager*
>
> *Wm McLaughlin Almada St Hamilton Wine Merchant,*
>
> *Michael Hughes 60 Tobago Street Glasgow Japanner*
>
> *M Dunbar 429 Gallowgate Glasgow Wine & Spirit Merchant*
>
> *T.E. Maley Slatefield Street Glasgow Superintendent of Industrial School*
>
> *James McKay 605 Gallowgate Glasgow Hairdresser*
>
> *John O'Hara 351 Gallowgate Glasgow Wine & Spirit Merchant*
>
> *Dated the Eighth day of April, Eighteen hundred and ninety-seven. Witness to the above Signatures:*
>
> *Donald Peffers,*
> *Clerk with Joseph Shaughnessy Solicitor*
> *83 Bath Street, Glasgow*

Club had been held. The men eventually elected to this temporary Board were: J.H.McLaughlin, John O'Hare, T.E. Maley, Michael Hughes, John Glass, Michael Dunbar and James McKay.

In the Memorandum of Association put forward by this Provisional Board, Article I stated that the name of the company should be 'Celtic Football and Athletic Company Limited', and Article *V.* declared that the 'The Capital of the Company is £5,000 divided into £5,000 shares of £1 each'.

The Articles of Association, registered on the same day – 12 April 1897 – go into considerable detail about Shares, Calls on shares, Transfer of shares, Transmission of shares, Forfeiture of Lien upon Shares, Surrender of Shares, Conversion of Shares, Reduction of Capital, Increase in Capital, General Meeting, Borrowing Powers, Duties of Directors etc, but it is not until Section 98 on page 18, that the original aim receives a mention. In an eleven-line paragraph on when directors may or may not recommend a dividend, the last sentence reads:

> ...the directors may also, after providing for payment of dividend of not less than five per cent per annum, devote such part of the profits for charitable purposes as they think fit.

One year later, when Celtic had an income of £16,267, the Company declared a 20 per cent dividend for its shareholders, dispersed £105 in directors' fees – and ignored Article 98! Some shareholders were a little uneasy over this 20 per cent figure and the lack of money for charity but their uncertainty did not last. For the following three years the dividend was 10 per cent.

There were probably some on the Provisional Board not too enamoured with the wording of the Articles or possibly another bout of in-fighting occurred when the shares were opened to purchase. Certainly, by the time the names of those on the First Board of Directors was announced in December 1897, three of the Provisional Board, Tom Maley, Michael Hughes and James McKay, had been dropped.

The new Board, still under the Chairmanship of J.H. McLaughlin, comprised John Glass (Club Chairman from 1890–1897), former players James Kelly (1888–1897) and Michael Dunbar (1888–1893), John O'Hare (Celtic's first Secretary 1888), John McKillop (a restaurateur) and new boy James Grant, a Wine and Spirits Merchant from Northern Ireland.

One of this Board's first decisions was to purchase the lease of Celtic Park – which still had four years to run – from the landlord Sir William Hosier for the sum of £10,000. A meeting of shareholders was held to allow the raising of additional capital to buy the field and a motion to raise £5,000 was agreed. These were to be offered as £5,000 shares at £1 each, none of which could be sold to an outsider. They were quickly snapped up, almost certainly by the existing Board members, thus strengthening their position. One year later, James Grant came to an agreement with the Club to build a special stand on the south side of the ground and receive a percentage of the takings from those using it. For reasons mentioned elsewhere, this was not a success and he eventually sold it to the club.

Celtic had so much success at this time and throughout the following 20 years that the workings of the Board were seldom apparent. The Provisional Board designated Willie Maley as Secretary/Manager in 1897 and his was the dominant name in the public's mind. Occasionally, various members of the Board came into the spotlight. James Grant, for instance, with his new stand; or Chairman John McLaughlin, when he had a public blast at the players on the pages of the *Glasgow Examiner* on 23 December 1891; or when it was announced that James Kelly and Michael Dunbar often turned up at training sessions to offer advice. Decisions which in other times may have caused comment, or even anger, were glossed over or ignored in view of the team's on-field success. There was no Reserve Team, for instance, yet the league was won from 1904–1910 and again from 1913–1917. Even the statement in 1909 that £2,200 had been given to charity since the Club had been incorporated as a limited company was treated lightly although £2,2,00 over 12 years was hardly munificent.

John O'Hara died in 1904, to be replaced by Thomas Colgan; John Glass passed away in 1906 and Tom White came onto the board. Three years later John H. McLaughlin was succeeded on his death as Chairman by James Kelly and two years after that John Shaughnessey, a Glasgow lawyer, was elected. In 1914, both James Grant and John McKillop passed away and the Chairmanship was taken over by Thomas White.

First Board of Directors 1897

J.H. McLaughlin	(Died 1909)
John Glass	(Died 1906)
John O'Hara	(Died 1904)
James Grant	(Died 1914)
John McKillop	(Died 1914)
Michael Dunbar	
James Kelly	

List of Directors 1920

Thomas White	Chairman
James Kelly	
Michael Dunbar	
John Shaughnessey	
Thomas Colgan	

1915–1916 Scottish League Division 1

	P	W	D	L	F	A	Points	Position
Celtic	38	32	3	3	116	23	67	1st

Fixtures

	H	A		H	A
Aberdeen	3-1	4-0	Kilmarnock	2-0	3-0
Airdrie	6-0	5-0	Morton	0-0	1-0
Ayr United	3-1	4-0	Motherwell	3-1	3-1
Clyde	5-0	3-1	Partick Thistle	5-0	4-0
Dumbarton	6-0	2-1	Queen's Park	6-2	1-0
Dundee	3-0	2-0	Raith Rovers	6-0	2-0
Falkirk	2-1	2-0	Rangers	2-2	0-3
Hamilton	5-1	3-2	St Mirren	0-2	0-5
Hearts	0-0	0-2	Third Lanark	4-1	4-0
Hibs	3-1	4-0			

A wonderful season for Celtic, both the goals for and against being very impressive, which left them a massive 11 points ahead of second place Rangers. 116 goals in a season is a Club record. Patsy Gallagher (28) and Jimmy McColl (35) were the main contributors although even the veteran Jimmy McMenemy (8) got his share. On April 15 1916, Celtic played Raith Rovers at Celtic Park in the afternoon (6-0) and Motherwell at Fir Park in the evening (3-1) due to fixture congestion.

1915–1916 Scottish Cup
The competition was suspended during wartime

1915–1916 GLASGOW CUP

	Third Lanark	(H)	2-0		
Final	Rangers	(Hampden)	2-1	70,000	07/10/15

Team: Shaw; McNair and Dodds; Young, Johnstone and McMaster; McAtee, Gallagher; McColl; McMenemy and Browning.

This was judged to be one of the poorest ever Glasgow Cup Finals. In fact, the gate was too good for the game. Rangers in particular were very poor and failed completely to mark Gallagher in eight minutes, who scored easily. Although Rangers equalised through outside-left Paterson, Celtic went ahead again thanks to Browning before half-time. In the second period, Rangers were seldom out of their own half; whilst Celtic passed well but finished poorly.

1915–1916 CHARITY CUP

	Rangers	(H)	3-0		
Final	Partick Thistle	(Hampden)	2-0	25,000	13/05/16

Alec McNair joined Celtic from Stenhousemuir in 1904 and retired in 1925. He was noted for his ability to jockey his opponents into positions advantageous to him and for his cool demeanour, which earned him the nickname of 'The Icicle'. He made 604 appearances in total.

Celtic were firm favourites in this Final which produced little excitement but occasional flashes of fine play. Thistle certainly made a game of it although their forwards were non-penetrative if clever, sometimes confused by the back-passing tactics of the very secure Celtic defence. Both goals came in the first half, when Celtic had the wind and sun in their favour. Jim Young scored the first with a high shot which the Thistle keeper had difficulty judging in the sun; and Patsy Gallagher got the second with an angled drive.

Team: Shaw; McNair and Dodds; Young, Johnston, McMaster; McAtee, Gallagher; O'Kane; McMenemy and Browning.

1916–1917 SCOTTISH LEAGUE DIVISION I

	P	W	D	L	F	A	Points	Position
Celtic	38	27	10	1	79	17	64	1st

FIXTURES

	H	A		H	A
Aberdeen	1-0	0-0	Kilmarnock	0-2	2-2
Airdrie	3-1	2-1	Morton	0-0	1-0
Ayr United	5-0	1-0	Motherwell	1-0	4-0
Clyde	0-0	5-0	Partick Thistle	0-0	2-0
Dumbarton	1-1	3-1	Queen's Park	3-2	3-1
Dundee	2-0	2-1	Raith Rovers	5-0	4-1
Falkirk	2-0	1-1	Rangers	0-0	0-0
Hamilton	6-1	4-0	St Mirren	3-0	5-1
Hearts	1-0	1-0	Third Lanark	2-0	0-0
Hibs	3-1	1-0			

Only ten points ahead of the pack this time, Celtic can thank their miserly defence for 24 shut-outs. The only defeat was at home to Kilmarnock, who proved to be their bogey team as they only drew 2-2 with them away. The double act was responsible for most of the goals – Gallagher (22) and McColl (24) – although John Browning assisted with a more than useful 12. This was Celtic's fourth consecutive championship win, their fourteenth overall. That defeat by Kilmarnock ended a long, unbeaten run in the league. Celtic had gone 62 matches (49 wins, 13 defeats), from losing to Hearts on 13 November 1915 until that Kilmarnock result.

1916–1917 SCOTTISH CUP

The competition was suspended during wartime

1916–1917 GLASGOW CUP

		Rangers	(H)	3-0		
Final	Clyde		(Celtic Park)	3-2	30,000	07/10/16

Celtic were very firm favourites but Clyde started well, took the lead and held onto it for the next three-quarters of an hour before Celtic found their rhythm. Goals from O'Kane, Browning and a Dodds penalty really made the score more reflect the play although Clyde got another just on the whistle after a mix-up between Shaw and McNair.

Team: Shaw; McNair and Dodds; Private Johnstone, Wilson, Private McAteer; McAtee, Gallagher; O'Kane; McMenemy and Browning.

1916–1917 CHARITY CUP					
	Rangers	(A)	2-0		
Final	Queen's Park	(Hampden)	1-0	30,000	19/05/17

Team: Shaw; McNair and Dodds; McStay, Cringan and Brown; McAtee, McMenemy; McColl; Browning and McLean.

No Gallagher in the team – and he was missed! Celtic were the better side and deserved their win but while the outfield play was reasonable, the shooting boots were not on, nevertheless Jimmy McColl showed the way in the tenth minute. Queen's Park, with Alan Morton at outside-left, claimed for three penalties, one of which seemed a sure decision, but the referee turned them all down.

1917–1918 SCOTTISH LEAGUE DIVISION I							
	P	W	D	L	F	A	Points	Position
Rangers	34	25	6	3	66	24	56	1st
Celtic	34	24	7	3	66	26	55	2nd

FIXTURES						
	H	A		H	A
Airdrie	3-3	0-2	Kilmarnock	2-3	3-1
Ayr United	4-0	2-1	Morton	2-0	1-1
Clyde	3-2	4-1	Motherwell	1-1	4-3
Clydebank	3-0	2-1	Partick Thistle	2-1	0-0
Dumbarton	3-0	2-0	Queen's Park	3-0	2-0
Falkirk	0-0	3-1	Rangers	0-0	2-1
Hamilton	1-0	2-1	St Mirren	1-0	0-0
Hearts	3-0	1-0	Third Lanark	1-3	2-0
Hibs	2-0	2-0			

Only one point in it at the end and astonishingly similar records for the season from the Old Firm. Since Celtic beat Rangers away and drew with them at home, they could be accused of not capitalising on their chances. Of the three defeats, two were at home – Kilmarnock and Third Lanark – while a draw against Motherwell on the last day of the season made all the difference.

1917–1918 SCOTTISH CUP

The competition was suspended during wartime

1917–1918 GLASGOW CUP		
Queen's Park	(A)	2-1
Rangers	(H)	0-3

1917–1918 CHARITY CUP

	Third Lanark (A)	2-1		
Final	Partick Thistle (Hampden)	2-0	25,000	25/05/18

This was Celtic's seventh consecutive Cup win in this competition. Thistle made it difficult for them but while their defence stuck to its task, the forwards lacked the guile necessary to outwit the green-and-white rearguard. Goals from Patsy Gallagher, a header 2 minutes into the second half and a rasper by John Browning took the Cup back to Parkhead.

Team: Shaw; McNair and Dodds; Brown, Hamill and Jackson; McAtee, McMenemy; Gallagher; Browning and Kelly.

The Great War – and Football

The war made a real difference to football in Scotland. Headlines began to appear in the papers about footballers enlisting. Letters appeared commenting on the great boost there would be to recruitment if popular footballers led the way. During matches, the slogan 'Kitchener wants you' was carried round at half-time on placards and there were many appeals for recruits to join the fun before it was all over!

In 1914, the FA and the SFA agreed to abandon International matches. The SFA also decided to scrap the Scottish Cup competition. Players' wages were to be reduced by 25 per cent and later fixed at £1 per week. No wages were paid during the close season and footballers were expected to take their place alongside the other workers in the munitions factories and shipyards. League matches were confined to Saturdays and holidays and players could only take part if they had worked the rest of the week. This could have worked to Celtic's disadvantage, in the third of their four-in-a-row seasons. The Club's away match against Motherwell on 25 March had been postponed due to snow. Since matches could only be played on Saturdays and as the season had to finish by the 29th April, they were forced to play two matches in one day. This was achieved on 15 April. Firstly they beat Raith Rovers 6-0 at Celtic Park, the match kicking off at 3.15 pm and at 6 pm, they trotted out at Fir Park and eventually defeated Motherwell by 2-1.

The war was horrendous but ironically, Celtic played some lovely football and set some new records, like 116 goals scored in 1915–1916, losing only 14 in 1913–1914 and going undefeated in 62 matches between 13 November 1915 and 21 April 1917. The team finished second in the Championship of 1917–1918, only one point behind their perennial rivals Rangers but one season later, won their fifteenth championship losing only two games in the process.

Celtic also played their part in promotion of the war effort. Appeals were made at half-time during matches at Parkhead for recruits; the Club sent footballs to army recruits in training and soldiers at the front; matches for

A 'Patriotic Card' issued in 1916, the purchase of which meant one half-penny donated to the National Belgian Relief Fund.

A charity match played at Hampden Park on 20 May 1916 to raise money for the Belgian Relief Fund. A Scottish League XI beat a Celtic XI 1-0. £938 was raised in total.

League XI (1): Stewart (Falkirk), Mandelson (Rangers), Private Wilson (Hearts), Gordon (Rangers), Mercer (Hearts), Nellies (Hearts), Simpson (Falkirk), McTavish (Part Time), Gunner Reid (Rangers), Cairns (Rangers), Morton (Queen's Park).

Celtic (0): Shaw, McNair, Dodds, Young, Johnstone, McMaster, McAtee, Gallagher, O'Kane, McMenemy, Browning.

Lance-Corporal William Angus VC. The other side of this card reads: 'For great devotion to duty displayed at Givenchy, June 12, 1915.' He left his trench voluntarily and in the teeth of terrible fire rescued a wounded officer from near the enemy trenches. He was wounded almost 40 times, sometimes seriously, during this episode.

War Relief Funds, initially for Belgian refugees, were played at Hampden Park in 1915, 1916 and 1917 when Celtic as League Champions, played against a select team representing the Rest of the League, before huge crowds. Celtic, though, like many other families, had their share of war dead. Peter Johnstone (Arras 1917), Donny McLeod (Flanders 1917), Bobby Craig (1918 Boulogne), Leighton Roose (1916 The Somme) all gave their lives for their country; while Willie Angus, a Lance Corporal in the Highland Light Infantry, who had been on Celtic's books before the war, won the VC for rescuing his Commanding Officer from no-man's-land near Givenchy.

1918–1919 SCOTTISH LEAGUE DIVISION 1							
	P	W	D	L	F	A	Points	Position
Celtic	34	26	6	2	71	22	58	1st

FIXTURES

	H	A		H	A
Airdrie	3-0	2-1	Kilmarnock	2-1	1-1
Ayr United	1-0	2-0	Morton	1-1	0-0
Clyde	2-0	3-0	Motherwell	0-0	1-3
Clydebank	3-1	2-0	Partick Thistle	2-1	1-0
Dumbarton	2-0	5-0	Queen's Park	2-0	3-0
Falkirk	4-0	2-1	Rangers	0-3	1-1
Hamilton	4-1	2-1	St Mirren	1-0	4-0
Hearts	1-1	3-2	Third Lanark	3-1	3-2
Hibs	2-0	3-0			

The reverse of the previous season, with Celtic finishing one point ahead of Rangers to take the title. Even more strange, this time Celtic drew one and lost another of the Old Firm matches. However, in a season of transition, this was an excellent result. Willie Cringan was now their regular centre-half; Charlie Shaw remained the capable last line; McNair and Dodds were dependable as ever at full-back, although Willie McStay came in for three appearances at right-back. Adam McLean had replaced John Browning on the left flank and the ammunition he provided allowed Patsy Gallagher and Jimmy McColl each to score 15 goals.

Another man to break into the team this season was Duggie Livingstone at left-back with ten appearances. He only played a couple of seasons with Celtic but made a bigger name for himself later as coach and manager. His career spanned Exeter, Sheffield United, Sheffield Wednesday, Sparta Rotterdam, Eire, Belgium, Newcastle United, Fulham and Chesterfield.

Late in 1918, Rangers outside-right Scott Duncan played for the Scottish League Select against the English League Select in a match at Hampden in aid of Belgian refugees. After the match, he was asked by Willie Maley if he

The team which won the War Fund Shield by beating Morton 1-0 in the final at Hampden Park on 4 May 1918. Back row, left to right: M. Quinn (Trainer), McNair, McGregor, Shaw, Livingstone, Wilson, McCall, Browning. Fonrt row: Gallagher, Brown, McMeneny, Cringan, McLean, Jackson.

would guest for Celtic the following Saturday. Duncan asked Rangers, who told him to please himself, so he did play for Celtic, against Third Lanark at Cathkin on 4 January 1919 (3-2) and Clydebank at home (3-1) one week later. Scott Duncan later managed Manchester United and Ipswich.

1918–1919 SCOTTISH CUP

The competition was suspended during wartime

1918–1919 GLASGOW CUP

	Clyde	(H)	3-1		
Final	Rangers	(Hampden)	0-2	65,000	5/10/18

1918–1919 CHARITY CUP

Queen's Park	(A)	1-3

1919–1920 SCOTTISH LEAGUE DIVISION I

	P	W	D	L	F	A	Points	Position
Rangers	42	31	9	2	106	25	71	1st
Celtic	42	29	10	3	89	31	68	2nd

FIXTURES

	H	A		H	A
Aberdeen	5-0	1-0	Hibs	7-3	2-1
Airdrie	1-0	0-0	Kilmarnock	1-0	3-2
Albion Rovers	3-0	5-0	Morton	1-1	2-1
Ayr United	4-0	1-1	Motherwell	5-0	0-0
Clyde	3-1	2-0	Partick Thistle	0-0	2-1
Clydebank	3-1	0-2	Queen's Park	3-1	2-1
Dumbarton	3-1	0-0	Raith Rovers	3-0	3-0
Dundee	1-1	1-2	Rangers	1-1	0-3
Falkirk	1-1	2-1	St Mirren	2-2	2-0
Hamilton	2-0	2-1	Third Lanark	2-1	4-1
Hearts	3-0	1-0			

Three points separated the teams but Celtic could not quite live up to the style of the year before. A new half-back line of Gilchrist; Cringan, and McMaster came in; McColl was replaced by Tommy McInally, who scored 29 goals in his first season. Unbeaten at home, the three reverses came at Clydebank, Dundee and Rangers. Generally, the away performances were less prolific in scoring terms; 54 goals at home but only 35 away. The Dundee match on 26 April at Celtic Park was full of incident. The visitors were getting a rough reception on their appearance for reputedly 'going down' against Rangers in a recent 6-1 defeat. Dundee at Parkhead, by contrast, were guilty of some very tough tackling and there was a great deal of tension in the crowd. A clash between McLean of Celtic and Rowlings of Dundee United led to a pitch invasion. Two Dundee players were assaulted; the referee was pushed and jostled and he eventually abandoned the match ten minutes from time. The resulting SFA inquiry decided that the result should stand but that Celtic Park should be closed to regular football until 31 August 1920, so the first three matches of the following season, Hamilton, Albion Rovers and Aberdeen were all played away from home.

	1919–1920 SCOTTISH CUP			
	Dundee	(A)	3-1	34,000
	Partick Thistle	(H)	2-0	65,000
QF	Rangers	(A\)	0-1	85,000

There were huge crowds, of course, in the after-war years. The attendance for the Partick Thistle tie at Celtic Park was particularly astonishing, although the bigger one for Rangers was to be expected. With Rangers heading for the League Title and Celtic pushing them hard, this old Firm quarter-final was expected to be close and lived up to expectations, a late goal by Tommy Muirhead separating the teams at the finish.

	1919–1920 GLASGOW CUP				
	Rangers	(H)	1-0		
	Queen's Park	(H)	3-1		
Final	Partick Thistle	(Celtic Park)	1-0	45,000	4/10/19

Celtic were right off their game on the day. In addition, an injury to Willie McStay caused him to be a passenger for most of the second half. Granted, Celtic were probably more often in Thistle's half than vice versa, but too many players played below-par. The only goal, 13 minutes from time, was rather an unusual one. Thistle left-back Bulloch cleared the ball and Tommy McInally met it first time with a high lob which completely deceived the keeper.

Team: Shaw; McNair, McStay; Gilchrist, Clingan, Cassidy; McAtee, Gallagher; McInally; McMenemy and McLean.

	1919–1920 CHARITY CUP				
	Rangers	(A)	2-1		
Final	Queen's Park	(Celtic Park)	1-0	45,000	15/05/20

Team: Shaw; McNair and Livingstone; Gilchrist, Clingan and McStay; Watson, McKay; McInally; McLean and Pratt.

This was the case of young guys up front, old hands at the back. Both had a say in victory but it was a sluggish performance. Shaw and McNair were immense for Celtic against a good Queens' attack, with Alan Morton in fine form on left-wing. The only goal came in the second half when McLean shot from close in and it slipped through the hands of the Queen's Park goalkeeper. Two 'new' names played in this final. David Pratt at outside-left played 22 league matches in total but moved on to Bradford after one season. David had won the Military Medal in the War. Inside-right John McKay was part of the intake from St Anthony's in 1919 and scored six goals in his ten League appearances.

Old Firm

The rivalry between these two premier clubs in Scotland deepened during the first 20 years of the 20th century. In fact, it was intensified by the incidents already discussed – the row over the Glasgow Exhibition Trophy, the choice of venue for the Charity Cup Final in 1901 and so on. Their image throughout British, European and even the World stage was badly tarnished by the aftermath of the Scottish Cup Final of 1909, the so-called Hampden Riot; while the religious divisions between them, always present after this upstart Irish Catholic-inspired team from Glasgow's East End suddenly rose to prominence, were made even more bitter when many Belfast Orangemen arrived to work in the new Harland and Wolff shipyard in Govan and gave support to the local team.

In terms of trophies won, however, these two decades belonged to Celtic. A review of their success shows just what a wonderful time it was, yet the old saying that fans are fickle even extended to the Celtic support, whose numbers dropped towards the end of the six-in-a-row League win between 1904–1910.

THE OLD FIRMS' RECORD IN COMPETITIONS 1900–1920

	LEAGUE	CUP	GLASGOW CUP	CHARITY CUP
1900–01	Rangers		Rangers	
1901–02	Rangers		Rangers	
1902–03		Rangers		Celtic
1903–04		Celtic		Rangers
1904–05	Celtic		Celtic	Celtic
1905–06	Celtic		Celtic	Rangers
1906–07	Celtic	Celtic	Celtic	Rangers
1907–08	Celtic	Celtic	Celtic	Celtic
1908–09	Celtic	witheld		Rangers
1909–10	Celtic		Celtic	
1910–11	Rangers	Celtic	Rangers	Rangers
1911–12	Rangers	Celtic	Rangers	Celtic
1912–13	Rangers		Rangers	Celtic
1913–14	Celtic	Celtic	Rangers	Celtic
1914–15	Celtic	—		Celtic
1915–16	Celtic	—	Celtic	Celtic
1916–17	Celtic	—	Celtic	Celtic
1917–18	Rangers	—	Rangers	Celtic
1918–19	Celtic	—	Rangers	Rangers
1919–20	Rangers		Celtic	Celtic
	Celtic 11	Celtic 6	Celtic 8	Celtic 11
	Rangers 7	Rangers 1	Rangers 8	Rangers 6

TOTAL: CELTIC 36 RANGERS 22

A modern complaint is that our League Championship is always between Rangers and Celtic. As we can see from the tables, it was ever so. Third Lanark won their only title in 1904; the so-called neutral had to wait until 1932 before Motherwell again broke the Old Firm dominance.

CHAPTER SIX (1920–1930)
Good Players – Poor Results

THAT CHAMPIONSHIP in the last year of the war, 1918, Celtic's 15th in total, proved to be something of a watershed in their history. The good times would soon prove to be behind them, with some years of woe to come.

In fact, if the period from 1888–1919 was dominated by Celtic, then Rangers soon gained the upper hand. From 1919 until the arrival of Jock Stein in 1965, they took the lead, winning 25 League Titles to Celtic's 5; 14 Scottish Cups to 8; and 6 League Cups to 2. Recent talk of nine or ten-in-a-row might have been irrelevant had not Celtic, on four occasions (1921–22, 1925–26, 1935–36, 1937–38) and Motherwell (1931–32) broken a Rangers 20-year run from 1919–1920 to 1938–1939. Yet during these two decades, Celtic had some very fine players and some good sides. So what went wrong? Before we look at Celtic's problems, let's first of all consider why Rangers improved.

As we have seen from the tables of success in the 1890s and also the first 20 years of the new century, Celtic was the more dominant team during this era. Rangers, however, were never very far behind, regularly runners-up in the League although having more difficulty with the Scottish Cup, their win in 1903 being the last triumph for an amazing quarter of a century. A criticism often applied to their teams at this time was 'unreliable', although others, more harsh or perhaps perceptive, suggested that they 'choked' at vital moments.

In the summer of 1920, after the tragic death of their manager, William Wilton, in a drowning accident near Gourock, their trainer, Bill Struth, took over. Struth had never played football but as an athlete in his younger days recognised the value of certain qualities. He immediately adopted a strict regime in which discipline, hardness and fitness were all important. He also insisted that the club travel in style, first-class preferably, and made the players dress accordingly.

Struth was very much a pragmatist, well aware of the crowd-pleasing value of a personality and soon signed the Queen's Park winger, Alan Morton, a player with an exciting turn of speed and a rare touch when sending over a cross. All these moves brought immediate success, with Rangers picking up the first two Championships after the war in 1919–1920 and 1920–1921, knocking Celtic out of the Cup at the quarter-final stage in

1919–1920 and reaching the final in both 1920–1921 and 1921–1922. As Rangers rose, so Celtic began to feel the pressure. In spite of admission prices rising from sixpence (2½p) to 1 shilling (5p) after the war, huge crowds attended matches in those years; 85,000 for the quarter-final cup tie against Rangers in 1920; 40,000 for the fourth round tie against Hearts the following season. The six ties in the Scottish Cup run of 1921–1922, for instance, attracted an average of 28,000 each, while Celtic's income from the 1920–1921 season amounted to £45,000.

But all was not well behind the scenes. Jimmy McMenemy left, on the grounds of 'irreconcilible differences' in June 1920. One year later, he led Partick Thistle to their one and only Scottish Cup Final. Two months later, Joe Dodds was transferred to Cowdenbeath although within one season he returned. In 1922, the Board made the fateful decision of withdrawing the Reserve Team, apparently on the grounds of cost. The predictable outcome was that the assembly-line of young players coming into the team dried up,

A fine youthful Jimmy McMenemy. This photograph was taken during his early years with Celtic. Around 1903–04, 'Napoleon', as he was known, was a tactical master, making better players out of those around him.

a very peculiar decision at a time when Rangers were going from strength to strength.

Success was occasional. A sixteenth League Championship was gained in 1921–1922, the title secured in a draw with Cup Winners Morton at Cappielow, amid scenes of anarchy and bigotry. One year later, Celtic won the Cup for the sixteenth time by disposing of Hibs 1-0 in front of 80,000 at Hampden. In between these victories, Tommy McInally had been transferred to Third Lanark. No one doubted his talents but the manager and Board disliked his lack of discipline.

1920–1921 Scottish League Division 1

	P	W	D	L	F	A	Points	Position
Rangers	42	35	6	1	91	24	76	1st
Celtic	42	30	6	6	86	35	66	2nd

Fixtures

	H	A		H	A
Aberdeen	3-1	2-1	Hibs	3-0	3-0
Airdrie 2-1	3-2		Kilmarnock	2-0	2-3
Albion Rovers 0-2	1-0	Morton 1-1	1-1	
Ayr United	3-1	1-3	Motherwell	1-0	1-1
Clyde 1-0	1-2		Partick Thistle 1-0	1-0	
Clydebank	1-1	2-0	Queen's Park	5-1	2-0
Dumbarton	1-1	3-1	Raith Rovers	5-0	0-2
Dundee 2-0	2-1		Rangers	1-2	2-0
Falkirk 4-1	3-1		St Mirren	6-0	2-0
Hamilton	2-1	1-1	Third Lanark	3-0	2-1
Hearts 3-2	1-0				

In boxing terms this was really no contest! Celtic lost too many goals during the season to compete with a very professional Rangers effort. The derby games were shared but Celtic lost badly at home to Albion Rovers in October, exactly one week after a home defeat by Rangers. From then on they stuttered away from home, the losses to Ayr United, Kilmarnock and Raith Rovers coming in a four-week period from the middle of March onwards. Tommy McInally again did well in the goal-scoring stakes with 28, while Joe Cassidy got 17.

1920–1921 Scottish Cup

	05/02/21	Vale of Leven	(A)	3-0	3,000
	19/02/21	East Fife	(A)	3-1	11,000
QF	05/03/21	Hearts	(H)	1-2	40,000

The Cup Campaign did not go as expected. Joe Cassidy got two goals in the first match against Vale of Leven and Tommy McInally two in the second match against East Fife up at Methil. After holding Hearts at home to 1-1 at half-time, however, the visitors scored a late winner which put them through eventually to the Final where they were beaten after a replay by Partick

Thistle. A most noticeable figure in the Partick Thistle line-up at inside-left was one Jimmy McMenemy, taking Partick Thistle to their one and only Scottish Cup triumph the season after he left Celtic.

1920–1921 GLASGOW CUP					
	Third Lanark	(H)	3-0		
	Rangers	(H)	2-1		
Final	Clyde	(Celtic Park)	1-0	40,000	2/10/20

Team: Shaw; McNair and McStay; Gilchrist, Cringan and Pratt; McAtee, Gallagher; McInally; Cassidy and McLean.

This was not a particularly exciting match but the five minutes before the interval were crucial. Outside-right Hugh Morris of Clyde was cutting in on goal when he was tackled by left-half David Pratt. Down he went, received some treatment on the pitch, but was carried off on a stretcher having broken a bone in his ankle. Before Clyde could re-organise, Andy McAtee took advantage of the situation to score the winner.

This must have been one of two highlights of David Pratt's career with Celtic. He had been in the Cameron Highlanders during the War, where he won a Military Medal, signed in the summer of 1919 and played some 22 league matches for the Club, before leaving for Bradford in 1921.

1920–1921 CHARITY CUP					
	Partick Thistle	(H)	2-0		
Final	Rangers	(Hampden)	2-0	55,000	14/05/21

Celtic FC 1920–21. Back row, left to right: W. Cringan, A. Longmuir, J. McMaster, P. Gallagher, J. McFarlane, W. McStay, J. Gilchrist. Middle row: W. Quinn (Trainer), A McNair, T. Craig, D. Livingstone, W. Lawrie, J. Murphy, J. McKay, C. Watson. Front row: D. Pratt, T. McInally, A. McAtee, H. Brown, C. Shaw, J. Price, J. Cassidy, A. McLean, W. Maley (Manager).
Note the name of Tully Craig in the middle row. He only played nine games for Celtic, but went on to star for Rangers.

Team: Shaw; Murphy, Dodds; Gilchrist, McStay, McFarlane; McLean, Gallagher; McInally; Cassidy and Pratt.

Celtic played an unusual team, with John McFarlane at left-half and David Pratt in front of him. Jamie Murphy, ex-Royal Scots Fusiliers, partnered Joe Dodds at the back. This was a very competitive match, many tempers rising to the surface. Celtic's main strength was their grit; the longer the game went on the more they upset Rangers' rhythm and the more disjointed the Light Blues became. Twenty minutes into the first half, Tommy McInally took a free-kick from 20 yards out which looked an easy catch for Rangers keeper Robb but right-back Candless got in the road of the ball and deflected it home. Celtic kept up the pressure from that point on and sealed the victory with another McInally shot 15 minutes from time.

1921–1922 Scottish League Division 1

	P	W	D	L	F	A	Points	Position
Celtic	42	27	13	2	83	20	67	1st

Fixtures

	H	A		H	A
Aberdeen	2-0	1-1	Hibs	3-1	1-2
Airdrie	2-0	1-0	Kilmarnock	1-0	3-4
Albion Rovers	3-1	2-0	Morton	1-0	1-1
Ayr United	2-1	0-0	Motherwell	2-0	1-1
Clyde	1-0	1-1	Partick Thistle	3-0	0-0
Clydebank	6-0	2-0	Queen's Park	3-1	3-1
Dumbarton	4-0	5-0	Raith Rovers	4-0	1-1
Dundee	4-0	0-0	Rangers	0-0	1-1
Falkirk	0-0	1-1	St Mirren	2-0	2-0
Hamilton	4-0	3-1	Third Lanark	2-0	0-0
Hearts	3-0	2-1			

Celtic finished only one point ahead of Rangers in this, their 16th Championship win, with 13 draws the most ever for a team winning the First Division. It was an unusual set of statistics for the season in general. Both the Old Firm matches were drawn; Celtic were unbeaten at home, scoring 51, losing only 4 in 21 matches; their two defeats were away at Hibs and Kilmarnock. Of the 13 draws, 5 were 0-0 and 7 were 1-1. In the goal-scoring stakes, McInally (17), Cassidy (17) and Gallagher (17) were the main men.

1921–1922 Scottish Cup

28/01/22	Montrose	(H)	4-0	6,000
11/02/22	Third Lanark	(A)	1-0	45,000
25/02/22	Hamilton	(H)	1-3	20,000

Typical Cup football. After a good victory, thanks to an Adam McLean goal, against Third Lanark in front of a huge crowd at Cathkin, Celtic stumbled badly two weeks later against a Hamilton side whom they had

Celtic FC 1921–22. Back row, left to right: Connor, Pratt, McKnight, Shaw, Cassidy. Middle row: Quinn (Trainer), Hilley, McNair, McStay (B), Dodds, McStay (W), McInally, Glasgow, Gilchrist. Font row: McFarlane, Collins, McMaster, McAtee, McKay, Gallagher, Murphy, McLean, W. Maley (Manager).

comfortably beaten 3-1 away on Hogmanay. One week after this Cup Tie, the teams met again in the League, this time at Parkhead – and Celtic won 4-0.

	1921–1922 GLASGOW CUP				
	Queen's Park	(H)	2-1		
	Partick Thistle	(H)	1-1		
Replay	Partick Thistle	(A)	2-0		
Final	Rangers	(Hampden)	0-1	80,000	1/10/20

1921–1922 CHARITY CUP		
Partick Thistle	(A)	3 goals 8 corners to 3 goals 6 corners
Rangers	(Hampden)	6 corners to 10 corners

The Players

By 1923, the Celtic team still had Charlie Shaw in goal and Alec McNair at right-back, in his 19th year of service. Willie McStay was at left-back, good in the air, solid in defence but capable of coming forward when necessary. His younger brother Jimmy was not flashy but gave little away at right-half or centre-half. On the other flank, John 'Jean' McFarlane was a fine passer of the ball; and in between, Willie Cringan was strength and security personified. The wingers were the strong-legged Andy McAtee and Adam McLean, the latter often compared favourably with Alan Morton. At centre-forward, Joe Cassidy (Trooper Joe) was a natural scorer, thriving on the service of the incomparable Patsy Gallagher and that greyhound of a player, Pat Connolly.

Gradually, the personnel changed. Peter Shevlin came in to replace Charlie

Shaw in the autumn of 1924, but his nervousness often betrayed him and he was succeeded by John Thomson in 1926. Willie McStay moved in to replace Willie Cringan at centre-half. Peter Wilson came in at right-half, a superb passer of the ball; as was Alec Thomson at inside-forward. Patsy Gallagher moved to Falkirk in 1925, Tommy McInally returned from Third Lanark in 1925; a genius but not a worker. And at centre-forward had appeared the incomparable Jimmy McGrory, first getting his chance when Joe Cassidy was transferred to Bolton Wanderers for £4,000. McGrory was a throwback to the days of Jimmy Quinn, not only skilful but fearless. Good players there were a-plenty but not always a cohesive force.

Tribute must be paid here to Patsy Gallagher. In any list of Celtic stars, he would be up near the top, yet he had such an unprepossessing figure to look at. Only 5ft 7in in height and less than 10 stone, he possessed a superb touch and a fine football brain turning in such performances during his career that superlatives to describe his play ran out. Physically, he should have been crushed. But few defenders ever managed to pin the little man down and he used his repertoire of wriggles, swerves, hops and occasional 'stops' to avoid the clumsy and evade even the talented. As if these gifts were not enough, his stamina and bravery were also of the very highest. Truly, he was phenomenal.

In addition to the parsimony displayed by the withdrawal of the reserve team, other problems concerning money continued through the 1920s. The harsh economic climate was having an effect on attendances. Jobs were becoming more scarce and a fairly rampant sectarianism prevailed. Celtic fans, by their very background, suffered more than most and eventually, a 'Buroo' gate for those not working was instituted.

Behind the scenes, there always seemed to be disputes over money. In the early part of season 1923–1924, the dressing room was an angry place. The captain, Willie Cringan, was asked to approach the Chairman, Tom White, and put some proposals to him. The players wanted a bonus of £1 per point in League matches, a not unreasonable request in their eyes. The Board refused. A very unhappy team lost the next match to Partick Thistle on 1 September and on 5 October, Cringan was transferred to Third Lanark.

The European tours had not been neglected. The Club had paid a quick visit to France at the end of May 1920 where they played the 'Lions of Flanders' at Lille, and other matches in Paris, including one against Newcastle United. In the summer of 1922, Celtic set out for the Continent again, a tour ridden with rough play. Against SK Slavia – ironically, the team coached by the Club's former player Johnny Madden – they were beaten 3-2 and had McStay and Gilchrist sent off. This was followed by a 2-1 defeat

The Celtic party outside the Central Hotel before catching the train south to start the Continental tour of 1922.

The players on a tour bus round Cologne, 1922.

against Sparta Prague, then a draw with the Prussian Select team at Grunewald. Attendances for the three matches were 52,000, 51,000 and 26,000 respectively, with admission prices ranging from one shilling (5p) to £1.

Just when Rangers' League dominance began to stretch, Celtic gave some joy to the faithful by winning the League Title in 1925–26. The defence leaked a fairly high level of a goal per game, but 97 were scored in total and only five matches lost. Another Cup Final appearance ended disappointingly when they lost to St Mirren in front of 98,620, both goals being blamed on

As part of the Continental tour 1922, Celtic played a match against the British Army at Weidenspecher Park, Cologne, on 31 May, winning 5-0.

goalkeeper Peter Shevlin's mistakes. The following season, even more goals were scored – 109 in total, including an astonishing 48 by Jimmy McGrory. Unfortunately, the defence was less than solid, letting in an expensive 55, which left Celtic only third in the table. Another Cup success, though, brightened the fans' day, this time against East Fife from the Second Division.

1922–1923 SCOTTISH LEAGUE DIVISION I

	P	W	D	L	F	A	Points	Position
Rangers	38	23	9	6	67	29	55	1st
Celtic	38	19	8	11	52	39	46	3rd

Fixtures

	H	A		H	A	
Aberdeen	1-2	1-3	Hibs	0-0	0-1	
Airdrie	1-1	0-1	Kilmarnock	1-2	3-4	
Albion Rovers	1-1	3-2	Morton	3-1	1-0	
Alloa Ath	1-0	3-2	Motherwell	1-0	0-0	
Ayr United	1-4	1-0	Partick Thistle	4-3	2-0	
Clyde	0-0	1-0	Raith Rovers	3-0	3-0	
Dundee	2-1	1-0	Rangers	1-3	0-2	
Falkirk	1-1	0-0	St Mirren	1-0	0-1	
Hamilton	2-1	1-1	Third Lanark	3-0	0-1	
Hearts	2-1	3-0				

A low-scoring season for everyone, possibly due to the defenders using the off-side law to their advantage. This was Celtic's lowest ever 'goals for tally' in the First Division Championship. Four of the defeats came at home; three teams, Rangers, Kilmarnock and Aberdeen beat Celtic home and away; the biggest shock came in the 4-1 home defeat to Ayr United. Joe Cassidy was top scorer with 20 goals and a young man called James McGrory made his league debut on 20 January at Cathkin against Third Lanark. The sporting papers were not all that enamoured with the new boy, one proclaiming that he was ' a trifle slow in executing his manoeuvres'. Jimmy was soon to answer that critic.

The biggest disappointment of the season was the failure of Willie Crilly. 'Wee Willy' had scored 50 goals for Alloa in 1921–1922 helping them to gain promotion before he was snapped up by Celtic. Unfortunately his lack of stature – 5ft 3in tall, 9 stone in weight – made him an easy target for the hard men in the League and after only three League matches he was back with Alloa.

		1922–1923 SCOTTISH CUP			
	13/01/23	Lochgelly Utd	(A)	3-2	9,000
	27/01/23	Hurlford	(H)	4-0	5,000
	10/02/23	East Fife	(H)	2-1	8,000
QF	24/02/23	Raith Rovers	(H)	1-0	30,000
SF	10/03/23	Motherwell	(Ibrox)	2-0	71,500
Final	11/04/23	Hibs	(Hampden)	1-0	82,000

Team: Shaw; McNair, W McStay; J. McStay, Cringan, McFarlane; McAtee, Gallagher; Cassidy; McLean and Connolly.

A not altogether comfortable passage for Celtic into the semi-final especially against weak opposition in two of the ties. Man of the tournament for Celtic was undoubtedly Joe Cassidy, who scored three against Lochgelly, four against Hurlford and two against East Fife. Joe missed out against Raith Rovers (in goals that is) but got one of the two against Motherwell to take Celtic into their first final of this decade.

In front of 82,000 people, the Battle of the Greens was a rather dour contest, in which Alec McNair, now 40 years of age, showed all his skills to

An aerial view of Hampden during this period of the 1920s. The ground could hold 80,000+, and 82,000 were present for the 1923 Scottish Cup Final.

129

The Celtic team which beat Hibs 1-0 in the Scottish Cup final of 1923. Back row, left to right: A. McNair, W. McStay, C. Shaw, J. McStay, J. McFarlane. Front row: A. McAtee, J. Cassidy, A. McLean, W. Cringan, P. Gallagher, P. Connolly.

frustrate the Hibs attack. In the second half, Joe Cassidy scored the only goal. A rather harmless lob forward by John McFarlane caught out the Hibs goalkeeper Willie Harper and Cassidy nodded the ball home, his 11th goal of a distinguished campaign.

1922–1923 GLASGOW CUP

Queen's Park	(A)	3-4

1922–1923 CHARITY CUP

Clyde	(Firhill)	1 goal 2 corners. to 1 goal 1 corner
Rangers	(H)	0-1

1923–1924 SCOTTISH LEAGUE DIVISION 1

	P	W	D	L	F	A	Points	Position
Rangers	38	25	9	4	72	22	59	1st
Celtic	38	17	12	9	56	33	46	3rd

FIXTURES

	H	A		H	A
Aberdeen	4-0	2-0	Kilmarnock	2-1	1-1
Airdrie	2-2	0-2	Morton	3-0	0-1
Ayr United	3-0	2-4	Motherwell	2-1	1-0
Clyde	4-0	0-0	Partick Thistle	1-2	1-1
Clydebank	1-2	0-0	Queen's Park	1-0	2-0
Dundee	0-0	1-2	Raith Rovers	0-0	0-1
Falkirk	2-1	1-3	Rangers	2-2	0-0
Hamilton	1-0	5-2	St Mirren	0-1	1-0
Hearts	4-1	0-0	Third Lanark	3-1	3-1
Hibs	1-1	0-0			

The 1920s was not a good time for Celtic, particularly after the success of the first 30 years. The team — which looked good on paper and could win the occasional cup — was very inconsistent in the League. In this season, the simple truth was that they did not score enough and let in too many.

In October and November, inconsistency was rife. Of eight matches played, Celtic won three and drew five, including four at 0-0. In March, they drew with Partick Thistle, lost to Clydebank, beat Kilmarnock, and lost to Falkirk, Raith Rovers and Airdrie. Ironically, one of the Clydebank goals was scored by Jimmy McGrory, on loan with them for most of this season. Joe Cassidy was top scorer with 25 goals. Towards the end of the season, Jimmy McStay moved to centre-half, a position he was to hold down for the next ten years. The defeat by Partick Thistle at Parkhead on 1 September 1923 was the first ever in the League by the Jags.

1923–1924 SCOTTISH CUP				
26/01/24	Kilmarnock	(A)	0-2	17,500

January 1924 had been a good month for Celtic. Draws against Rangers (2-2) and Clyde (0-0) had been followed by wins over Hamilton (1-0), Third Lanark (3-1) and Aberdeen (4-0). One week later, though, the players failed to maintain that momentum and the team crashed out of the Scottish Cup in the opening round, for the first time since the Arthurlie disaster of 1897.

1923–1924 GLASGOW CUP		
Rangers	(A)	0-1

1923–1924 CHARITY CUP				
	Queen's Park	(A)	2-0	
Final	Rangers	Hampden	2-1	27,000 10/05/24

Rangers were firm favourites to take the trophy but good performances by Patsy Gallagher and Joe Cassidy made all the difference. At the back, though, Celtic were uncertain, and up front rather scrappy. Rangers had many chances but took only one 13 minutes before the interval, Alan Morton equalising Patsy Gallagher's headed opener. Shortly into the second half, Willie McStay grabbed the winner after a goalmouth scrabble and then, with brother Jimmy and John McFarlane, formed a half-back line which Rangers could not breach.

Team: Shaw; McNair and Hilley; J. McStay, W. McStay and McFarlane; Connolly, Gallagher; Cassidy; Thomson and McGrory.

1924–1925 SCOTTISH LEAGUE DIVISION I								
	P	W	D	L	F	A	Points	Position
Rangers	38	25	10	3	77	27	60	1st
Celtic	38	18	8	12	77	44	44	4th

FIXTURES

	H	A		H	A
Aberdeen	3-1	4-0	Morton	2-1	0-1
Airdrie	1-1	1-3	Motherwell	4-0	0-1
Ayr United	2-0	2-1	Partick Thistle	1-2	2-2
Cowdenbeath	3-1	0-3	Queen's Park	1-1	1-3
Dundee	4-0	0-0	Raith Rovers	2-0	2-2
Falkirk	6-1	2-1	Rangers	0-1	1-4
Hamilton	0-2	4-0	St Johnstone	2-1	0-0
Hearts	1-0	1-3	St Mirren	5-0	1-2
Hibs	1-1	3-2	Third Lanark	7-0	1-1
Kilmarnock	6-0	1-2			

The same number of goals scored as the Champions but look at the difference in goals against and games lost. Only three of the defeats were at home (51 scored, 13 against) but the away form was nightmarish, 9 defeats, 5 draws (26 for and 31 against).

Jimmy McGrory had been brought back from Clydebank at the end of the previous season and shared the number nine shirt with Willie Fleming. In spite of missing December and January with a knee injury, he scored 17 in the league. His deputy, Fleming, notched 10 in his absence. By the beginning of the following season, he was with Ayr United.

The Celtic team which won the Cup against Dundee in 1925. This photograph was taken before a charity match at the end of that season. The 'Linesman' on the extreme left is Jimmy Quinn.

1924–1925 SCOTTISH CUP

24/01/25		Third Lanark	(A)	5-1	42,000
07/02/25		Alloa	(H)	2-1	12,000
21/02/25		Solway Star (Annan)	(H)	2-0	7,000
07/03/25	QF	St Mirren	(A)	0-0	47,428
10/03/25	Replay	St Mirren	(H)	1-1	36,000
16/03/25	Replay	St Mirren	(Ibrox)	1-0	47,492
21/03/25	SF	Rangers	(Hampden)	5-0	101,714
11/04/25	F	Dundee	(Hampden)	2-1	75,317

Team: Shevlin; W. McStay and Hilley; Wilson, J. McStay and McFarlane; Connolly, Gallagher; McGrory; Thomson and McLean.

If the cup win of 1923 had been greatly helped by the goals from Joe Cassidy, then Jimmy McGrory did the same in 1925, with 11 in total. The semi-final at Hampden turned into a rout, the goals coming from McGrory (2), Adam McLean (2) and Alec Thomson, yet the attendance of 101,714, obviously expecting a closer match, was the first six-figure crowd at any match between Scottish clubs.

In the final itself, Dundee were in front at half-time after showing their strength and power. Unfortunately, they decided to sit on their lead and left only one man up front in the second half. Celtic pressed ferociously and won corner after corner but could not get the goal they needed until the 75th minute, when Patsy Gallagher took a hand in the proceedings. This goal has been described and embellished in so many ways over the years that we are not sure just what happened and, of course, there were no TV cameras there to record the moment. What can be said with certainty is, that Patsy went on some form of miraculous run before forcing the ball over the line with the ball jammed between his feet and perhaps even performing a partial somersault as he did so! No matter the precise details, it was a wonder goal which got Celtic back into the match and demoralised Dundee. Just before the end, Jimmy McGrory got the winner with a characteristic full-length diving header from the John McFarlane cross. It was Celtic's eleventh Cup success in total — a new record.

1924–1925 Glasgow Cup

	Third Lanark	(A)	4-2		
Final	Rangers	(Celtic Park)	1-4	76,000	4/10/25

1924–1925 CHARITY CUP

Partick Thistle	(H)	1-2

1925–1926 SCOTTISH LEAGUE DIVISION 1

	P	W	D	L	F	A	Points	Position
Celtic	38	25	8	5	97	40	58	1st

Fixtures

	H	A		H	A
Aberdeen	4-1	4-2	Kilmarnock	0-0	1-2
Airdrie	3-2	1-5	Morton	3-1	5-0
Clydebank	1-1	2-1	Motherwell	3-1	1-2
Cowdenbeath	6-1	1-1	Partick Thistle	3-0	0-0
Dundee	0-0	2-1	Queen's Park	4-1	4-1
Dundee United	6-2	0-1	Raith Rovers	1-0	2-1
Falkirk	3-1	1-1	Rangers	2-2	0-1
Hamilton	2-0	3-1	St Johnstone	4-1	3-0
Hearts	3-0	2-1	St Mirren	6-1	2-0
Hibs	5-0	4-4			

Celtic FC 1925–26. Back row, left to right: E Corrigan*, A. McLean, J. McGrory, J. McFarlane, V. McCrogan*, D. Blair*, W. Gordon*. Middle row: T. McInally, E. Gilfeather*, W. Fleming, P. Shevlin, D. McColgan*, A Thomson, M. Callaghan. Front row: W. Leitch*, P. Connolly, J. McStay, W. McStay, M. Hilley, P. Gallagher, E. McGarvey (Trainer).
The players marked with an asterisk played five, or fewer, games for the first team.

A fine championship win, Celtic's 17th. Ironically, the team was little different from the year before, apart from two vital areas. McGrory played a full season, scoring 36 league goals; and Tommy McInally, returned from Third Lanark, provided both the skill and a finishing touch, ending with 17 goals. Add to these Adam McLeans's 15 from outside-left, Alec Thomson's 15 at inside-right, plus Paddy Connolly's 5 on the right-wing and we have a fairly useful forward line. This was a vital Championship, as it stopped Rangers' momentum. The Light Blues, in fact, had a very poor season, finishing sixth on 44 points. Unfortunately, their demise was not to last. Note the name of Dundee United appearing in this Division for the first time.

1925–1926 SCOTTISH CUP					
23/01/26		Kilmarnock	(A)	5-0	24,174
06/02/26		Hamilton	(H)	4-0	28,000
20/02/26		Hearts	(A)	4-0	52,000
06/03/26	QF	Dumbarton	(H)	6-1	19,000
20/03/26	SF	Aberdeen	(Tynecastle)	2-1	24,000
10/04/26	Final	St Mirren	(Hampden)	0-2	98,000

Team: Shevlin; W. McStay, and Hilley; Wilson, J. McStay, and McFarlane; Connolly, Thomson; McGrory; McInally and Leitch.

A high-scoring passage to the final watched by very respectable crowds all the way. Celtic were firm favourites, the crowd willing them to do the 'double' for the fourth time in their history. St Mirren, though, were determined not to be overawed and kept plugging away, getting two goals in the first period, both of which could be attributed to a lack of height on the part of goalkeeper Peter Shevlin. Celtic tried hard, but it was not their day, the team formation having been broken up before the start due to an injury to Adam McLean. Without a Reserve Team and with only a small group of players, Celtic were forced to play Willie Leitch at outside-left, having only recently recalled him from a loan period with Ayr United. This was Willie's only Scottish Cup outing, although he also has 5 league appearances to his credit.

	1925–1926 GLASGOW CUP				
	Partick Thistle	(A)	1-1		
Replay	Partick Thistle	(H)	5-1		
	Rangers	(H)	2-2		
Replay	Rangers	(A)	1-1		
Replay	Rangers	(A)	2-0		
Final	Clyde	(H)	1-2	23,000	10/10/25

	1925–1926 CHARITY CUP				
	Partick Thistle	(A)	2-1		
	Third Lanark	(H)	2-0		
Final	Queen's Park	Ibrox	2-1	24,000	15/05/26

Queen's made quite a contest of this match, particularly during the first half, even though Tommy McInally had opened the scoring in 14 minutes. After half-time, they continued to give as good as they got and equalised after 65 minutes. Three minutes later, though, McGrory got another and from then on Celtic's strength and pace told and they held out to win 2-1.

Team: Shevlin; W. McStay and Callachan; Wilson, J. McStay, McFarlane; Connolly, Thomson; McGrory; McInally and McLean.

Celtic FC, League Champions 1925–26. Willie McStay (with ball) as captain. One of only two Championships in this decade.

Henry Callachan was signed from Parkhead Juniors in 1925 and made 11 league appearances over the next two seasons, the most important of which was the match against Morton at Celtic Park on the 14 April 1926 when Celtic clinched their second championship of the 1920s.

Tactics

In the early 1920s, players probably began to think more about the game, the laws and their implications. Soon, a few defenders began to take advantage of the 'off-side law' as it was then. This stated that a player was off-side if there were fewer than three opponents between him and his opponent's goal when the ball was last played by a team-mate. Three players in particular, Morley and Montgomery of Notts County plus Bill McCracken of Newcastle United, realised the full implication of this. They would advance as near the half-way line as possible, then move up quickly and with good timing, so that the forward pass caught players off-side. This tactic was difficult for forwards to counteract, was immensely unpopular with press and public, but did cause the goal-scoring rate to decrease.

A glance at Celtic's record during the 1920s shows that for a period, even for a team with such an attacking emphasis, their forwards found it very difficult to stay on-side.

CELTIC'S GOAL-SCORING RECORD DURING THE 1920s

Year	Matches	Goals	Position in League
1920–21	42	86	2nd
1921–22	42	83	1st
1922–23	38	52	3rd
1923–24	38	56	3rd
1924–25	38	77	4th
1925–26	38	97	1st
1926–27	38	101	3rd
1927–28	38	93	2nd
1928–29	38	67	2nd
1929–30	38	88	4th

In those two very poor years of 1922–1923 and 1923–1924 Rangers won the Championship with 67 and 72 goals. In the high-scoring year of 1926–1927, the defence lost a staggering 55 goals.

In 1925, the law was altered at the instigation of the SFA to read two opponents instead of three. This change made the use of the off-side trap extremely risky, so that goal-scoring rose once more. Once again, though, a tactical change in football was made in defence at the expense of attacking play. With the law change, the centre-half's role was altered. If he continued to push forward as in the 2-3-5 formation, he left big gaps in defence, so his role changed quickly to more of a third centre-back, his job now to police the opposing centre-forward. Full-backs now pushed wider and began to mark the wingers. Wing-halves who originally played closer to the touch lines when the centre-half was controlling the middle, now moved in there to cover and mark opposing inside-forward. Attacking moves, instead of coming through the centre-half were switched to the wings. Wing-halves and inside-forwards were told to get the ball out there and it was then the winger's job to beat his full-back and cross the ball to the centre-forward.

Unfortunately, Celtic did not alter their style appreciably while other teams did. Their close-passing game was loosely based on the 2-3-5 formation which was very successful in its time. A review of the team which won the Scottish Cup in 1926-1927 one year after the law was changed, may gave us some idea of their formation and style.

1.	John Thomson	188 appearances	64 shut-outs	5ft 8in	10st 8lbs
2.	Willie McStay	446 appearances	39 goals	5ft 9in	12st
3.	Hugh Hilley	195 appearances	0 goals	5ft 8in	11st
4.	Peter Wilson	395 appearances	15 goals	5ft 10in	11st 2lbs
5.	Jimmy McStay	472 appearances	8 goals	5ft 8in	11st
6.	John McFarlane	304 appearances	13 goals	5ft 7in	10st 10lbs
7.	Paddy Connolly	296 appearances	46 goals	5ft 8in	11st
8.	Alec Thomson	451 appearances	98 goals	5ft 9in	11st
9.	Jimmy McGrory	445 appearances	472 goals	5ft 8in	12st
10.	Tommy McInally	213 appearances	127 goals	5ft 8in	11st 4lbs
11.	Adam McLean	408 appearances	138 goals	5ft 6in	10st 10lbs

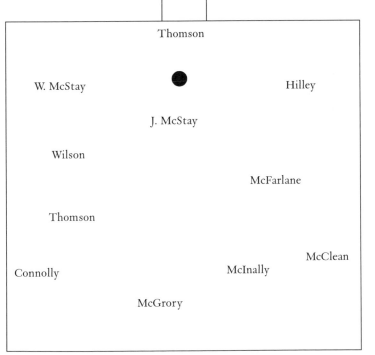

The lay-out of positions for the Celtic team which won the Scottish Cup in 1926–27. Note the forward position of Jimmy McStay in his centre-half role. The black circle denotes the position which the centre-halfs of most other teams were adopting, forming a strong back line with the two full-backs.

John Thomson was a very secure last line of defence. The team however still played a 2-3-5 formation. Hugh Hilley was a very defensive left-back with no goals in his career at Celtic Park. Willie McStay at right-back (but much more comfortable at left-back) was a prolific penalty-taker and free-kick taker, three-quarters of his total coming from penalties alone. From 1918-1933 the number five for Celtic was worn by Willie Cringan followed by Willie McStay then Jimmy McStay. All three could be described as defenders who attacked, responsible for urging the ball up-field from the back, passes either to one-half or inside-forward in the time-honoured Celtic passing game. Neither wing-half could be described as a prolific scorer. John McFarlane was not only master of the cross-field pass but loved the fast dribble; Peter Wilson was more a surveyor of the field before passing. I suspect, then, that Wilson played the deeper of the two.

Paddy Connolly, the greyhound (for obvious reasons), and Adam McLean were both out and out wingers but McLean, as can be seen from his scoring record, was as keen as McGrory to get on the end of Connolly's crosses. Alec Thomson was another fine passer but scored just under 100 goals in 451 games. Again he probably played slightly deeper leaving the enigmatic Tommy McInally to give McGrory close support. Various Celtic biographers are critical of McInally's attitude, even going so far as to call him a wastrel but a goal-scoring record of better than a goal every two games for an inside-forward is excellent. Even the great Patsy did not achieve that. As for McGrory, 472 goals in 445 games is simply phenomenal!

1926–1927 SCOTTISH LEAGUE DIVISION 1

	P	W	D	L	F	A	Points	Position
Rangers	38	23	10	5	85	41	56	1st
Celtic	38	21	7	10	101	55	49	3rd

FIXTURES

	H	A		H	A
Aberdeen	6-2	0-0	Kilmarnock	4-0	3-2
Airdrie	2-1	2-2	Morton	3-0	6-2
Clyde	7-0	2-2	Motherwell	3-2	1-0
Cowdenbeath	2-0	1-2	Partick Thistle	2-1	3-0
Dundee	0-0	2-1	Queen's Park	2-3	6-1
Dundee United	7-2	3-3	Rangers	0-1	1-2
Dunfermline	2-1	6-0	St Johnstone	4-0	0-1
Falkirk	3-1	1-4	St Mirren	6-2	1-3
Hamilton	2-2	3-3			
Hearts	1-0	0-3			
Hibs	2-3	2-3			

An even better goal-scoring performance than the previous year, when Celtic won the championship, but a very shaky defence. Not that Rangers

John Thomson, who moved into the first eleven in season 1926–27. In the ensuing four years he made 188 appearances with 64 shut-outs (34 per cent).

were very much better. This was the first full season after the change in the off-side law (see *Tactics*) so perhaps it would be fair to say the defences were having problems coping with the new law. McGrory alone hit 49 goals, five on three occasions – Aberdeen (H), Motherwell (A), and Clyde (H). At centre-half, the position most altered in its scope by the change in off-side law, the matches were split between Jimmy McStay and John Donoghue. A young man called John Thomson made his debut against Dundee at Dens Park on the 12 February 1927.

	1926–1927 Scottish Cup			
22/01/27		Queen of The South	(A)	0-0	8,000
26/01/27	Replay	Queen of The South	(H)	4-1	7,000
05/02/27		Brechin City	(A)	6-3	4,000
19/02/27		Dundee	(A)	4-2	37,471
05/03/27	QF	Boness	(A)	5-2	9,000
26/03/27	SF	Falkirk	(Ibrox)	1-0	73,000
16/04/27	Final	East Fife	(Hampden)	3-1	80,000

Celtic's defence leaked quite heavily through the early rounds but looked better against a strong Falkirk side in the semi-finals and were firm favourites in the Final against a team from the Second Division.

East Fife provided a shock start when they scored in only 7 minutes, with new goalkeeper John Thomson, in only his fourth Scottish Cup tie, looking rather static as the ball went in. Within a minute, however, the scores were level when Paddy Connolly's cross was diverted into the net by a Fifer's defender. Adam McLean got the second ten minutes before the interval after a fine piece of play by the whole forward line. The second half could not have started worse for the Second Division team as Paddy Connolly scored almost from the re-start and although East Fife never gave up trying, Celtic turned the screw, playing lovely football and creating lots of chances which the rather profligate forwards, especially Tommy McInally at his infuriating worst, refused to take. This was the first final to be broadcast on the new invention – 'the wireless'.

Team: Thomson; W. McStay, and Hilley; Wilson, J. McStay, and McFarlane; Connolly, Thomson; McInally; McMenemy and McLean. John McMenemy was the second of Jimmy McMenemy's family of footballing sons, who made his debut in the League match against Falkirk on the 6 April 1927 and 10 days later made a successful cup debut appearance in the Final.

Celtic FC, Scottish Cup and Glasgow Cup winners 1926–27. Back row, left to right: Wilson, McGrory, W. McStay, J. Thomson, McMenemy, McFarlane, McGarvie (Trainer). Front row: McInally, Connolly, A. Thomson, McLean, J. McStay, Hilley.

1926–1927 GLASGOW CUP

	Partick Thistle (H)		3-1		
Final	Rangers	(Hampden)	1-0	51,000	9/10/26

The match was won – and lost – on the initial toss of the coin to determine ends. Rangers won and forced Celtic to play against a very strong wind in the first half but Celtic, showing superb teamwork, defended well in that period then opened out their play in the second half with the wind now behind them and tortured a Rangers team which was not on song. The only goal of the match – a powerful shot from Jimmy McGrory – came early in the second half.

Team: Shevlin; W. McStay and Hilley; Wilson, Donoghue, McFarlane; Connolly, Thomson; McGrory; McInally and McLean.

1926–1927 Charity Cup

Rangers   (H)   1-4

———— ✿ ————

1927–1928 SCOTTISH LEAGUE DIVISION 1

	P	W	D	L	F	A	Points	Position
Rangers	38	26	8	4	109	36	60	1st
Celtic	38	23	9	6	93	39	55	2nd

FIXTURES

	H	A		H	A
Aberdeen	1-1	1-3	Hibs	3-0	2-2
Airdrie	3-2	1-3	Kilmarnock	6-1	2-2
Bo'ness	4-1	1-0	Motherwell	1-2	1-3
Clyde	3-0	1-0	Partick Thistle	0-0	3-3
Cowdenbeath	1-1	2-0	Queen's Park	3-0	3-1
Dundee	3-1	4-1	Raith Rovers	0 3	3-0
Dunfermline	9-0	1-1	Rangers	1-0	0-1
Falkirk	3-0	3-1	St Johnstone	3-0	5-3
Hamilton	4-0	0-0	St Mirren	6-0	2-0
Hearts	2-1	2-2			

Much the same as the previous season, although the defence was tighter. The Old Firm matches were shared; there were only two home defeats (Motherwell and Raith Rovers) but winning only 9 games from 19 away from home made the difference. In the match against Dumfermline, on 14th January 1928, Jimmy McGrory scored 8 goals in the 9-0 victory.

Tommy McInally was suspended for missing training and missed five matches in February and March. He was brought back for the vital run-in but defeats against Motherwell at Fir Park (27/4/28) Airdrie at Broomfield (10/4/28) and Raith Rovers at Parkhead (23/4/28) were expensive. The loss of Peter McGonagle in the Motherwell match through injury meant he was out for the remainder of the season, to the detriment of the defence.

1927–1928 Scottish Cup					
21/01/28		Bathgate	(H)	3-1	3,000
04/02/28		Keith	(A)	6-1	5,800
18/02/28		Alloa	(H)	2-0	7,000
03/03/28	QF	Motherwell	(A)	2-0	23,000
24/03/28	SF	Queen's Park	(Ibrox)	2-1	54,000
14/04/28	Final	Rangers	(Hampden)	0-4	118,115

A comfortable run to the final, although an unnamed player was rumoured not to have travelled back with the party from Keith, preferring instead to sample some Highland hospitality! McGrory with six and McInally with four were the main scorers, although a tight rearguard was the more impressive feature in the run to the Final, where Rangers were the opponents – the fifth Old Firm clash at this stage. The loss of McGonagle from the defence was crucial. Rangers had not won the Cup since 1903 and started the match in determined fashion, although Celtic with the wind behind them, set up many attacks.

Ten minutes after the interval, Rangers were awarded a penalty when Willie McStay punched a shot off the line. Captain Davie Meiklejohn took the kick and blasted it home, boosting Rangers confidence. They now began to play with freedom and scored further goals from Sandy Archibald (2) and Bob McPhail, winning comfortably in the end.

Team: Thomson; W. McStay, and Donoghue; Wilson, J. McStay and McFarlane; Connolly, Thomson; McGrory; McInally and McLean.

Photograph given out by a drink company in 1927–28. Back: J. Thomson. Second row: W. McStay, McGonagle. Third row: Wilson, J. McStay, McFarlane. Fourth row: A. Thomson, McInally. Front row: Connolly, McGrory, McLean.

The Celtic forward line which played in the 1928 Scottish Cup final. From left to right: Paddy Connolly, Alec Thomson, Jimmy McGrory, Tommy McInally, Adam McLean. Perhaps the jersey out of the shorts shows McInally's individuality, but autocratic managers like Willie Maley tended to disapprove of such players.

1927–1928 GLASGOW CUP					
	Queen's Park	(A)	4-1		
	Third Lanark	(H)	7-0		
Final	Rangers	(Hampden)	2-1	84,536	8/10/27

Team: Thomson; W. McStay and McGonagle; Wilson, J. McStay and McFarlane; Connolly, Thomson; McGrory; McInally and McLean.

Two goals in two minutes sealed the match for Celtic. In the 32nd minute of a typical tense Old Firm match, Tommy McInally lobbed the Rangers keeper to put Celtic one up. Two minutes later, they got a second, Paddy Connolly knocking in an Adam McLean cross. Rangers threw everything at Celtic in a determined second-half push but the defence coped well, the Light Blues' only goal in the 86th minute coming too late to prevent the Cup going back to Parkhead.

1927–1928 CHARITY CUP		
Rangers	(H)	0-2

Behind The Scenes

The relative lack of success at Celtic Park through these years was a worrying time for all involved and towards the latter quarter of the 1920s, the management and directors took action.

The waywardness of Tommy McInally could be stood no longer and he was transferred to Sunderland for £2,500 in May 1928; he was soon joined

Celtic Park in the late 1920s. Note the spacious terracings behind both goals.

at Wearside by Adam McLean in August of the same year. The Club made known that other players were available for transfer, even the great McGrory, for whom Arsenal had offered a blank cheque. Fortunately for Celtic, this superb servant decided to stay at Parkhead. But the directorate and manager had made life difficult for themselves by even suggesting such a move. Granted, money was required to replace the Grant Stand but the financial report in the *Glasgow Observer* of May 1928 suggested that Celtic 'were quite snug and comfy' with assets of £23,217. In seasons to come, the Club made profits of £2,027 (1927/1928) £5,221 (1928/1929) and £3,500 (1929/1930). This Stand was ready for the start of the 1929/1930 season.

Whenever a team fails to reach the expectations expected of it, an analysis of the various factors involved is necessary. Firstly the players. While the teams of 1904–1910 and 1913–1917 were exceptional, there can be little doubt that the personnel involved in the mid-20s were of a similar quality. Charlie Shaw was a sound goalkeeper and he was replaced by the highly talented John Thomson. They were behind a fairly strong defence (apart from one very bad season in 1926–1927) while forwards like McAtee, Gallagher, McGrory, McLean, Connolly, McInally and the Thomsons, were at least the equal of yesteryear.

The manager's role must be considered. Willie Maley had performed wonders for Celtic since his appointment in 1897. Initially, he dealt with players who were his contemporaries – players not only of talent but mercurial in nature like Doyle, Divers and McMahon. As these faded out at the turn of the century, he brought in a team of youngsters which eventually matured enough to win six-in-a-row between 1904 and 1910. To these players, he was a strong figure – 'The Boss' in name, as well as fact. He chose them, brought them into the team, very often in a position for which they thought they were not suitable, and, in the midst of terracing and newspaper criticism, calmly experimented until the blend was right. What he achieved was two excellent sides between 1904 and 1917. The fact that he been with the Club since its very inception and had been an officer of some sort or another ever since, gave him rather a special status, with a freedom of decision which few managers have ever enjoyed.

Celtic had indeed much to thank him for. He seemed to be, along with Chairman J.H. McLaughlin, the instigator of several 'novel' ventures at that time, like the improvement of the ground to international match standard, the accommodation for the Press, stands for convenience of spectators and Club visits to the Continent. The cycle track alongside the terracings hosted the World Championships in 1897 and The Celtic Sports, directly controlled and organised by Willie Maley, were a popular feature for many years.

By the end of the First World War, though, he had just passed his 50th birthday, many of those years having been spent working long hours under stress and strain. It would be surprising if he had been unaffected by this, plus the added sorrow of losing personal friends – and some players – in that horrendous conflict. He had always been stand-offish, even unapproachable. Now that a generation gap appeared between players and manager, this distancing became more apparent. Given the circumstances, it should come as no surprise that relationships within the Club soured occasionally. After the austerity of the war period, people were out to have fun in the early 20s, and Celtic players were no different. Maley always appeared more comfortable with the quiet self-effacing type – McGrory, McNair – rather than the flamboyant ones, Gallacher, and McInally. That he remained in the job until the early 40s is a tribute to his staying power but one must wonder if a younger man might have stopped the decided decline in these years? The question must also be asked, what was the Board doing about it all through these two decades?

After the death of Michael Dunbar in 1921, the Board consisted of Thomas White, Chairman since 1914, Thomas Colgan, John Shaughnessey, John McKillop and James Kelly. The relationship between these men and the manager could not have been an easy one. Willie Maley had been at Celtic Park longer than any of them, including James Kelly and I suspect some of them would have found him cantankerous and difficult. The 20s and 30s was also a period when the Directorate received criticism from several quarters – press, supporters and former players – and it may have suited them to have Maley as the figurehead to take the flak.

Sometimes, comments made to justify their actions seemed almost laughable, as when James Kelly, asked when a Reserve Team should be introduced, said that youngsters could improve their game more by watching the First Team rather than playing! Whatever the reason, the 20s had proved to be a miserable time for Celtic. The rest of the football world seemed to be rethinking their styles and tactics after the off-side law change of 1925, whereas Celtic seemed content to continue with their once-successful 2-3-5 formation. The decade belonged to Rangers, and for all their success, they were not averse to new thinking.

1928–1929 SCOTTISH LEAGUE DIVISION I

	P	W	D	L	F	A	Points	Position
Rangers	38	30	7	1	107	32	67	1st
Celtic	38	22	7	9	67	44	51	2nd

FIXTURES

	H	A		H	A
Aberdeen	2-2	2-2	Kilmarnock	3-0	3-2
Airdrie	4-1	1-0	Motherwell	2-0	3-3
Ayr United	3-0	2-0	Partick Thistle	1-0	0-3
Clyde	4-0	1-0	Queen's Park	1-2	4-4
Cowdenbeath	1-0	1-0	Raith Rovers	3-1	4-1
Dundee	2-1	1-0	Rangers	1-2	0-3
Falkirk	3-0	0-3	St Johnston	0-0	1-1
Hamilton	3-0	1-1	St Mirren	0-3	1-0
Hearts	1-0	1-2	Third Lanark	3-1	2-0
Hibs	1-4	1-2			

Celtic just could not live with the Rangers juggernaut which scored 107 goals on the back of their 'double' win the year before and finished 16 points ahead. The defence was almost unchanged all season – Thomson; W. McStay, McGonagle; Wilson, J. McStay, McFarlane – but the forward line was chopped and changed, McGrory making only 21 League appearances. Equally bad blows were the loss of McInally and McLean to Sunderland, the former for 'disappointing reasons'. The Celtic Stand caught fire on 28 March 1929, so Celtic finished the season with five 'home' matches played at various venues. Third Lanark at Shawfield (30/03/29), Partick Thistle at Firhill (1/04/29); Hibs at Easter Road (13/04/29); Queen's Park at Hampden (17/04/29); Falkirk at Shawfield (20/04/29).

1928–1929 SCOTTISH CUP

19/01/29		Arthurlie	(H)	5-1	8,000
02/02/29		East Stirlingshire	(H)	3-0	7,500
16/02/29		Arbroath	(H)	4-1	7,000
06/03/29	QF	Motherwell	(H)	0-0	47,000
13/03/29	Replay	Motherwell	(A)	2-1	32,000
23/03/29	SF	Kilmarnock	(Ibrox)	0-1	40,000

After poor crowds in the early rounds, the two matches in the quarter-final must have warmed the treasurer's heart. Kilmarnock had twice lost to

Celtic in the League, so the Parkhead faithful were full of confidence, but the team did not perform well on the day and went down 1-0. Kilmarnock deserved their win and went on to beat Rangers in the Final.

	1928–1929 GLASGOW CUP				
	Rangers	(A)	2-1		
	Third Lanark	(A)	2-2		
Replay	Third Lanark	(H)	5-1		
Final	Queen's Park	(Hampden)	2-0	40,000	6/10/29

Queen's Park had most of the play in the first half and enough scoring opportunities to be two or three up by half-time, but some bad luck and superb goalkeeping by John Thomson kept them out.

Seven minutes into the second half, Celtic punished them. From a pass by Paddy Connolly, Jimmy McGrory rammed the ball home; 13 minutes later, another Connolly cross, this time a McGrory header and it was all over.

Team: Thomson; W. McStay, McGonagle; Wilson, Donoghue, McFarlane; Connolly, Thomson; McGrory; Gray and McCallum.

	1928–1929 CHARITY CUP				
	Queen's Park	(A)	6-5		
	Clyde	(Hampden)	3-1		
Final	Rangers	(Ibrox)	2-4	25,288	11/05/29

1929–1930 SCOTTISH LEAGUE DIVISION I								
	P	W	D	L	F	A	Points	Position
Rangers	38	28	4	6	94	32	60	1st
Celtic	38	22	5	11	88	46	49	4th

FIXTURES						
	H	A		H	A	
Aberdeen	3-4	1-3	Hibs	4-0	2-0	
Airdrie	1-2	1-0	Kilmarnock	4-0	1-1	
Ayr United	4-0	3-1	Morton	0-1	2-1	
Clyde	0-2	3-2	Motherwell	0-4	1-2	
Cowdenbeath	2-1	2-1	Partick Thistle	2-0	2-3	
Dundee	1-1	2-2	Queen's Park	2-1	1-2	
Dundee United	7-0	2-2	Rangers	1-2	0-1	
Falkirk	7-0	1-0	St Johnstone	6-2	6-1	
Hamilton	3-0	3-2	St Mirren	3-0	0-0	
Hearts	2-1	3-1				

A very inconsistent season in the league, infuriating their support by their poor away form. Johnny Thomson missed nine matches, after breaking his collar-bone, lower jaw, a rib and loosing two teeth against Aberdeen on 5 February. Six different right-backs were tried (Geatons, McCallum, Hughes, Barrie, Wilson, Cook); as were four outside-lefts (Kavanagh, Napier,

Connolly, Hughes). The one certainty was McGrory's goal touch. Although missing ten matches, he scored 33 goals, including five hat-tricks. Bogey teams were Aberdeen, Motherwell and Rangers, with Celtic losing twice to each. Of the Old Firm league matches played during the 1920s, Celtic won two, Rangers 13 and five were drawn.

1929–1930 Scottish Cup				
18/01/29	Inverness Caledonian	(A)	6-0	6,500
01/02/29	Arbroath	(H)	5-0	6,500
15/02/29	St Mirren	(H)	1-3	32,000

A romp for Celtic at Inverness, the goals coming from McGrory with a hat-trick, Charlie Napier, Paddy Connolly and a Peter Wilson penalty. In the second round an equally impressive score against Arbroath and this time McGrory got two, the two Thomsons, Bert and Alec, one-a-piece, and Peter Scarff getting his name on the score sheet. But in the third round against St Mirren, also at home in front of a good crowd of 32,000, Celtic after holding them 1-1 at half time, lost two goals late in the second half and went out at a disappointing stage.

1929–1930 Glagow Cup					
	Clyde	(A)	1-1		
Replay	Clyde	(H)	6-0		
	Queen's Park	(H)	3-1		
Final	Rangers	(Hampden)	0-0		12/10/29
Replay	Rangers	(Hampden)	0-4	41,500	16/10/29

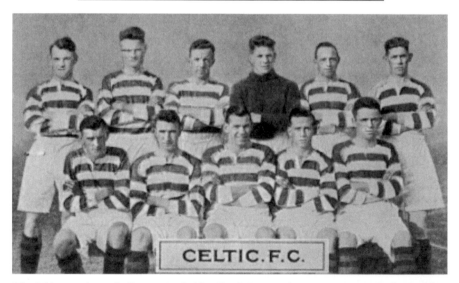

The Celtic team beaten by Rangers in the New Year's Day match, season 1929–30. Back row, left to right: Geatons, Robertson, J. McStay, J. Thomson, McGonagle, Wilson. Front row: A. Thomson, Connolly, McGrory, Kavanagh, Scarff.

Within two years Celtic would lose John Thomson because of a terrible accident and Peter Scarff to TB.

1929–1930 CHARITY CUP			
	Queen's Park	(A)	4-1
	Clyde (H)	1-0	
Final	Rangers	2-2	35,667 10/05/30
			Rangers won by toss of coin

A review of this decade shows an entirely different story from earlier years. A Struth-led Rangers emergence was a very successful one and apart from the Scottish Cup with which they always had a problem, trophy after trophy went to Ibrox.

THE OLD FIRM s RECORD IN COMPETITIONS 1920–1930

	LEAGUE	CUP	GLASGOW CUP	CHARITY CUP
1920–21	Rangers		Celtic	Celtic
1921–22	Celtic		Rangers	Rangers
1922–23	Rangers	Celtic	Rangers	Rangers
1923–24	Rangers		Rangers	Celtic
1924–25	Rangers	Celtic	Rangers	Rangers
1925–26	Celtic			Celtic
1926–27	Rangers	Celtic	Celtic	
1927–28	Rangers	Rangers	Celtic	Rangers
1928–29	Rangers		Celtic	Rangers
1929–30	Rangers	Rangers	Rangers	Rangers
	Celtic 2	Celtic 3	Celtic 4	Celtic 3
	Rangers 8	Rangers 2	Rangers 5	Rangers 6

TOTAL: CELTIC 12 RANGERS 21

CHAPTER SEVEN (1930–1939)
Second Best

ALTHOUGH THE LEAGUE CHAMPIONSHIP had not been won since 1925–1926, the Celtic management, players and support entered the decade of the 30s full of optimism. The Directors had decided to re-instate the reserve team in the Alliance League and it was felt sure that this would bring some new talent through to the first team. For most of the season, that team picked itself. The defence of Thomson, Cook and McGonagle; Wilson, McStay and Geatons was tried and tested, although still playing without the 'stopper centre-half' deployed by most clubs. Still, the system was reasonably effective, particularly in Cup matches. On both flanks were newcomers, eye-catching and efficient. Bert Thomson, full of pace and skill on the right-wing; Charlie Napier on the left, full of dribbles and tricks. Between them, Alec Thomson, Jimmy McGrory and Peter Scarff.

An early season victory in the Glasgow Cup against Rangers was followed after Christmas by a good run in the Cup, sixteen for – four against, which took them to the Final where Motherwell would be their opponents. Celtic were particularly keen to win this match, as a long-awaited tour of North America was planned for the summer. It is fairly easy to be paranoid about the treatment Celtic receive in the media but a review of the papers just before this match would concur with a conspiracy theory. Perhaps a so-called 'provincial' team would receive a more favourable Press than one going into its twenty-first Scottish Cup Final, but there was no doubt that the sports writers were keen for a Motherwell victory.

Not that Motherwell needed the help. They were possibly the most attractive team of the period, the left-wing duo of George Stevenson and Bob Ferrier a particularly potent force plus there was the added attraction for Celtic fans of seeing John McMenemy, son of the famous Jimmy, at inside-right. In fact, with eight minutes to go in the Final, they were still two up. The homing pigeons were being sent back to Motherwell with the good news, while in the Directors' Box at Hampden, the SFA Secretary no doubt had the claret and amber ribbons ready to be attached to the Cup!

However, fine work by Charlie Napier from a free-kick and quick thinking by Jimmy McGrory pulled one back. Then there occurred one of the most unfortunate incidents ever in Scottish Cup history. In the very last minute,

Charlie Napier joined Celtic in 1928 and soon showed his repertoire of skills. He played 200 times for the club, scoring 92 goals before leaving for Derby County.

Bert Thomson, on the right-wing, wriggled past his opponent and sent a swirling ball into the middle. 'Go for it, Alan!', somebody is reputed to have shouted. Unfortunately the wrong Alan did. Instead of goalkeeper Alan McClory gathering the ball, centre-half Alan Craig dived at it but did not make full contact and the ball skidded off his head into the net.

In view of what was to come later in the season, this could hardly be classed as a tragedy and yet it was a disaster for Alan Craig. In a long career, he never got the chance to sample Cup glory again; for the rest of his life, the incident rested like a millstone around his neck and caused him much heartache.

So, 2-2 it was and a replay the following Wednesday, in front of another six-figure crowd. The old maxim that you only got one chance in the Cup against Celtic proved true in this case, Celtic winning comfortably by 4-2.

Goalkeeper and left-back: the superb Johnny Thomson with Willie 'Peter' McGonagle. The latter held down the Celtic left-back spot for almost ten years, making 325 appearances, with eight goals.

This made for a very happy party to gather at Glasgow to board the TSS Caledonia on the 13 May. The group included four Directors – Messrs Colgan, Kelly, McKillop and White – manager Willie Maley and 17 players, J. Thomson, W. Cook, W. McGonagle, J. Morrison, P. Wilson, J. McStay, C. Geatons, R. Whitelaw, D. Currie, W. Hughes, R. Thomson, A. Thomson, J. McGrory, P. Scarff, C. Napier, J. McGhee and H. Smith.

They arrived in New York on 22 May and played their first match the following day. It proved to be a pleasant but exhausting tour. Thirteen matches were played in high humidity, the players having to contend with hard narrow pitches, embryonic refereeing and tough, enthusiastic opponents. The team also had to cope with constant entertaining, exiles travelling for miles around to see the Scottish Cup then waiting to talk to the players.

USA Tour Dates			
May	23	Pennsylvania All-Stars	6-1
	24	New York Giants	3-2
	30	New York Yankees	3-4
	31	Fall River	0-1
June	6	Pawtucket Rangers	1-3
	7	Brooklyn	5-0
	13	Carsteel	7-0
	14	Hakoah	1-1
	21	Bricklayers	6-3
	25	Michigan All-Stars	5-0
	27	Ulster United	3-1
	28	New York Yankees	4-1
	29	Baltimore	4-1

Of the 13 games played, nine were won, three lost and one drawn, 48 goals for 18 against. It had certainly been an exhausting trip but an unforgettable experience for the players, who like players since then who also made this trip, would have realised just what a pull the Club has on supporters all over the world.

A happy group of Celtic players on the American tour of 1931. This photograph was taken in Detroit, with Jimmy McGrory holding the Scottish Cup.

1930–1931 Scottish League Division 1								
	P	W	D	L	F	A	Pts	Position
Rangers	38	27	6	5	96	29	60	1st
Celtic	38	24	10	4	101	34	58	2nd

FIXTURES

	H	A		H	A
Aberdeen	1-0	1-1	Hibs	6-0	0-0
Airdrie	3-1	2-1	Kilmarnock	3-1	3-0
Ayr United	4-1	6-2	Leith Ath	4-0	3-0
Clyde	0-1	2-0	Morton	4-1	1-0
Cowdenbeath	6-0	1-1	Motherwell	4-1	3-3
Dundee	2-2	0-0	Partick Thistle	5-1	0-1
East Fife	9-1	6-2	Queen's Park	1-1	3-3
Falkirk	3-0	2-3	Rangers	2-0	0-1
Hamilton	2-1	0-0	St Mirren	3-1	3-1
Hearts	2-1	1-1			

A much better season for Celtic, with only two points in it at the end. Three draws in the last seven matches were crucial in the final analysis. The team was slowly changing at this time. Willie Cook and Peter McGonagle were the regular full-backs; Chic Geatons had come in at left-half; the two Thomsons, Bert and Alec formed the right-wing and Charlie Napier at inside – or outside – left. McGrory, as usual, was prolific, amassing 36 in total, even though he missed nine matches through injury. Johnny Thomson missed only two matches all season, his replacement – 24-year-old David Robertson – only having these two matches for Celtic in his career at Parkhead. Thomson was playing in Internationals, firstly against Wales and then against Ireland. This was Leith Athletic's first appearance in the First Division since 1894–1895.

A relaxed group of players training at Parkhead. From left to right: Willie Cook, Jimmy McStay, Chic Geatons, Jimmy McGrory, John Thomson. The latter two are wearing spikes. Notice the very heavy sweaters with round necks, still a feature of the training kit in the early 60s.

1930–1931 SCOTTISH CUP

17/01/31	East Fife	(A)	2-1	9,000
04/02/31	Dundee Utd	(A)	3-2	13,000
14/02/31	Morton	(A)	4-1	20,000
28/02/31 QF	Aberdeen	(H)	4-0	64,499
14/03/31 SF	Kilmarnock	(Hampden)	3-0	53,973
11/04/31 Final	Motherwell	(Hampden)	2-2	104,863
15/04/31 Replay	Motherwell	(Hampden)	4-2	98,509

A good run for the Final, McGrory scoring eight goals in the whole campaign, well supported by Bert Thomson, who got a hat-trick against Aberdeen, Charlie Napier on four and Peter Scarff with three.

This Motherwell team was one of the most attractive footballing sides of the period and were expected to give Celtic a run for their money. That proved to be something of an under-statement (for fuller description see page 150).

Team: J. Thomson; Cook, McGonagle; Wilson, J. McStay and Geatons; R. Thomson, A. Thomson, McGrory; Scarff and Napier.

The winning team in the 1931 Scottish Cup final, with Manager Maley (left) and Trainer McGarvie (right). Back row, left to right: Geatons, Cook, J. Thomson, McGonagle, Wilson. Front row: Napier, Scarff, McGrory, McStay, R. Thomson, A. Thomson.

Only John Thomson, Jimmy McStay, Peter Wilson and Alec Thomson survived from the team which won the Scottish Cup four years before.

1930–1931 GLAGOW CUP

	Clyde	(A)	3-1		
Final	Rangers	(Hampden)	2-1	71,800	11/10/30

Before this match, there was a tribute to those who died in the R101 Airship Disaster and, according to many reports, that was the most memorable thing about it. Rangers had the better of the out-field play but the finishing of their forwards was deplorably weak; Celtic, on the other hand, relied on doggedness and pluck, although a touch of good fortune was also theirs.

Charlie Napier opened the scoring for Celtic in five minutes. Unfortunately, a few minutes later, he was knocked unconscious following a collision with Rangers' right-back Dougie Gray and from then on, always looked slightly dazed. Seven minutes into the second-half, Jimmy McGrory got the second, running onto a long pass from Alec Thomson and, although under pressure from the full-backs closing in and the keeper coming out, he found the net. Rangers pulled one back through centre-forward Jimmy Smith 18 minutes into the second-half. They must also have felt that their chances increased when Bert Thomson was ordered off after a clash with left-back Buchanan but, in a finale too frequently marred by fouls, Celtic held out to take the trophy.

Team: Thomson; Cook and McGonagle; Geatons, J. McStay and Whitelaw; R. Thomson, A. Thomson, McGrory, Scarf and Napier.

1930–1931 CHARITY CUP		
Rangers	(Hampden)	2 goals 1 corner to
		2 goals 3 corners

Disaster

The new season opened well, the team playing attractive football, winning five and drawing two of their first seven matches. During the summer, when Celtic were training in North America, Rangers on 29 June had signed a very promising and prolific centre-forward from Yoker Athletic, Sam English. He quickly made the first team and showed up well, recovering from a slight injury to take the field for his first Rangers-Celtic match at Ibrox on 5 September 1931.

The crowd was large on a fine, sultry afternoon – 75,000 – but the play was nervous, with many errors creeping in. Five minutes after the interval, the game still goalless, Rangers' right-winger Fleming pushed the ball in front of Sam English and he raced towards the goal. Just as he prepared to shoot, Johnny Thomson came out of the Celtic goal and dived to block the shot. English rose limping; Thomson lay where he fell. Trainer, manager and doctor raced onto the field; a stretcher was called for. The incident occurred at the Rangers end and their support, like fans everywhere, were not unhappy to see an opponent down and a section even cheered. Rangers captain Davie Meiklejohn was quick to go behind the goal and gesture for silence; it was an effective appeal and Thomson was stretchered off in peace and quiet; Chic Geatons went into goal for Celtic but the heart had gone out of the play and it petered out into a goalless draw. Some six hours later, Johnny Thomson died from his injuries in the Victoria Infirmary. He was 32 years old.

The fatal save. As Sam English of Rangers, playing in his first-ever Old Firm match, pushes the ball past Johnny Thomson. The goalkeeper collides with his knee, and is fatally injured. There were stories afterwards – not helped by an injudicious comment by Willie Maley – that it was not an accident. This picture would suggest otherwise. At the moment of collision, English's eyes are firmly fixed on the ball ahead.

I am obviously too young to have seen John Thomson in the flesh and newsreel pictures of those days are very amateurish to our more sophisticated tastes. One must also be wary of over-emphasising the talent of a player who died so young and in such distressing circumstances. However, in his five-year career with Celtic and Scotland, John Thomson's skills were constantly praised and admired by a whole range of football enthusiasts. He was blessed with great balance, good positional sense and exceptional agility plus that most essential attribute for a keeper in that era of the charge – bravery. He truly must have been exceptional.

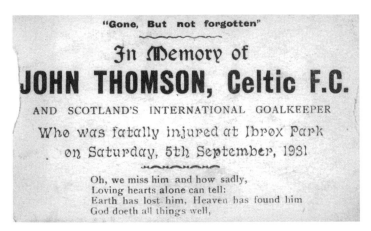

From a newspaper of the time.

Memorial to late J. Thomson at Celtic Park

Everyone connected with Celtic Football Club were deeply shocked by John Thomson's death but with the next match against Queen's Park only seven days after the tragedy, a successor to Thomson was needed quickly. John Falconer was tried out in four consecutive league matches and lost eight goals; Joe Coen played in three games and lost five goals.

Then Willie Maley remembered how thwarted Celtic had been in Massachusetts during the summer tour by Joe Kennaway of the Fall River Club and invited him over. The keeper made his debut on 31 October against Motherwell and soon proved his worth. It proved more difficult replacing outside-left Adam McLean who had departed for Sunderland in 1928. During this season five players – Peter Kavanagh, Willie Hughes, Jerome Solis, Joe McGhee and Jimmy Cameron – were all tried but none stamped their authority. Even Charlie Napier had a spell there, although his unorthodox play made him more effective at inside-forward. By Christmas, Celtic were still in contention for the League but a number of defeats in the second half

After the death of John Thomson, Celtic tried out two other goalkeepers without much success, before bringing John 'Joe' Kennaway over from Fall River in Massachussets. Kennaway made his debut against Motherwell on 31 October 1931 and was an instant hit with the fans.

of the season left them third. The winners were Motherwell, thus stopping Rangers from equalling Celtic's record of six-in-a-row.

1931–1932 SCOTTISH LEAGUE DIVISION I

	P	W	D	L	F	A	Pts	Position
Motherwell	38	30	6	2	119	31	66	1st
Celtic	38	20	8	10	94	50	48	3rd

FIXTURES

	H	A		H	A
Aberdeen	2-0	1-1	Kilmarnock	4-1	3-2
Airdrie	6-1	1-1	Leith Ath	6-0	3-0
Ayr United	4-2	3-2	Morton	6-3	3-3
Clyde	1-1	1-2	Motherwell	2-4	2-2
Cowdenbeath	7-0	2-1	Partick Thistle	1-2	2-0
Dundee	0-2	0-2	Queen's Park	2-2	3-0
Dundee Utd	3-2	0-1	Rangers	1-2	0-0
Falkirk	4-1	0-2	St Mirren	1-0	2-1
Hamilton	6-1	0-1	Third Lanark	5-0	3-3
Hearts	3-0	1-2			

The most tragic season in Celtic's history, with the loss of John Thomson at Ibrox on 5 September 1931. Frankly, after such an event, it would have been surprising if any of the players could concentrate their minds on the task at hand. Two other goalkeepers, John Falconer and Joe Coen were given a chance before Joe Kennaway was brought over from Fall River. Before the year was out, the Club was struck by another blow. Peter Scarff played what proved to be his last match against Leith Athletic on 19 December. Complaining of illness, he had tests which confirmed the presence of TB; was forced to retire and died on 9 December 1933.

All in all, a desperate time for Celtic with football far from the minds of many at the Club. Tribute must be paid, though, to the Champions, a very fine side who were five points clear at the finish and whose 119 goals was the second best ever in the First Division Championship.

		1931–1932 SCOTTISH CUP			
	16/01/32	Falkirk	(H)	3-2	14,000
	30/01/32	St Johnstone	(A)	4-2	19,158
QF	13/02/32	Motherwell	(A)	0-2	36,000

Motherwell got some measure of revenge for their Cup Final defeat of the season before. They were much the better team against a Celtic side whose manager seemed unsure of his best forward-line permutation. Even the presence of Jimmy McGrory playing his first match after injury since the Ne'erday defeat could not inspire the team. Unfortunately for Motherwell, they could not summon up a similar display against Rangers in the quarter-final, going down 2-0 and thus losing the chance of the 'Double'.

One of the early photographs showing Joe Kennaway in the goalkeeping berth. Taken somewhere in 1932.

1931–1932 GLASGOW CUP

	Rangers	(H)	1-1
Replay	Rangers	(A)	2-2
Replay	Rangers	(A)	0-1

1931–1932 CHARITY CUP

Partick Thistle	(A)	2-1
Third Lanark	(H)	1-2

1932–1933 SCOTTISH LEAGUE DIVISION I

	P	W	D	L	F	A	Pts	Position
Rangers	38	26	10	2	113	43	62	1st
Celtic	38	20	8	10	75	44	48	4th

FIXTURES

	H	A		H	A
Aberdeen	3-0	0-1	Kilmarnock	0-0	2-2
Airdrie	2-1	3-0	Morton	7-1	1-0
Ayr United	4-1	1-0	Motherwell	4-1	2-4
Clyde	2-1	2-0	Partick Thistle	1-2	0-3
Cowdenbeath	3-0	5-1	Queen's Park	2-0	1-4
Dundee	3-2	0-3	Rangers	1-1	0-0
East Stirling	3-0	3-1	St Johnstone	5-0	0-1
Falkirk	0-1	1-1	St Mirren	0-0	1-3
Hamilton	0-3	1-1	Third Lanark	4-2	4-0
Hearts	3-2	1-1			

A team suitable for winning cups but not for the relentless pursuit of the League Title. Celtic were particularly poor away from home, winning only seven out of nineteen matches. Willie Cook was sold in mid-season to Everton, to be replaced by 18 year old Bobby Hogg. Hugh O'Donnell came in at outside-left for Charlie Napier, his brother Frank McGrory's occasional deputy at centre-forward. Jimmy, as usual, was on song scoring 22 in 25 league matches. Malcolm McDonald made his league debut against Third Lanark on 16 August at Cathkin.

1932–1933 SCOTTISH CUP

21/01/33		Dunfermline	(A)	7-1	8,394
04/02/33		Falkirk	(H)	2-0	26,733
18/02/33		Partick Thistle	(H)	2-1	55,595
04/03/33	QF	Albion Rovers	(A)	1-1	14,000
08/03/33	Replay	Albion Rovers	(H)	3-1	23,810
18/03/33	SF	Hearts	(Hampden)	0-0	87,000
02/04/33	Replay	Hearts	(Hampden)	2-1	63,756
15/04/33	Final	Motherwell	(Hampden)	1-0	102,339

Team: Kennaway; Hogg, McGonagle; Wilson, J. McStay, Geatons; R. Thomson, A. Thomson; McGrory; Napier and H. O'Donnell

Jimmy McGrory shows hos power against Partick Thistle in a Scottish Cup tie on 18 February 1933.

Celtic FC 1933–34. Back row, left to right: W. Maley (manager), A. Thomson, R. Hogg, J. Kennaway, C. Napier, J. McGrory, W. McGonagle. Front row: J. Crum, C. Geatons, J. McStay, P. Wilson, M. O'Donnell.

Bobby Hogg was only 18 years old when he made his debut against Rangers on 2 January 1933.

After the easy demolition of Dunfermline, in which McGrory and Hugh O'Donnell both got hat-tricks, Celtic made heavy weather of reaching the final. Joe Kennaway missed the Partick Thistle match and both games of the quarter-final through injury, his replacement being John Wallace. So, for the third time in three seasons and the second time in a Final, Celtic were paired with a Motherwell side keen to get their hands on this trophy. The Steelmen had been impressive on their way to this stage, scoring 27 goals (with only one reply) in total and felt that this was their year. Considering Celtic's uncertain league form, many of their supporters might have agreed with that prediction.

Motherwell fielded the same forward-line as two years before, Celtic the same half-back line, but, in truth, the match was a disappointing one, having none of the excitement or incidents of the previous occasion. Almost inevitably, McGrory scored the only goal in the second half and the delighted Celtic fans cheered their team all the way back to Celtic Park. Success was not a regular feature of Celtic's life in the 1930s. Hugh O'Donnell and Bobby Hogg thus gained Scottish Cup medals in their first season in senior football. Willie Cook, whose place Hogg had taken, won an English cup medal the same year when Everton beat Manchester City 3-0 at Wembley, before a smaller attendance of 92,950. Thanks to that Cup win, Celtic made a profit of £5,664 for the season.

1932–1933 GLASGOW CUP

	Clyde	(A)	1-1
Replay	Clyde	(H)	3-1
	Partick Thistle	(A)	0-1

1932–1933 CHARITY CUP

Clyde	(H)	3-1
Queen's Park	(A)	2-3

The following season 1933–1934, proved something of a non-event. Bert Thomson left for Blackpool at the beginning of the season and Jimmy McStay for Hamilton at the end, while Alec Thomson and Peter Wilson were put on the transfer list. Injuries to McGrory and Napier allowed new names from the reserves to appear, with Hughes, Buchan, Crum, Paterson, McDonald, Divers and the O'Donnell brothers all getting their chance.

1933–1934 SCOTTISH LEAGUE DIVISION 1

	P	W	D	L	F	A	Pts	Position
Rangers	38	30	6	2	118	41	66	1st
Celtic	38	18	11	9	78	53	47	3rd

FIXTURES

	H	A		H	A
Aberdeen	2-2	0-3	Kilmarnock	4-1	3-1
Airdrie	4-2	4-2	Motherwell	3-0	1-1
Ayr United	0-3	1-3	Partick Thistle	2-0	3-0
Clyde	2-1	1-1	Queen of South	0-1	2-3
Cowdenbeath	7-0	1-0	Queen's Park	3-1	3-2
Dundee	3-2	2-3	Rangers	2-2	2-2
Falkirk	2-2	0-2	St Johnstone	0-0	1-1
Hamilton	5-1	1-1	St Mirren	3-0	2-1
Hearts	0-0	1-2	Third Lanark	3-1	1-1
Hibs	2-1	2-1			

Nineteen points adrift at the end, Celtic's defence once more let them down. This was Jimmy McStay's last season and since Celtic, unlike other teams in these years, still expected their centre-half to be a ball-player rather than a stopper, then I suspect Jimmy's legs were beginning to feel the pace. Peter Wilson, at 28, was also in his last season with the club, while Johnny Crum became more of a regular fixture. Up front, Alex Thomson was in his last season, Willie Buchan moved more into the picture and McGrory in only 23 matches, scored 16 goals. The away record was grim; only five games won from nineteen.

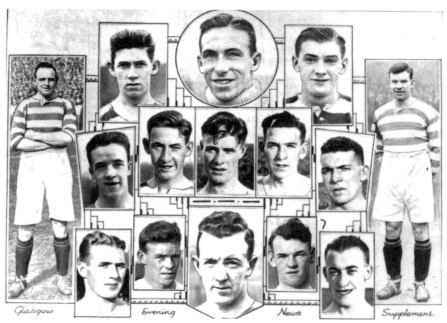

A supplement from the Evening News *on the night of the Charity Cup final 1934. Left hand side: W. McGonagle. Right hand side: J. McGrory. Back row, from left to right: P. Wilson, J. Kennaway, A. Thomson. Middle row: J. Crum, W. Buchan, W. Dunn, H. O'Donnell, F. O'Donnell. Front row: R. Hogg, W. Hughes, J. McStay, C. Geatons, C. Napier.*

Centre-forward Willie Dunn, one of nine footballing brothers, opened his Celtic career against the Chile/Peru touring team at Parkhead on 4 October 1933, but played only another nine league matches before moving to Brentford.

Both clubs put out very strong sides for this benefit match, as befits any Old Firm encounter. On the day, Rangers wom easily by four goals to nil.

McGrory himself was injured, and he could not take part in the game. The 'dressed' linesmen are Alan Morton (left) and Jimmy Quinn.

1933–1934 SCOTTISH CUP					
20/01/34		Dalbeattie Star	(A)	6-0	2,376
03/02/34		Ayr United	(A)	3-2	23,651
17/02/34		Falkirk	(H)	3-1	43,000
03/03/34	QF	St Mirren	(A)	0-2	33,434

The match against Dalbeattie Star provided one of the smallest attendances at a Celtic cup tie for many years. Johnny Crum scored four in this game. In the quarter-final, though, St Mirren sprang a surprise in front of a huge Love Street crowd, which saw Celtic miss two penalties and St Mirren one.

St Mirren went on to reach the Final but were outclassed 5-0 on the day by Rangers.

1933–1934 GLASGOW CUP			
	Third Lanark	(A)	4-1
	Rangers	(H)	1-1
Replay	Rangers	(A)	1-2

1933–1934 CHARITY CUP				
	Clyde	(H)	2-1	
	Third Lanark	(Hampden)	4-1	
Final	Rangers	(Hampden)	0-1	34,000 12/05/34

The next season was no better, as predicted by Willie Maley. 'We have been drifting for a year or two due to the final dissolution of our fine team of 1931 which through a series of tragic mishaps never attracted the success which it at one time promised. The deaths of Thomson and Scarff robbed the team of its fire and the other members of that brave side seemed to sag under these tragedies; (*Celtic Handbook 1935–1936*). Various combinations of players were tried without success and a slow reduction in the numbers attending the matches prompted the Board to take an unprecedented step. 'Napoleon' himself, Jimmy McMenemy was appointed coach in 1934 and almost immediately an improvement in the team was noted. Although the trophy cabinet still remained bare there were encouraging signs of team play as, after a poor start, they finished second in the table.

1934–1935 SCOTTISH LEAGUE DIVISION I	P	W	D	L	F	A	Pts	Position
Rangers	38	25	5	8	96	46	55	1st
Celtic	38	24	4	10	92	45	52	2nd

FIXTURES	H	A		H	A
Aberdeen	4-1	0-2	Hibs	4-0	2-3
Airdrie	2-0	2-0	Kilmarnock	4-1	3-2
Albion Rovers	5-1	1-2	Motherwell	3-2	0-1
Ayr United	7-0	0-1	Partick Thistle	3-1	3-1
Clyde	0-2	3-0	Queen of South	1-2	4-3
Dundee	4-0	0-0	Queen's Park	4-1	0-1
Dunfermline	3-0	3-1	Rangers	1-1	1-2
Falkirk	7-3	2-1	St Johnstone	0-0	1-0
Hamilton	3-1	2-4	St Mirren	2-1	4-2
Hearts	4-2	0-0			

Not a vintage season for football. A great Rangers team on the slide beating a Celtic one not quite up to it. Seemingly determined never to see sense, Celtic played two out-and-out footballers at centre-half – Chic Geatons and Malcolm McDonald – a complete contrast to the successful teams of the time. Jimmy Delaney came into forward-line at outside-right, showing his powers with fifteen goals; Willie Buchan got 13, McGrory 18. The damage was done at the start of the season. After winning the first match comfortably against Kilmarnock at Celtic Park, a bad run followed, only one win (Hibs) in the next seven, including defeats by Motherwell (A), Queen's Park (A) and Hamilton. From that point on, Celtic were always chasing.

1934–1935 SCOTTISH CUP					
26/01/35		Montrose	(H)	4-1	15,000
09/02/35		Partick Thistle	(H)	1-1	54,180
13/02/35	Replay	Partick Thistle	(A)	3-1	39,644
	Bye				
	QF	Aberdeen	(A)	1-3	40,104

In the earlier cup ties, the O'Donnell brothers stamped their authority on the matches, Frank scored two against Montrose, Hugh getting three of the Celtic goals against Thistle over the two legs.

Celtic had decided not to have a reserve team during most of the 1920s, a decision much criticised by many fans. At the beginning of the 1930s, the board members decided to re-enter a team in the Alliance League, with almost immediate success. The above squad won the 2nd XI Cup in 1935. Several went on to star in the first team, like Malcolm MacDonald (back row, extreme left), Jimmy Delaney (front row, extreme left) and Johnny Crum (from row, third from right). On the extreme right of the front row is John Fitzsimmons, later Doctor to both Celtic and Scotland in the 1960s and 1970s.

The reason for the bye is obvious. There were 14 teams in the draw for the fourth round, with only eight required for the quarter-finals, so six ties were drawn leaving two teams to go through as byes. Why that should have been necessary is more difficult to work out. In the end, both teams which received the bye, Celtic and Motherwell were knocked out at the quarter-final stage.

1934–1935 GLASGOW CUP		
Queen's Park	(H)	1-0
Rangers	(H)	1-2

1934–1935 CHARITY CUP		
Queen's Park	(H)	1-4

Expectations among the support were high for 1935–1936, although a few players were transferred in the early months. Charlie Napier went to Derby; the O'Donnell brothers to Preston North End. The crucial moment, though, was when Celtic signed Willie Lyon, a dominant 'thou-shalt-not-pass' type of centre-half from Queen's Park. Celtic had never had such a central defender (see *Tactics*) and he immediately tightened an always suspect defence, so much so that only 33 goals were lost in 38 games compared to 45 the season before.

1935–1936 SCOTTISH LEAGUE DIVISION I

	P	W	D	L	F	A	Pts	Position
Celtic	38	32	2	4	115	33	66	1st

FIXTURES

	H	A		H	A
Aberdeen	5-3	1-3	Hibs	4-1	5-0
Airdrie	4-0	3-2	Kilmarnock	4-0	1-1
Albion Rovers	4-0	3-0	Motherwell	5-0	2-1
Arbroath	5-0	2-0	Partick Thistle	1-1	3-1
Ayr United	6-0	2-0	Queen of South	5-0	3-1
Clyde	2-1	4-0	Queen's Park	3-0	3-2
Dundee	4-2	2-0	Rangers	3-4	2-1
Dunfermline	5-3	0-1	St Johnstone	2-0	3-2
Hamilton	1-0	2-0	Third Lanark	6-0	3-1
Hearts	2-1	0-1			

Commanding centre-half Willie Lyon joined Celtic in April 1935 and proved just what the team needed to solidify the defence and organise the play.

This was a super season for Celtic, with everyone on song. Seventy-one goals were scored at home, the best ever. Jimmy McGrory hit 50 in total, including seven hat-tricks, one of which, against Motherwell on 14 March

1936, was reputedly completed in three minutes. Ironically, the team lost the first match of the season against Aberdeen (1-3) at Pittodrie, then went 18 undefeated before losing to Dunfermline at East End Park. The 33 goals lost was the lowest since 1923–1924 but that included only 34 matches. Rangers finished five points adrift.

Celtic won 2-1 at Ibrox, the first League win there since 1921, and also beat Motherwell 2-1 at Fir Park, for the first League victory over the Steelmen since 1926. Rangers came from behind to take the Old Firm match 4-3 on New Year's Day but their challenge faltered against Hamilton in mid-April.

1935–1936 SCOTTISH CUP				
25/01/36	Berwick Rangers	scratched	(walkover)	
08/02/36	St Johnstone	(H)	1-2	26,647

This was a curious episode. The match against Berwick Rangers was scheduled for Celtic Park, but that proved unplayable on the day. As Berwick was a non-league side, they could have insisted on a Saturday re-match. Willie Maley offered them £100 to play on Wednesday, an offer which the Berwick directors accepted then scratched from the competition, allowing Celtic to carry on with their important league match against Hearts the following Saturday. In the second round, Celtic did not play very well, but made many chances which were spurned. St Johnstone, by contrast, were only allowed two chances by a miserly Celtic defence but took both of them.

1935–1936 GLASGOW CUP					
	Third Lanark	(H)	1-1		
Replay	Third Lanark	(A)	1-0		
Final	Rangers	(Ibrox)	0-2	40,000	12/10/35

1935–1936 CHARITY CUP					
	Partick Thistle	(H)	1-0		
Final	Rangers	(Hampden)	4-2	63,000	9/05/36

Team: Kennaway, Hogg and Morrison; Geatons, Lyon and Paterson; Delaney, Buchan; McGrory; Crum and Murphy.

With five minutes to go in this exciting match, the teams were locked at two goals each, with Celtic 7-6 ahead on corners. Jimmy Delaney then took the ball towards the corner flag, cut back towards goal and let fly. 3-2. Back came Celtic on the attack again, some quick passing between the forwards, before McGrory let fly with one of his specials. 4-2 to Celtic and the Charity Cup was on its way to Parkhead for the first time since 1926. Celtic had gone one up in 34 minutes through Delaney. Rangers equalised five minutes before half-time through McPhail. Early in the second half, Turnbull made it 2-1 for Rangers, with Delaney again getting the equaliser. Then came those vital five minutes.

The Celtic team which won the Charity Cup in 1936. Back row, left to right: C. Geatons, R. Hogg, J. Kennaway, J. Morrison, W Buchan, G. Paterson. Front row: J. McMenemy (Trainer), J. Delaney, J. McGrory, W. Lyon, J. Crum, F. Murphy, W. Maley (Manager).

Willie Lyon, who joined Celtic from Queen's Park in 1933, was a natural leader and quickly took over as captain until the outbreak of war. At that point, he joined the Scot's Greys with whom he won the Military Cross in 1943.

Tactics

By the end of season 1935-1936, everybody could see that the Celtic ship was sinking and even the traditionalists, reared on an attacking philosophy, acknowledged that a stopper centre-half might be required.

Season	Matches Played	Goals For	Goals Against	Position
1930–31	38	101	34	2nd
1931–32	38	94	50	3rd
1932–33	38	75	44	4th
1933–34	38	78	53	3rd
1934–35	38	92	45	2nd

From this list goal-scoring would not appear to be a problem, but a leaking defence was certainly in evidence. Willie Maley signed Willie Lyon from Queen's Park in April 1935 and he proved just what Celtic required. An ever-present in the following season, he scored six goals (four penalties) but more importantly, settled the rearguard so much that the team picked up Celtic's 18th Championship.

Season	Matches Played	Goals For	Goals Against	Position
1935–36	38	115	33	1st

170

Possibly buoyed up by the defence's strength, Jimmy McGrory scored 50 League goals in this season, a Club record, as was the 71 goals scored in home matches. A look at how this team was re-arranged in the fairly new W/M formation is as follows.

Joe Kennaway	295 appearances	83 shut-outs
Bobby Hogg	322 appearances	0 goals
John Morrison	178 appearances	1 goal
Chic Geatons	319 appearances	13 goals
Willie Lyons	163 appearances	17 goals
George Paterson	195 appearances	16 goals
Jimmy Delaney	160 appearances	73 goals
Malcolm McDonald	147 appearances	37 goals
Jimmy McGrory	445 appearances	472 goals
Johnny Crum	211 appearances	88 goals
Willie Buchan	134 appearances	59 goals
Johnny Divers	82 appearances	48 goals
Frank Murphy	161 appearances	58 goals

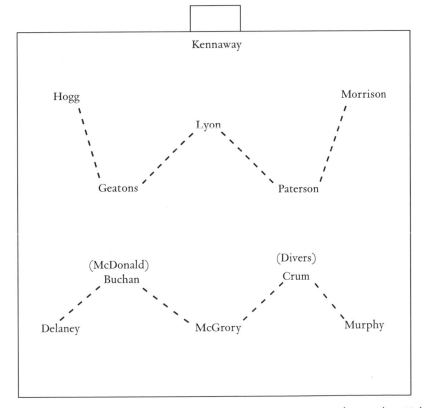

The W/M formation, successfully used by Celtic to win the 1935–36 League Championship. With a stopper centre-half like Willie Lyon at one end and a forward scoring a goal a game in Jimmy McGrory at the front, the makings of a good team were there. Add to this some solidity at full-back, strength at wing-half and four other forwards all capable of frequent scoring, the result was two League Championships, one Scottish Cup and an Exhibition Cup in four years. Then, unfortunately, came the Second World War.

It was almost a miraculous transformation by Celtic and makes the modern reader wonder why those behind the scenes took so long to fall into line with other teams. In England, for instance, Arsenal adopted the stopper centre-half by 1926 and most teams had adopted a similar style by 1928. In Scotland, Rangers had Jimmy Simpson to shut the gate and this father of Ronnie, the future Lisbon Lion, plied his role to great effect.

However a quote by the former Rangers director and player George Brown may put Celtic's apparent lack of foresight in a different light. He said:

> About 1930, there was a charity game in which a Rangers/Celtic Select played a Heart/Hibs Select. Davie Meiklejohn was at right-half, I was at left-half and Celtic's Jimmy McStay was at centre-half. Things did not go very well for us in the first-half and by the interval we were one goal down. So during half-time, Meiklejohn said to McStay, 'all the trouble is coming through the middle because you are too far up the field. We play with Jimmy Simpson well back and this leaves the backs free'. McStay agreed to try this and we eventually ran out comfortable winners. So from then on he played the same type of game for Celtic.

Perhaps he did, but the statistics would tend to suggest that it was not working effectively. Bringing in Willie Lyon as an out-and-out stopper, gave the Club immediate success, that League Championship of 1935–1936, followed by a Cup win the following season, then another Championship in season 1937–1938 plus the Exhibition Cup. Not a bad result from a new system – and it took the great Brazilians in 1958 to make it redundant!

McGrory

McGrory also had a wonderful season in 1935–1936 scoring 50 in total, and perhaps at this point, I may pay tribute to a great player.

Jimmy McGrory breaks Steve Bloome of England's record number of goals scored. He scored this goal in the 5-3 victory over Aberdeen on 21 December 1935 at Celtic Park.

I was fortunate enough to meet and get to know Jimmy McGrory in the 60s and early 70s. In fact I was signed by him in 1965, only months before he

McGrory's powerful physique made him a trial to opposing defenders. However, players had to be strong during this period just to wear the very heavy jersey, shorts and stockings, plus those huge boots.

was relieved of the manager's job, to be replaced by Jock Stein. It was hard for me to reconcile the quiet, gentlemanly personage I met at Celtic Park with the image that football history has presented to us when Jimmy McGrory was at his peak. He was not only a strong, enthusiastic chase everything type of centre-forward but, judging by the number of goals he scored in not always successful teams, he must have had two very accurate feet, a powerful shot, great positional sense, sharpness over the ten yards so vital round the box, a good first touch, as they say nowadays, plus a great spring to meet the many crosses thrown in to power home with that bull-like neck.

The lack of consistent success for Celtic in the 20s and 30s may have contributed towards the paltry collection of caps – seven – which McGrory collected in a long career but no-one at Celtic Park, or even non-Celtic fans around the country, were ever in any doubt about Jimmy McGrory's values to this Club and country.

1936–1937 Scottish League Division 1

	P	W	D	L	F	A	Pts	Position
Rangers	38	26	9	3	88	32	61	1st
Celtic	38	22	8	8	89	58	52	3rd

Fixtures

	H	A		H	A	
Aberdeen	3-2	0-1	Kilmarnock	2-4	3-3	
Albion Rovers	4-0	3-1	Motherwell	3-2	0-8	
Arbroath	5-1	3-2	Partick Thistle	1-1	1-1	
Clyde	3-1	1-1	Queen of South	5-0	0-1	
Dundee	1-2	0-0	Queen's Park	4-0	2-0	
Dunfermline	3-1	4-3	Rangers	1-1	0-1	
Falkirk	1-0	3-0	St Johnstone	3-2	1-2	
Hamilton	3-3	2-1	St Mirren	3-0	2-1	
Hearts	3-2	1-0	Third Lanark	6-3	2-4	
Hibs	5-1	2-2				

In spite of almost the same personnel as the year before, Celtic slumped badly allowing their chief rivals through to the title. Granted, McGrory played in only 22 matches (18 goals) but again the defence would appear to have let the side down, 58 goals a lot to lose for such a settled foundation. Carelessness seemed to be very prevalent. Of the first 22 matches, 14 were won and four drawn so the collapse came after that, culminating, on the last day of the season, in Celtic's heaviest-ever defeat 0-8 against Motherwell at Fir Park, on 30 April.

1936–1937 Scottish Cup

30/01/37		Stenhousemuir	(A)	1-1	5,000
03/02/38	Replay	Stenhousemuir	(H)	2-0	8,000
13/02/37		Albion Rovers	(A)	5-2	19,000
27/02/37		East Fife	(A)	3-0	12,690
17/03/37	QF	Motherwell	(H)	4-4	36,150
24/03/37	Replay	Motherwell	(A)	2-1	35,023
03/04/37	SF	Clyde	(Ibrox)	2-0	76,000
24/04/37	Final	Aberdeen	(Hampden)	2-1	147,365

Team: Kennaway; Hogg and Morrison; Geatons, Lyon and Paterson; Delaney, Buchan; McGrory; Crum and Murphy.

Good crowds, reasonable performances by both the team and individuals. McGrory scored nine in all, Willie Buchan six, Johnny Crum two.

For the fourth time in the 30s, Motherwell were drawn against Celtic in the Cup and this time it required a replay to settle the tie. For the Final, against a very attractive Aberdeen side, 147,365 packed into Hampden, the record attendance for both a Scottish Cup Final and any match in Europe, with what was reckoned to be another 30,000 or so locked outside. Aberdeen worked hard but Celtic had the edge over 90 minutes. The score was all-square at half-time – Crum scoring for Celtic, Armstrong for Aberdeen – but Celtic turned the heat on in the second half and it came as no surprise

Fir Park, the very basic Motherwell ground where Celtic received an embarrassing 8-0 defeat on 20 April 1937.

Celtic v. Sunderland, 1936. This match, and the return leg at Celtic Park two weeks later, were promoted as a British Championship. The first game at Roker park ended in a 1-1 draw. Celtic won the second 3-2 thus taking the unofficial 'British Club Championship' by four goals to three.

The famous English star, Raich Carter, is second from the right in the second-front row.

when Willie Buchan got the winner. It was Celtic's 23rd Scottish Cup Final, their 22nd on Hampden and 15th Final victory.

1936–1937 Glasgow Cup		
Third Lanark	(A)	3-1
Rangers	(A)	1-2

This Celtic team had the unique experience of playing in front of the largest attendance for any match in Europe when beating Aberdeen 2-1 in the 1937 Scottish Cup final. Back row, left to right: Geatons, Hogg, Kennaway, Morrison, Buchan, Paterson. Front row: W. Maley (Manager), Delaney, McGrory, Lyon, Crum, Murphy, J. McMenemy (Trainer). This was McGrory's last big occasion in a Celtic jersey.

	1936–1937 CHARITY CUP				
	Clyde	(H)	3-1		
Final	Queen's Park	(Hampden)	4-3	21,000	15/05/37

Just one month after the Scottish Cup Final, Celtic met Queen's Park in the Charity Cup Final without their regular eleven. Hogg and Delaney were touring Austria with the SFA; Morrison and Crum were injured, while Kennaway, although he played, was far from 100 per cent fit.

Team: Kennaway; Geatons and Paterson; Dawson, Lyon and Duffy; McDonald, Buchan; McGrory; Divers and Murphy.

This was a really entertaining end-to-end match, in which Celtic were behind three times yet came back to win. A rather static Celtic defence allowed Queen's Park to score in 26 minutes; Divers equalised in 40. Queens made it 2-1 in 58 minutes, Murphy equalised in 73. In the 80th minute a headed goal made it 3-2 for the Spiders but just before the end McGrory equalised and then, with about one minute left, Willie Lyon raced forward and blasted an unstoppable shot into the net for a 4-3 win.

There were a few personnel changes for the following season. Matt Lynch came in for a few games at right-half or outside-right, Willie Buchan left suddenly for Blackpool in November to be replaced by Malky McDonald, but the bigger loss was McGrory, who played his last match in November against Queen's Park scoring as ever. Joe Carruth got the nod to replace him but after seven matches in which he scored nine goals, Carruth was replaced by Johnny Crum who kept the position for the rest of the season. John Divers made the inside-left position his own, the team gelled together very well and went on to win the Championship, Celtic's 19th, scoring an excellent 114 goals.

One year after the teams met as league Champions of their respective countries, Celtic and Sunderland met again as cup winners. At stake was an unofficial British Cup which Celtic won by beating Sunderland 2-0 at Roker Park on 6 October 1937. No trophy, though, ever appeared. Captain Willie Lyon is holding the Scottish Cup.

1937–1938 SCOTTISH LEAGUE DIVISION I

	P	W	D	L	F	A	Pts	Position
Celtic	38	27	7	4	114	42	61	1st

Fixtures

	H	A		H	A
Aberdeen	5-2	1-1	Morton	4-0	3-2
Arbroath	4-0	0-2	Motherwell	4-1	2-1
Ayr United	1-1	1-1	Partick Thistle	6-0	6-1
Clyde	3-1	6-1	QOS	2-2	2-2
Dundee	3-0	3-2	Queen's Park	4-3	3-0
Falkirk	2-0	0-3	Rangers	3-0	1-3
Hamilton	4-2	2-1	St Johnstone	6-0	2-1
Hearts	2-1	4-2	St Mirren	5-1	3-1
Hibs	3-0	3-0	Third Lanark	1-1	1-1
Kilmarnock	8-0	1-2			

Celtic were three points clear as they won their 19th Championship. This was Jimmy McGrory's last season and he played in only a handful of matches. Even so, he scored five goals, that 114 tally coming from a variety of other sources; Willie Buchan (12), Johnny Crum (24), Joe Carruth (16), Jimmy Delaney (7), Malcolm McDonald (12), John Divers (20) and Frank Murphy

Jimmy McGrory's last match for Celtic was at Parkhead on 16 October 1937 against Queen's Park. Ironically, he scored against Desmond White, then in goal for the Spiders, later Secretary and Chairman of Celtic.

(10). Celtic's record home attendance was recorded in the match versus Rangers on 1 January 1938, 83,500 being the generally accepted figure. Jimmy McGrory's last match was against Queen's Park on 16 October 1937, when he scored against Queen's Park goalkeeper, Desmond White, later to be Celtic's Chairman.

1937–1938 SCOTTISH CUP				
22/01/38	Third Lanark	(A)	2-1	43,877
12/02/38	Nithsdale	(H)	5-0	6,000
05/03/38	Kilmarnock	(H)	1-2	39,390

A large attendance for the local derby at Cathkin, after which the players prepared for the second round by having a few days' relaxation at Symington at the Tinto Hills. However, one round later, Kilmarnock, now managed by Jimmy McGrory, created a sensation by knocking Celtic out of Parkhead, a result which seemed to harm the relationship between the newish manager and his former boss, Willie Maley.

League Champions 1937–38. Malky McDonald, now in the team, with Willie Buchan gone south. Back row, left to right: Geatons, Hogg, Kennaway, Morrison, Crum, Paterson. Front row: Delaney, McDonald, Lyon, Divers, Murphy.

1937–1938 GLASGOW CUP

Rangers	(H)	1-2

1937–1938 CHARITY CUP

	Queen's Park	(A)	3-1		
	Partick Thistle	(H)	3-2		
Final	Rangers	(Hampden)	2-0	40,000	14/05/38

At no time did Rangers ever look like scoring. Their attack lacked imagination and inspiration and was easily held by a Celtic defence superbly marshalled by Willie Lyon. The first goal came in 8 minutes, when Rangers left-back Cheyne failed to control the ball, Divers latched onto it, took it to the by-line and cut it back for Delaney to score. After 19 minutes Celtic went two up, a corner kick by Murphy met at the far post by Divers for what proved to be the winning goal.

Team: Kennaway; Hogg and Morrison; Geatons, Lyon and Paterson; Delaney, Carruth; Crum; Divers and Murphy.

Earlier in the season, on 6 November, Celtic reached the Golden Jubilee of its birth. The jubilee year proved a good one, not only in football terms but in finance, the balance sheet showing a profit of £7,105, a total of £21,515 in credit, £1,905 on deposit and a War Loan Investment of £10,206. To celebrate the Jubilee in style, the Club held an official banquet on 16 June

1938 in the Grosvenor restaurant in Glasgow, to which were invited officials of the SFA, representatives of Scottish League teams, every living Celtic player together with the Lord Provost of the City and senior members of the council, over 200 guests in all. In an evening of much speech-making, the toast to Celtic FC was proposed by Sir John Cargill, Honorary President of Rangers, but the highlight of the evening was the presentation of a cheque to Willie Maley from the Celtic Board of Directors for all his efforts during those 50 years.

Willie Maley

There seems little doubt that the presentation of the cheque by the Board was an inducement for Willie Maley to retire. He had become increasingly autocratic as he grew older and the Directors would not have found him an easy man to deal with. They would also have been well aware that the fans were unhappy with the team's performances over the last two decades and, like supporters everywhere wanted change – for the better! Perhaps this was suggested to Willie Maley. Certainly, Jimmy McMenemy was brought in as coach in 1934 and that led to some improvement, but it is hard to imagine that Maley himself felt that his position was under any threat. His own conduct, though, had given room for criticism on several occasions. On the summer tour of 1931 to North America, dismayed by the refusal of the Board to allow his brother Tom to travel with the party, he sulked in his cabin claiming illness. Maley then requested that they send for his brother to escort him home. The Board did so only to find that when Tom arrived, brother Willie had made a complete recovery and Tom joined the rest of the trip.

Willie Maley's comment after the death of John Thomson, when in answer to a question about the collision he replied 'I *hope* it was an accident' was a rather unfortunate reply which should immediately have been withdrawn. Such a proud man was unlikely to do so and the words were very wounding, not only to the luckless Sam English, who had clashed with Thomson, but to relationships between Celtic and Rangers.

The death of John Thomson, the inquest, the burial and subsequent events put an enormous strain on the Club and Maley in particular. It was he who faced the press at all times, not the Directors or the players, and was then forced to continue with the season. Within a few months, he had to cope again with tragedy when Peter Scarff retired at 23 with TB in December 1931. Scarff deteriorated rapidly and died in 1933.

At the Golden Jubilee dinner on 16 June 1938, Tom White was effusive in his praise of Willie Maley's contribution and presented him with a cheque for 2,500 guineas, in token of all he had done for Celtic in those 30 years. Unfortunately, for the last two years of his career at Celtic Park, this gift caused no end of trouble. It was undoubtedly a generous gesture by the

Board, although possibly could be construed as an inducement to his retirement. But Maley was extremely annoyed. He had already rejected one suggestion that Jimmy McGrory be brought in alongside him to learn the ropes of management; now he was very annoyed at having to pay tax on the honorarium, especially as the Club had declared a profit of £7,105 on the year.

This was slightly ironic. Shortly after the Exhibition Cup Final, captain Willie Lyon was appointed by the players to discuss with the manager the bonus promised by one of the Directors, of which only 20 per cent had been paid. Maley, at his most autocratic, told Lyon to go and see the Director in question, adding rather bitterly, that he would no doubt take the money out of his own pocket.

Maley was off ill for a period in the last season before the war and there was evidence to suggest that dressing-room discipline was not as strict as normal during this period. He was eventually 'retired' on New Year's Day 1940, the reins passing to Jimmy McStay. For the rest of his life and, indeed a new life away from Parkhead, which must have been difficult to cope with after 62 years, Maley was fairly bitter about the treatment he had received. He chose not to attend a match at Celtic Park again until the early 50s but was then touched to be recognised and remembered fondly by many fans. Willie Maley died on 2 April 1958.

As so often happens, the good team of one season is not the team of the next and so it proved with Celtic in 1938–1939. After a good start, culminating in a Glasgow Cup win, a series of indifferent displays resulted, causing Willie Maley to write in his annual report; 'this year will certainly be written down as one of the most disappointing, (if not *the* most disappointing) in over 51 years of existence'. He had been ill for much of the season and during this particular report was in very contemplative mood, often looking back to earlier and happy days. He admits that he does not know 'how to explain the form of our side last year' but then goes on to give a little dig at his players, perhaps showing some lack of rapport between them and the manager. 'In every game it is possible to have the breaks against you but the law of averages counts in all sports and what is lost one day, comes back another day. That, of course, does not apply to clearly indolent play backed by an imaginary superiority which is, like foolish pride in oneself, a sin.'

After the success in League and Exhibition Cup of the year before, perhaps the players did take things too casually. There were very few changes in personnel all season. The Exhibition Final team of Kennaway; Hogg and Morrison; Geatons, Lyon and Paterson; Delaney, McDonald; Crum; Divers and Murphy was the stable choice, Matt Lynch and Joe Carruth being the main replacements. Jimmy Delaney broke his arm badly at Arbroath on 1

April, an injury which kept him out of football for nearly two years. He was replaced by Oliver Anderson and John Watters stood in for Malcolm McDonald when he went down with appendicitis in November 1938. So the team was much the same but the performances just lacked the consistency of the year before.

1938–1939 SCOTTISH LEAGUE DIVISION 1							
	P	W	D	L	F	A	Pts	Position
Rangers	38	25	9	4	112	55	59	1st
Celtic	38	20	8	10	99	53	48	2nd

FIXTURES					
	H	A		H	A
Aberdeen	1-2	1-3	Motherwell	1-3	3-2
Albion Rovers	4-1	8-1	Partick Thistle	3-1	0-0
Arbroath	2-0	2-0	Queen of South	5-1	1-1
Ayr United	3-3	4-1	Queen's Park	0-1	2-1
Clyde	3-1	4-1	Raith Rovers	6-1	0-4
Falkirk	1-2	1-1	Rangers	6-2	1-2
Hamilton	1-2	1-0	St Johnstone	1-1	1-1
Hearts	2-2	5-1	St Mirren	3-2	1-2
Hibs	5-4	0-1	Third Lanark	6-1	2-0
Kilmarnock	9-1	0-0			

Another slump. Both teams scored goals – and lost them! Rangers' 55 goals against was the highest ever for a First Division Championship win. Inconsistency was Celtic's downfall. The defence was little changed from week to week, but up front the line changed frequently. Five outside-rights and five inside-rights were tried, while the talisman – McGrory – was now manager of Kilmarnock. That same Kilmarnock was beaten 9-1 in the first match of the season as the goals came early, 72 in the first 24 matches. From then on, form dipped, fewer goals went in and six matches were lost. Still, the interest was obviously there, the Old Firm match at Ibrox on 2 January 1939 attracting a British record (for a League match) of 118,567.

When discussing the destination of League Championships, much emphasis is given to Old Firm matches. Yet, in the 1930s neither side won both matches in any one season. Overall, Celtic won four, Rangers seven and seven were drawn.

1938–1939 SCOTTISH CUP					
21/01/39		Burntisland	(A)	8-3	3,000
04/02/39		Montrose	(A)	7-1	6,389
18/02/39		Hearts	(A)	2-2	49,572
22/02/39	Replay	Hearts	(H)	2-1 AET	80,840
	QF	Motherwell	(A)	1-3	31,000

An easy start to the campaign at Burntisland and Montrose but Hearts brought Celtic down to earth before one of the biggest ever attendances at

Tynecastle, nearly 50,000. Four days later, another 30,000 on top of that crowded into Parkhead to see the replay, two goals by Johnny Divers taking Celtic through to the quarter-final, where they met old rivals Motherwell, who proved too good for them on this occasion.

1938–1939 GLASGOW CUP				
	Third Lanark	(A)	1-1	
Replay	Third Lanark	(H)	8-1	
	Queen's Park	(H)	2-1	
Final	Clyde	(Hampden)	3-0	43,976 14/10/38

Team: Kennaway; Hogg, Morrison; Geatons, Lyon, Paterson; Delaney, McDonald; Crum; Divers, Birrell.

The Clyde Chairman, Mr John McMahon summed up the match succinctly; 'Undoubtedly the better team won'. Celtic had the wind behind them in the first-half and made many chances, some of which were missed and others saved by goalkeeper Brown. Against the wind in the second-half the flood-gates opened, goals by Delaney in 49 minutes, Geatons in 80 minutes and Crum in 85 minutes, giving Celtic a comfortable 3-0 victory, the first in this competition since 1930.

1938–1939 CHARITY CUP		
Clyde	(H)	?-3

A decade which once again, in term of trophy success, belonged to Rangers. Ironically Celtic had many good players at this time, in the eyes of good judges, at least the equal of their Ibrox counterparts. What they lacked though, was firstly some discipline.

THE OLD FIRM S RECORD IN COMPETITIONS 1930–1940				
	LEAGUE	CUP	GLASGOW CUP	CHARITY CUP
1930–31	Rangers	Celtic	Celtic	Rangers
1931–32		Rangers	Rangers	Rangers
1932–33	Rangers	Celtic	Rangers	Rangers
1933–34	Rangers	Rangers	Rangers	Rangers
1934–35	Rangers	Rangers		
1935–36	Celtic	Rangers	Rangers	Celtic
1936–37	Rangers	Celtic	Rangers	Celtic
1937–38	Celtic		Rangers	Celtic
1938–39	Rangers		Celtic	Rangers
1939–30			Rangers	Rangers
	Celtic 2	Celtic 3	Celtic 2	Celtic 3
	Rangers 6	Rangers 4	Rangers 7	Rangers 6

TOTAL: CELTIC 10 RANGERS 23

Willie Maley during this decade was in his sixties and had less and less to do with the everyday work of the players, leaving details like that to Jimmy

McMenemy. At the beginning of the decade, he had to cope with the loss of John Thomson and Peter Scarff and towards the latter stages of the 1930s his own health was uncertain. Taking all these factors into account, it would not be surprising if he lacked the passion and drive of his younger years.

There was also a lack of organisation around the playing system. The attacking centre-half had fallen into disfavour after the off-side law change in 1925, with most teams now adopting styles where the centre-half was more of a 'stopper'. It took Celtic a long time to change to a similar pattern; indeed it was only when Willie Lyon arrived in 1935 that this system was adopted, with immediate success. Three other factors prevalent at Ibrox but lacking at Parkhead during this decade were consistency, confidence and strength. Rangers radiated strength and power. They could play as well, of course, but their rearguard provided a strong base from which the confidence, and therefore, the consistency radiated, with successful results. Celtic, by contrast, were occasionally dazzling, frequently effective but often uncertain. Their fans could easily go from the heights to the depths in one match; unfortunately, in this decade, as in the 20s, there were more of the latter.

CHAPTER EIGHT
Various Trophies — and an Exhibition Cup

As well as the major trophies, the League Championship and the Scottish Cup, plus local competitions for the Glasgow and Charity Cups, Celtic Football Club has taken part in a number of 'special' tournaments, either to commemorate or celebrate a specific occasion. The first of these was in 1888, as part of the first Glasgow International Exhibition. After drawing their first match against Abercorn (Paisley) 1-1, Celtic then beat Dumbarton 3-1 and Partick Thistle 1-0 before losing 0-2 to Cowlairs in the final.

For the Glasgow International Exhibition of 1901, another trophy was put up for competition, and the eight leading Scottish clubs took part. All matches were played, as in 1888, at Glasgow University's Recreation ground in Kelvingrove, just to the west of the main building. Celtic reached the final by beating two Edinburgh sides, Hibs on 21 August 1901 by a single goal and Hearts two weeks later, by 2-1. On both occasions, the goal-scoring hero was James Drummond, an inside-left from Bellshill, who only managed four league appearances in his Celtic career before leaving for Manchester City. In the final, Celtic faced Rangers at the same venue on 9 September, and the match deteriorated into a rowdy and unpleasant affair. Celtic opened the scoring after fifteen minutes but Rangers came back strongly to win 3-1, the actual trophy so impressing the Directors that they insured it for a large sum, in those days, of £100.

One year later, Ibrox was given the nod over Celtic Park for the international match of 1902 between Scotland and England. At the time, the decision was quite a blow to everyone connected with Celtic. Tragically, though, wooden planking on a section of the west terracing at Ibrox gave way, resulting in 25 deaths and more than 500 injuries. Rangers immediately organised a competition to raise money for compensation to the victims. A select field was invited to join them, Sunderland, the English league champions, Everton the runners-up, and Celtic, the runners-up in the Scottish league. The winning club would receive the Glasgow Exhibition Trophy of 1901.

Both Scots teams beat their English opponents in the semi-final matches, Celtic crushing Sunderland by five goals to one and Rangers equally impressive against Everton. The final was held at Cathkin Park on 17 June 1902 and was memorable, not only for a Celtic victory by three goals to two, but for a hat-trick for Jimmy Quinn in his first major game as centre-forward at Celtic. The teams had been level at 2-2 after 90 minutes, so extra time was played, Quinn's winning header coming two minutes from the end.

So, the very fine trophy, much admired at Ibrox moved to Celtic Park, but not without some controversy. For some reason, Rangers expected the trophy to be returned at the end of the tournament and were not pleased at Celtic's decision to keep it. In the years prior to the First World War, Rangers directors made several requests to their counterparts at Parkhead to return the trophy, all to no avail; in fact, Celtic's refusal to fall in with their wishes was a source of some friction between the clubs for some years.

In 1919, the Victory Cup was put up for competition by the Scottish League, to commemorate the allied victory in the First World War. In the first round, Celtic beat Vale of Leven 2-0 at Celtic Park on 1 March 1919 watched by a crowd of 12,000, Andy McAtee and Joe Cassidy getting the goals. Two weeks later, also at Parkhead, Albion Rovers proved worthy opponents before going down 3-1. McAtee, Jimmy McColl and Patsy Gallagher all scored with 25,000 present. On 29 March, Celtic stumbled to a 1-0 defeat at the hands of St Mirren at Love Street in front of a similar attendance. The team just did not perform well on the day and Patsy Gallagher missed a penalty. St Mirren went on to win the trophy.

Another one-off competition occurred in 1928 when the Glasgow Dental Hospital Cup was promoted by the Glasgow Football Association. The aim of this event was to raise funds for the local dental hospital which eventually opened in 1931 and the fixtures, held in midweek, were played under the charity cup rules that is, corners would count in the event of a drawn game. In their first tie, Celtic comfortably beat Queen's Park 4-0 at Parkhead on 14 November, goals from Joe Riley (2) and Owen McNally (2) sending the majority of the 4,000 home in happy mood. Two weeks later, Partick Thistle were Celtic's semi-final opponents at Hampden in what turned out to be something of a farce. Perhaps the organisers had forgotten that darkness falls in Glasgow in November just after 4pm, but a 2.30 pm kick-off time was an illogical decision. Only 3,000 were present and, after 90 minutes the teams were level at 1-1 in failing light. The referee instructed the teams to play on as long as possible in extra time. Thistle scored two goals in the semi-darkness and were leading 3-1 when the referee called a halt with about ten minutes left. The organisers later decided that the result should stand, an appropriate decision, as Thistle were the better team on the day. Later in the final they beat Rangers to take the Dental Hospital Cup back to Firhill.

Tait's Tower, or more correctly, 'The Tower of Empire', in Bellahouston Park, the eye-catching feature of the Empire Exhibition.

In 1938, the Empire Exhibition was staged in Glasgow's Bellahouston Park. It was a most impressive, well laid-out display which covered many countries and aspects of the British Empire.

The scene was dominated by Thomas F. Tait's 300ft high tower, rising from a hill in the centre of the park. Unfortunately, this tower, intended to be a permanent feature of the park, had to be dismantled early in the Second World War when someone realised it was providing some navigational assistance to German planes! Glasgow's weather was at its worst for the summer but hopes and enthusiasms were high, with football fans especially eager to witness the knock-out tournament devised as a special attraction.

The best Scottish and English sides were invited. From England, Sunderland, FA Cup winners in 1937; Everton, Chelsea and Brentford. Current league champions Arsenal were invited, but had to decline due to touring commitments. Ironically, this tour was later cancelled and they were keen to join in but the organisers stuck to their original choice. From

An aerial view of the Empire Exhibition site, Bellahouston Park, Glasgow. Ibrox Park is at the top left.

Scotland, Celtic league champions, Rangers, champions the previous year, Aberdeen, second to Rangers, and Hearts, runners-up to Celtic. All the matches would be played at Ibrox Park just across the road from the exhibition site. There was no doubt that the competition was to be treated in a serious fashion, although, naturally, the English and Scottish sides were kept apart in the first round. When the draw was made, some interesting ties came up. Celtic were drawn against Sunderland; Rangers against Everton; Hearts were paired with Brentford and Aberdeen with Chelsea.

On 12 May 1938, the following communiqué was issued from the headquarters from the SFA at 48 Carlton Place: 'At a meeting held today at the exhibition between Messrs D Bowie and G Graham, representing the Control Committee and Lord Elgin and Captain Graham, representing the exhibition, it was agreed;

1. that the trophy to be presented to the winning team should take the form of a replica of the tower in the exhibition made of silver, standing about 18 inches high on a suitable plinth.

2. that the players of the winning team in the final should receive a minature of the trophy in silver.

3. that all other players taking part in the competition should receive a miniature plate.

This was a very generous gesture by the organisers, a replica of Tait's Tower much more interesting than a medal to most players.

Naturally, the traditional rivalry between England and Scotland, plus the normal competitive spirit between teams in the same league, made the tournament a keenly contested affair. Celtic were strongly fancied,

A most interesting and attractive feature of the Celtic Park trophy room, The Empire Exhibition Cup, is made of silver, and is a replica of 'The Tower of Empire' at the Exhibition.

particularly after the ease with which they beat Rangers in the Charity Cup only a few days before. Of the visiting English clubs, it was felt that Everton was the most skilful and would provide the main challenge

Celtic 0 Sunderland 0

The opening match, on 25 May 1938, was between Celtic and Sunderland. The Wearsiders had three Scots in their team all down the left side, Hall at full back, Hastings at left-half and Gallagher at inside-left. Two other English internationals were also in the team, Bobby Gurney at centre-forward and Raich Carter at inside-right. All in all, Sunderland was a formidable proposition and had been doing special training for what they regarded, as did many others, as a British Football Championship.

The Celtic team which took the field was the same one which beat Rangers in the Charity Cup final: Kennaway, Hogg and Morrison; Geatons, Lyon and Paterson; Delaney, Carruth, Crum, Divers and Murphy.

On the night, 50,000 turned out to see a fascinating contest. Celtic looked early on as though they would take command but the longer the match went on the better Sunderland became. Both sides made some good openings in the first-half but could not finish off their work and they reached the interval without a score. The best chance for Sunderland came in the 51st minute when Raich Carter directed a powerful header towards the corner of the net and only a superb save by Joe Kennaway saved Celtic. Just on the final whistle, a good move between Divers and Crumb left the latter with a whole goal to aim at but he drove his shot wide.

And so to extra time, the first half of which was fairly even but in the second period, Sunderland looked the more likely team to score with Kennaway making another fine save, this time from left-winger Burnbanks. For all their pressure though, the Celtic defence held out and the match finished as a goalless draw.

The Replay – Celtic 3 Sunderland 1

By the rules of the competition, the replay was on the following evening, a showery night making the pitch rather spongy. This time round though, the Celtic eleven all rose to the occasion and dominated the match, with inside-left Johnny Divers the mastermind behind the victory. Celtic had been forced to make changes from the first match, Matt Lynch and Malcolm MacDonald replacing the right-wing combination of Jimmy Delaney and Joe Carruth. In the midst of the wind and rain, Sunderland made the first chance when Raich Carter blasted in an 18 yarder which Joe Kennaway did well to knuckle over the bar. From that point on, though, Celtic took control, with Divers showing his class on the wet surface.

Yet Sunderland opened the scoring, inside-left Saunders taking the ball along the by-line in a wonderful run beating three Celtic defenders before tricking Joe Kennaway to score. This was much against the run of play but Celtic equalised just before the interval; Johnny Crum sending in a looping shot which Mapson, in goal for Sunderland, got his hands to but could not keep out of the net. Celtic must have been disappointed to be level at the interval, as they had most of the play. Within 13 minutes of the second half, it was all over as a contest. In 48 minutes, a combined move between Crum and Divers and the latter scored from six yards: then in 58 minutes a pass from Frank Murphy to Divers who pulled the ball out to the left then tucked it into the net off the bottom of the post. It was a comfortable victory for Celtic in front of a disappointing crowd of 20,000, the heavy rain no doubt affecting the attendance. John Divers received much praise for his two goals and overall play although the subtle skills of Malcolm MacDonald were not overlooked.

Aberdeen 4 Chelsea 0

On the Friday evening, 27 May, the second match in the competition took place, when Aberdeen met Chelsea. The English team were very disappointing and the crowd of 20,000 were not slow in letting their disapproval show, particularly in the first half when Aberdeen went 3-up. With the wind now behind them, Chelsea did improve a little in the second period but the Dons were always in control and eventually won 4-0.

Rangers 0 Everton 2

On the following Monday, Rangers versus Everton was the attraction and 48,000 turned out expecting another Scots team to go through. Unfortunately, Rangers were under the lash for most of the first-half against a talented Everton team who were one up at half-time thanks to a goal by Tommy Lawton. After only 14 minutes of the second half, Everton got another, Jerry Dawson being injured as he collided with the scorer inside right Cunliffe. Dawson left the field, centre-half Jimmy Simpson (father Lisbon Lion Ronnie) went into goal and a ten-man Rangers could not make any impression on a strong Everton rearguard.

Hearts 1 Brentford 0

The last of the first round matches was played on Wednesday 1 June, attended by another large crowd of 46,000. They saw an engrossing battle which could be summed up as follows: Brentford played some delightful football. Hearts didn't, but the men from Tynecastle went through. Only in the early stages could Hearts be compared with their opponents. From then on, the English team gave a fine display of attacking football while their defence coped comfortably with the sporadic Hearts attacks.

One goal settled the tie though, and that came in 26 minutes, at a time when Brentford were temporarily down to ten men due to an injury to outside-right Hopkin. Hearts inside-left Black went down the wing and logged the ball over the keeper's head. It looked a certain score until left-back Poiser nodded the ball out but it only went as far as right-winger Briscoe and he hammered the ball home to give Hearts a victory.

Celtic 1 Hearts 0

So, the four teams through were Celtic, Everton, Aberdeen and Hearts, with the draw pairing Celtic-Hearts and Aberdeen-Everton.

The former tie was first up, on Friday 3 June, with Hearts having had only two days to recover from their efforts from Brentford while Celtic had the benefit of a week's rest since their Sunderland matches. Hearts, regarded as fortunate winners in their first round, were not expected to have much chance against a confident Celtic team, the same eleven who put out

Sunderland, Matt Lynch and Malcolm McDonald continuing on the right wing.

Another 48,000 were present to see the all Scottish affair and a rejuvenated Hearts team, showing no sign of their exertions only 48 hours previously, gave a very good account of themselves. In fact for 70 or so minutes, they were the better team and the fact that Celtic's two outstanding players were goalkeeper Joe Kennaway and centre-half Willie Lyon is perhaps significant. In the first half, Hearts hit the bar and had a goal disallowed for off-side; early in the second, they had what looked like a good penalty claim turned down after a foul by Bobby Hogg. Midway through the second half though, came the turning point in the match. A cross by Matt Lynch was diverted into the middle by John Divers and Johnny Crum hooked the ball in from six yards or so, the Hearts goalkeeper getting his hands to the ball but unable to stop it going into the net. From then on, Celtic's confidence grew, they took a tighter grip on the match and might have scored one or two more if Hearts keeper Waugh had not been in such outstanding form.

Aberdeen 2 Everton 3

On Monday 6 June, the second semi-final went ahead, in front of a rather disappointing 20,000. This turned out to be a keenly contested affair which Everton narrowly won 3-2 although Aberdeen could be regarded as unlucky losers.

The English side scored within the first minute, Aberdeen equalised six minutes later and went ahead just before the interval. Everton equalised in 51 minutes, then scored what proved to be the winner in 56 minutes, Joe Mercer making a strong run down the right and sending over a perfect cross which Tommy Lawton met with power and precision.

The Empire Exhibition Cup Final – Celtic v. Everton

That set up a classic clash for the final, a combination which the organisers had hoped for, a Scottish team against an English one. One worry for all those fans of good football was the state of the Ibrox pitch. The weather had been wet for the fortnight of the tournament and the ground was soggy and rather cut up.

Biased as the Scottish press may have been, there was keen optimism that Celtic would triumph. The skill of Everton was much admired, although Rangers were so bad in their first round tie that the English side's level could not be truly assessed and it was generally agreed that they were a shade fortunate to beat Aberdeen. Celtic, on the other hand, seemed to be running into form at the right time. Their Silver Jubilee Dinner was due to be held the Wednesday after the final and the team were determined that the new trophy would occupy a special place at that function. Celtic's only selection problem was at outside-right, the choice between a fit again Jimmy Delaney or his very capable replacement in the two previous matches, Matt Lynch. In the end, Willie Maley plumped for Delaney's speed and direct approach. Everton were also forced into a change in that same position. Ex-Ranger Torry Gillick failed a fitness test, his place going to England international Geldard, another speedster. He would be well supported by the skill of ex-Celt Willie Cook at right-back and the industry of Joe Mercer at right-half and had the perfect target for his crosses in Tommy Lawton, centre-forward. The teams were:

Celtic: Kennaway, Hogg, Morrison; Geatens, Lyon, Patterson, Delaney, McDonald; Crum; Divers and Murphy.

Everton: Sagar, Cook and Greenhalgh; Mercer, Jones, Thomson; Geldard, Cunliffe, Lawton, Stevenson and Boyes

There had been one or two complaints, especially from unsuccessful English teams, about the quality of Scots referees. We will never know of course whether the organisers allowed this to influence their choice but the man in charge was an Englishman, Mr Thomson of Northumberland.

Empire Exhibition Cup Final Programme. Everton proved strong opponents all through the competition, with ex-Celtic player Willie Cook at right-back, the industry of Joe Mercer at left-half, the skill of Torry Gillick at outside-right and the power of Tommy Lawton at centre-forward.

Celtic: Kennaway, Hogg, Morrison, Geatons, Lyon, Paterson, Delaney, MacDonald, Crum, Divers, Murphy.

Everton: Sagar, Cook, Greenhaugh, Mercer, Jones, Thomson, Gillick, Cunliffe, Lawton, Stevenson, Boyes.

Another variation of the League Championship winning team in 1937–38. Back row, left to right: Geatons, Hogg, Kennaway, Morrison, Paterson, Murphy. Front row: Delaney, Divers, Lyon, Carruth, Crum.

Joe Carruth was feted as the new McGrory, but although a great trier, he never held down a permanent place in the teams of the period. Still, 30 goals in 42 matches was a very good performance.

The final on 10 June, watched by 82,000 people, turned out to be a classic, a close contest played at a tremendous pace, in which each and every player rose to the occasion.

As often happens in such a case, those defending (and in the comfortable position of facing the play) allow their opponents room for nice passes and quick attacks but shut the space down in the vital areas, so few goals are scored. For Celtic, Joe Kennaway was superb; Willie Lyon outstanding. In the Everton team, the main area was the half-back line of Mercer, Jones and Thomson, strong in positional play with good distribution.

Play ranged from end to end in hectic fashion, but after 90 minutes the game was still goalless, so the teams went into extra time. The deadlock was eventually broken in the 96th minute, Johnny Crum scoring with a well-placed shot. In his excitement, Crum ran behind the goal and did a little dance while waving to the Celtic fans, an action which more than one newspaper correspondent commented on unfavourably the following day! Everton did get the ball in the net near the end, a header by left-winger Boyes, but he was clearly in an off-side position and the goal was chalked off.

Scorer of the winning goal in extra-time in the Empire Exhibition Cup Final, Johnny Crum joined Celtic in 1932 from Ashfield. Smallish, and on the light side, he nevertheless gave his all for the club, scoring 88 goals in 211 appearances.

It was a fine win by Celtic, who thus added the Empire Exhibition Trophy to the League Championship and the Charity Cup as their honours for the season. The trophy was presented by Lord Elgin to Captain Willie Lyon on a special platform erected in the grandstand enclosure and the players received their miniatures there as well. In retrospect, the tournament had been a great success. The weather had not been perfect but the players were enthusiastic, the majority of the matches had been tense and exciting, the final had been a fitting finale and a total of 334,000 had attended. From a Celtic viewpoint, of course, the important matter was that the team had risen to the occasion in distinguished company and brought back to Parkhead a distinctive – and permanent – addition to the Trophy Room.

CHAPTER NINE
'Greetin' Malky' – Malcolm MacDonald

Malcolm MacDonald was born in Glasgow in October 1913. After playing as a juvenile with Linwood St Convals, then St Anthony's for one year as a junior, he joined Celtic in March 1932. He was signed as a centre-half but was a very talented, all-round footballer, part of the team which won the League in 1935–1936 and the Empire Exhibition Trophy of 1938. Malcolm received several war-time caps for Scotland and has always been recognised as one of the finest, pure footballers to pull on the hooped jersey. During his career he made 147 appearances, scoring 37 goals. Malcolm now lives in Ardrossan, on the Ayrshire coast.

Q When you first arrived at Celtic Park in 1932 the manager was Willie Maley. How did you get on with him?

A I was terrified of him. Terrified. He would come in occasionally to training to keep an eye on us. Sometimes when they were dishing out the wages on a Friday, my wages wouldn't be there. I would then get a message from the manager's secretary that he wanted to see me. I would go in and he would be sitting behind his desk with an air of surprise.

'What can I do for you?', he would say.

'I'm in for my wages'.

'Oh! Certainly', and he would make a great play of looking for my wages and then he would say

'Oh! By the way, Malcolm' and then pick you up on something. He was very shrewd. He would pick an incident I couldn't put up any defence against and he would not let me mention any incidents which were in my favour. He would always finish then in exactly the same way,

'Malcolm, if you don't do as I tell you, you won't be here long.' But he wouldn't tell me what to do – he only told me what not to do.

Q Could you have a close relationship with him?

A Oh no, it was more of a headmaster/pupil type of thing.

Q Did Maley take the training?

A No, but he would come down to the bottom of the tunnel a lot of the time and speak to the trainer.

Q Who was the trainer?

A Jimmy McMenemy and then later Alec Dowdalls.

Q What sort of training did you do? Did you train with a ball?

Malcolm MacDonald.

A No, you didn't get a ball. Just running. You got a ball if you managed to pinch one by yourself!

Q Did you use a stopper centre-half as many teams did at that time?

A No, we didn't use a stopper centre-half but my job playing centre-half was to mark the centre-forward. If I moved away, I asked one of the other players to pick him up and I marked another man.

Q Did you practice free-kicks or corner-kicks?

A No, not really. If you did you didn't practice it as a team, maybe just two or three players would work things out.

Q When you first arrived there, what was the team and how did you get on with them?

A Well, Joe Kennaway was in goals, always a good keeper, but he also always had an excuse when he lost a goal. Peter McGonagle was a hard man. I don't know how many times he was going to kick my bloody arse! The same boy would have done it too! Peter Wilson was my mentor. He would criticise me but would do it in a logical way. He would say 'If you lose the ball there, Malcolm, you will put us all in trouble'. He would remember just what happened and remind me afterwards.

My biggest problem, and this sounds bigheaded and I don't mean it to be, is that I was a good two-footed footballer. I would dribble in areas where other, maybe less skilful defenders, would just put the ball away.

Jimmy McStay was, how do you say, a passive centre-half; he didn't push himself, he was quite content to stop anything coming through. He wasn't the type to come forward and combine with his inside-forward. Happier in defence. Bobby Hogg was the same.

Chic Geatons was also defensive but a very talented player and we worked well together. They were extraordinarily good to me. You must remember I was still a schoolboy when I started but they would criticise me in the right way.

McGrory? Jimmy took me under his wing because I came out of St Rochs, same as himself. He wasn't a good manipulator of the ball; they used to say that when McGrory started dribbling, he blinded himself with ignorance; but he was a good positional player. He was great at taking the man away and leaving space for somebody else.

Charlie Napier; Charlie was a comedian but he was a good player, too. He liked to take free-kicks and always took them the same way. He put the ball down, stepped back a couple of paces then walked forward and blasted the thing. From the minute it left his foot, it was in the back of the net. I was lucky meeting all these good players. They cosseted me but at the same time, they got on to me.

My first game was at outside-left (against Partick Thistle on 30 April 1932), and I was taking a corner-kick, thinking about dropping the ball just in front of goal, taking it with my right foot on the left wing and curling it in. McGrory said 'I don't want these, I want them swinging out and landing just about the penalty spot'.

(Author's note: This was in many ways a tribute to Malcolm MacDonald. Here was an experienced player telling a novice to change feet when taking the corners. Obviously Malcolm had two good feet – and McGrory knew it.)

Q Unfortunately, the team was not always successful at this time?

A Frankly, they were just an ordinary team.

Q Willie Lyon came in as centre-half in 1935 and solidified the defence. It looks as though he was an out-and-out stopper?

A Oh yes, he was, Willie couldn't play football but he could stop.

Q Had the forward-line started to change at the time?

A Yes, the forward-line when I started was, Bert Thomson, Alec Thomson, McGrory, Scarff and Napier. Peter (Scarff) lost his life early; he was a good player with whom I got on well. We had something in common. I had played for Linwood St Convals as a juvenile and he came from Linwood – that was a common start for us. Of the Thomsons, Bert was a fine player but a poor trainer and in the end fell out with Willie Maley. The poor man died young (in 1937 aged 30). Alec Thomson was an older player when I arrived. If he stood sideways you couldn't see him. He was always on at me, 'Malky, son, you cannae dae that!'

Q When Celtic played Aberdeen in the Cup Final in 1937 it was the biggest ever attendance but you were not in the team. Were you injured?

A I don't think so. I can't remember why I wasn't in. Willie Buchan took my place, just before he went to Blackpool.

Q The next season, of course, was the Exhibition Cup Final. The forward line had changed a bit by this time?

A Yes, although the defence was much the same, Bobby Hogg – dead keen and fit at right-back. Jock Morrison was at left-back. He didn't have much skill but was just an old-fashioned back of the time. No left foot, but that didn't stop him. He used to get on to me when I was having a wee dribble in the penalty area. He used to come after me when I did that and say 'Malky, Malky' and give me a mouthful!

George Patterson – he and I formed a great friendship as we arrived at roughly the same time. Jimmy Delaney was very direct. He could catch pigeons but you had to play to him or in front of him, seldom with him. He was an out-and-out winger, as was Frank Murphy. John Crum played up front. He was a fly wee man. He was great at dragging centre-halfs out of the middle and leaving space for me and others. I was the one who played the deeper role and I was more of a defensive player. Johnny Divers was the one who played up. He had good height and was good in the air. I was hopeless in the air. Frank Murphy was another good player but he never forced himself on the play. When he wasn't there, we missed him but he just did things so naturally that you just took him for granted.

Q Willie Maley went out in 1940 and Jimmy McStay came in. Did that make a difference?

A It didn't differ much, we just had a different man in control. It didn't alter the team any. The format was the same, the training never varied.

Q How did the war affect football?

A It was a very difficult time. We didn't know from week to week just what the team was. Some players were in the forces, some in reserved occupations; and of course Celtic didn't play any English stars.

Q Why were Rangers so successful at this time?

A Well, Struth made a difference and I think they took war-time football much more seriously than we did.

Q In 1945 Jimmy McGrory came in for Jimmy McStay? Were either of these guys really allowed to manage?

A Oh! I think that the Board made its presence felt. They took advantage of the fact that they did not have a say when Old Man Maley was there. Once he went away, they took the chance to impose themselves on the manager such as not agreeing with him in certain selections – that sort of thing.

Q Which of the Board would have interfered most?

A Well, White was Chairman with Colgan and Shaughnessey. The Colonel (Shaughnessey), he was, well, I don't know what he was like in the Boardroom, but he was a nondescript sort of a guy. He was an awfully nice man. You couldn't fall out with him. No matter what he said to you, it would be said in such a way that you couldn't take offence at it.

Q Did they ever come into the dressing room?

A Oh yes, they would come in and they all had their favourites. The older players, for instance, like Alec Thomson, Jimmy McGrory and Peter McGonagle, they would go to the Directors and discuss the game man-to-man. The players would be criticised but they would pick up from the conversation something that they could use, maybe a complaint about the way we were playing for instance, and from there it went round the team.

Q If the manager did not say very much, how did you know what to do in a game? Did you discuss it amongst yourselves?

A He didn't discuss that sort of thing, for example, how to play. He only discussed what you were doing wrong.

Q At the Exhibition Cup Final, for instance, would someone have been to see Everton?

A No, you had to find out for yourself just what type of players you were playing against. You didn't know beforehand what your opponent did. There was just a player in front of you and you got on with the job and he got on with his.

Q Did the condition of Celtic Park deteriorate during the war?

A Yes, it did in a way but I always felt anyway that the spectators were too far away behind the goal. It was fine along the touchline. The pitch, though, was always in a good state. All the training was done behind the goals, there was no other place to use.

Q You are obviously an intelligent man and everyone agrees that you were an exceptional player, so did you ever wonder why you were not as successful as Rangers?

A Well, they were more physical than us. Our forward-line was slight, we had to play football. Any high-balls were left to John Divers. We tried to play in triangles. It was an unwritten law; then later that changed to squares. They played a more direct game, were very strong at the back, very physical.

Q Was there any player at the time who probably deserved more praise than he received?

A Yes, Frank Murphy. Frank was a quiet lad, never flaunted his ability but was always there. He never got into arguments about anything but just made his presence felt. You only realised his worth when he was missing. Somebody would say that they heard a good piece of advice or information and we would ask 'Who said that?' The answer would be Frank Murphy.

Q How good a player was Malcolm MacDonald?

A Oh! Greetin' Malky! I don't think I had seen Celtic play until I had signed for them. I was just a supporter. I was good with my feet, I suppose, with both of them. And even if I do say it myself, I was a good positional player. You must remember that the experienced players took up all the right positions and I would just fill in where required. Their answer was, if we had the ball the opposition didn't have it, so 'just be careful with your passing, Malky!'

Q Malcolm, you were fourteen years at Celtic Park, do you look back on it as an enjoyable time?

A Oh yes, I enjoyed the whole time. When I arrived I was a young boy and the older players were good to me. Then, later on, I was the experienced player helping all the wee boys. But they were all good lads and Celtic Park was a great place to play football.

CHAPTER TEN (1939–1946)
The Nation at War –
Celtic in Turmoil

WITH THE WAR CLOUDS showing above the horizon, season 1939–1940 began in an atmosphere of some uncertainty. A bad start at Aberdeen was followed by a good win against Hearts at home, when the forward line showed in glimpses just what they could do. A week later, though, Aberdeen repeated their win by the same score at Celtic Park and gloom set in again. The following two matches – at Cowdenbeath and home to Clyde – finished in victories for Celtic; but the day after the Clyde match, 3 September 1939, war was declared.

RESULTS IN 1939–1940		
	H	A
Aberdeen	1-3	1-3
Clyde	1-0	
Cowdenbeath	2-1	
Hearts	2-0	

The following day, an edict was issued stating that professional football, along with all other forms of mass entertainment, was to be abandoned. Players' contracts would be suspended, but registrations would remain valid. In simple terms, no money for the players – but they were still tied to their clubs. As the days passed, and the authorities realised that there would be no mass bombing campaign in cities, a relaxation in the original ban was permitted. Football matches could take place but only on Saturdays and public holidays. They must be confined to regional and district groupings; while crowds could not exceed 8,000, or, for large stadia, 15,000. The Scottish League and Scottish Cup competitions were abandoned for the duration of the war but the Glasgow and Charity Cups, both local tournaments, were allowed to continue. Celtic were allocated to the West division of the Regional Leagues set up by the Scottish League management committee along with fifteen others, the clubs being allowed to pay their players £2 a week and use the services of any Anglo-Scots returned or stationed here during the war period.

The new set-up began on 21 October with a defeat by Hamilton Academicals at Celtic Park, the first of 15 in this season. Frankly, it was a difficult, if not to say farcical time, to attempt to run any club. Some players like Willie Lyon (Scots Guards), Oliver Anderson (Royal Artillery), Willie Gallagher (Royal Engineers) and John Watters (Navy) enlisted during that season. Others were caught by the 'call-up' which was spread over successive age-groups, while those in the yards or factories were working longer hours for the war effort and often turned up for a match straight from work. Managers were never sure just which players would be available and were often scratching round for names to fill the places of those who failed to appear. Nevertheless, it was a very poor season for Celtic, finishing 13th in the table.

1939–1940 WEST REGIONAL LEAGUE

	P	W	D	L	F	A	Pts	Position
Rangers	30	22	4	4	72	36	48	1st
Celtic	30	9	6	15	55	61	24	13th

The league was divided into East and West sections with sixteen teams – Airdrie, Albion Rovers, Ayr United, Celtic, Clyde, Dumbarton, Hamilton, Kilmarnock, Morton, Motherwell, Partick Thistle, Queen's Park, Queen of the South, Rangers, St Mirren and Third Lanark – all in the West section. After six months' experience of wartime football, Cowdenbeath folded from lack of money and by May 1940, eight of the 38 pre-war League clubs were out of action. To help meet the ongoing costs of the clubs, a five per cent levy was put on the gates of the others and a special fund set up.

Gates were generally poor at this time and to give them a boost, a cup competition was started, the first round of which was to be played on a home and away basis, the Club with the greater number of goals going through.

	Celtic	4	Raith Rovers	2
	Raith Rovers	3	Celtic	0
Aggregate:	Celtic	4	Raith Rovers	5

A New Manager

The really big news that winter, however, came on 1 February 1940, when after 52 years of service, Willie Maley relinquished his post as Secretary/ Manager. His leaving was not voluntary but very definitely at the behest of the Directorate. Maley seems to have been particularly disappointed to not retain the post of Secretary, feeling that he could still have something to contribute to the Club, even at 72 years of age.

The post of Manager was offered to ex-Celtic captain Jimmy McStay, who had been very successful in his first season at Alloa. The new Secretary was Desmond White, the Chairman's son. Unfortunately as is the case in football, the latter post was much more secure than the former. McStay in fact, was quite badly treated by the Celtic Board of Directors in his years in charge, on several counts. Firstly, he had to cope with the break-up of a reasonably

Willie Maley bids farewell to his beloved Parkhead, escorted by Jimmy McMenemy, Willie Loney and Joe Dodds.

talented side. A comparison of the list of retained players for two successive seasons shows the effect of war. Secondly, there was strong evidence that McStay was very much an 'interim' manager. The Board – by this time, consisting of Thomas White, Thomas Colgan, John Shaughnessey, John McKillop and Robert Kelly – seemed split on his appointment, some preferring another former star, Jimmy McGrory. McStay initially got the nod, but as time went on, it would appear that they regarded their choice as the wrong one and inclined towards McGrory. McStay would no doubt be well aware of this, with a resulting blow both to his esteem and to his relationship with the Board.

Thirdly, the Directorate did not seem to take war-time football seriously and flatly refused to allow McStay to use top players usually based in England but stationed in Scotland. Perhaps the biggest mistake was not to allow Matt Busby to play with the Club. He did offer his services to Celtic and manager McStay was only too delighted to accept the offer, fully aware of the benefits such a personality would bring, but the Board refused and Busby turned out instead for Hibs. This lack of interest in war-time football was in direct contrast to Rangers' attitude. Their manager, Bill Struth, thought that clubs should be fully committed to sport at such a time so that

Willie Maley, just before he 'relinquished' his post as secretary/manager, with King George VI in Glasgow.

their support received a boost to morale by their success. Rangers won every league open to them during the war and played their reserve team in the North-Eastern Section to help make it financially viable.

CELTIC PLAYERS 1939–40

NAME	YEAR JOINED	FIRST CLUB
Oliver Anderson	1937	Arthurlie
James Birrell	1938	Blairhall Colliery
James Campbell	1939	Petershill
Joseph Carruth	1936	Petershill
John Crum	1932	Ashfield
Michael Davitt	1935	St Francis
James Delaney	1934	Cleland
John Divers	1933	Renfrew Juniors
John Doyle	1936	Dublin Bohemians
Robert Duffy	1936	Lochee Harp
Chas Geatons	1928	Lochgelly Celtic
Robert Hogg	1931	Royal Albert
John Kelly	1939	Arthurlie
John Kelly	1939	Shawfield Juniors
Jas Kennaway	1939	Fall River, USA
Matthew Lynch	1935	St Anthony's
William Lyon	1935	Rob Roy
John Morrison	1938	Croy Celtic
Andrew Mullen	1937	Port Glasgow Juniors
Francis Murphy	1933	Croy Celtic
James McDonald	1939	Blairhall Colliery
Malcolm MacDonald	1932	St Anthony's
Joseph McLauchlin	1939	Blairhall Colliery
Hugh O'Neill	1938	Blairhall Colliery
Kinniard Ouchterlonie	1939	Lochee Harp
George Paterson	1932	Dunipace Juniors
James Shields	1939	Arthurlie
Thomas Paterson	1939	Petershill
John Watters	1936	St Aloysius College

Four all-time greats: Jimmy Quinn, Willie Maley, Jimmy McGrory, Patsy Gallagher.

The initial Regional League only lasted that one season of 1939–1940 before the Scottish Football League brought it to a close. Attendances had been poor, probably because no team news could be given until kick-off in an era when teams were announced the day before. At their AGM in June 1940, it was decided to suspend league competition until further notice, although there was nothing to stop clubs forming a competition of their own. Accordingly, 16 clubs got together to form the new 'South Scottish League' which began on 10 August 1940. The Charity and Glasgow Cup competitions were allowed to continue during the war, but Celtic's record in them during this first year of the war was equally disappointing.

1939–1940 GLASGOW CUP

	Queen's Park	(H)	2-2
Replay	Queen's Park	(A)	0-1

1939–1940 CHARITY CUP

Third Lanark	(H)	3-2
Rangers	(A)	1-5

1940–1941 SOUTHERN LEAGUE

	P	W	D	L	F	A	Pts	Position
Rangers	30	21	4	5	79	33	46	1st
Celtic	30	14	6	10	48	40	34	5th

The season started on 10 August 1941 with a 2-2 draw against Hamilton Accies at Parkhead but from then on the team gave a repetition of the previous year's performance. By November, only 12 goals had been scored in 13 matches. Admittedly, Celtic were still without the services of the injured Delaney and had lost players like Paterson and Milne to the forces. By Christmas, though, play had improved and a 3-2 win over Rangers in the Ne'erday fixture set the standard for the latter half of the season, during which they lost only two matches.

CELTIC PLAYERS 1940–41

Name	Year Joined	First Club
John Crum	1932	Ashfield
James Delaney	1934	Cleland
John Divers	1933	Renfrew Juniors
Harry Ferrier	1940	Barnsley
Cornelius Ferguson	1940	Alloa
Charles Geatons	1928	Lochgelly Celtic
George Gillan	1940	Alloa
Robert Hogg	1931	Royal Albert
George Johnstone	1940	Aberdeen
John Kelly	1939	Arthurlie
Matthew Lynch	1935	St Anthony's
Patrick MacAuley	1940	Douglas Hawthorn
Malcolm MacDonald	1932	St Anthony's
Alex. Miller	1940	Preston North End
John Morrison	1930	Croy Celtic
Francis Murphy	1933	Croy Celtic
George Paterson	1932	Dunipace Juniors
William Waddell	1939	Aberdeen

Only 18 players listed compared to 29 the previous year.

A Scottish League Cup competition followed the league season, 16 teams divided in four sections, the winners of the sections to meet in the semi-finals.

1940–1941 SCOTTISH LEAGUE CUP

Airdrie	1	Celtic	2
Celtic	3	Motherwell	2
Celtic	2	Partick Thistle	4
Celtic	3	Airdrie	1
Motherwell	4	Celtic	2
Partick Thistle	0	Celtic	1

LEAGUE CUP POSITION

	P	W	D	L	F	A	Pts	Position
Celtic	6	4	0	2	13	12	8	1st

LEAGUE CUP SEMI-FINAL

SF	Hearts	2	Celtic	0

A Summer Cup was also instituted that year, each match played on a home and away basis.

SUMMER CUP

1st Round	Celtic	2	Partick Thistle	1
	Partick Thistle	0	Celtic	2
Aggregate	Celtic	4	Partick Thistle	1
2nd Round	Celtic	1	Motherwell	2
	Motherwell	2	Celtic	1
Aggregate	Celtic	2	Motherwell	4

1940–1941 GLASGOW CUP

	Queen's Park	(H)	3-2	
	Clyde	(H)	1-0	
Final	Rangers	(Hampden)	1-0	28/10/40

The Glasgow Cup. This trophy was first put up for competition in season 1887–88, when it was won by Cambuslang. Even during the two World Wars, the Glasgow Cup maintained its status. By the 1970s, however, as fixture lists grew with European competition, the big-name clubs were more reluctant to take part and in some years, no tournament was held. Since 1989–90, the competition has been limited to clubs' under-18 teams, a move which has proved very popular.

A mixed first-half was only notable for a magnificent save by goalkeeper George Johnstone at the top left-hand corner of his goal from Alec Venters. The goal which mattered came 15 minutes into the second-half, George Gillan raced on to a through ball by Johnny Crum and scored from just inside the penalty area. The Rangers players protested that he had been off-side but the linesman and referee were not to be moved. Celtic's man of the match was undoubtedly Malcolm McDonald.

Team: Johnstone; Hogg, McCulloch; McDonald, Waddell (Aberdeen), Paterson; Kelly, Conway; Crum; Gillan, Murphy.

1940–1941 CHARITY CUP

Queen's Park	(A)	5-3
Partick Thistle	(H)	1-2

1941–1942 SOUTHERN LEAGUE

	P	W	D	L	F	A	Pts	Position
Rangers	30	22	4	4	97	35	48	1st
Celtic	30	15	9	6	69	50	39	3rd

This was a better performance by Celtic, in spite of players coming and going. Unfortunately the season had started in the worst possible way with trouble in the first Old Firm match of the season, at Ibrox on 6 September 1941. Rangers were two up just before the interval when Celtic were awarded a penalty for a violent push on Jimmy Delaney which sent him into the net. The referee (Mr W. Webb from Glasgow) pointed to the spot but was immediately surrounded by protesting Rangers players. When order was restored, Frank Murphy missed the penalty, amid disturbances on the West terracing, which continued into the second half.

This led the SFA, on 17 December, to close Celtic Park for one month. Celtic felt hard done by, as the match had been held at Ibrox, but newspapers pointed out that the idea of clubs being responsible for the conduct of their fans had been noted and agreed at a meeting back in 1922 between the SFA, (President Tom White of Celtic) and the Scottish League (President Willie Maley). These incidents had occurred on the West terracing or 'Celtic end' at Ibrox and by the dictates of the 1922 meeting, a ban seemed reasonable. Rangers, in fact, were also rapped for the dissent of their players

1941–1942 SCOTTISH LEAGUE CUP

Queen's Park	1	Celtic	2
Celtic	4	Hibs	3
Celtic	1	Hamilton	0
Celtic	6	Queen's Park	2
Hibs	1	Celtic	0
Hamilton	1	Celtic	2

LEAGUE CUP POSITION

	P	W	D	L	F	A	Pts	Position
Celtic	6	5	0	1	15	7	10	1st

LEAGUE CUP SEMI-FINAL

SF	Rangers 2	Celtic 0

CELTIC PLAYERS 1941–42

NAME	YEAR JOINED	FIRST CLUB
Austin Collier	1941	Partick Thistle
John Conway	1940	Glencraig Celtic
William Corbett	1941	Maryhill
John Crum	1932	Ashfield
James Delaney	1934	Stoneyburn Juniors
John Divers	1933	Renfrew Juniors
Harry Dornan	1941	Kilmarnock
Robert Hogg	1931	Royal Albert
John Hunter	1941	Kilmarnock
Matthew Lynch	1935	St Anthony's
Patrick McAuley	1940	Douglas Hawthorn
James McDonald	1939	Blairhall Colliery
Malcolm MacDonald	1932	St Anthony's
Joseph McLaughlin	1939	Blairhall Colliery
Francis Murphy	1933	Croy Celtic
James Nelson	1941	Douglas Water Primrose
John Riley	1941	Perthshire
William Waddell	1940	Aberdeen
George Paterson	1932	Dunipace Juniors

1941–1942 SUMMER CUP

1st Round	Celtic	2	Hibs	5
	Hibs	0	Celtic	1
Aggregate	Celtic	3	Hibs	5

1941–1942 GLASGOW CUP

Rangers (Hampden) 2-3

1941–1942 CHARITY CUP

Third Lanark (A) 2-0
Rangers (Hampden) 1-2

1942–1943 SOUTHERN LEAGUE

	P	W	D	L	F	A	Pts	Position
Rangers	30	22	6	2	89	23	50	1st
Celtic	30	10	8	12	61	76	28	10th

Another disappointing season for Celtic, although the team was very inexperienced. With stars like Lyon, Milne, Corbett, Paterson, Airlie, Gallagher and Paton in the forces, and both Johnny Crum and John Divers

Jimmy Delaney spent 13 years at Celtic Park, where his attacking skills made him a legend with the fans. A bad injury to his arm kept him out of the game for two years but he came back, first to Celtic, then to several other clubs with which he achieved cup success.

Scottish Cup winner, with Celtic in 1937; FA Cup winner with Manchester United in 1948; Irish FA Cup winner with Derry City in 1954; FAI Cup finalist with Cork Athletic in 1956.

moved to Morton, Celtic were forced to play some boys still in their teens. The biggest problem was the loss of three experienced centre-halves – Lyon, Waddell and Corbett.

In the New Years match against Rangers, when Celtic lost 8-1, Malcolm McDonald was ordered off for disputing the referee's decision, to be followed five minutes later by Matt Lynch for the same offence. Both players were suspended; McDonald for the rest of the season, but Lynch only until 27 March.

1942–1943 SOUTHERN LEAGUE CUP

Celtic	2	Hibs	1
Rangers	3	Celtic	0
Celtic	2	St Mirren	0
Hibs	2	Celtic	1
Celtic	0	Rangers	2
St Mirren	5	Celtic	1

LEAGUE CUP POSITION

	P	W	D	L	F	A	Pts	Position
Celtic	6	2	0	4	6	13	4	3rd

Celtic failed to quality for the quarter final.

CELTIC PLAYERS 1942–43

NAME	YEAR JOINED	FIRST CLUB
William Corbett	1941	Maryhill
John Crum	1932	Ashfield
James Cully	1941	Alloa
James Delaney	1934	Stoneyburn Juniors
Harry Dornan	1941	Kilmarnock
Robert Fisher	1941	New Herrington
Robert Hogg	1931	Royal Albert
Matthew Lynch	1935	St Anthony's
Patrick MacAuley	1940	Douglas Hawthorn
James McDonald	1939	Blairhall Colliery
Malcolm MacDonald	1932	St Anthony's
Joseph McLauchlin	1939	Blairhall Colliery
John McPhail	1940	Strathclyde
William Miller	1942	Maryhill Harp
Francis Murphy	1933	Croy Celtic
James Nelson	1940	Douglas Water Primrose
John Paton	1942	Dennistoun Waverley
John Riley	1941	Perthshire

Note the names of John McPhail and Willie Miller appearing for the first time.

1942–1943 SUMMER CUP

1st Round	Motherwell	2	Celtic	2
	Celtic	3	Motherwell	2
Aggregate	Celtic	5	Motherwell	4
2nd Round	Celtic	0	Rangers	4
	Rangers	4	Celtic	1
Aggregate	Celtic	1	Rangers	8

1942–1943 GLASGOW CUP

Rangers	(A)	1-2

1942–1943 CHARITY CUP

	Queen's Park	(H)	3-0		
	Clyde	(H)	3-1		
Final	Third Lanark	(Hampden)	3-0	25,000	22/05/43

Team: Miller; Hogg and Dornan; Lynch, McLaughlin, Corbett; Delaney, McPhail; Rae; McGinley, Long.

In terms of team balance and forward superiority, Celtic were streets ahead. Third Lanark defended courageously but never threatened in attack. Celtic were one up at half-time, a fine combined movement ending with a well- placed shot by Charley McGinley.

Thirds had lost their captain Blair after 30 minutes and although they started the second-half more brightly, Celtic soon took control once more.

Goals by McGinley again and then a spectacular effort by Hugh Long, after a run in which he beat four opponents, meant there was no way back for Third Lanark. This was the 24th time in its history Celtic had won the Charity Cup.

1943–1944 SOUTHERN LEAGUE							
	P	W	D	L	F	A	Pts	Position
Rangers	30	23	4	3	90	27	50	1st
Celtic	30	18	7	5	71	43	43	2nd

John Divers — the second of three players with this name to grace Celtic Park. John was highly regarded in his years at Parkhead. He had two good feet and a silky pass, and his 48 goals in 82 matches testifies that he could score as well.

This was a better season for Celtic in the league although there was a seven point gap between the two leaders at the end. John Divers had returned to Celtic from Morton and gave a boost to the forward line; while Jimmy Delaney played as well as ever on the right wing, but the team's failings can be seen on the statistics. For all their good outfield play, there was nobody to put the ball in the net on a consistent basis; while, at the back, 43 goals lost in 30 matches would tend to suggest the middle of the defence was fairly suspect. Even so, the performances were better than in previous years and the large crowds which rolled up were very appreciative.

1943–1944 SCOTTISH LEAGUE CUP

Celtic	8	Hamilton	1
Falkirk	1	Celtic	3
Partick Thistle	0	Celtic	1
Hamilton	0	Celtic	3
Celtic	3	Falkirk	0
Celtic	6	Partick Thistle	0

LEAGUE CUP POSITION

	P	W	D	L	F	A	Pts	Position
Celtic	6	6	0	0	24	2	12	1st

LEAGUE CUP SEMI-FINAL

SF	Celtic	2	Rangers	4	(Hampden)	87,121	28/04/44

CELTIC PLAYERS 1943–44

NAME	YEAR JOINED	FIRST CLUB
A. Boden	1943	Duntocher Boys' Guild
William Corbett	1941	Maryhill
James Cully	1941	Alloa
James Delaney	1934	Stoneyburn Juniors
James Devine	1943	Mossend Boy's Guild
Harry Dornan	1941	Kilmarnock
John Gribbon	1943	Duntocher Boys' Guild
Robert Hogg	1931	Royal Albert
F. Kelly	1943	Renton Boys' Guild
H. Long	1942	Maryhill Harp
Matthew Lynch	1935	St Anthony's
Patrick MacAuley	1940	Douglas Hawthorn
H. McCluskey	1942	St Annes Boys' Guild
Malcolm McDonald	1932	St Anthony's
P. McDonald	1942	Shawfield Juniors
C. McGinlay	1943	Clydebank Boys' Guild
J. McGowan	1942	St Bride's BG & Armadale
J. McHugh	1943	Coatbridge St Patrick's
Joseph McLauchlin	1939	Blairhall Colliery
John McPhail	1940	Strathclyde
J. Mallan	1942	Pollok
William Miller	1942	Maryhill Harp
George Paterson	1932	Dunipace Juniors
John Paton	1942	Dennistoun Waverley
J. Rae	1922	Arthurlie

1943–1944 SUMMER CUP
Celtic did not take part

1943–1944 GLASGOW CUP

Partick Thistle	(H)	1-3

1943–1944 CHARITY CUP

Queen's Park	(A)	4-1
Clyde	(H)	1-4

1944–1945 SOUTHERN LEAGUE

	P	W	D	L	F	A	Pts	Position
Rangers	30	23	3	4	88	27	49	1st
Celtic	30	20	2	8	70	42	42	2nd

Almost the same statistics and the same story as the previous year. Having won their first four matches, Celtic then lost six from their next fourteen. The team was forever being chopped and changed to find the right combination, and from early December went on a good unbeaten run of 17 matches, including a victory over Rangers on New Year's day at Ibrox.

1944–1945 SOUTHERN LEAGUE CUP

Clyde	0	Celtic	0
Celtic	3	Falkirk	2
Partick Thistle	0	Celtic	1
Celtic	1	Clyde	1
Falkirk	1	Celtic	0
Celtic	1	Partick Thistle	2

LEAGUE CUP POSITION

	P	W	D	L	F	A	Pts	Position
Celtic	6	2	2	2	6	6	6	2nd

Celtic failed to qualify for the semi-final.

1944–1945 SUMMER CUP

1st Round	Albion Rovers	1	Celtic	1
	Celtic	4	Albion Rovers	2
Aggregate	Celtic	5	Albion Rovers	3
2nd Round	Bye			

SUMMER CUP SEMI-FINAL

SF	Celtic	0	Hearts	2	(Tynecastle)

1944–1945 GLASGOW CUP

	Third Lanark	(A)		2-1	
Final	Rangers	(Hampden)		2-3	07/10/44

CELTIC PLAYERS 1944–45

NAME	YEAR JOINED	FIRST CLUB
James Delaney	1934	Stoneyburn Juniors
James Devine	1943	Mossend Boys' Guild
J. Divers	1933	Renfrew Juniors
R. Evans	1944	St Anthony's
J. Gallacher	1943	Armadale
Robert Hogg	1931	Royal Albert
F. Kelly	1943	Renton Boys' Guild
Matthew Lynch	1935	St Anthony's
Patrick MacAuley	1940	Douglas Hawthorn
G. McAloon	1943	Wolverhampton
Malcolm McDonald	1932	St Anthony's
P. McDonald	1942	Shawfield Juniors
C. McGinlay	1943	Clydebank Boys' Guild
J. McGowan	1942	St Bride's BG & Armadale
Joseph McLauchlin	1939	Blairhall Colliery
John McPhail	1940	Strathclyde
J. Mallan	1942	Pollok
William Miller	1942	Maryhill Harp
J. Mulligan	1943	McDonald's Amateurs
R. Quinn	1943	Blantyre Celtic
R. Ugolini	1944	Armadale
A. Young	1944	Steelend Victoria

1944–1945 CHARITY CUP

	Third Lanark	(H)	5-0		
	Partick Thistle	(A)	1 goal 9 corners		
			to 1 goal 2 corners		
Final	Rangers	(Hampden)	1-2	50,000	21/05/45

The Supporters Association

September 1944 seems an unlikely time for a Supporters' Association to be formed. But in the case of Celtic, that is exactly when it occurred. While the Allies were fighting their way up through France and the Americans were pushing up through the Pacific Islands towards Japan, a Celtic fan named Willie Fanning, from Caroline Street in Parkhead wrote a letter to 'Waverley's' column in the *Daily Record*. Willie Fanning was no troublemaker. The 27-year-old was in despair over his team's performances during the war years and wanted an improvement. He felt that a Supporters' Association might help by bringing closer contact between fans, manager and players. His letter ended with these cajoling words, 'Would any Celtic supporters interested in a Supporters Club please write me. All letters will be answered'.

Many letters arrived but only 14 people were interested enough to attend the inaugural meeting at a Church Hall in Chester Street in Shettleston. A Committee was formed, Willie Fanning was chosen as President and Waverley gave the new venture some free publicity in his column. The second meeting in a hall beside Alexandra Parade was packed and had to be adjourned to an open-air site nearby. Shortly afterwards, the Celtic FC Supporters' Association was duly constituted. By late 1946, the Association had built up to 12 branches in Central Scotland, of which the Glasgow branch was by far the largest. Interest in the Assocation kept going, as did the numbers. Just after the Coronation Cup was won in 1953, the Supporters' Association Handbook listed 102 branches, including one in Northern Ireland.

These words were penned during June 1998, upon my return from a visit to the convention of the American Celtic Supporters' Association in Las Vegas, Nevada. As an example of how much the Celtic family has grown, it was announced at their main meeting that the 42nd club in America – in Tampa Bay, Florida – has just been affiliated to the North American Celtic Supporters' Federation!

Setting The Scene

For the first post-war season, the Scottish League re-arranged those clubs which had taken part in the Southern and North-Eastern Leagues plus those which had temporarily folded during the war years. These were grouped into 'A' and 'B' sections, the 'A' section comprising the 16 clubs with the largest drawing power. The 'B' division had 14 clubs and there was a Reserve League of 16 teams (the second elevens of the 'A' division sides).

The guarantee for 'A' division visiting teams was fixed at £100 and it was decided that players should not receive more than £3 per week. The players were very unhappy with this figure, particularly as attendances rose considerably after the war and clubs, naturally, took in more money. Since English players, through their Union, had managed to gain an increase in their wages, Scottish players decided to follow suit.

The 'A' division players formed a Union and appointed delegates to place before the League Management Committee demands for wages of £6 per week. A meeting of club Directors, though, decided to fix the wages at £4 per week, with a £2 bonus for a win and £1 for a draw. The players wanted another meeting but the Scottish League informed them that the Directors' decision was unanimous and binding. There were threats of strike action if the League Management Committee refused to meet them but even when they did, the players received no joy and so the club's terms were met under protest.

1945–1946 SOUTHERN LEAGUE								
	P	W	D	L	F	A	Pts	Position
Rangers	30	22	4	4	85	41	48	1st
Celtic	30	12	11	7	55	44	35	4th

For the 1945–1946 season, Celtic could choose from a list of 29 signed players, with another 13 due to come back from active service. The fans were delighted that normality had returned to the football scene but the fare served up for them was far from successful. Malcolm McDonald had gone to Kilmarnock and John Divers had received a free transfer. Just after New Year in this season, Jimmy Delaney joined Manchester United.

Inconsistency was once more the problem, the team capable of some sparkling form but seldom in every match.

CELTIC PLAYERS 1945–46		
NAME	YEAR JOINED	FIRST CLUB
W. Bolland	1944	Muirkirk Hibs
James Delaney	1934	Stoneyburn Juniors
James Devine	1943	Mossend Boys' Guild
J. Divers	1933	Renfrew Juniors
R. Evans	1944	St Anthony's
G. Ferguson	1945	St Anthony's
J. Gallacher	1943	Armadale
H. Gilmartin	1945	Market Star
J. Gilroy	1945	Market Star
D. Hill	1945	Ashfield Juveniles
Robert Hogg	1931	Royal Albert
C. Kelly	1945	Cambuslang Rangers
F. Kelly	1943	Renton Boys' Guild
A. Kiddie	1945	Dundee Stobswell
T. Kiernan	1945	Albion Rovers
Matthew Lynch	1935	St Anthony's
Patrick MacAuley	1940	Douglas Hawthorn
Malcolm McDonald	1932	St Anthony's
P. McDonald	1942	Shawfield Juniors
C. McGinlay	1943	Clydebank Boys' Guild
H. McLafferty	1945	St Roch's
Joseph McLauchlin	1939	Blairhall Colliery
John McPhail	1940	Strathclyde
J. Mallan	1942	Pollok
William Miller	1942	Maryhill Harp
R. Quinn	1943	Blantyre Celtic
P. Rodgers	1944	Bowhill St Ninian's
R. Ugolini	1944	Armadale
A. Young	1944	Steelend Victoria

1945–1946 SOUTHERN LEAGUE CUP			
Queen's Park	3	Celtic	1
Celtic	4	Clyde	0
Third Lanark	0	Celtic	4
Celtic	2	Queen's Park	0
Clyde	6	Celtic	2
Celtic	1	Third Lanark	1

	P	W	D	L	F	A	Pts	Position
CELTIC	6	3	1	2	14	10	7	2nd

Celtic failed to qualify for the semi-final.

1945–1946 GLASGOW CUP		
Rangers	(A)	1-3

1945–1946 CHARITY CUP		
Rangers	(H)	1-3

Change

If the Celtic fans were disappointed by their team's lack of success in these years, particularly when they were compared to their main rival, then manager Jimmy McStay must have felt worse. From the comments of former players, it is quite apparent that he had little authority over normal managerial concerns and towards the end, he did not even pick the team. After many years of dealing with the autocratic, and at times, irascible Willie Maley, the Board seemed quite determined to have a manager of more malleable temperament, like McStay. They were, though, still wanting to replace him, but handled the matter with a decided lack of tact. The scenario unfolded fairly quickly. In early July 1945, while on holiday with his family at Ayr, McStay read rumours in the papers concerning his impending sacking. On 10 July, reports announced that Jimmy McGrory had met with the Kilmarnock directors to inform them that he was considering another offer. On 15 July, the *Sunday Mail* announced that McGrory is 'as good as at Parkhead'.

In the *Daily Record* of 21 July, Waverley stated that he had been informed (on the QT) that McGrory would start work on 23 July. On that day, Jimmy McStay returned to Celtic Park from his holiday and had a short meeting with Tom White, the Chairman, who asked for his resignation. This was duly given and Jimmy McGrory arrived the following day to take the reins. It was an unfortunate way to do business and a very cruel way to treat a fine former player. As a manager, McStay had received a glowing report from his previous employers at Alloa, but at Parkhead, not only was he in the sometimes impossible position of trying to find and field teams in war-time, he was obviously not given the backing of the Board.

Perhaps McStay might have done better if he had adopted some of Willie Maley's strength and cussedness, but not everyone is built like that and even so, it is doubtful whether his tenure would have lasted any longer as a Board split originally on his appointment had become united in their desire to bring in a new man. As for that new man, it seems ironic that McGrory was of the same diffident personality as his predecessor. No doubt the Celtic fans thought that the man who was such a dazzling hero as a player would bring those talents to his new post. Unfortunately, football management does not always work like that. Even if Jimmy McGrory had been an extrovert, charismatic personality, it seems that the Board wanted to continue to impose its presence on any manager, and he would always do the job with 'Big Brother' not just watching from above, but 'hands on' in his office.

The Victory-in-Europe Cup

At the end of World War Two, the Glasgow Cup Committee, as part of the joyful celebrations, invited the Old Firm to compete for a special trophy with the match proceeds going to charity. Rangers were unable or unwilling to take part, due to their preparation for a Southern League Cup Final against Motherwell, so, at short notice, Queen's Park replaced them.

The teams met at Hampden on 9 May 1945 in warm weather before a crowd of 28,000. The Celtic team was Miller; Hogg, P. McDonald; Lynch, Mallon, McPhail; Paton, M. McDonald; Gallacher; Evans and McLaughlin. Queen's Park proved the more lively side right from kick-off and opened the scoring after 25 minutes. Two minutes later, however, Johnny Paton equalised, after the Queens' defence had been caught out by a simple cross ball. In the second-half, play was fairly even, although the class of Malcolm McDonald was always evident. Nine minutes from the end, Johnny Paton rose to the occasion again when he won the decisive corner-kick off a Queens' defender, which gave Celtic the narrowest of winning margins, by one goal (three corners) to one goal (two corners), so taking the Victory-in-Europe Cup to Parkhead.

The Victory Cup

This trophy was put up to celebrate the end of World War Two after the surrender of Japan and was played over a three-month period at the end of season 1945-46. The first-round matches were two-legged affairs and Celtic started well, crushing St Johnstone 8-2 at Perth, Jackie Gallacher scoring four and Tommy Kiernan a hat-trick. In the second leg, back at Parkhead, the formality turned into a procession of goals, with Celtic winning 5-0, making the aggregate 13-2. From them on, the tournament was a straight knock-out affair and Celtic advanced comfortably to the semi-finals by beating Queen of the South 3-0 at Parkhead, then Raith Rovers 2-0 at Kirkcaldy.

In the semi-final, on 1 June 1946, Celtic faced a strong Rangers team which had already beaten them four times out of four during the season. To the surprise of just about all of the 66,000 present, though, Celtic played very well and held the Light Blues to a 0-0 draw.

In the replay, also at Hampden, on the following Wednesday, Rangers won the toss, chose to have the wind at their backs for the first half and went in

A packed Hampden Park (top) with the North Stand now in place. Attendances like this were common for matches after Second World War, but there was only a crowd of 28,000 the night Celtic beat Queen's Park on corners to take this Victory-in-Europe Cup back to Parkhead.

at the interval 1-0 up, thanks to a Willie Waddell goal. Their changing room was a happy place. Celtic's, by contrast, was bedlam. Several players were furious over some of the referee's decisions; others complained that they could smell liquor on his breath. The captain, George Paterson, even complained to the Celtic officials about it, but play continued. The second-half was chaotic. Jimmy Sirrell – later to become manager of Notts County – received an ankle injury, leaving him limping on the wing. Rangers were then awarded a doubtful penalty when Willie Thornton fell in the box. The protests from Celtic were long and loud; the referee decided to assert his authority. George Paterson and Jimmy Mallan were ordered off, a decision which enraged the Celtic support, several of whom came over the retaining wall to remonstrate with the referee but the police intercepted them and they were ejected. When order was restored, George Young took the kick and scored to give Rangers a 2-0 lead. Shortly afterwards, Jackie Gallacher was injured and carried off, leaving Celtic with only seven fit men to finish the match.

Some days later, the SFA met to consider their response to the referee's report. Not unsurprisingly, Paterson and Mallon were suspended – for three months. That was harsh, but their next decision was illogical. Matt Lynch – who had taken great pains to distance himself from the proceedings, was also suspended, for one month. This decision was taken in spite of his immediate opponent, Jimmy Duncanson, sending a letter to the SFA stating the he and Lynch had been standing off to one side talking while all the furore was going on! The Celtic Board, to the disgust of many fans, did not appeal against all three decisions. They merely contented themselves with a comment in the Handbook: 'History will surely record that indiscretions in refereeing and harshness of punishment have imposed an undeserved penalty on club and player alike'. History has recorded these penalties. But the Victory Cup, for all that, went to Ibrox.

CHAPTER ELEVEN
The Last Line of Defence —
Willie Miller

WILLIE MILLER joined Celtic from Maryhill Harp in May 1942 and almost immediately made the goalkeeping position his own. In those days, he got plenty of work to do behind a poor defence so his record of 28 shut-outs in 123 appearances (23 per cent) is an excellent one. Time after time, Willie received rave notices in the papers for his special saves — and his courage. During his career at Parkhead, he received six caps for Scotland. After spells with Clyde, Stirling Albion and Hibs, Willie retired in 1954 and worked for many years in the whisky trade. He now lives with his wife Pat in Bearsden on the north west of Glasgow.

I signed for Celtic in May 1942 from Maryhill Harp. At the time, I was training to be an engineer in the railways so I worked all day and went along to Parkhead at night. The manager at the time was Jimmy McStay, a thorough gentleman, whose manner was very much up-market. I always felt that the Board was very much in control and he was never able to do the things he wanted to do. At night we did all our own training. Alec Dowdalls looked after all the injuries but no one supervised the training at all. In fact, there was very little organisation. I generally did about 2-3 laps around the track without stopping, then some sprints but most of my training was done in the gym — bending, stretching, throwing the ball against the wall and catching it at different heights and speeds. Wartime being the way it was, the surroundings at Celtic Park suffered a little but the pitch was always in good order.

Rangers were very much the top dogs at that time. They were, frankly a superior team to us. They had a hard manager in Bill Struth and the players had to toe his line, although I personally got on well with him. A mis-behaviour when he was there and you were really in the bad books! I think that is why there was more put into the game at Ibrox than at Celtic Park. It was a bad time to be at Parkhead from the results point of view. When I worked full-time after finishing my apprenticeship, I was still a young man and as you well know, when you are young, you do not need to train as much as when you get older. We only trained in the morning, finished off about mid-day, went into town to Ferraris or the Bank Restaurant where we had lunch on the Club. I felt I had too much time on my hands and I worked with Connells, the gent's outfitters, in the afternoon.

The system at training was the same as at night. We saw Jimmy McStay there occasionally but Alex Dowdalls was the only one who came around the players and even he did not oversee training. You did it on your own. We never practised free kicks or corner kicks. We played a five-a-side behind the goals near the end of training, but most of it was done without a ball. Rolando Ugolini and I used to train together — he was a

Willie Miller.

great keeper. We always got on very well with each other and practised together — throwing, catching, diving, as well as stretching and bending.

The system we used then was not like most of the other teams. Nearly all of them had a 'stopper' centre-half but ours were good players in their own right — players like Willie Corbett, John McPhail or, during the war, big Joe McLaughlin. Because these were good footballers, it left more space than normal and that meant more work for me, but you could say I had more chance to shine. People nowadays will think it strange but the manager never discussed what they now call tactics before the match. He just gave an encouraging talk. Even if we were two down at half-time, he would just try to pick you up. The captain — Malky McDonald during the war — was the man who tended to organise teams much more so than the manager.

When Jimmy McStay went in 1945 and Jimmy McGrory came in, there was no real difference. McGrory was a true gentleman but not right for the role of manager. He had some tough years ahead of him. There was no real change in training or conditions under McGrory. I still felt that the Board — or really Bob Kelly — picked the team. The Board seldom got involved with the players. There was a Board meeting every Thursday and that is the only time they came in during the week. I always had the feeling that the Chairman — Tom White — was more concerned with administration and business and Bob Kelly was the man who always oversaw team selection. I never knew how or why

Celtic chose not to play stars from England, like Stanley Mathews or Matt Busby, but afterwards it seemed daft not to. The only people we used were actual Celtic players in the forces home on leave, that sort of thing. It would have made a difference if we had been able to use some of these English stars or Scots or Anglo-Scots stars and that is why we were inferior to Rangers as far as play was concerned. The defence was not so bad but the forward line could not score goals. I can remember just how annoyed the crowds were about the results in these war years. As a goalkeeper, I was in the perfect position to hear the crowds' remarks and they were not sympathetic!

Curiously enough, although Rangers were the top dogs, the Old Firm players got on very well. There was obviously some needle between the teams and the occasional incident but generally no bitterness. My first Old Firm match is one I will always remember; we lost 8-1! Another match I will always remember is the one at Dundee in 1947-1948 when we were in danger of relegation. There were some nerves before the game and some celebration afterwards – thanks to three goals by Jock Weir whom I never thought was a very good player.

There were good players at Celtic Park at that time. John McPhail was always a good player, always a potential goal scorer. Tully was an exceptionally talented ball player who always played with the head. One thing about Tully – he could make other players play. Bobby Evans was not only a good player but a nice type of boy. He was a natural footballer – able to play in any position. But one of the best players I ever played with was Malcolm McDonald – the supreme player, who could play anywhere but was also one of the best captains in my years. In fact, when I arrived, the Exhibition Cup forward-line was still there. Jimmy Delaney – a very nice man – Johnny Crum, Johnny Divers – a real character from Maryhill – and Frank Murphy.

Goalkeepers, of course were used to being charged in those days. I got injured quite a bit but never missed any games. Where I used to get injured was my habit of diving at the forward's feet, I got a few bad knocks there. In general, you got the ball, took one step and kicked it away. That is how you survived. My worst injuries were split heads but, as I said, I just played on.

We never received a fortune in those days. My best ever wage was £10 a week, with £2 for a win and £1 for a draw. The bonus was bigger for beating Rangers. I thoroughly enjoyed my football career! It was wonderful to play for Celtic; they were a great club with such a wonderful support and I have very happy memories of my days there!

CHAPTER TWELVE (1946–1950)
A Flirt with Relegation

THE FIRST PROPER post-war season of 1946–1947 saw the introduction of a new trophy, the Scottish League Cup, which made many a Celtic fan's eye twinkle. Traditionally, cups were just made for Celtic's style of play and this one would be no different. The format, unlike the Scottish Cup, was for teams to be drawn in sections of four. The matches were then played home and away, with the winner going through to the quarter-finals, which were also played home and away. The semi-final and final were straight knock-out matches.

CELTIC PLAYERS 1945–46

NAME	YEAR JOINED	FIRST CLUB
S. Airlie	1942	St Anthony's
J. Baillie	1946	St Roch's
T. Bogan	1946	Hibernian
J. Cantwell	1946	Glenboig St Joseph's
J. Campbell	1946	St Anthony's
W. Corbett	1941	Maryhill
J. Devine	1943	Mossend Boys' Guild
R. Evans	1944	St Anthony's
G. Ferguson	1945	St Anthony's
J. Gallacher	1943	Armadale
W. Gallacher	1937	St Anthony's
G. Hazlett	1945	Pollokshaws Boys' Guild
D. Hill	1945	Ashfield Juveniles
R. Hogg	1931	Royal Albert
F. Kelly	1943	Renton Boys' Guild
T. Kiernan	1945	Albion Rovers
P. Lamb	1946	St Anthony's
M. Lynch	1935	St Anthony's
P. MacAuley	1940	Douglas Hawthorn
P. McDonald	1942	Shawfield Juniors
J. McGrory	1946	Maryhill Harp
M. McLafferty	1945	St Roch's
D. McMillan	1945	Maryhill Harp
J. McPhail	1940	Strathclyde
J. Mallan	1942	Pollok
W. Miller	1942	Maryhill Harp
R. Milne	1940	Polkemmet
P. O'Sullivan	1945	Airdrieonians
G. Paterson	1932	Dunipace Juniors
J. Paton	1942	Dennistoun Waverley
R. Quinn	1943	Blantyre Celtic
J. Rae	1948	St Peter's Boys' Guild
J. Sirrel	1946	Royal Navy
R. Ugolini	1944	Armadale
J. Watters	1936	St Aloysius College

The biggest pool of players for some years was available to manager Jimmy McGrory – 35 in all. The entire terracing at Celtic Park had been tidied up and strengthened with concrete edging. Basic ticket prices were similar to the year before; 40/- (£2) for the Stand, 24/8d (£1.25p) for the enclosure and 17/4d (87p) for the ground.

In the Celtic Football Guide, manager Jimmy McGrory had written: 'It is with confidence that I predict a bright season in 1946–1947 provided the present players are inspired by the traditions of the past and we are not visited with more than an average dose of misfortune'. True, misfortune certainly did not happen, yet this season and the following three were amongst the worse in the Club's history.

1946–1947 SCOTTISH LEAGUE DIVISION I

	P	W	D	L	F	A	Pts	Position
Rangers	30	21	4	5	76	26	46	1st
Celtic	30	13	6	11	53	55	32	7th

FIXTURES

	H	A		H	A
Aberdeen	1-5	2-6	Motherwell	3-2	2-1
Clyde	3-3	2-2	Partick Thistle	2-0	1-4
Falkirk	0-0	4-1	Queen of South	2-0	1-3
Hamilton	2-1	2-2	Queen's Park	1-0	3-1
Hearts	2-3	1-2	Rangers	2-3	1-1
Hibs	4-1	0-2	St Mirren	2-1	1-0
Kilmarnock	4-2	2-1	Third Lanark	1-4	0-0
Morton	1-2	1-2			

By the time the first Old Firm match for 1946–1947 came round on 7 September, Celtic had won only one out of seven League games, suffering particularly heavy defeats at Aberdeen (2-6) and home to Third Lanark (1-4). They had also gone out of the Glasgow Cup in the first round to Clyde. The Rangers match, for which the prices had been raised, ended in another defeat and in the League Cup section, which started two weeks later, they finished second to Hibs. A draw in the return Ne'erday fixture with Rangers might have heralded a better second half of the season, but the First Round Cup defeat by Dundee brought them back to reality. During the season, George Paterson had left for Brentford in a straight swap for Gerry McAloon, but the biggest transfer bid in the season, according to manager McGrory's report, was Celtic's bid for the great Will Mannion. Celtic were apparently prepared to pay the money but Middlesbrough would not let him go.

The first post-war season proved to be a disappointing one for Celtic. Under new manager Jimmy McGrory, only Willie Miller seemed sure of his place. Other positions saw a few incumbents, some sensible, some surprising. For instance, while three right-backs were tried out (Hogg, Lamb and McDonald) and three left-backs (Milne, McDonald and Lamb), no fewer

A Celtic team from just after the Second World War. Back row, left to right: Lynch, McMillan, Hogg, Miller, McDonald, Milne. Front row: Jordan, Kiernan, Rae, McAloon, Hazlett.

This particular team played only three matches together in 1946: against Motherwell on 23 November, Kilmarnock on 30 November and Morton on 7 December.

than nine names were listed at outside-right (Sirrell, Cantwell, Hazlett, Rae, Bogan, Evans, Jordan, Docherty, Quinn) and five at centre-forward (Rae, Cantwell, Airlie, Kiernan, Bogan). Few were successful, with the result that only 53 goals were scored, top scorers being Kiernan (10) and McAloon (11). There were five home defeats; and four losses in the first eight matches meant that Celtic were always chasing the rest.

1946–1947 SCOTTISH LEAGUE CUP

	H	A
Hamilton	3-1	2-2
Hibs	1-1	2-4
Third Lanark	0-0	3-2

LEAGUE CUP POSITION

	P	W	D	L	F	A	Pts	Position
Celtic	6	2	3	1	11	10	7	2nd

Celtic failed to qualify for the second stage.

In the first year of this new competition, a defeat by Hibs at Easter Road got Celtic off to the worst possible start and three subsequent draws saw Celtic finish in second place.

1946–1947 SCOTTISH CUP

25/01/47	Dundee (A)	1-2	36,000

A packed house, but a jittery team lacking confidence. Outside-right Hugh Doherty, playing his only Scottish Cup tie, missed an absolute sitter in the first half when Celtic were a goal down. Bobby Evans was at outside-left in this game, one of three forward positions he filled that season.

1946–1947 GLASGOW CUP

Clyde	(H)	0-2

1946–1947 CHARITY CUP

	Queen's Park	(A)	6 corners to 1 corner		
	Third Lanark	(H)	1 goal 7 corners to 1 goal 2 corners		
Final	Rangers	(Ibrox)	0-1	38,000	14/05/47

1947–1948 SCOTTISH LEAGUE DIVISION I

	P	W	D	L	F	A	Pts	Position
Hibs	30	22	4	4	86	47	48	1st
Celtic	30	10	5	15	41	56	25	12th

FIXTURES

	H	A		H	A
Aberdeen	1-0	0-2	Motherwell	0-1	3-0
Airdrie	0-0	2-3	Partick Thistle	1-2	5-3
Clyde	0-0	0-2	Queen's Park	4-0	2-3
Dundee	1-1	3-2	Queen of South	4-3	0-2
Falkirk	0-3	1-0	Rangers	0-4	0-2
Hearts	4-2	0-1	St Mirren	0-0	2-1
Hibs	2-4	1-1	Third Lanark	1-3	1-5
Morton	3-2	0-4			

A second championship for Hibs and Celtic's worst-ever performance in the league.

This season the League Cup matches were played at the beginning of the season and away from Celtic Park, Rangers, Dundee and Third Lanark all proved too good. Thirds repeated the dose in the semi-final of the Glasgow Cup. Injuries took their toll but there would appear to have been some desperation in the continual chopping and changing of the team, particularly up front. For most matches, the defence read: Miller: Mallan, Milne; McPhail, Corbett and McAuley; but Oh! The changes up front! Five outside-rights, eight inside-rights, nine centre-forwards, five inside-lefts, with Johnny Paton the left-wing regular apart from seven appearances by Konrad Kappler.

Celtic started badly, losing six of the first nine matches and a further collapse occurred after losing the Ne'erday fixture against Rangers (0-4). Of the 13 matches left, seven were lost and two drawn. A change was needed and a big name was brought in. Jock Weir, who had only moved from Hibs to

Blackburn Rovers the year before for £10,000 was bought for £7,000 in February and made his debut against Falkirk. He was to repay that fee within two months. As the slump continued in the League, Celtic also went out of the Scottish Cup at the semi-final stage by a single goal at extra time. Successive defeats in the League to Hibs (2-4) and Third Lanark twice (1-5 and 1-3) made the final match against Dundee at Dens Park the vital one.

CELTIC'S POSITION BEFORE THE FINAL LEAGUE MATCH

	PLAYED	POINTS
Celtic	29	23
Morton	27	23
Queen of South	29	23
Airdrie	27	20
Queen's Park	28	17

The League table at that point is shown above. Queen's Park were already doomed, but who would join them was still in some considerable doubt.

The Celtic team at Dundee charged with the onerous task of keeping Celtic up was Miller; Hogg, Mallan; Evans, Corbett, McAuley; Weir, McPhail, Lavery; Gallagher and Paton. With only minutes to go, Dundee were 2-1 ahead but an equaliser and then a winner just before the whistle, making a hat trick for Jock Weir, saved the day for Celtic with Airdrie eventually accompanying Queen's Park to the Second Division.

1947–1948 SCOTTISH LEAGUE CUP

	H	A
Dundee	1-1	1-4
Rangers	2-0	0-2
Third Lanark	3-1	2-3

LEAGUE CUP POSITION

	P	W	D	L	F	A	Pts	Position
Celtic	6	2	1	3	9	11	5	3rd

Celtic failed to qualify for the next stage.

Defeats away from home sank Celtic's chances, the match against Third Lanark being played at Hampden due to ground alterations at Cathkin. The final this year was eventually between East Fife and Falkirk, with the Fifers, then a Second Division side, wining 4-1.

1947–1948 SCOTTISH CUP

07/02/48		Cowdenbeath	(H)	3-0	19,931
21/02/48		Motherwell	(H)	1-0	55,231
06/03/48/ QF		Montrose	(H)	4-0	39,077
27/03/48 SF		Morton	(Ibrox)	0-1	80,000
				(AET)	

Astonishing attendances, typical of the post-war years, with John McPhail getting four of the eight goals scored. Unfortunately, Morton proved too strong in the semi-final, although the only goal came in extra time.

1947–1948 GLASGOW CUP

	Clyde	(H)	1-1
Replay	Clyde	(A)	2-0
	Third Lanark	(H)	1-3

1947–1948 CHARITY CUP

	Third Lanark	(H)	1-0		
Final	Rangers	(Hampden)	0-2	69,500	08/05/48

Change

The Club had been saved from relegation but the shock of the near-miss spurred the Directorate into action. Jimmy Hogan, the old Burnley player who had coached successfully both on the Continent and with the English FA, was brought in to help the manager. Charles Tully was bought from Belfast Celtic for £8,000; and Bobby Collins arrived eventually from Pollok Juniors, after initially agreeing to join Everton for a much bigger fee. The fans responded to the Board's initiative. For the opening game against Morton, 55,000 were present and attendances remained high throughout the early months.

The team was slowly evolving into a more settled side. Willie Miller was still in goal, although now being challenged by John Bonner. Bobby Hogg moved to Alloa in December, Roy Milne his successor. Willie Corbett had been transferred to Preston North End in the summer and new boy Alec Boden replaced him. Bobby Evans was first choice right-half, although a young man called Tommy Docherty got a couple of games, with Pat McAuley at left-half. Jock Weir held down the right-wing berth, where Jimmy Sirrell also made a few appearances; John McPhail and Leslie Johnstone (signed from Clyde in October 1948) challenged for the inside-right position; centre-forward rotated between Jackie Gallagher and Dan Lavery, while Charlie Tully and John Paton invariably made the left side their own. Individually, the players all had their moments but collectively they disappointed. Attendances were quite outstanding; 55,000 were at Parkhead for the opening match against Hibs in the League Cup. The Old Firm matches in the same trophy attracted 70,000 to Celtic Park and 105,000 to Ibrox. By Christmas, the average home attendance was 48,000.

Such gates were not unusual just after the war, but Celtic were exceptional. One reason may have been Charlie Tully, whose subtlety and impertinence had the sports writers comparing him to Patsy Gallagher and Tommy McInally. For all his guile, though, the presence of other talented players and the huge attendances, the fact remained that Celtic failed to gather any of the three trophies.

Obituary.

I annouce with deep sorrow that

Mr. JOHN MADDEN,

Being a Scotsh football international,
for many years trainer of football club S. K. SLAVIA Prague, Czechoslovakia,

died peacefully, at his home, after a long illness bravely born in the age of 83 years.

His body will be burried on Wednesday 21 st of April 1948.

The Funeral will take place just this day at 13·30 p. m. at Olšanské cemetary in Prague, to the family sepulchre.

PRAGUE, 19 th of April 1948.

Františka Madden.

A star of the early Celtic teams, Johnny Madden scored 49 goals in 119 appearances. After giving service to Dundee and Tottenham Hotspur, he moved to Czechoslovakia, where he becamce coach to Slavia Prague FC.

In 1938, Johnny Madden took SK Slavia all the way to win the Mitropa Cup, a central-European cup for club champions, forerunner of the three current European competitions.

Johnny Madden's memorial and final resting place in Prague.

1948–1949 SCOTTISH LEAGUE DIVISION I

	P	W	D	L	F	A	Pts	Position
Rangers	30	20	6	4	63	32	46	1st
Celtic	30	12	7	11	48	40	31	6th

FIXTURES

	H	A		H	A
Aberdeen	3-0	0-1	Morton	0-0	0-0
Albion Rovers	3-0	3-3	Motherwell	3-2	1-0
Clyde	2-1	4-0	Partick Thistle	3-0	2-1
Dundee	0-1	2-3	QOS	2-2	0-1
East Fife	0-1	2-3	Rangers	0-1	0-4
Falkirk	4-4	1-1	St Mirren	2-1	1-1
Hearts	2-0	2-1	Third Lanark	1-2	2-3
Hibs	1-2	2-1			

Some improvement over the previous seasons was evident but Celtic were not in any way a threat to those at the top. Only one win from the first seven matches set the standard. By Christmas, six had been recorded, against five defeats. Charlie Tully had arrived from Northern Ireland and scored five goals in three positions (inside-right, inside-left and outside-left). Jock Weir got seven, John Paton five and the top scorer was Jackie Gallagher with thirteen. A young Glasweigan named Tommy Docherty made his debut on 21 August 1947. He later scored from inside-right against East Fife and Falkirk but was transferred to Preston North End in November 1949.

The impact that Charles Patrick Tully had on the Celtic scene was astonishing. Within a short space of time, stories of his on and off the field activities were all over Glasgow and the Celtic support received a real boost. Forty-seven goals in 319 matches tells only half the story.

1948–1949 Scottish League Cup

	H	A
Clyde	3-6	2-0
Hibs	1-0	2-4
Rangers	3-1	1-2

League Cup Position

	P	W	D	L	F	A	Pts	Position
Celtic	6	3	0	3	12	13	6	3rd

Celtic failed to qualify for the next stage.

The League Cup results also continued to disappoint – defeats to Clyde at home, and both Hibs and Rangers away put Celtic in third place for the second successive season.

1948–1949 Scottish Cup

22/01/49	Dundee Utd	(A)	3-4	25,000

Jackie Gallagher (2) and Charlie Tully scored for Celtic, but although the players played well individually, collectively they were just not a team, with the defence in particular causing problems.

1948–1949 Glasgow Cup

	Partick Thistle (H)		1-1	Game abandoned: pitch flooded after heavy shower of rain.
Replay	Partick Thistle (H)		2-1	
	Queen's Park	(A)	3-0	
Final	Third Lanark	(Hampden)	3-1	87,000 27/09/48

Team: Miller; Milne, Mallan; Evans, Boden, McAuley; Weir, W. Gallagher; J. Gallagher; Tully and Paton.

This was Celtic's first Glasgow Cup win since 1940 but most of the crowd must have expected the trophy to be destined for Cathkin. Seven minutes into the second half, with Third Lanark one up and in control, they were awarded a penalty. Mitchell took the kick, the shot beat Willie Miller, but the ball hit the post and ran along the line, with Mitchell, of course, unable to touch it.

The Celtic players breathed a sigh of relief and put their heads down. Eight minutes later, Willie Gallagher equalised from a Jock Weir pass. Seven minutes from time, Jock Weir scored from 30 yards and four minutes later, he headed the third from a Johnny Paton corner.

1948–1949 Charity Cup

	Queen's Park (H)	0-0	Celtic won on toss of a coin
	Third Lanark (Hampden)	2-0	
Final	Partick Thistle (Hampden)	1-2	51,813 7/05/49

Parkhead, Ibrox — and Rome!

The following season was little better. For the first time, the League Cup sectional games preceded the League campaign and the team rose to the occasion, beating Rangers 3-2 at Parkhead in the first match of the season and losing 2-0 in the return, before 95,000 at Ibrox. The latter match had some unpleasant moments both on and off the field. In the eyes of most observers, at least in the Celtic end and in the Press Box, Sammy Cox's boot caught Charlie Tully in the pit of the stomach as the Celtic player over-reached himself in trying to control the ball. Tully fell to the ground, obviously in pain, but the referee waved play on and this led to some fighting in the crowd and bottle throwing. Police moved in to quell the trouble while Tully rolled over the touchline to receive treatment. After the match, the Celtic Directorate asked the SFA to look into the matter. Their decision was astonishing. It stated that the terracing trouble had been caused by the actions of two players, Cox and Tully, both of whom were severely reprimanded. The findings surprised the football public and were not acceptable to Celtic.

By 14 September, the Old Firm had already met twice that season in the League Cup and once in the Glasgow Cup. To attempt to take some heat out of the situation, the Celtic Directorate wrote to the League Management Committee asking that the League match against Rangers at Ibrox due on 24 September be postponed or delayed. This request was refused, but much of the support decided to boycott the game, where a reduced attendance saw Rangers comfortably win 4-0. Four days later, the SFA Council meeting approved the Referees Committee decision on the Cox-Tully case by 25 votes to five.

Two new boys had come into the team early that season. Bobby Collins, received rave notices in both his 'assumed' position of outside-right and the two matches played in his 'natural' inside-right berth. He scored eight during the season. The other newcomer Mike Haughney from Newtongrange Star, gave creditable displays at both centre-forward and outside-left, notching 15 goals. It was also old faithful Willie Miller's last season and he moved to Clyde during the summer. Johnny Bonnar replaced him. Again, none of the major trophies came back to Parkhead, but the season finished in fine style with a visit to Rome to mark the 50th anniversary of the founding of Lazio FC. Stops were made on the way out at London, Brussels, Lucerne and Milan and on the way back at Genoa, Montreux and Paris. On 30 May, the match was played on an afternoon of fierce heat and resulted in a 0-0 draw, two Lazio players being sent off. In the return match at Parkhead in September, on a much cooler evening, Celtic won 4-0.

CELTIC

Official Programme

BOBBY COLLINS (Pollok)

GLASGOW CUP—1st ROUND

CELTIC v. PARTICK THISTLE

Wednesday, 8th September, 1948

Kick-off 6.20 p.m.

PRICE 2d.

The 'Wee Barra'. Only 5ft 4in, and 9st 4lbs, yet Bobby Collins gave no quarter throughout his career. Played out of position frequently with Celtic, whose management seemed to want him on the wing, he blossomed further when he played in the engine room of inside-forward or midfield. In ten years and 320 games with Celtic, he scored 116 goals before going on to further success with Everton and Leeds.

1949–1950 SCOTTISH LEAGUE DIVISION I

	P	W	D	L	F	A	Pts	Position
Rangers	30	22	6	2	58	26	50	1st
Celtic	30	14	7	9	51	50	35	5th

FIXTURES

	H	A		H	A
Aberdeen	4-2	0-4	Partick Thistle	1-0	0-1
Clyde	4-1	2-2	Queen of South	3-0	2-0
Dundee	2-0	0-3	Raith Rovers	2-2	1-1
East Fife	4-1	1-5	Rangers	1-1	0-4
Falkirk	4-3	1-1	St Mirren	0-0	1-0
Hearts	3-2	2-4	Stirling Albion	2-1	1-2
Hibs	2-2	1-4	Third Lanark	2-1	0-1
Motherwell	3-1	2-1			

The immediate post-war years were disappointing for Celtic. There were some fine players in several positions but inconsistency was the bugbear, not helped by continual chopping and changing up front. Collins, Haughney and Weir all competed for the number seven jersey; McPhail, Collins, Haughney, Fernie and Taylor for the number eight and so on. Worst of all was at outside-left, where six players were tried (Taylor, Tully, McAuley, Peacock, Docherty and Haughney). Only 14 goals were scored away from home, the lowest ever in a league season for Celtic. The home record was comparatively good; the 8 games and 35 goals lost away from home were the problem.

1949–1950 SCOTTISH LEAGUE CUP

	H	A
Aberdeen	1-3	5-4
Rangers	3-2	0-2
St Mirren	4-1	0-1

League Cup Position

	P	W	D	L	F	A	Pts	Position
Celtic	6	3	0	3	13	13	6	2nd

Celtic failed to qualify for the next stage.

Another tough section in the League Cup proved too much for Celtic. Good victories in the first two matches – Rangers (H) 3-2 and Aberdeen (A) 5-4 – were made irrelevant as the team lost the next three – St Mirren (A) 0-1, Rangers (A) 0-2 and Aberdeen (H) 1-3 – to go out of the competition. Rangers, the winners of the section, went out in the semi-final to East Fife, the latter going on to lift the Trophy for the second time in three years.

1949–1950 SCOTTISH CUP

	28/01/50	Brechin	(A)	3-0	6,500
	15/02/50	Third Lanark	(A)	1-1	35,000
Replay	20/02/50	Third Lanark	(H)	4-1	24,000
	25/02/50	Aberdeen	(H)	0-1	65,112

The first match in the second round between Third Lanark and Celtic was uncannily like the incidents of the 'snow' Cup final between the same teams in 1889. On 15 February 1950, snow fell so heavily on Cathkin that the referee, five minutes before the kick-off, decided that the game should be abandoned but the clubs agreed to play a 'friendly', just as in 1889. Some of the crowd wanted their money back and chanted for some time outside the pavilion. Later, it was announced that the monies involved would be returned on the following Monday at Celtic Park, where the Celtic Treasurer found, to his dismay, that the small number doing the complaining at Cathkin, had now grown into a large crowd wanting their money back.

In a rather strange Third Round draw, only two ties – Celtic *v.* Aberdeen and Dunfermline *v.* Stenhousemuir – were arranged. The other six teams all received byes into the Quarter Final. Celtic's effort in the tie was to be applauded, but the skill, and solitary goal, came from Aberdeen.

1949–1950 GLASGOW CUP

Rangers	(H)	1-2	

1949–195 CHARITY CUP

	Clyde	(H)	1-0		
	Third Lanark	(A)	1-0		
Final	Rangers	(Hampden)	3-2	81,000	06/05/50

This became known as the 'Danny Kaye' Charity Cup Final as the result of a piece of clowning by the American comedian before the kick-off.

The Celtic team was Bonnar; Haughney, Milne; Evans, McGrory, Baillie; Collins, Fernie; McPhail; Peacock, Tully.

Celtic were one up at half-time, neat work by Charlie Tully allowing him to lob the ball to John McPhail whose glancing header went in off Willie Woodburn in 41 minutes. In 48 minutes, another deflection, this time off Sammy Cox, from a rather soft shot by McPhail made it two and four minutes later, Tiger Shaw mis-controlled Tully's cross allowing 'Hookey' McPhail to complete his hat-trick. Rangers came back with goals from Gillick in 67 minutes and Thornton in 78, but Celtic refused to buckle and finished 3-2 winners.

The Charity Cup-winning team of 1950. Back row: Haughney, Milne, Bonnar, Evans, McGrory, Baillie. Front row: Collins, Fernie, McPhail, Peacock, Tully.

John McGrory only played 58 matches during his nine-year Celtic career (1946–53). This Charity Cup final was his first big occasion and he coped well with Willie Thornton. In his last season he played all his games at centre-forward, scoring 11 goals.

CHAPTER THIRTEEN (1950–1952)

A Comeback of Sorts

THERE WAS RENEWED OPTIMISM among Celtic fans for the advent of the 1950s. Frankly, both the war years and post-war years had been horrendous in their results. This review of the period from 1946–1950 shows just how few trophies Celtic picked up in that period.

CELTIC'S RECORD IN COMPETITIONS 1946–1950

	LEAGUE	SCOTTISH LEAGUE CUP	SCOTTISH CUP	GLASGOW CUP	CHARITY CUP
1946–47					
1947–48					
1948–49				Celtic	
1949–50					Celtic

If we review the same period and put in the trophy wins of Celtic's chief rival, the extent of Rangers domination becomes clear.

RANGERS' RECORD IN COMPETITIONS 1946–1950

	LEAGUE	SCOTTISH LEAGUE CUP	SCOTTISH CUP	GLASGOW CUP	CHARITY CUP
1946–47	Rangers		Rangers		
1947–48		Rangers		Rangers	Rangers
1948–49	Rangers	Rangers	Rangers	Celtic	
1949–50	Rangers	Rangers		Rangers	Celtic

A trophy count of eleven to two in Rangers' favour should have had the Celtic fans worried about the new decade, but they were hopeful, as were the Celtic players and officials, boosted by the end-of-season trip to play Lazio. While in Rome, they were present at an audience with the Pope, when Pius XII read out Celtic's name as one of the groups present.

New players for the season included John Higgins, George Hunter and John McAlindon. During the close season a great deal of work had been done around Celtic Park in the way of redecoration, the provision of new entrances, and the renewing of crush-barriers. Unfortunately, the club lost the services of Jimmy Hogan, recognised as one of Britain's top coaches but the many players who had benefited from his stay at Celtic Park were soon to match the desires of the support for success.

Charles Patrick in action.   *A youthful John McMcPhail.*

1950–1951 LEAGUE CUP		
Section Games	H	A
East Fife	2-0	1-1
Raith Rovers	2-1	2-2
Third Lanark	3-1	2-1

LEAGUE CUP POSITION								
	P	W	D	L	F	A	Points	Position
Celtic	6	4	2	0	12	6	10	1st

		H	A		
QF	Motherwell	1-4	1-0	Aggregate:	2-4

The section perhaps looks an easy one to our eyes, but in 1950 East Fife had an excellent record in this competition, so Celtic's qualification for the quarter-final stage was to be praised. Unfortunately, a poor result at home in the first leg of the Motherwell tie left them with too much work to do.

1950–1951 SCOTTISH LEAGUE DIVISION I								
	P	W	D	L	F	A	Points	Position
Hibs	30	22	4	4	78	26	48	1st
Celtic	30	12	5	13	48	46	29	7th

FIXTURES

	H	A		H	A
Aberdeen	3-4	1-2	Morton	3-4	2-0
Airdrie	0-1	4-2	Motherwell	3-1	1-2
Clyde	1-0	3-1	Partick Thistle	0-3	1-0
Dundee	0-0	1-3	Raith Rovers	2-3	2-1
East Fife	6-2	0-3	Rangers	3-2	0-1
Falkirk	3-0	2-0	St Mirren	2-1	0-0
Hearts	2-2	1-1	Third Lanark	1-1	0-2
Hibs	0-1	1-3			

This year, the Celtic team was the most settled in formation since the war in many positions. Bonnar and Hunter each had half a season in goal, Fallon only missed three matches at right-back, Milne or Rollo was at left-back. Up front, the left-wing combination was usually Peacock and Tully, while Collins, Weir, Fernie, Haughney, McPhail, McAlindon and Walsh competed for the other three. Unfortunately, while the forward line did play some very neat football, all too often it lacked punch, as 48 goals in 30 matches would testify. The goal-scoring was disappointing; Peacock (5), Tully (3), Jock Weir (8), McPhail (13), Collins (15), Haughney (1), Donald Weir (1), McAlindon (2). After the successful campaign in the League Cup sectional matches, Celtic started the league campaign full of optimism and did defeat Rangers at home 3-2 in their second match. However, in September and early October they also lost three league games (Morton H, Raith Rovers H, Aberdeen A) as well as crashing heavily at home to Motherwell in the quarter-final of the League Cup.

Thereafter, the team tightened up, going ten matches without defeat. Unfortunately, three successive losses (Rangers A, Motherwell A, Aberdeen H) stopped their momentum and from then on their form was very inconsistent. Six matches were lost at home in total and they were beaten by the champions both home and away.

1950–1951 SCOTTISH CUP

27/01/51		East Fife	(A)	2-2	22,000
31/01/51	Replay	East Fife	(H)	4-2	36,185
10/02/51		Duns	(H)	4-0	22,907
24/02/51		Hearts	(A)	2-1	48,000
10/03/51	QF	Aberdeen	(H)	3-0	75,000
31/03/51	SF	Raith Rovers	(Hampden)	3-2	84,327
21/04/51	Final	Motherwell	(Hampden)	1-0	131,943

The earlier rounds were not problem-free. East Fife were leading 2-1 with ten minutes left but some clever play by Charlie Tully out on the left gave him the opportunity to cross and Bobby Collins, all 5ft 4in of him, outjumped everyone else for the equaliser. At Tynecastle, goalkeeper George Hunter, only 20 years of age, gave a wonderful display and defied Hearts time and time again. For the quarter-final, against Aberdeen, the crowd was so big that the gates were locked; and Raith Rovers never gave up in the semi-final before yet another big crowd. So the scene was set for another Celtic versus Motherwell Final. Twenty years before, the same two protagonists had met, with the winners, Celtic, taking the Scottish Cup on tour to North America. Celtic had already arranged a similar tour in 1951, but would they go as Cup-winners?

The answer, eventually, was yes; Celtic held on to the single-goal lead scored in the first half by John McPhail, thus winning the Cup for the sixteenth time. McPhail's contribution in total was seven goals, the rest coming from Jock Weir (5), Bertie Peacock (2), Charlie Tully (2), Bobby Collins (2) and Donald Weir (1).

Celtic FC, Scottish Cup-winners 1951. Back row, left to right: Fallon, Rollo, Hunter, Evans, Boden, Baillie. Front row: Weir, Collins, McPhail, Peacock, Tully.

George Hunter had an excellent Scottish Cup campaign but only months later he developed TB and was sent to Switzerland to aid his recovery. He recovered well enough to play another two seasons at Celtic Park. In 38 appearances, he had nine shut-outs (24 per cent).

1950–1951 GLASGOW CUP

	Clyde	(H)	3-0		
	Queen's Park	(A)	2-1		
Final	Partick Thistle	(Hampden)	1-1		
Replay	Partick Thistle	(Hampden)	2-3	29/05/50	52,000

1950–1951 CHARITY CUP

Rangers	(Hampden)	1-2

The bedlam which marked Celtic's departure for the USA in 1951. This photograph was taken in Central Station in Glasgow, and shows Bobby Evans (just in front and to the right of the policeman) making his way to the train.

The US Tour

The touring party to the United States left on 8 May from Central Station in Glasgow. Those travelling were the Chairman Robert Kelly, Directors Desmond White and Tom Devlin, Manager Jimmy McGrory, Trainer Alec Dowdalls and players John McPhail, George Hunter, Sean Fallon, Alex Rollo, Bobby Evans, Alex Boden, Joe Baillie, Jock Weir, Bobby Collins, Bertie Peacock, Charlie Tully, Jimmy Mallan, Roy Milne, John McGrory, Willie Fernie and John Millsopp. At Southampton, the party boarded the Queen Mary, and made the crossing in luxury to New York, where the headquarters were in the Paramount Hotel. It was much of a repetition of the previous tour in 1931, civic receptions, hospitality by fans and, of course, football – in the heat!

Nine matches were played between 20 May and 20 June, of which seven were won, one drawn and one lost; New York Stars (5-1), Fulham (2-0: New York), Eintracht Frankfurt (3-1: New York), Philadelphia All-Stars (6-2), the National League XI (2-1: Toronto), the Chicago Polish Eagles (4-0: Detroit), Fulham (1-1:Toronto), the Kearney Select 2-0 in New Jersey and Fulham (3-2: Montreal). The enthusiasm of the American fans was tremendous and it was matched by those who greeted the team on its return for a well-earned rest. Unfortunately for the players, it proved a short close-season. The touring party arrived back on 29 June and by mid-July the players had reported back for training. The team would start the season early

Jock Weir in Philadelphia during the 1951 tour when his double-act with Charlie Tully wowed the fans — off the field and on! His 106 appearances were graced by 33 goals.

Alec Boden was a good servant to Celtic during the late 1940s and early 1950s, settling down in the centre-half berth, although he also had a few games at inside-forward and outside right. His 158 appearances spanned 13 years. But the highlight was surely the Scottish Cup win against Motherwell in 1951, with the half-back line of Evans, Boden and Baillie.

247

by playing in the St Mungo Cup Competition, run as a combined Glasgow Corporation and SFA contribution to the 'Festival of Britain'. All sixteen First Division Clubs took part in this competition.

St Mungo Cup

14/07/1951 FIRST ROUND:
Celtic 2 Hearts 1 (51,000)
Scorers: McPhail and Walsh

19/07/1951 SECOND ROUND
Celtic 4 Clyde 4 (29,000)
Scorers: Collins (2, 1 penalty), Walsh and McPhail

20/07/1951 REPLAY
Celtic 4 Clyde 1 (29,000)
Scorers: Fallon (2), Peacock and Walsh

28/07/1951 SEMI-FINAL, Hampden
Celtic 3 Raith Rovers 1 (48,000)
Scorers: Walsh (3)

01/08/1951 FINAL
Celtic 3 Aberdeen 2 (81,000)
Scorers: Fallon (2), Walsh

Aberdeen scored in 14 minutes through Harry Yorston, George Hunter being injured after colliding with a post and having to go off for ten minutes. Bobby Evans took over in goal. In 35 minutes, Aberdeen went two up through former Celt Tommy Bogan. Just before the interval, Charlie Tully won Celtic a corner when he shied the ball against an Aberdeen defender. From the corner on the right, taken by Tully, Sean Fallon scored Celtic's first goal. Celtic dominated the second half. Within five minutes, a great run by Jimmy Walsh and a fine pass gave Fallon the chance to score his second with a strong drive and Walsh soon got the third after fine work by Charlie Tully. The team: Hunter; Haughney, Rollo; Evans, Hallan and Baillie; Collins, Walsh; Fallon, Peacock and Tully.

So Celtic collected another of the 'one-off' trophies which were their speciality and this one looked good. It was a heavy silver cup, embellished by the Glasgow Coat-of-Arms, with salmon masquerading as handles. Unfortunately, one of these came off when handled by a Celtic official and after some investigation, the truth came out. The Trophy was a second-hand one, originally a yachting award in 1894 and hastily re-fashioned as a football trophy. The affair caused some correspondence between the Celtic Chairman and the Lord Provost, some of it aired in the pages of the *Glasgow Herald*.

Inside-forwards of great skill, with a desire to compete: Bertie Peacok (left) and Bobby Collins (right).

But nothing came of it and the St Mungo Cup still adorns the Boardroom of Celtic Park.

The season had started well for another recruit. Jimmy Walsh had been signed from Bo'ness United and had made his first team debut against Hibs in the last match of the previous season. He scored in every round of the St Mungo Cup and continued this good form into the League Cup and early stages of the League. George Hunter had been sent to Switzerland for a cure for TB so Johnny Bonnar returned, although when he lost three goals to Rangers in the League Cup on 13 October, Andy Bell was brought in for twelve matches. To shore up the centre-half berth, Jock Stein was brought home from Llanelli, for which thanks must be given for a long memory to Jimmy Gribben, the Assistant Trainer. Considering just what Stein gave overall to Celtic's cause, the fee of £1,200 would appear to have been something of a bargain.

One surprise recruit for this season came from America. In 1931 fine work by Joe Kennaway in Fall River made him the choice to replace John Thomson a few months later. On the more recent tour, a Jamaican called Gil Herron had impressed club officials in Detroit with his physique, his pace and shooting ability. He came over to Celtic Park in August 1951, played in the public trial, where he scored twice and was signed shortly afterwards. He made his debut later that month in the League Cup against Morton, scoring against the great Jimmy Cowan, and played another four times for the first team. In the reserves, he scored fifteen goals in fifteen games, was ordered off against Stirling Albion on 2 January 1952, played for Jamaica against Trinidad and Cuba in March and was freed on 17 May 1952. A short but fascinating career.

1951–1952 League Cup

Section Games	H	A
Airdrie	2-0	1-1
Morton	2-0	0-2
Third Lanark	1-1	1-0

League Cup Position

	P	W	D	L	F	A	Points	Position
Celtic	6	3	2	1	7	4	8	1st

League Cup Quarter- and Semi-Finals

			H	A	
15/09/51	QF	Forfar	4-1	1-1	Aggregate 5-2
13/10/51	SF	Rangers	0-3		(Hampden)

This League Cup campaign was the most successful so far, the team qualifying rather uncomfortably from their section (only 0.08 of a goal better than Morton) and then disposing of Forfar in the quarter-final. The home leg on 15 September 1951 was an important victory, the goals coming from Baillie, Collins, Walsh and Peacock. Rangers however, proved just too strong in the semi-final even before an injury to Alec Boden hindered Celtic's play. Surprisingly, the Light Blues were beaten by Dundee in the Final.

1951–1952 Scottish League Division I

	P	W	D	L	F	A	Points	Position
Hibs	30	20	5	5	92	36	45	1st
Celtic	30	10	8	12	52	55	28	9th

Fixtures

	H	A		H	A
Aberdeen	2-0	4-3	Partick Thistle	2-1	4-2
Aidrie	3-1	1-2	Queen of South	6-1	0-4
Dundee	1-1	1-2	Raith Rovers	0-1	0-1
East Fife	2-1	1-3	Rangers	1-4	1-1
Hearts	1-3	1-2	St Mirren	2-1	1-3
Hibs	1-1	1-3	Stirling Albion	3-1	1-2
Morton	2-2	1-0	Third Lanark	2-2	3-3
Motherwell	2-2	2-2			

A review of the league seasons since the war shows quite clearly why the Celtic fan of the time was so perplexed and angry over his team's league form.

This was another dreadful season, with 55 goals lost. Jock Stein came in at centre-half for his first match in early December but by then the damage had been done. Of the first 11 matches four were lost and four drawn. The goals came from a variety of scorers: Collins (12), Millsopp (2), Jock Weir (3), Walsh (7), McPhail (11), McAlindon(1), Lafferty (3), Peacock (6), Tully (4). During the season, 16 forwards were tried out in different positions.

This had been a long season for many players, what with the tour of North America the previous summer, then the St Mungo Cup and straight into a long campaign. None felt it more than John McPhail, who had returned from that very hospitable tour tired and overweight but whose presence, at the apex of the forward line, meant so much to the team that he was regarded as essential. Unfortunately, he was being asked to do too much – his team-mates looking for him rather than others as the recipient of a pass and he broke down as a result in November. By mid-January, though, he was back and the team perked up, his own nine goals in the final run helping to keep Celtic in a safe, if mid-table, position.

1951–1952 SCOTTISH CUP				
30/01/52		Third Lanark (H)	0-0	30,000
04/02/52	Replay	Third Lanark (A)	1-2 (AET)	27,334

This was the end of an era, the first time in more than 50 years that Celtic had lost in a Scottish Cup replay.

1951–1952 GLASGOW CUP			
		Third Lanark (A)	5-2
24/09/51	Final	Clyde (Hampden)	1-2	50,000

1951–1952 CHARITY CUP			
Clyde	(H)	0-0	Clyde won on toss of coin

Willie Fernie in typical mode, effortlessly keeping the ball away from a defender. Willie was present for most of the major Celtic occasions of the 1950s, but the highlight must be his display in the 1957 League Cup final when Celtic beat Rangers 7-1. Unlike many Scottish players of those years, Willie Fernie played in two World Cup Finals, 1954 and 1958.

CHAPTER FOURTEEN (1952–53)
The Flag Incident

DURING THE SEASON of 1951–1952, a dispute over a decision made by the SFA almost put Celtic FC out of football. The 'flag incident' as it became known, had its cause in football but thereafter, politics, jealousy and, dare one say it, sectarianism all played a part. It was a time when those involved with Celtic found out which clubs regarded their image and traditions with respect and which were happy to see them fall. There were some surprising alliances.

The Background

As we reviewed in an earlier chapter, Celtic had its origins among the Irish Catholics of the East End and its initial mission was to raise money to help the poor in that area. Unfortunately, as the Club became more 'professional' in the business sense, there seemed, among the directorate, less and less interest in this charitable aspect, at least in the passage of hard cash to those in need. To be fair, the Club has always been happy to send a team to play for worthy causes. In my own time at Parkhead, many a free mid-week was filled with friendlies, not only against the lesser-known professional sides but also non-league teams up North, in the Borders or even England. Through the years, the Club has also allowed collections for charity on various occasions both within and outside the ground.

That the Club, from its beginnings, was a notable success on the field of play pleased everybody. The humblest fan felt that he or she was as much part of Celtic Football Club as the Chairman of the Board of Directors. They were full of admiration for those who had brought the Club into being, all men with Irish backgrounds and to honour this association Celtic have always flown the Irish flag above the enclosure. Initially, this was the old Irish flag of golden heart on green background, but when Ireland became the Free State in 1921, the new tricolour flag was raised in its place.

The Initial Cause: 3 November 1951

Charlie Tully was ordered off against Third Lanark for kicking George Aitken. He was later suspended for a month.

A youthful Charlie Tully (left).

The Response

The Club was instructed to post warnings around the ground until the end of the season about good conduct by spectators. The officials in the Celtic-Third Lanark match had complained of a very hostile reception as they left the field, one of the linesmen also making an allegation of spitting.

Repercussions

At the subsequent SFA council meeting on 12 December 1951, Celtic Chairman Robert Kelly objected to both the warnings and the allegations. Celtic, though, were warned that further trouble could lead to serious action against the Club, 'including possible closure of the ground'.

Further Developments

During the Old Firm match on 1 January 1952, played at Celtic Park in miserable weather, which Rangers won 4-1, bottles were thrown and eleven spectators arrested.

The Outcome

Worried about the violence, the Glasgow Magistrates, on 15 January 1952, made several recommendations which they invited the SFA and Scottish League to consider:

1. That the Rangers and Celtic clubs should not again be paired on New Year's Day when passions were more likely to be inflamed by drink and when more bottles were likely to be carried than on any other day.
2. That on any occasion when these clubs meet, admission should be by ticket only and the attendance limited to a number consistent with public safety, the number to be decided by the Chief Constable.

3. That in the interest of the safety of the public, Celtic FC should be asked to construct numbered passageways at each end of Celtic Park.

4. That the two clubs should avoid displaying flags which might incite feeling among the spectators.

There was a delay before the official statement came out. In the meantime, the 11 transgressors were dealt with. Two were sentenced to 20 days imprisonment, three were fined £10, four were fined £5 and the other two £2 each.

Eventually, the Referee Committee of the SFA issued its own recommendations.

a) They were not in favour of the New Year's Day game being transferred to another date.

b) The responsibility for the conduct of its supporters, in accordance with Article 114 of the SFA's regulations, lay with Celtic.

c) It was not sufficient for Celtic to say they had a sufficient number of policemen present, who in any event could not take action until misconduct had occurred.

d) Celtic was advised to warn its 'irresponsible' supporters that further trouble would possibly mean no matches played at Celtic Park for a prolonged period.

e) The Club was instructed to refrain from displaying on match days any flag or emblem which has no association with Scotland or the game itself.

f) Both clubs were ordered to take all steps to prevent a display by spectators of provocative flags or emblems and to discourage any display of sectarian sentiments which, the Committee felt, were at the root of the disturbances.

Reaction

1. The Press

While agreeing with the SFA that the responsibility for the condutct of its supporters lay with Celtic, the *Glasgow Herald's* correspondent raised two topics; 'if the police, according to the SFA 'cannot take any action until after misconduct has occurred', then how can Celtic? And secondly, I am glad to see that the SFA has at last recognised that sectarian sentiments are the root cause of the trouble. They have taken a long time to realise that'. (4 February 1952).

A few days later, other papers had a photo of the Irish flag flying above the Parkhead enclosure, with the caption; 'Celtic still haven't taken down the Eire flag'. This was before the Magistrates or the SFA had even considered the recommendations of the Referee Committee.

2. The Authorities

The Glasgow Magistrates endorsed the recommendations of the Referee Committee, although expressing dissatisfaction that their own suggestion of transferring the date of the New Year game had not been adopted.

3. *The SFA*

After a meeting of the SFA Council on 25 February 1952, Celtic Chairman Robert Kelly, backed by Rangers Chairman John F. Wilson, moved that as the SFA had no power to make such an order they should reject the section dealing with the banning of the flag. The Council, however, went ahead and also endorsed the recommendations of the Referee Committee by 26 votes to seven, having firstly ordered the Chairmen of Celtic and Rangers to leave the chamber.

Celtic, made more sure of their position by Council's position, continued to fly the flag.

At their meeting on 10 March 1952, the SFA Council proposed to give Celtic three days to comply with the order or suffer suspension. After discussion, though, it was realised that, if Celtic decided to ignore the instruction, the League programme would suffer and clubs would be inconvenienced, so an amendment that the period of grace be extended to 30 April, the official end of the season, was carried by 16 votes to 13.

Mr Kelly was under considerable pressure to conform. The *Glasgow Herald* commented:

the feelings of the Referee Committee, who met before the Council did, now are that in ordering Celtic to take down the flag, they are not inflicting any penalty or punishment – they are simply doing something to stop hooliganism at football matches.

More than once during yesterday's long discussion Mr R. Kelly, Celtic's Chairman was asked to realise that. He was also asked to realise that the whole matter was no longer one of taking down or flying the flag; it was a matter of Celtic having defied the Council's instructions and that if only he would make a gesture and take the flag down, even without prejudice to further discussion of the case, everyone would be happy. At different stages, several councillors made extravagant demonstrations of sympathy for Celtic – even though they latterly voted for a shorter period of grace being given to them. Not even Mr Kelly, I am sure, appreciated that he had so many friends – up to a point, the point where finance joins forces with principles. 'You'll be the biggest man in football', he was informed. 'You'll establish a reputation never possessed by anyone in the football world if only you'll take this flag down, even temporarily, and enable us as the Council to say you've accepted our decision'. That was the gist of the many appeals for 'bigness'. Perhaps Mr Kelly does not wish to be the biggest man in football or perhaps he wishes to maintain or increase his present reputation – almost everyone in the Council sympathises with him and his Club – by adhering to his principles. There can be little doubt he struck the shrewdest blow of all when he said that in the history of Scottish football, suspension had been ordered only when a rule had been broken and that no-one had proved that Celtic had broken any rules.

At a further meeting on 7 April 1952, the SFA then decided to cancel their order for the time being. The acting Chairman of the Referee Committee which had given the original instruction to Celtic to take down the flag, proposed that his decree be suspended until the Scottish League and the SFA met to consider the matter. This latter meeting was held on 28 April 1952 but it was agreed to adjourn until 14 May if in the interim Celtic had not agreed to accept the Council's decision. At the same time, the Secretary of the SFA noted that 'the Association must reserve complete freedom of action to the Council in any matter for which the Association alone holds responsibility.

The Celtic party in St Louis on the American tour of 1957. Robert Kelly (centre); Jimmy McGrory (extreme right).

The SFA were looking for a way out of their dilemma. On one hand, if the Secretary's statement was followed, then Celtic should have been suspended. On the other, the SFA was quite well aware that a large body of football legislators were of the opinion that such a punishment would be both unfair and unwise. They decided to save face. Since it was the end of the season the flag was furled now for the summer. If Celtic then agreed to a nominal submission to the SFA's decision, then the matter could be re-opened before the new season and the decision could be reversed. This suggestion was put to the Club and accepted, the Celtic Secretary writing to the SFA stating that while his Directors were bowing to the order, they were doing so under protest.

The face of the SFA was saved. Just before the start of the season 1952–1953, a Council meeting of the SFA defeated – by 18 votes to 12 – a motion from the Referee Committee to the effect that the flag should come down. And so ended what had become a farcical position for the SFA. Lessons were there to be learned, none more so than at the beginning, when Celtic's refusal to bend was publicly backed by the Chairman of their chief rivals; and, at the end, when, in spite of all the advice regarding the strength of Celtic's position, 12 clubs were still determined that the flag of a neutral country should not fly over Parkhead.

After the trauma of the 'flag incident' the Celtic faithful might have expected some light relief when football came round again, but it was not to be. Indeed, a series of injuries struck the club throughout this season. Bobby Collins broke an arm in a pre-season friendly in Ireland and was out until Christmas. John McPhail fractured his jaw in several places at Kirkcaldy in the second league match. Joe Baillie tore ligaments in his knee in November and missed the rest of the season. And Sean Fallon twice fractured his arm, once in December and again in February.

Add to this a three-week suspension for Charlie Tully and the uncertain form of George Hunter, recently returned from Switzerland after treatment for TB. Unfortunately, Hunter was often barracked by the normally supportive Celtic fans and his confidence slumped. On New Year's Day he was badly at fault for Rangers' winning goal and his uncertainty spread through the defence, which looked very indecisive in the following three matches, defeats by Motherwell, Clyde and Queen of the South.

1952–1953 League Cup

Section Games	H	A
Hibs	1-0	0-3
Partick Thistle	2-5	1-0
St Mirren	3-1	1-0

League Cup Position

	P	W	D	L	F	A	Points	Position
Celtic	6	4	0	2	8	9	8	2nd

Celtic failed to qualify for the next stage.

Bad defeats at home to Partick Thistle and away to Hibs scuppered the League Cup campaign. Dundee won for the second year running, beating Kilmarnock in the Final.

1952–1953 Scottish League Division I

	P	W	D	L	F	A	Points	Position
Rangers	30	18	7	5	80	39	43	1st
Celtic	30	11	7	12	51	54	29	8th

Fixtures

	H	A		H	A
Aberdeen	1-3	2-2	Motherwell	3-0	2-4
Airdrie	0-1	0-0	Partick Thistle	3-1	0-3
Clyde	2-4	2-1	Queen of South	1-1	1-2
Dundee	5-0	0-4	Raith Rovers	0-1	1-1
East Fife	1-1	1-4	Rangers	2-1	0-1
Falkirk	5-3	3-2	St Mirren	3-2	2-1
Hearts	1-1	0-1	Third Lanark	5-4	3-1
Hibs	1-3	1-1			

Very much the same story as the year before, with not enough goals scored and too many given away. The season started in tragic fashion when John Millsopp, who had played at outside-left only a few days before in the League match against Falkirk was taken ill with appendicitis. He was operated on immediately but complications set in and he died one week later. This was another of those seasons with frequent personnel changes, particularly up front. Seven different names appeared at outside-right, five at inside-right, six at centre-forward, six at inside-left and four at outside-left. Worst of all was at left-back, with eight listed!

By contrast, Bobby Evans was ever-present at right-half and Jock Stein missed only three matches. But the end product was the same – a mid-table position and frustration for the fans.

1952–1953 SCOTTISH CUP				
24/01/53		Eyemouth United (A)	4-0	4,131
07/02/53		Stirling Albion (A)	1-1	24,763
11/02/53	Replay	Stirling Albion (H)	3-0	25,000
21/02/53		Falkirk (A)	3-2	23,100
14/03/53	QF	Rangers (A)	0-2	95,000

The Eyemouth match, in pouring rain, was easy in the end but the local goalkeeper, who had put up a brave resistance, was cheered off the pitch by the Celtic fans at the end.

The tie at Brockville has gone down in history for one incident in the second half. At half-time, Falkirk with two ex-Celts in their line-up, Jimmy Delaney and Jock Weir, were two goals up. After the interval, Celtic increased the pressure. Charlie Tully took a corner kick, which beat all who jumped for it, swerved in the air and curled into the net. Unfortunately, any celebrations were halted by Referee Gerard, who had seen some infringement (Tully, as usual, placing the ball just outside the quarter-circle?) and ordered the corner to be re-taken. Not one whit annoyed, the bold Charlie put the ball down and repeated the feat, to the astonishment of all present. Falkirk were flabbergasted, but the Celtic players gained momentum from the incident, further goals from Willie Fernie and John McGrory taking them through. Unfortunately, Rangers were a stiffer test in the quarter-final and won deservedly by 2-0.

1952–1953 GLASGOW CUP			
	Queen's Park (H)	0-0	
Replay	Queen's Park (A)	2-2	
		Queen's Park won on toss of coin	

1952–1953 CHARITY CUP				
	Clyde (H)	4-0		
	Third Lanark (H)	1-1		
		Celtic won on toss of coin		
09/05/53	Final Queen's Park Hampden	3-1	40,600	

Team: Bonnar; Haughney, Rollo; Evans, Stein, McPhail; Collins, Fernie; Mochan; Peacock, Tully.

New boy Neil Mochan had been signed from Middlesborough only days before this final and was chosen for his Celtic debut in this match, the ninth player to wear the number nine shirt during the season.

The day was beautiful, the ground was firm, the crowd were in shirt-sleeves – and Mochan delivered. Queen's Park were the more attractive side, Celtic more direct. In 30 minutes, Mochan went on a good run, beat two defenders and crossed to the far post, where Willie Fernie scored. Only seconds later, Queens left-back Bell failed to control the ball and Mochan blasted home a fine shot, as he did again in 65 minutes, although the Queen's Park players complained that he used his hand to control the ball. That spurred the Amateurs into action but Johnny Bonnar was in inspired form and made a number of good saves, only being beaten once three minutes from the end.

CHAPTER FIFTEEN
A Coronation — and a Surprise Victory

TO COMMEMORATE the year of the Coronation in 1953, the Scottish Football Association and Scottish League, together with the FA and English League, put up a special Coronation Cup for competition between teams representing the two countries. Eight teams were chosen in total, with the matches to be played at Ibrox and Hampden.

Not since the Empire Exhibition Trophy of 1938 had there been a chance for one team to be crowned Cup Kings of Britain and the fans were suitably excited. Charity was also to benefit. In each match, the two clubs involved would split 50 per cent of the gate money after expenses while the remaining 50 per cent was divided among charities such as The King George VI Memorial Fund, the National Playing Fields Association and the Central Council of Physical Recreation.

The English representation was a strong one. Newcastle United, FA Cup Winners in 1952, Arsenal, League Champions in 1953; Manchester, League Champions in 1952 and Tottenham Hotspur, runners-up in the same competition.

The Scots were represented by Hibs, League Champions in 1951–1952; Rangers, just about to complete the League and Cup 'double' that season and Aberdeen, finalists in the Scottish Cup.

Many Celtic fans, while delighted that their team was taking part, were surprised to see them involved at all, as from recent performances, other Scottish teams were probably more deserving of the honour. After all, in season 1952–1953, Celtic had failed to qualify from their League Cup section; had been knocked out in the quarter-final of the Scottish Cup and finished eighth in the league.

There was also a few problems behind the scenes. These are the words of Jock Stein, taken from an interview I recorded with him at the SFA offices in Park Gardens in 1981:

Q There were some doubts as to Celtic's participation in the Coronation Cup?

A Well. I think Celtic's participation in it was purely financial. It was supposed to be the top two in the League and obviously we did not qualify, but it was felt that Celtic's pull at the gate was important and that was the way Celtic got in.

Q Is it true there were some behind-the-scenes problems at Celtic Park over pay and conditions?

A Yes. John Hughes was the union official and he felt that, as it was a big competition and there would be a lot of money drawn at the turnstiles, the players should be paid a guaranteed £100 per match. There was some consultation between the players and officials of each league club, but it never got to any great length.

Bob Kelly, the Chairman at the time, brought us all in individually and asked us our opinion. We all wanted to play in the competition but each club had to make their mind up. It wasn't as if the Scottish clubs could get together. The two Scottish clubs certain to go in were Celtic and Rangers, the other teams had to play to get in. There was no way we could make any decisions for the Rangers players.

At the outset we were talking about a strike but at the end of the day, I think with the pull of the big game and everything else, we were not long in deciding we wanted to be in it. Anyway, the Chairman did say at that time, it didn't matter who wouldn't play, there would certainly be a Celtic team in the competition. It didn't matter where they came from, there would be a team of green-and-white jerseys there. That frightened quite a lot of people and in the end, we were going to play.

Celtic 1 Arsenal 0

On the first evening of the Tournament, 11 May 1953, Celtic met Arsenal at Hampden. Their performance that night was a very rare one by a team more used to mediocrity. As the *Glasgow Herald* football correspondent put it:

> It was almost incredible. Celtic, who had had their supporters in a frenzy of anguish with a serious of displays unworthy of the Club, in the season just ended, have beaten Arsenal, the English League Division One Champions – not only beating them but taught them how to play football…Celtic produced combined football of such brilliance as to make even their most fervid follower wonder whence it came.

59,300 were there to witness this display and had Arsenal lost by 5 or 6 they would have had no valid complaint. Their goalkeeper George Swindon had several outstanding saves and many other shots were just inches high or just wide.

The Celtic team was Bonnar; Haughney, Rollo; Evans, Stein, and McPhail; Collins, Walsh; Mochan; Peacock and Tully. All of them played well but three men stood out. John McPhail at left-half and Bobby Evans on the right stamped their authority in the middle of the park and gave the Arsenal inside-men little space; while Neilly Mochan, newly signed from Middlesborough, was all skill and thrust. The only goal, in 23 minutes, was really not worthy of the occasion. A corner-kick by Bobby Collins was hoisted high up into the wind behind Celtic in the first half, and as goalkeeper Swindon jumped for it, the ball swerved violently, hit his hands and spun into the net.

Hibs 2 Tottenham Hotspur 1

At Ibrox, on the same evening, only 15,000 were present to watch the other quarter-final tie when Hibs met Tottenham Hotspur. A combination of a bare, bumpy pitch and a light ball did little for the standard of play, although, as at Hampden, the Scottish team was much superior to the English. Typically, though, Spurs opened the scoring in 28 minutes through outside-left McLellan and then tried to hold their lead by packing their defence. Gradually, Hibs raised their game. Lawrie Reilly scored the equaliser with the header in the 60th minute from a Govan free-kick and, just when the crowd was expecting the match to go into extra-time, repeated the effort this time from a Bobby Johnstone cross, to give his team a 2-1 victory and a place in the semi-finals.

Rangers 1 Manchester United 2

Two nights later, Rangers and Manchester United took the field at Hampden for the third quarter final. A crowd of 75,000 reflected the interest in this game, although one suspects a goodly number of Celtic fans – on the night supporting Manchester United – helped to swell the crowd.

Rangers were under-strength, without their wing-halfs, Ian McColl and Sammy Cox, and also their high-scoring inside-forward, Derek Grierson. As the match progressed, their absence became apparent. Although Rangers opened the scoring through young reserve player Peter McMillan in 7 minutes, Manchester United controlled the game, thoroughly making up for the poor displays of their compatriots – Arsenal and Spurs – on the opening night. Their two goals came just after the interval, the first in 52 minutes when Stan Pearson latched on to a short pass from Willie Woodburn to George Young and scored from close range; the second by Jack Rowley in 56 minutes, when, after a fine three-man move, he had all the time to pick his spot for the winner.

Aberdeen 0 Newcastle United 4

Meanwhile, over at Ibrox, Newcastle ran out easy winners over Aberdeen by 4-0. Yet Aberdeen, with the wind behind them, started brightly enough and struck the post three times in the first half. However, Newcastle looked a very composed team and soon showed their class. In 14 minutes outside-right Glen White scored from a free-kick and inside-left George Hannah got the second 6 minutes later with a 20 yard drive.

The second-half developed into an exhibition by the Magpies. When challenged by Jackie Millburn, George Young sent the ball past his own keeper Norrie Martin and seven minutes from the end, Millburn met a White free-kick on the turn and sent a fine shot past the Rangers goalkeeper. A crowd of only 5,000 was present to see Aberdeen's humiliation.

Celtic 2 Manchester United 1

On Saturday 16 May, in front of a disappointing 7,300 crowd, Celtic met Manchester United in the first of the semi-finals. A strong, gusty wind made conditions difficult, yet in the circumstances, this was an excellent match between two teams capable of some fine play.

Celtic fielded the same eleven which had beaten Arsenal and once again could thank their half-back line – Bobby Evans, Jock Stein and John McPhail – for inspiring the side to victory. But everyone played well. Bertie Peacock harried United's captain John Carey the whole match, never allowing him to use his tactical brain; Neilly Mochan made life difficult for centre-half Allenby Chilton, moving away from the middle frequently, thus dragging him out of position; and Charlie Tully gave his opponent Tom McNulty something of a roasting. It was Tully's fine play and good pass that gave Peacock the chance to open the scoring in the 34th minute. His powerful drive from just inside the box gave keeper Jack Crompton no chance. Manchester United opened the second half with the wind in their favour and fully expected to come into it as they had against Rangers. After only eight minutes however, Tully controlled a Rollo pass and sent a long ball into the path of Neilly Mochan, who placed a right-foot shot into the corner of the net. United had their chances, a miss right in front of goal by inside-left Pearson and a penalty claim against Alec Rollo; on the other hand Celtic might have gone further ahead when Bobby Collins only managed to hit the cross-bar from six yards out. Manchester United did pull one back through Jack Rowley 13 minutes from time and came at Celtic from then to the finish. Cool play, though, by Mike Haughney and Jock Stein kept them at bay and Celtic were through to the Final. Happy as the Celtic crowd were, the sight of Charlie Tully limping towards the dressing room gave them cause for concern.

Hibs 4 Newcastle United 0

Over at Ibrox, an excellent attendance of 45,000 were rather disappointed by a lacklustre display by Newcastle, who made a fairly lifeless contribution to the match.

On a dusty and bare pitch, in the strong swirling wind, Hibs gave a nice display of teamwork, combining good passing with strong shooting. Newcastle, on the other hand, were dainty but not direct and their efforts were never sustained.

Future Lisbon Lion Ronnie Simpson was unfortunate to lose the first goal in 16 minutes when an Eddie Turnbull shot was deflected past him by his centre-half Frank Brennan; and he was not at fault, either, in 33 minutes, when Lawrie Reilly knocked past him a cross-cum-shot, again by Turnbull, which was heading past the post.

Two further goals, by Johnstone in 54 minutes and Turnbull in 62, wrapped up the match for Hibs, leaving the fans happy but rather confused at the lack of zest in the English team's play.

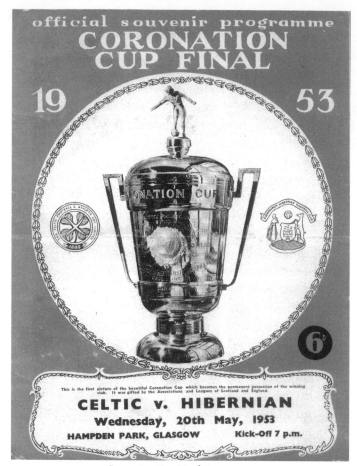

Coronation Cup Final Programme.

The Coronation Cup Final, Celtic v. Hibs

The Coronation Cup Final on 20 May 1953, was eagerly anticipated by press and fans alike. Because of the competition, the football season had been an unusually long one, but there was no end-of-season feeling about the Celtic-Hibs clash. Heavy rain fell on the dry Hampden pitch the day before the match, making the underfoot conditions well-nigh perfect on the night. Hibs were at full strength and favourites for the trophy. The forward line was well known as the Famous Five and more than compensated for an uncertain defence. Celtic were without Charlie Tully, injured in the last minute of the semi-final and drafted in Willie Fernie as his replacement. The full teams were:

Celtic: Bonnar; Haughney, Rollo; Evans, Stein, McPhail; Collins, Walsh; Mochan; Peacock and Fernie.

Hibs: Younger; Govan, Paterson; Buchanan, Howie, Combe; Smith, Johnstone; Reilly; Turnbull and Ormond.

Willie Fernie missed the first two matches of the Coronation Cup tournament, but came back for the final. Later, he went to Middlesborough for two seasons where he provided the ammunition for Brian Clough. He served as Celtic reserve coach during 1967–73, then as Kilmarnock manager from 1973–77.

Rather than rely on the newspapers for a description of this match, we can hear the words of Jock Stein from the same interview mentioned above.

Q The team had not been playing well all season, but from the Arsenal match, your form suddenly improved. Why?

A Well, a week before, we had a match against Ayr United. The manager, Mr McGrory – and the directors – were not happy with the form of the side at the time. I don't think they had any reason to be pleased with it and there was talk of various signings etc. We lost the Ayr match 3-1 and that put us back a bit, but in-between, there was talk of signing somebody and we then signed Neil Mochan at that time. This made a big difference because we had a Charity Cup Final coming up and this was his debut for the Club. He came on and did well and I think we all got a lift from that.

Q In the Manchester United match, was one of the star players a certain Mr Stein?

A Aye, I had quite a good game that night. Maybe there were so few I remember that one. Jack Rowley was playing at centre-forward and he was a prolific goal scorer. We had got Arsenal out of the way with a Bobby Collins corner-kick, he scored direct from a corner-kick. Manchester United had already beaten Rangers in the competition and everyone felt that they were favourites for the trophy. Johnny Carey was a big name in their side at that time, they had players like Dennis Violett and others who would be involved in the Munich Air disaster as well. But, it's true to say that I had a good game that night.

Q Now in the final, there were some famous names on either side?

A Oh! Hibs had a tremendous side at that time. I think that, when you look back at the five forwards they had at that time, the Famous Five, they were well named. But we had played well in the competition. I don't think that we were too worried about them.

John McPhail was a revelation for us in this competition. He played in mid-field and had a sort of free role, like the one Jim Baxter would later play. He didn't worry about picking up any players, as they talk about nowadays. He was the playmaker for us. Bertie Peacock worked hard for us and Charlie Tully obviously was on the wing for the early rounds. He wasn't fit for the final and Willie Fernie came in.

It was a big job for us because Hibs were a good side and had played well right through the competition. But on the night – lots of people say that we were lucky and that John Bonnar saved us but then, that's what he was there for. Celtic played good football that night and played good open football. We scored a goal – if my memory serves me right – in the first half. I made a tackle on Lawrie Reilly on the half-way line and the ball broke to Neilly Mochan. He just dragged it in and from the inside-left position – I still say it was 40 yards but he says it wasn't as far as that – he hit it with his right foot – the late Tommy Younger was in goals that day – I'm sure the only time he saw it was when it came back out of the net.

But Celtic played well on the night and one outstanding feature for us was Johnny Bonnar's display in goal. He had some unbelievable goal-line saves. John wasn't a good keeper off his line – I had charge of everything that came across. Again, that night, I think the whole team played well. I played particularly well myself against Lawrie Reilly, I remember it well, and Bobby Johnstone had played well because he was against John McPhail, who as I said, had a free role and Bobby then got some space. But Bonnar that night had some tremendous saves, and in the end, we ran out good winners.

Q Was the victory an important one for Celtic?

A The important thing for the Club and the players was that the Club had played in many of these competitions. There was a Victory Cup, there was the Exhibition Cup in 1938 and then this Coronation Cup. Each time a Cup had been put up for competition we had won it and this time round, we had won it well. Luckily, – if you want to say that – the following year 1953-1954 we won the League and Cup and obviously that was a very good season for us. It was a long time since Celtic had won the League before that.

107,000 fans had been present at this tremendous advert for football. Not only Jock Stein, but everyone who was there acknowledged with praise the performance of goalkeeper Johnny Bonnar. Yet only weeks before, he was so out of favour that Celtic made an unsuccessful bid for Morton's international keeper Jimmy Cowan. I once asked Neilly Mochan how far out he had been when he struck that famous goal. 'Never 40 yards, Jim' he disclaimed modestly, 'I would say about 35 yards – yes, 35 yards'. 'With the big brown ball too' I reminded him. He smiled at the memory; 'Aye Jim – the big brown ball'. He reflected for a moment then in vintage Mochan mode, blew through his cheeks and waved both hands in a dismissive gesture, 'some of these modern guys couldn't have kicked that ball 35 yards!'

The Coronation Cup.

Coronation Cup winning team. Back row, left to right: Alec Dowdalls (physiotherapist), Mike Haughney, Alec Rollo, John Bonnar, John McPhail, Bobby Evans, Charlie Tully, Jimmy McGrory. Front row: Bobby Collins, Jimmy Walsh, Jock Stein, Neilly Mochan, Bertie Peacock, Willie Fernie.

The Coronation Cup was brought back to Celtic Park and placed proudly in the trophy cabinet, to join the other 'one-off' cups so much a feature of Celtic's history. It had been a superb victory – and sparked off an air of renaissance which resulted in a League/Scottish Cup 'double' the following season.

267

CHAPTER SIXTEEN
'Hookey' — John McPhail

JOHN MCPHAIL was only 17 when he joined Celtic in 1941. He started off his career as a wing-half but later moved to the forward line, where his height and power were very effective. He also had a very good touch on the ball for such a big man and a fine eye for goals, as 87 in 204 appearances will testify.

Nicknamed 'Hookey' because of the spin he could put on a ball, John scored the only goal of the 1951 Scottish Cup Final win against Motherwell, was a 'revelation' at wing-half (according to Jock Stein) in the Coronation Cup of 1953 and played his part in the League Cup 'Double' season of 1953–1954. Unlike many players, John McPhail's only senior club was Celtic.

Q You arrived at Celtic Park in 1941, just after the war had started. It must have been a strange time to be playing professional football.

A It certainly was. I had only come out of school – St Mungo's Academy – and played one or two games for Junior teams to earn some pocket money on a Saturday. I played for Ashfield, Blantyre Celtic and one or two others. When I played for Blantyre Celtic, Tommy Bogan was also playing that day and we turned up after the game, which we had won, for the cash. So this old boy gave the rest 30 shillings (£1.50) each and says to me, 'you're gettin £2.00 son'. 'That's lovely', I replied 'very generous. What's that for?' 'To make sure you don't come back!' The next week I played for Strathclyde and Celtic signed me shortly afterwards, Strathclyde getting about £250 – in those days a lot of money.

Q Did the war make a difference to the play?

A Oh yes! Tom White, who was the Chairman at the time, refused to have guest players, under any manner or means. Rangers had them, other teams had them, it was one way of getting the best players, but Tom White said no! He refused Matt Busby and Matt went to Hibs and that helped them enormously. Several other players were refused, like Gerry McAloon, who eventually came to us. Then, the Directors eased up a bit on the rule but by then there was no-one available to come. Many of our players were in the Army or Navy at the time. Fortunately I was only 17. But in general, it was a bad period.

Q Near the end of the war there was a change of manager at Celtic Park. Did that make a difference?

A Well, old Jimmy (McStay) was always under starters orders! He was a good old chap, well meaning and what not, but we never though he would last too long. When Jimmy McGrory came in though, we were looking for big things from him. He was a hero of mine. There was a bit of an upset for a period and then we got players like Charlie

John 'Hookey' McPhail in his early days at Parkhead. Due to injury, John never played as many games as he might have, but he did play in the important ones in the 1950s, e.g. the 1951 Scottish Cup final and the Coronation Cup final.

(Tully) and Bertic (Peacock) from Ireland and things took a turn for the better. We got the Glasgow Cup, something we had not had for a while and played good football. Shortly, we went on to win the Scottish Cup.

Q But in between John there had been some terrible years. Why was that? I mean, there were some good players there at the time.

A There were several good players. You couldn't put your finger on anything in particular. However, I must be honest and say that although there were several good players there, there were also some very poor players. As a Celtic fan, I was weaned on the Exhibition team and the team of the 30s, so when I went there, and walked in among players who were, let's say, non-Celtic class players, that was disappointing. So while we had several really good ones, there were many of the other type as well.

Q How did Celtic compare to Rangers of that time?

A Oh! They were great. They were very strong and they had two or three of these guest stars — they were tremendous — and their whole team was dynamite. They used to play their Reserve team in the North-Eastern League during the war. They did fairly in it at times because they had so many good players in the whole squad.

Q The season of 1947–48 was a disastrous one for Celtic. At the end of it you had to play in a most important game at Dundee. A win was required to avoid relegation.

A That was a classic. We had signed wee Jock Weir, from Middlesborough and wee Jock was a character. Bob Kelly was Chairman by that time. Tom White had died in 1947, so Bob was now headman. When we got to Dundee for the actual game, he said 'I don't know what to do with you all, so just go out and relax'. Now had that been modern times, with events as they were, we would have been better watched. But, we all felt a devotion to the Club, so we went out and merely had a beer or two, something like that, and went to bed.

    The next day, we all went onto that park brand new, fit as fiddles. We scored first through wee Jock Weir and they equalised just before half-time. Wee Jock was right on form. They had made me captain that day and I was getting onto the wee man all the time to do something for us. Then Dundee went 2-1 ahead but in the last 10 minutes, marvellous, two hoaching great goals by Jock, 3-2, and that saved us. As it worked out, we finished fifth from the bottom. Supposing we had been beaten in that particular game, we would still have been safe. But that didn't matter, we just knew we had to win that particular match and we did it.

Q There were stories at that time about Jimmy McGrory not picking the team and Bob Kelly being the man controlling everything. Was that true?

A Just about that period, I think Jimmy let go of the reins himself. He felt he hadn't been making good choices. I liked the old chap enormously, but he wasn't a dominant figure and quietly, without any great fuss or announcement, Bob (Kelly) gradually took control.

Q The Scottish Cup Final of 1951 seemed to be a rather special day for John McPhail.

A It was indeed. Oh! I enjoyed that one thoroughly. Strangely enough, I had been bothered all that year by a bad groin injury. After two or three matches, I would have to stop playing, then after a wee rest, I would come back in again. It wouldn't be allowed nowadays. Towards the end of the season. I was only playing in the Cup matches, then getting a couple of weeks rest before the next one and so on. I could only last 10–15 minutes; so everything I had to do had to be packed into that period.

    When it came to the Cup Final against Motherwell, I'm looking up at the clock and saying, 'its about time my groin went again!' It was about the 14th or 15th minute, Joe Baillie, I think, won the ball, banged it through and I was onto it, beat a couple of men then lobbed it over the keeper. The first thing I did was look up at the clock and say to myself, 'well, my groin's about to go any minute!' And it did.

Q The aftermath of that victory of course was that the Club went on tour to the USA. That must have been quite a trip?

A We went over by boat. That was a three to four day trip, we were in the lap of luxury and all that kind of thing. We had a very successful tour. I think we won seven, lost one and drew one. We had several hard matches against Fulham and an awful game against Eintracht Frankfurt, break-ins and what not, with a large support for them from the German community in New York. But overall it was a marvellous experience.

Q When I interviewed Jock Stein many years ago about the Coronation Cup, he commented that McPhail's play was, in his words, a 'revelation'. For Jock to say that you must have played well.

A Well, during that tournament I was just recovering from the groin strain, which took nearly two years before I felt O.K. again. It was Bob Kelly who then suggested that, since I had started off as a mid-field man, I should go back and play there. So there was Bobby Evans, Jock and myself. We beat Arsenal, then Manchester United to go on to the Final to meet Hibs, who were really bouncing along then. They had the Famous Five forward line and loved to move about, so I said to myself — playing left-half — anything we do, we've got to do early on. If we don't do something early on, this team will smother us. I kept feeding Neilly Mochan with the ball and he eventually scored that glorious goal before half-time. In the second-half — I think I was 15 stone and 90 years old at the time — in that second-half, I felt like that and they absolutely came on top of us like an avalanche. How they didn't score, I'll never know. With five minutes to go, Gordon Smith beat a couple of men, crossed the ball, and Lawrie Reilly had a shot. It hit Johnny Bonnar on the head, hit the cross-bar and then dropped back down into Johnny's hands. I just stood there with my hands on my hips, hysterical with laughter, as Reilly was going off his nut. I quickly took a look up at that old Hampden clock, then suddenly, there was a shout from the other end and Jimmy Walsh had put us 2-up! I couldn't believe the score but was just happy to win.

Q And of course success in that competition led to a great season the following year.

A Yes, I was very lucky to be part of that wonderful season. Not many players in Celtic's history have ever done a League and Cup 'Double', so it was wonderful for us.

Q Tell me about some of the players at Celtic Park at the time.

A Well, Charlie Tully was really good. I was responsible for getting him to Parkhead in the first place. My throat had been giving me bother and they sent me over to Coleraine in northern Ireland, where I had some friends. Every Saturday, I used to go into Coleraine or up to Belfast to see Belfast Celtic and Tully impressed me immensely.

When I came back I mentioned him to Chic Geatons who was coaching for Celtic and McGrory and said 'there's a man over there worth taking a look at' and next thing they have got him over and signed. By the time I got back, he had played against Rangers — which obviously I missed — and I couldn't believe all the jubilation. I knew he was good, but I didn't think he was that good. I joined the team again and then realised he was something else. What we needed then was a lift and Charlie gave us that.

Bobby Collins was a great wee player. Industrious, hard. Not the same ability as Jimmy Johnstone, for instance, but he had pace and he crossed some great balls to me at centre, crosses driven hard, you just had to touch it and it was in the back of the net. Bertie Peacock was the engine room for Charlie and also played some good stuff. Bobby Evans, of course, was another engine room at the back. And of course, there was Jock Stein, the old steadying head, and the full-backs like Sean Fallon. We had a great keeper for a while in 1951 — George Hunter — who unfortunately later took ill. Johnny Bonnar came in for the Coronation Cup and the 'Double' and he certainly did his bit. But we all did our best and the Club achieved a recovery, or partial recovery.

Q How did you get on with the Rangers players?

A Well, my opponent was usually Willie Woodburn for a long time and I got on fine with him. Mind you, I was 14–15 stone and he was only 13 stone! But I do remember a game, a Charity Cup tie or a Glasgow Cup tie, and we beat them. For the first goal, the ball came over from Charlie, his crosses were never as hard as Bobby Collins's, so you had to jump and direct them. So I jumped, and Woodburn jumped and the ball

John McPhail and Ella McPhail in 1998.

went into the net. Woodburn turned to me and said in a quiet voice, 'John I touched that before it went in!' I replied 'Willie, I'm delighted that a Rangers player scored the opening goal for Celtic in an Old Firm tie'. I was credited with a hat-trick, yet the first came off Woodburn, the second hit Sammy Cox's toe on the line before going into the net, but I definitely got the third myself.

Q John, suppose a manager like Jock Stein had been in charge then, would the players have responded to him?

A We had too many sort of, well its hard to define. You see, I played with a lot of Exhibition Cup chaps and they were not only great players in their own right but introduced a new format which suited them. They might not have listened to a modern coach-type figure.

Once the older players went out, Jock came in, had a bunch of fairly young guys around him, and even then, he spoke a lot of good sense.

Q You were nearly in the unusual position of having two brothers there at Celtic Park. I believe you just missed each other.

A Yes, I left to join the *Daily Record* and Billy, who was with Clyde came in about a month later. Apparently, at one time, the Chairman made a remark such as 'Oh! I've made a mistake paying two and a half grand for this fellow!' Well, to be honest, Billy's legs were bad even then, he hadn't done much, then scored three against Rangers. After that, he was the greatest thing since sliced bread!

Q How do you look back on your whole 14-year career at Celtic Park?

A I enjoyed every minute of it – the good, the bad, the miserable. It was something I wanted to do, never thought it would happen and it did happen. But if I regret something, it was that we were never properly guided – and while we had four or five stars in the team, there was still a lot of questionable players.

Now, Jock rubbed that out because when it came to the Lisbon Lion situation, every guy could hold his own position, there was no dead wood about. In my time we had, although I won't mention names – some people might think I was one of them! But, as I say, Jock got it with new faces, new people, people of talent, ones he could talk to, or even bully occasionally. However, I don't think he could have handled any better than McGrory did, the type of player that was there in the early 50s.

CHAPTER SEVENTEEN (1953–1960)
In Sunshine — then in Shadow

A VERY JUBILANT GROUP of players arrived back in July for pre-season training, confident that the success in the Coronation Cup would lead to further glory. The more astute supporters, however, were not expecting too much. In contrast to the early years of the century, when cups were regarded more highly, now the league was the major trophy and Celtic's recent record there was deplorable. A glance at the table below shows just how poor the league record had been since the the Second World War.

		Celtic's League Record 1946–53		
SEASON	GAMES PLAYED	POSITION	GOALS FOR	GOALS AGAINST
1946–47	30	7th	53	55
1947–48	30	12th	41	56
1948–49	30	6th	48	40
1949–50	30	5th	51	50
1950–51	30	7th	48	46
1951–52	30	9th	52	55
1952–53	30	8th	51	54

In four of these seven seasons more goals were lost than scored; in another, parity was almost achieved. The best goals scored per game (in 1946–47) was a measly 1.7; the worst goals lost (in 1947–48) WAS a disastrous 1.8. Unfortunately, this latter figure was nearly equalled in three other seasons.

No wonder the Celtic fans of the time felt frustrated and annoyed. Only the Scottish Cup win of 1951 had lightened the gloom. Yet, this same team, which had finished eighth in the League, failed to qualify from their League Cup section and went out of the Scottish Cup at the quarter-final stage, had taken on the best of Britain to win the Coronation Cup. The faithful had been delighted but still looked forward to season 1953–54 more in hope than expectation.

1953–1954 LEAGUE CUP		
Section Games	H	A
Aberdeen	0-1	2-5
Airdrie	2-0	1-2
East Fife	0-1	1-1

			LEAGUE CUP POSITION					
	P	W	D	L	F	A	Points	Position
Celtic	6	1	1	4	6	10	3	4th

Celtic failed to qualify for the next stage

This was the worst League Cup campaign so far, Celtic winning only one match. The fans were bitterly disappointed, as this competition came only two months after Celtic had beaten the best of Britain's teams to win the Coronation Cup. Despair settled on Celtic Park, yet within a matter of months, the same squad of players would achieve the 'double' of League and Cup.

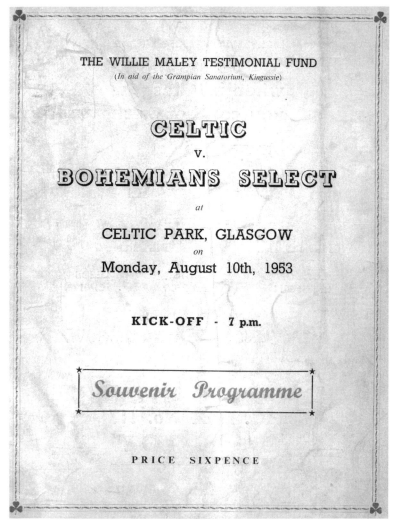

THE WILLIE MALEY TESTIMONIAL FUND
(In aid of the Grampian Sanatorium, Kingussie)

CELTIC

v.

BOHEMIANS SELECT

at

CELTIC PARK, GLASGOW

on

Monday, August 10th, 1953

KICK-OFF - 7 p.m.

Souvenir Programme

PRICE SIXPENCE

Willie Maley was in his 86th year when this match was played. Celtic fielded the team that had just won the Coronation Cup; the Bohemians Select was boosted by two players from Cliftonville and three from Queen's Park.

Willie Maley sits in the middle of the front row, surrounded by the players of Celtic and the Bohemians Select. Unfortunately for the visitors Celtic rather hogged the proceeding, winning 10-1.

1953–1954 Scottish League Division 1							
	P	W	D	L	F	A	Points	Position
Celtic	30	20	3	7	72	29	43	1st

Fixtures					
	H	A		H	A
Aberdeen	3-0	0-2	Hibs	2-2	3-0
Airdrie	4-1	6-0	Partick Thistle	2-1	3-1
Clyde	1-0	7-1	Queen of South	3-1	1-2
Dundee	5-1	1-1	Raith Rovers	3-0	0-2
East Fife	4-1	1-4	Rangers	1-0	1-1
Falkirk	1-0	3-0	St Mirren	4-0	3-1
Hamilton	1-0	0-2	Stirling Albion	4-0	1-2
Hearts	2-0	2-3			

The defence was much tighter than the year before. Whichever goalkeeper played (the appearances were split between Johnny Bonar, George Hunter and Andy Bell) the back line was sound, with full-backs Mike Haughney and Frank Meechan also playing their parts. The half-back line of Bobby Evans, Jock Stein and Bertie Peacock was very solid, both wing-halves capable of some fine football. Up front, while 2.4 goals per match was not vintage scoring at that period in football, the forward line was certainly entertaining and/or infuriating, depending on which minute of which match. Various permutations were used, the choice from Collins, Walsh, Fernie, Tully, Fallon, Mochan and Higgins. However, they did well enough to help Celtic take their 20th Championship, the first since 1937–38, finishing five points clear of Hearts. Top scorer was Neil Mochan, with 20 goals.

The challenge for the Title seemed to falter when Celtic were beaten by their closest rivals at Tynecastle on 6 February 1954, Jimmy Wardhaugh scoring a controversial winner by bundling George Hunter over the line. The prospective Champions, though, showed their mettle by winning their last nine matches scoring 22 goals.

1953–1954 SCOTTISH CUP

17/02/54		Falkirk	(A)	2-1	20,000
27/02/54		Stirling Albion	(A)	4-3	26,300
13/03/54	QF	Hamilton	(A)	2-1	22,000
27/03/54	SF	Motherwell	(Hampden)	2-2	104,424
05/04/54	Replay	Motherwell	(Hampden)	3-1	96,200
24/04/54	Final	Aberdeen	(Hampden)	2-1	130,060

Team: Bonnar; Haughney, Meechan; Evans, Stein, Peacock; Higgins, Fernie; Fallon; Tully and Mochan.

A well-deserved victory for Celtic in this competition, particularly when all the matches were played away from Celtic Park. Celtic had received a bye in the first round and had to wait an extra four days before the second round tie could go ahead, as Brockville had been unplayable on the Saturday. Against Stirling, they were 2-0 down and also 2-3 at one point, but a fierce free-kick from Neilly Mochan 30 yards out was the turning point in the match. In the semi final, Motherwell equalised in the last minute to force an equaliser, but nine days later, a superb performance on the wing by John Higgins provided the inspiration for victory. Fernie, Mochan and an O.G. by right-back Kilmarnock were the scorers. The Final was eagerly anticipated, as Aberdeen had beaten Rangers 6-0 in the other semi-final and were regarded as worthy opponents. Celtic opened brightly, won corner after corner but the Aberdeen defence held firm and at half-time, there was still no scoring. Early in the second half, Celtic went ahead when a fierce cross-cum-shot from Neilly Mochan was deflected into his own net by centre-half Young. Shortly afterwards, Buckley equalised for Aberdeen but as the battle continued, Celtic became the stronger side. The winner came from a classic and typical run by Willie Fernie, who received the ball from a throw-in, swerved his way along the line past several defenders before rolling the ball back into the path of Sean Fallon, who tapped it into the net.

It was a perfect ending to the season, one during which the team, against all expectations, had won Celtic's fourth League and Cup 'double'. A grateful Board of Directors then took them to Switzerland to see the World Cup Tournament, eventually won by West Germany.

1953–1954 GLASGOW CUP

Rangers	(Hampden)	0-1

1953–1954 CHARITY CUP

	Queen's Park	(H)	0-0
Replay	Queen's Park	(A)	1-0
	Rangers	(A)	1-1
Replay	Rangers	(H)	0-4

———— ✤ ————

1954–1955 SCOTTISH LEAGUE CUP

Section Games	H	A
Dundee	0-1	1-3
Falkirk	3-0	2-2
Hearts	1-2	2-3

LEAGUE CUP POSITION

	P	W	D	L	F	A	Points	Position
Celtic	6	1	1	4	9	11	3	3rd

Celtic failed to qualify for the next stage.

After the glories of the previous year's double it was the same old story in the League Cup. At least, Celtic had the consolation, slight though it was, of losing to the eventual winners, Hearts.

1954–1955 SCOTTISH LEAGUE DIVISION 1

	P	W	D	L	F	A	Points	Position
Aberdeen	30	24	1	5	73	26	49	1st
Celtic	30	19	8	3	76	37	46	2nd

FIXTURES

	H	A		H	A
Aberdeen	2-1	2-0	Motherwell	1-0	2-2
Clyde	2-2	2-2	Partick Thistle	0-0	2-4
Dundee	4-1	1-0	Queen of South	1-1	2-0
East Fife	2-2	4-3	Raith Rovers	4-1	3-1
Falkirk	3-1	1-1	Rangers	2-0	1-4
Hearts	2-0	3-0	St Mirren	5-2	1-1
Hibs	1-2	5-0	Stirling Albion	7-0	3-2
Kilmarnock	6-3	2-1			

The League campaign was disappointing, at least in terms of final position. A glance at the respective years' final results, though, shows that this year's unsuccessful team only won one less game, lost four fewer, scored four more goals and finished with three more points.

CELTIC'S LEAGUE PERFORMANCE 1953–1955

	P	W	D	L	F	A	Points	Position
1953–1954	30	20	3	7	72	29	43	1st
1954–1955	30	19	8	3	76	37	46	2nd

The eight extra goals lost, though, was probably critical, as was the challenge by Aberdeen in their first ever championship year. In 1953–54, even with a comparatively small total of 43 points, the joint lowest ever in the nine seasons since the war, Celtic finished five points clear of the rest.

The team had started the season well, unbeaten in the first nine matches then losing away to Partick Thistle (2-4). Then came a run of five unbeaten before falling heavily to Rangers on New Year's Day (1-4) and a further successful sequence of ten before losing to Hibs (1-2). However, among the unbeaten runs, were poorish draws, St. Mirren (1-1), Falkirk (1-1), Queen of the South (1-1) and East Fife (2-2). Two players – Haughney and Evans – played in every match, Peacock only missed one and Stein two. John McPhail started in only four, his aerial power badly missed. Perhaps most surprising was that Bobby Collins played in only 20 of the league matches and Neilly Mochan in 17, especially when the scoring rate was taken into account. Collins notched five and Mochan nine. Top scorers were Walsh (19), Fernie (13) and Higgins (9), with Jock Stein, for the second successive season, scoring one league goal.

		1954–1955 Scottish Cup			
05/02/55		Alloa Athletic	(A)	4-2	15,000
19/02/55		Kilmarnock	(A)	1-1	31,000
23/02/55	Replay	Kilmarnock	(H)	1-0	40,000
05/03/55	QF	Hamilton	(H)	2-1	49,000
26/03/55	SF	Airdrie	(Hampden)	2-2	88,840
04/04/55	Replay	Airdrie	(Hampden)	2-0	71,800
23/04/55	Final	Clyde	(Hampden)	1-1	106,234
27/04/55	Replay	Clyde	(Hampden)	0-1	68,831

Team: Bonnar; Haughney, Meechan; Evans, Stein, Peacock; Collins, Fernie; McPhail; Walsh, Tully. Replay: Fallon replaced Collins.

Not an easy passage through the earlier rounds, in front of large crowds. In the first match against Kilmarnock, a block on his own line by Alec Rollo saved the day; while in the quarter-final, Hamilton fought all the way before Celtic scored the winner in the second-half. Nearly 89,000 were present for the semi-final, in which Airdrie scored in 20 seconds, but Celtic were level at half-time, thanks to Willie Fernie. Another goal by Jimmy Walsh made it 2-1 for Celtic, who had most of the pressure, although Airdrie surprisingly equalised near the end. For the replay, Celtic brought back John McPhail, now fit again and his controlled play made life difficult for the young Airdrie centre-half Doug Baillie. McPhail led the line in exemplary fashion and scored two fine goals in the second-half.

Celtic started the final in exuberant mood and scored in 35 minutes through Jimmy Walsh after a fine through ball by Willie Fernie. Gradually, though, particularly in the second-half, Celtic withdrew into a defensive shell and allowed Clyde more and more of the play. With less than two minutes left, a corner on the right was taken by Archie Robertson. To his disgust, it was flighted too near the Celtic keeper to do any damage.

Unfortunately, Johnny Bonnar, in the Celtic goal, completely misjudged the swirling cross, which merely touched his fingers before dropping down to bounce over the line.

For the replay, the Celtic management made one of those selection decisions quite common in the 50s and 60s which the fans could only wonder about. Bobby Collins, who had given Clyde's international left-back Harry Haddock a hard time on the Saturday, was dropped. Jimmy Walsh moved to inside-right, Sean Fallon was brought in at centre-forward and John McPhail moved to inside-left. The reason for the change was never revealed; in practice, the momentum has been given to Clyde. They took advantage of it and did what Celtic were noted for under pressure. They raised their game, struck at the Celtic defence with speed and eagerness, eventually getting the winning goal through Tommy Ring. Thanks to a goalkeeper's error in the first match and poor forward play in the second, Celtic had lost a great chance to retain the Scottish Cup. They would have to wait ten years before it returned to Parkhead.

1954–1955 GLASGOW CUP

	Partick Thistle	(A)	2-2
Replay	Partick Thistle	(H)	2-2
Replay	Partick Thistle	(H)	4-5

1954–1955 CHARITY CUP

Rangers	(H)	0-1

1955–1956 SCOTTISH LEAGUE CUP

Section Games	H	A
Falkirk	5-1	1-1
Queen of the South	4-2	2-0
Rangers	0-4	4-1

League Cup Position

	P	W	D	L	F	A	Points	Position
Celtic	6	4	1	1	16	9	9	2nd

Celtic failed to qualify for the next stage.

The same old story in the League Cup – non-qualification for the quarter-final. This season's competition, though, started well for Celtic, as they beat Queen of the South in successive matches and then hammered Falkirk 5–1 at Parkhead. Rangers had also won their three matches, so the scene was set for a deciding match on 27 August at Ibrox. The Celtic fans in the 75,000 were treated to a superb, determined display by their team, which never allowed Rangers to settle and won handsomely by 4 goals to 0, the scorers being Mochan, McPhail and new boy Eric Smith (2).

Four days later, the teams met again, this time at Parkhead, with the Celtic contingent already anticipating a quarter-final place. There was the usual surprise in the Celtic selection, Matt McVittie being brought in for his very first match. Within two minutes, Sammy Baird gave Rangers the lead and just before the interval, Jock Stein left the field in obvious pain from an ankle injury. He resumed in the second half, but as a passenger at outside-left, with Bobby Evans moving into the pivotal position. Almost immediately, Sean Fallon pulled up lame with a muscle problem and Celtic had to reshuffle once again. Rangers took control, scored through Sammy Baird, and then got two further goals in the last ten minutes, thus wiping out Celtic's better goal average.

1955–1956 SCOTTISH LEAGUE DIVISION I

	P	W	D	L	F	A	Points	Position
Rangers	34	22	8	4	85	27	52	1st
Celtic	34	16	9	9	55	39	41	5th

FIXTURES

	H	A		H	A
Aberdeen	1-1	0-1	Kilmarnock	0-2	0-0
Airdrie	3-1	2-1	Motherwell	2-2	2-2
Clyde	4-1	3-1	Partick Thistle	5-1	0-2
Dundee	1-0	2-1	Queen of South	1-3	3-1
Dunfermline	4-2	1-1	Raith Rovers	2-0	1-1
East Fife	0-0	0-3	Rangers	0-1	0-0
Falkirk	1-0	1-3	St Mirren	3-0	2-0
Hearts	1-1	1-2	Stirling Albion	3-0	3-0
Hibs	0-3	3-2			

In a league increased to 18 teams, this campaign was disappointing, with too few goals scored. Apart from goalkeeper Dick Beattie, who only missed three matches, the team was chopped and changed in every position, including centre-half, where Jock Stein eventually retired with ankle trouble in January and Bobby Evans took over for the rest of the season. In the first five matches (two won, two lost, one drawn), five different outside-rights were tried, (Craig, Smith, Docherty, Collins and Higgins) and by the season's end, another three players (Walsh, McVittie and McAlindon) had also been given a run in the same positions.

1955–1956 SCOTTISH CUP

04/02/56		Morton	(A)	2-0	17,000
18/02/56		Ayr United	(A)	3-0	24,000
03/03/56	QF	Airdrie	(H)	2-1	59,000
24/03/56	SF	Clyde	(Hampden)	2-1	62,500
21/04/56	Final	Hearts	(Hampden)	1-3	132,840

Team: Beattie; Meechan, Fallon; Smith, Evans, Peacock; Craig, Haughney; Mochan; Fernie, Tully.

A competition played in diverse conditions. At Cappielow, there was a sodden pitch, with occasional hidden icy patches, a drizzling rain which soaked the whole crowd and play to match the conditions. Two first-half goals by Tully and Collins sealed the victory.

At Somerset Park, by contrast, the match began with a rock-hard pitch underfoot and a wintry sun overhead, not the conditions liked by the Celtic players. One goal in the first half and two in the last minute of play (Collins and Mochan) took the team into the quarter-finals.

At Parkhead, there was pale sunshine and a stiff breeze blowing straight down the length of the pitch. Celtic took advantage of it in the first-half and scored through Collins; Airdrie equalised in 74 minutes, stunning the Parkhead faithful. Within four minutes, though, Tully eased fears of a replay with a typical neat effort.

Against Clyde in the semi-final, Celtic went two up early on but then allowed the Bully Wee back into it, just like the year before. However, although McPhail pulled one back for Clyde, Celtic held out to make the Final for the third successive year. There were obvious problems of selection for this last match. Collins was unfit, as was Higgins, so an unknown youngster – Billy Craig – was brought in for his first Scottish Cup tie. As Jock Stein and Alec Boden were also injured, Eric Smith was chosen at right-half and Bobby Evans moved to centre-half. Mike Haughney partnered Craig in attack and Frank Meechan came in at right-back. There was much shaking of heads in the Celtic fans' section over these moves, ones obviously received with delight by Hearts. They fully deserved their victory, tackling hard, striking with venom and refusing to allow an increasingly dispirited Celtic eleven any say in the match. Goals by Ian Crawford (2) and Alfie Conn to one by Mike Haughney meant the Cup went back to Edinburgh for the first time since 1906.

		1955–1956 Glasgow Cup			
		Clyde	(H)	4.0	
		Partick Thistle	(A)	2.0	
26/09/56	Final	Rangers	(Hampden)	1-1	53,000
26/12/56	Replay	Rangers	(Hampden)	5-3	39,000

Team: Beattie; Haughney, Fallon; Evans, Stein, Peacock; Smith, Fernie; Sharkey, Collins and Mochan.

The final replay was keenly anticipated, especially the clash between the centre-halves, Jock Stein and George Young, and the new boys, Jim Sharkey of Celtic and 'The Rhino' Don Kichenbrand from South Africa. On the day, Celtic won mainly because Sharkey's clever dribbling discomforted George Young whereas Jock Stein, in one of his last performances, managed to contain the 'Rhino'. The goals came from Collins (2), Sharkey (2) and Fernie.

1955–1956 CHARITY CUP

Clyde	(H)	4-1
Third Lanark	(A)	0-0
		Third Lanark won on toss of coin

1956–1957 SCOTTISH LEAGUE CUP

Section Games	H	A
Aberdeen	3-2	2-1
East Fife	2-1	1-0
Rangers	2-1	0-0

LEAGUE CUP POSITION

	P	W	D	L	F	A	Points	Position
Celtic	6	5	1	0	10	5	11	1st

LEAGUE CUP QUARTER- AND SEMI-FINALS

	QF	Dunfermline	6-0 0-3	Aggregate: 6-3	
	SF	Clyde	2-0	(Hampden)	
27/10/56	Final	Partick Thistle	0-0 (AET)	(Hampden)	58,973
31/10/56	Replay	Partick Thistle	3-0	(Hampden)	31,126

Team: Beattie; Haughney, Fallon; Evans, Jack, Peacock; Walsh, Collins; B. McPhail; Tully and Fernie. Replay: Mochan for Walsh.

For only the second time in the competition's history, Celtic topped the League Cup section. A tough one it was, too, but Celtic disposed comfortably of the Dons and East Fife both home and away, won a tight Old Firm encounter at Parkhead thanks to goals by Collins and Tully, then held out at Ibrox.

The defence was quite set at this period; Beattie, Haughney, Fallon, Evans, new boy John Jack and Peacock, while a good addition to the forward line was Billy McPhail, signed from Clyde for £2,500.

He scored two against Dunfermline in the first leg of the quarter-final, along with Mochan (2) and Collins (1), as with an own goal thrown in for good measure, Celtic gave the Pars a 6-0 hammering. Some frailties were still evident, though, as they crashed 0-3 in the return, but still went through on aggregate.

Billy McPhail was on target twice more against his old team Clyde in the semi-final to take Celtic through to the Final, where the fans' expectations were high as they faced Partick Thistle at Hampden. 89,973 were present but, in truth, it was a disappointing match. Four days later, with one change in the Celtic line-up – Mochan in for Walsh, the match was again scoreless by the interval. Four minutes into the second half, Billy McPhail was on the spot to punish defensive dithering by clipping the ball past Tommy Ledgewood in Thistle's goal. Shortly after, he flicked Neilly Mochan's cross into the net from close in. In the 60th minute, Bobby Collins raced clear of an opposing defence claiming off-side and shot low and hard into the net to seal a Celtic victory. It was their first ever League Cup win – but only 31,126 were there to witness the event.

1956–1957 SCOTTISH LEAGUE DIVISION I

	P	W	D	L	F	A	Points	Position
Rangers	34	26	3	5	96	48	55	1st
Celtic	34	15	8	11	58	43	38	5th

FIXTURES

	H	A		H	A
Aberdeen	2-1	1-0	Kilmarnock	1-1	0-0
Airdrie	3-0	7-3	Motherwell	2-1	0-1
Ayr United	4-0	3-1	Partick Thistle	1-1	1-3
Dundee	1-1	1-2	Queen of South	0-0	3-4
Dunfermline	3-1	1-0	Queen's Park	2-0	0-2
East Fife	4-0	0-2	Raith Rovers	1-1	1-3
Falkirk	4-0	1-0	Rangers	0-2	0-2
Hearts	1-1	1-3	St. Mirren	2-3	0-2
Hibs	2-1	3-3			

In the League, Celtic finished in the same disappointing fifth position of the year before. Unfortunately, Billy McPhail, who had missed only one of the 11 League Cup fixtures, started only 13 of the 34 League matches. A disappointing 11 games were lost, only two of which were at home – Rangers in the second match on the 22 September and St. Mirren on 17 April. The home record, in fact, was very good, 9 won, 6 drawn, 33 for, 14 against, but oh, that away form, 9 lost and 29 goals against. Rangers won both league matches, the first time since 1948–49.

The forward line was seldom the same two weeks running, with two new names, Alex Bryne and Vince Ryan getting a few games at inside-forward and centre-forward. Top scorers were Mochan (8), Higgins (9), Collins (5), Ryan (3), McPhail (4), Fernie (6) and Haughney with 7 penalties. As one McPhail (John) came to the end of his Celtic career (May 1956) brother Billy joined the same month from Clyde and played a big part in the League Cup win – the first ever. His best moments for Celtic, however, were yet to come.

1956–1957 SCOTTISH CUP

02/02/57		Forres Mechanics	(A)	5-0	7,000
16/02/57		Rangers	(H)	4-4	55,000
20/02/57	Replay	Rangers	(A)	2-0	80,000
02/03/57	QF	St Mirren	(H)	2-1	49,000
23/03/57	SF	Kilmarnock	(Hampden)	1-1	109,145
27/03/57	Replay	Kilmarnock	(Hampden)	1-3	76,963

After an easy first round victory over Forres Mechanics, Celtic faced their Old Firm rivals in the sixth round at Parkhead. It turned out to be a rousing match, 2-2 at half-time, the goals coming from Billy McPhail (2), Higgins and Collins. Four days later, in the replay, Higgins and Mochan scored the first-half goals which took Celtic through. The fans must have felt that the team could go all the way after that and certainly the team coped comfortably with St Mirren in the quarter-finals. Kilmarnock, though, proved to be made of sterner stuff, were one up at half-time in the semi-final, before Collins equalised. In the replay though, Killie always had the upper hand and ran out worthy winners, much to the disgust of the Celtic support.

1956–1957 GLASGOW CUP

Rangers	(H)	3-4

1956–1957 CHARITY CUP

Rangers	(A)	0-1

The American Tour 1957

Celtic set sail on the *Mauretania* for North America on the Club's third tour of that continent at the end of the season. On previous tours, most of the matches had been confined to the East Coast and environs but this time, thanks to air travel, Celtic also played in St Louis, Vancouver, and San Francisco.

Everywhere they went, the players and officials received great hospitality, most fans wanting to discuss the winning of the League Cup for the first time when they beat Partick Thistle. Perhaps it was a pity the tour was not one year later, when a second League Cup win was even more memorable.

FIXTURES

19/05/57	Celtic 3	Tottenham Hotspur 4	New York
25/05/57	Celtic 4	Philadelphia Uhriks 0	Philadelphia
26/05/57	Celtic 2	Hapoel (Israel) 1	New York
29/05/57	Celtic 3	Catholic Youth Council Select 0	St Louis
01/06/57	Celtic 3	Tottenham Hotspur 6	Vancouver
05/06/57	Celtic 5	San Fransico Select 0	San Fransico
08/06/57	Celtic 1	Tottenham Hotspur 3	Toronto
09/06/57	Celtic 2	Tottenham Hotspur 2	Montreal

AMERICAN TOUR RESULTS

	P	W	D	L	F	A
Celtic	8	5	0	3	23	14

1957–1958 SCOTTISH LEAGUE CUP

Section Game	H	A
Airdrie	3-2	2-1
East Fife	6-1	4-1
Hibs	2-0	1-3

LEAGUE CUP POSITION

	P	W	D	L	F	A	Points	Position
Celtic	6	5	0	1	18	8	11	1st

LEAGUE CUP QUARTER- AND SEMI-FINALS

			H	A	
	QF	Third Lanark	6-1	3-0	Aggregate: 9-1
	SF	Clyde (Ibrox)	4-2		
19/10/57	Final	Rangers	(Hampden)	7-1	82,293

Team: Beattie; Donnelly, Fallon; Fernie, Evans, Peacock; Tully, Collins; McPhail; Wilson and Mochan.

Another successful League Cup section, with only Hibs offering any real challenge. Qualification was made more tense by Hibs winning the first of the section meetings at Easter Road, but Celtic rose to the challenge in the home match at Parkhead, with Billy McPhail and his new-found partner Sammy Wilson – a bargain free from St Mirren – getting one goal each. Two other young boys were blooded – John Donnelly at right-back and Bertie Auld at outside-left.

A comfortable double win against Third Lanark in the quarter-final and a stiffer test by a flu-stricken Clyde in the semi-final, set the team up for their second consecutive League Cup Final, and, as it transpired, the first ever such Old Firm Final. What a day it was for the Celtic fans! The players all rose to the occasion, giving their opponents a torrid time. Willie Fernie showed great skill and stamina; the wingers, Charlie Tully on the right and Neilly Mochan on the left, caused torment to their immediate opponents Shearer and Caldow; the defence, to a man, dealt with Rangers' infrequent attacks with almost contemptuous ease; and at centre-forward, Billy McPhail teased John Valentine, Rangers centre-half, so much that this match effectively ended his career.

All around Glasgow, in the pubs, the buses and the subway, Celtic fans were dancing and singing and paraphrasing the words of a Harry Belafonte hit of the time: 'This is my island in the sun; Celtic 7, Rangers 1'! It was a wonderful time for such long-suffering fans and they revelled in their success. The goal-scoring for the whole League Cup campaign was shared between McPhail (13), Wilson (7), Collins (7), Fernie (3), Mochan (40), Peacock (1), Smith (1) and 2 for the young débutant Bertie Auld.

1957–1958 SCOTTISH LEAGUE DIVISION I

	P	W	D	L	F	A	Points	Position
Hearts	34	29	4	1	132	29	62	1st
Celtic	34	19	8	7	84	47	46	3rd

The team which beat Rangers 7-1 in the 1957 League Cup final. Back row, left to right: Donnelly, Fallon, Beattie, McPhail, Fernie, Evans. Front row: A. Dowdalls (Physio), Tully, Collins, Peacock, Wilson, Mochan.

The scorers in the 1957 League Cup final. From left to right: Willie Fernie, Billy McPhail, Neil Mochan, Sammy Wilson.

FIXTURES

	H	A		H	A
Aberdeen	1-1	1-0	Motherwell	2-2	3-1
Airdrie	4-2	5-2	Partick Thistle	2-3	1-0
Clyde	6-2	6-3	Queen of South	1-2	3-4
Dundee	0-0	3-5	Queen's Park	5-1	3-0
East Fife	4-0	3-0	Raith Rovers	1-1	2-1
Falkirk	2-2	1-0	Rangers	0-1	3-2
Hearts	0-2	3-5	St Mirren	2-2	1-1
Hibs	4-0	1-0	Third Lanark	4-1	2-0
Kilmarnock	4-0	1-1			

Thanks to, and probably because of, the success in the League Cup campaign, the long haul of the League season was also going well early on. Celtic were unbeaten in their first 11 matches, scoring 28 goals in the process. However, in the typical unpredictable form of the period, they lost the next four over Christmas and New Year. In the first of the defeats, against Partick Thistle (2-3) at Parkhead, Willie Fernie was carried off and Billy McPhail badly injured. Fernie was out for a month and McPhail till March, but unfortunately there were no obvious successors as this generation of players came to the end of their Celtic careers.

The other defeats at that festive period, all at home, were to Queen of the South (1-2), Hearts (0-2) and Rangers (0-1). New boys like Mike Jackson, Jim Conway and John Colrain all made their debut during this campaign; whereas it was the last full season for Bobby Collins and Willie Fernie although the latter later returned from Middlesborough. After New Year, the team did pick up a little, but further away – defeats to Hearts (3-5), Dundee (3-5) and Queen of the South (3-4) prevented any late surge, Celtic finishing third behind Hearts and Rangers. In the last match of the season, a 4-1 victory over Third Lanark, Frank Haffey played his first match. Forty-eight goals scored at home was the best since the war.

It would be remiss of me not to acknowledge the astonishing display by the Champions, Hearts. One hundred and thirty-two goals in a season is phenomenal, 13 better than the previous record (Motherwell 1931–32). However, to score that number at one end and only lose 29 at the other is the hallmark of an extremely fine team, one fully deserving of our praise.

1957–1958 SCOTTISH CUP

01/02/58	Airdrie	(A)	4-3	26,000
15/02/58	Stirling Albion	(H)	7-2	30,200
01/03/58	Clyde	(H)	0-2	65,000

Celtic were three up at half-time in the Airdrie match, thanks to goals by Collins, Byrne and Fernie, and only carelessness allowed the Diamonds to come close. Alec Bryne, who also got the winner at Broomfield, got another two in the comfortable win against Stirling Albion, the other goals coming from Sammy Wilson, with a hat-trick, Neilly Mochan and Eric Smith. The third-round tie was a home match for Clyde but as Shawfield was undergoing some repairs, it went ahead at Celtic Park but not to Celtic's advantage. They just did not play at all, were two down at half-time and failed to make any impression on an enthusiastic Clyde team which went all the way to the Final, where they won the trophy 1-0 against Hibs.

1957–1958 GLASGOW CUP

Partick Thistle	(H)	1-0	
Rangers	(A)	1-1	
		Rangers won on toss of coin	

1957–1958 Charity Cup

Rangers	(A)	0-1

1958–1959 SCOTTISH LEAGUE CUP

Section Games	H	A
Airdrie	3-3	2-1
Clyde	2-0	4-1
St Mirren	3-0	3-6

LEAGUE CUP POSITION

	P	W	D	L	F	A	Points	Position
Celtic	6	4	1	1	17	11	9	1st

LEAGUE CUP QUARTER- AND SEMI-FINALS

		H	A	
QF	Cowdenbeath	2-0	8-1	Agg: 10-1
SF	Partick Thistle	1-2	(Ibrox)	

Celtic once again qualified from a fairly comfortable League Cup section, where the only shocks were the home draw with Airdrie and the away defeat to St. Mirren. An unflattering 2-0 win over Cowdenbeath in the home leg of the quarter-final thanks to goals by Collins and Auld was followed by an 8-1 thrashing of the same opponents in Fife, Sammy Wilson scoring four and one of the 'new boys', John Colrain, getting two. At Ibrox in the semi-final, Celtic had made some changes but hoped for success against Thistle. The Jags, though, played very intelligently with old heads in the right position, catching Celtic out on breakaways to score their two goals in 72 and 81 minutes. This victory, a great disappointment to Celtic, was particularly merited by Partick Thistle since their goalkeeper, Tommy Ledgerwood, had been injured early in the second half and eventually had to leave the field.

1958–1959 Scottish League Division 1

	P	W	D	L	F	A	Points	Position
Rangers	34	21	8	5	92	51	50	1st
Celtic	34	14	8	12	70	53	36	6th

Fixtures

	H	A		H	A
Aberdeen	4-0	1-3	Motherwell	3-3	0-2
Airdrie	1-2	4-1	Partick Thistle	2-0	0-2
Clyde	3-1	1-2	QOS	3-1	2-2
Dundee	1-1	1-1	Raith Rovers	3-1	1-3
Dunfermline	3-1	0-1	Rangers	2-2	1-2
Falkirk	3-4	2-3	St Mirren	3-3	0-1
Hearts	2-1	1-1	Stirling Albion	7-3	1-0
Hibs	3-0	2-3	Third Lanark	3-1	1-1
Kilmarnock	2-0	4-1			

Very much a transitional season for Celtic, as the Old Guard went out and many new boys came in. Unfortunately, that meant another bout of chopping and changing of positions, particularly in the forwards. Billy McPhail and Sean Fallon were injured in the pre-season public trial and both later retired. Within a few months, Bobby Collins was on his way to Everton and Willie Fernie to Middlesborough. These were unusual moves, in that both were at the height of their powers and seemed happy enough. It was suggested by the cynics that the fees collected – around £40,000 – just about covered the costs of the long-awaited floodlights installed shortly after. Whatever the reason, it weakened the team.

As would be expected with any team in the throes of alteration, inconsistency was rife in the League campaign. Goalkeeping duties were split between the experienced Dick Beattie and new boy Frank Haffey. Dunky McKay, the first of the ball-playing full-backs, came in to make the right-back berth his own, while Neil Mochan dropped back to left-back. After Willie Fernie moved on, Eric Smith took over at right-half, although the young Paddy Crerand got a few outings. Bobby Evans remained the regular centre-half, except for missing 14 matches, when Billy McNeill, recently signed from Blantyre Vics, took over. At left-half, Bertie Peacock remained the man in possession.

When it came to the forward line, however, new names and old vied for every position. At outside-right, seven different names were tried (Tully, Smith, Colrain, Higgins, McVittie, Slater and Wilson); at inside-right, nine (Collins, Tully, Smith, Fernie, Jackson, McVittie, Wilson, Chalmers and Colrain); at centre-forward four (Byrne, Colrain, Conway, Lockhead); at inside-left, five (Wilson, Collins, Divers, McVittie, Colrain); and at outside-left, three (Auld, McVittie and Divers).

Many of those players had came up through the reserve ranks under the guidance of Jock Stein and had quality, but young players generally settle better if introduced into a set formation with good players around about them, not thrown in at the deep end.

The League campaign tended to demonstrate that fact, when 12 matches were lost in total. Only two were at home, Airdrie (1-2) and Falkirk (3-4) and indeed, the team did the Parkhead faithful proud, scoring 48 goals in 17 matches. The away form, though, was abysmal. Ten matches lost and three drawn. The new boys contributed towards the goals tally – Jackson (3), Colrain (12), Auld (9), Lockhead (3) and Divers (8) – but a sixth place finish was the worst for five years.

1958–1959 SCOTTISH CUP

31/01/59		Albion Rovers	(H)	4-0	27,000
14/02/59		Clyde	(H)	1-1	32,500
23/02/59	Replay	Clyde	(A)	4-3 (AET)	26,087
28/02/59		Rangers	(H)	2-1	42,000
14/03/59	QF	Stirling Albion	(A)	3-1	28,600
04/04/59	SF	St Mirren	(Hampden)	0-4	73,855

This campaign provided thrills a-plenty for the support. An easy first-round win over Albion Rovers; a tough tie and replay with Clyde, which Celtic eventually won in extra-time after being behind three times; and then a classic Old Firm encounter, Rangers looking strong in defence and quick in attack, but Celtic gave their all and that made up for some lack of quality. In the semi-final, though, an extremely talented St Mirren side both out-fought and out-played Celtic, using the pace of Gerry Baker and Alistair Miller to unsettle the Celtic defence. Saints went on to win the Cup against Aberdeen by three goals to one.

1958–1959 GLASGOW CUP

Third Lanark	(H)	2-4

1958–1959 CHARITY CUP

	Rangers (A)		1-1		
			Celtic won on toss of coin		
Final	Clyde	(Hampden)	5-0	26,082	09/05/59

Team: Haffey; Donnelly and Mochan; McKay, Evans and Peacock; Smith McVittie; Byrne, Colrain and Divers.

For the first 20 minutes of this match, Clyde played most attractive football but were guilty of timidness in the tackling which allowed their opponents to control their early efforts. By the end, Celtic were so much in control that it was almost embarrassing and could have had many more goals but for careless finishing. The five goals were scored by Alec Byrne (3) and two strong free-kicks by Neilly Mochan.

The Kelly Kids

During this season, two more 'star' names left the club. In October 1959, Charlie Tully returned to Ireland as player-manager with Cork Hibs; and towards the end, Bobby Evans, after missing only three matches, requested a transfer 'for personal reasons' and moved to Chelsea. The two previous years had seen the gradual break-up of, frankly, a very intermittently successful side and the replacement by what became known, in a direct copy of the Busby Babes at Manchester, as the Kelly Kids.

This always struck me as a very unusual comparison. Matt Busby had worked wonders with Manchester United since taking over in 1945. They had won the English First Division Championship in 1951–52, 1955–56 and 1956–57 and were runners-up in 1946–47, 1947–48, 1948–49 and 1950–51. The English Cup was won in 1948 and Manchester United were beaten finalists in 1957 and 1958; and the club had reached the semi-final of the European Cup in 1956–57 and 1957–58.

Throughout this period, Busby had overseen the break-up of a fine side and the development of a new one so there is every reason to name the team after him – the 'Busby' Babes. By contrast, at a time when a journalist in the Daily Express coined the label 'Kelly Kids' for Celtic's young generation of players, Jimmy McGrory was Manager of Celtic, had been since 1945 and would be until 1965. The Celtic support were so sure that his input into team selection was minimal that the irony of naming a promising group of kids after the Chairman of the club seemed lost on them. It was just common knowledge that Bob Kelly picked the team, so much so that after every major defeat, even the newspapers made allowances for Jimmy McGrory's position.

1959–1960 Scottish League Cup

Section Games	H	A
Airdrie	2-2	2-4
Partick Thistle	1-2	2-0
Raith Rovers	1-0	1-2

League Cup Position

	P	W	D	L	F	A	Points	Position
Celtic	6	2	3	1	9	10	5	3rd

Celtic failed to qualify for the next stage.

The three other teams involved in this section looked beatable on paper, but Celtic could not rise to the challenge. A home defeat by Partick Thistle, and away losses to Airdrie and Raith Rovers in successive games infuriated the fans, who were becoming really exasperated by the constant changing of the team. In these six League Cup matches, for instance, four different inside-lefts (Colrain, Divers, Gallagher and O'Hara) were tried out. Typical of the selection decisions of the time is the story of Thomas Mackie. He had only joined Celtic that year, played well in the public trial in early August and was selected for the first League Cup match against Raith Rovers at outside-left. The regular incumbent, Bertie Auld, was out of favour after being ordered off against Holland in May of that year.

Mackie scored Celtic's goal in the 1-2 defeat, played in the following match against Partick Thistle (also lost), whereupon he was dropped and replaced by Alec Byrne. Three further chances came his way in the early stages of the League campaign but by 19 September, he was out of the first team picture. One year later, he was out of Celtic Park.

1959–1960 SCOTTISH LEAGUE DIVISION I

	P	W	D	L	F	A	Points	Position
Hearts	34	23	8	3	102	51	54	1st
Celtic	34	12	9	13	73	59	33	9th

FIXTURES

	H	A		H	A
Aberdeen	1-1	2-3	Kilmarnock	2-0	1-2
Airdrie	0-0	5-2	Motherwell	5-1	2-1
Arbroath	4-0	5-0	Partick Thistle	2-4	1-3
Ayr United	2-3	1-1	Raith Rovers	1-0	3-0
Clyde	1-1	3-3	Rangers	0-1	1-3
Dundee	2-3	0-2	St Mirren	3-3	3-0
Dunfermline	4-2	2-3	Stirling Albion	1-1	2-2
Hearts	3-4	1-3	Third Lanark	4-0	2-4
Hibs	1-0	3-3			

In the league, a disastrous 13 matches were lost, equalling the second worst ever performance in 1950–51. Apart from seasons during the Second World War, 59 goals against *was* the worst ever. Six of these defeats came in the first 15 matches and by Christmas, the team was in 11th place in the table. The fans were disillusioned, and stayed away. Inconsistency again was the problem, not helped by the constant changes in the forward line.

A list of the goal scorers may give some idea of the range of players involved: Steve Chalmers (14), Bertie Auld (3), Thomas Mackie (1), Bobby Carroll (1), Jim Conway (6), Mike Jackson (8), Dan O'Hara (1), John Colrain (4), Alec Byrne (4), Neil Mochan (13), and John Divers (10).

Bobby Evans played his last match for the club at Parkhead on 30 April, while new boy John Clark made his debut at Arbroath on 3 October.

1959–1960 SCOTTISH CUP

13/02/60		St Mirren	(A)	1-1	36,220
24/02/60	Replay	St Mirren	(H)	4-4 (AET)	38,000
29/02/60	Replay	St Mirren	(H)	5-2	51,000
05/03/60		Elgin City	(A)	2-1	11,200
13/03/60	QF	Partick Thistle	(H)	2-0	41,000
	SF	Rangers	(Hampden)	1-1	79,786
	Replay	Rangers	(Hampden)	1-4	70,977

A tough opening tie against St Mirren, who had beaten Glasgow University 15-0 in the previous round. The teams were very well matched in the first two matches, although Celtic were 3-1 down at half-time in the replay. In the second replay, though, Neilly Mochan, in his last Scottish Cup campaign, scored all five goals, three by half-time. There was surprise all round the country when news came through that Elgin City were one up at half-time, but goals by John Divers and Eric Smith within the last six minutes pulled Celtic through; while the same Smith and John Colrain got the two goals in the quarter-final against Partick Thistle.

In the semi-final, Celtic played well in the first match to hold Rangers to a draw. In the replay, however, after a well-matched first half, Celtic folded after the interval and crashed out of the Cup by four goals to one. As a measure of the strength of Scottish football at this time, Rangers within weeks were thrashed 12-4 over two legs by Eintracht Frankfurt, the Germans later losing 7-3 to Real Madrid in the European Cup Final at Hampden Park!

Against continental opposition that summer, Celtic made a dramatic change to their strip. Criticised for years for not having numbers on the back of the jersey, which those in charge always insisted would ruin the look of the hoops, the players turned out for the friendly against Sparta Rotterdam on 14 May 1960, with numbers on their shorts.

1959–1960 GLASGOW CUP

Rangers	(H)	1-2

1959–1960 CHARITY CUP

Clyde	(H)	3-3	Celtic won on toss of coin
Rangers	(A)	1-1	Rangers won on toss of coin

For the Celtic fan of this decade, frustration was a constant state of mind. Yet, there were definite signs of improvement from the immediate post-war years. Not perhaps in the League Championship, where the late 1940s run of poor placings – 7th (1946–47), 12th (1947–48), 6th (1948–49) and 5th (1949–50) – continued into the 1950s. Astonishingly, though, this same squad of players, playing as a more settled team, tightened up at the back and became more positive up front, thanks to the directness of new boy Neil Mochan and won the title in 1953–54.

Traditionally, Cup competitions were always regarded as Celtic's forte. As can be seen from the table, however, few trophies ended up in the Parkhead Trophy Room during these years. For the fans, and this was where their frustration really surfaced, there were enough near-misses in the various cups at the quarter-final, semi-final and final stages.

CELTIC'S RECORD IN COMPETITIONS 1950–60

	LEAGUE	SCOTTISH CUP	SCOTTISH League CUP	GLASGOW CUP	CHARITY CUP
1950–51	7th	Celtic	QF		
1951–52	9th		SF		
1952–53	8th	QF			Celtic
1953–54	Celtic	Celtic			
1954–55	2nd	Final			
1955–56	5th	Final		Celtic	
1956–57	5th	SF	Celtic		
1957–58	3rd		Celtic		Celtic
1958–59	6th	SF			
1959–60	9th	SF			

The decade had started well with a 16th Scottish Cup Final win in 1951, a feat repeated three years later. In 1953, Celtic became Kings of Britain by winning the Coronation Cup against an inspiring list of opponents. After seasons of disappointment in the League Cup, they reached successive finals in 1956 and 1957, and won them both, with the latter triumph a superb 7-1 victory over Rangers which entered into folklore.

Buoyed up as they were by these moments of glory, nevertheless the Celtic fans were equally angry and despondent over the failures. What annoyed them most were two facets of team selection prevalent all through the 40s, 50s and to an extent, the early 60s. The first was the constant chopping and changing of personnel, particularly in the forward line; and the second the frequent decision to make a 'shock', often illogical choice, in big matches, for example, the dropping of Bobby Collins in the 1955 Scottish Cup Final replay against Clyde or the choice of Billy Craig in the 1956 Final against Hearts.

Unlike other decades in Celtic's history, when their chief opponent was Rangers, the list of winners for the various competitions in this decade shows a wide range of names, many of these having a final flurry at the top before the Old Firm re-asserted their domination from the 1960s onwards.

COMPETITION WINNERS 1950–60

	LEAGUE	SCOTTISH CUP	SCOTTISH League CUP
1950–51	Hibs	Celtic	Motherwell
1951–52	Hibs	Motherwell	Dundee
1952–53	Rangers	Rangers	Dundee
1953–54	Celtic	Celtic	East Fife
1954–55	Aberdeen	Clyde	Hearts
1955–56	Rangers	Hearts	Aberdeen
1956–57	Rangers	Falkirk	Celtic
1957–58	Hearts	Clyde	Celtic
1958–59	Rangers	St Mirren	Hearts
1959–60	Hearts	Rangers	Hearts

As for the tactics involved, the W/M Formation would have been the basic pattern for most of the decade. From the comments of players in our various interviews, training was mainly without the ball and there was certainly no imposition of a tactical style from above. As intelligent players, though, there would have been much discussion amongst themselves over methods and systems. The visit to the World Cup Finals in Switzerland would have opened many an eye to other ways of playing the game; while the free-flowing *4-2-4* arrangement of Brazil in winning the 1958 Tournament in Sweden – with the matches on television – would have been noticed.

In that same year, in fact, Dunky McKay became a regular in the Celtic team – the first, in Scotland anyway, of the ball-playing attacking full-backs which shocked the older generation. In the space of ten years, a team of players had come together, had some success, been broken up and replaced by a new group, ready to take Celtic's message into a new era. A comparison of two Cup-Final selections, ten years apart, shows the difference;

1950–1951 Team: Hunter; Fallon, Rollo; Evans, Boden and Baillie; Weir, Collins; McPhail (J.); Peacock, Tully.

1960–1961 Team: Haffey; McKay, Kennedy; Crerand, McNeill, Clark; Gallagher, Fernie, Hughes; Chalmers, Byrne.

In the unique way that fans remember great days, however, the 50s will remain memorable for certain moments. The Scottish Cup wins of 1951 against Motherwell and 1954 against Aberdeen; the League and Cup 'double' – Celtic's fourth – of 1954; their first League Cup victory against Partick Thistle in 1956; probably their most prestigious acquisition of the period, the Coronation Cup of 1953; but, most of all, that wonderful day when their chief rivals were put to the sword with a 7-1 victory in the League Cup Final of 1957.

CHAPTER EIGHTEEN
A Reluctant Transfer –
Paddy Crerand

PAT CRERAND joined Celtic in 1957 and quickly made the right-half position his own in a fairly young team. Pat had a superb long pass and a fine shot, got nine caps during his time with Celtic but was transferred to Manchester United early in 1963 after a row with the coaching staff in the dressing-room at Ibrox at half-time during the Ne'er Day clash with Rangers. With Manchester United, he won an FA Cup medal in 1963, League Championships in 1965 and 1967 and a European Cup medal in 1968.

Q When you first joined Celtic from Duntocher Hibs, what was the set up like?

A Well, I was lucky in that Jock (Stein) was there when I went there. Jock was in charge of the Reserve team and was way ahead of his time, trying out different formations and so on. I learned a great deal from Jock. Neilly (Mochan) was there and Bertic Peacock. We used to go to the George Hotel after matches and I would must sit there and listen. I learned a lot from the three of them, as it happens.

Q There were rumours that Jimmy McGrory didn't pick the team etc. What did you think?

A He didn't. There were so many different situations that made that quite clear. Like Mike Jackson turning up at Hampden Park for the semi-final of the Cup against Rangers, just coming from his work, in fact, coming to see the game, and finished up playing. Or Willie Goldie. On the way to Airdrie, the coach passed him standing at a bus stop with a Celtic scarf on. Bob (Kelly) said 'stop and give the boy a lift', and he ended up playing too. How the hell could you accept anything like that in the situation we were in!

Q What was a day at Parkhead like back then?

A You reported for training at 10 o'clock. All the gear was there on the table, we just put it on and went out round the pitch. We never saw a ball, that was for Saturday! Willie Johnstone was the trainer at the time. He stood at the bottom of the tunnel in a white coat and the only time he took his hands out of his pockets was to smoke a cigarette. But then again, that was the days when Willie was trying to be a physio and a trainer. Probably he didn't know a great deal anyway in those days, very different from today. But once Jock went to Dunfermline, the whole thing was a shambles, it was a nightmare.

Q The defence at the time seemed quite settled, but up front, the changes were unbelievable.

Pat Crerand (left) after Manchester United's European Cup win 1968 with a young George Best and manager Matt Busby.

A Well, it didn't make a great deal of difference to us playing defensively because there was no tactics or anything. You went on the pitch and just played and tried to work out some form of tactics as you went along. Free-kicks were an absolute shambles. No-one knew what to do. You just put the ball down and whatever came into somebody's mind, you just tried to create.

Corner kicks, nothing, no idea whatsoever of anything. I mean, people used to wonder why Celtic never won anything. Well, there were a lot of good young players, but all they needed was a little bit of guidance and there was nobody there to guide us.

Q What was your attitude to some of the older players?

A Jim, my attitude. My God, I was a Celtic fan. I had been watching Celtic as far back as I could remember. They were all heroes of mine. You would go out onto the track and you would be frightened to go by them in case they said 'hello' to you and you got embarrassed. The ones I found great were Big Jock, Neilly Mochan and Bertie Peacock. They were all marvellous to listen to and very good to me.

Q When you became an international in the early 1960s, did that make a financial difference to you at Celtic Park?

A Not really, no! I mean, at that time, people said we didn't care about money and for me that was true. We were playing for Celtic and you thought it was great. As you got a bit older and a little bit wiser, things change. There was no great bickering in football clubs those days about anybody getting more money than anybody else. We were all getting roughly the same anyway.

But then I went with the Scottish International team, that was a bigger shambles than there was at Celtic Park. Tactically, they were very unaware as well. I always maintain that the team I played with in 1961–1962 was as good a Scottish team as there has ever been. When you think of Denis Law, Alex Scott, John White, Davie Wilson, Jim Baxter, Ian St John – great players, but no organisation. I think if Jock had been manager of that Scottish team we would have gone to Chile and probably done well because the Czechs beat us qualifying for the 1962 Finals and they got to the Final itself but they were beaten 3-1 by Brazil.

Q You got into some trouble playing the Czechs.

A Well, when we played Czechoslovakia, there was a big guy kicking lumps out of me. Coming from Glasgow, the first thing you do when somebody kicks you is kick them back. That turning the other cheek is a load of crap. So, when he kicked me hard, I kicked him back and the two of us got sent off. Well, that didn't go down too well with Bob Kelly, who fined me I think.

Then, a few weeks later, in a five-a-side match at Falkirk, well, you know what a Falkirk crowd is like to Celtic, they are very anti-Celtic. So we are standing there, getting a lot of abuse from the crowd, while watching the other game. Then we go on and we played Falkirk. Now, daft as it may seem now, in five-a-side matches back then, you couldn't pass backwards in your own half. That guy Davidson (Bobby) was refereeing the game and – I can't remember who threw the ball back – but I claimed, saying, 'you can't do that, that's a foul', Davidson disagreed with me and told me to get on with the game. Then I started arguing with him and he sent me off for absolutely nothing. After that, the five-a-side deteriorated into a shambles with trouble on the pitch and off the pitch, where we were getting calls of 'Fenien B's' which did not go down well with us, we were all young and mad. We tried to get into the dressing rooms but Falkirk had kept them well-barred. Then some guy, I think his name was Danny McLennan, he coached in the Middle East, came in and had a go at us, telling Bob Rooney, on his first trip with the Club, that it was typical of us. Poor Bob lost his temper and went for Danny and we all had to pull him off.

Back at Celtic Park, that day did not meet with approval. I was called back from holiday in Ireland and fined again. I don't mind getting fined, but we weren't in the wrong. Bob Kelly, though, just seemed to take the part of anyone but me in those cases. I ask you, if somebody comes up and does something to you, if it's not right, then you have to kick against it!

Q Are you not always judged at Celtic Park by how you do against Rangers?

A I cannot remember how we did against Rangers. I know we beat them a few times when I was there but I'm not sure of the record.

Q But, Pat, it was their period.

A Oh! I know they were successful and the fact that they were winning things – but I think we were as good as them, but we had no organisation, none whatsoever.

I played with a lot of good players in the early 60s. A few years later, they won the European Cup. Jock came back and got them organised. Just think what would have happened if Jock had come back earlier. It was sad when Jock left and went off to Dunfermline. The only reason Jock left was that Bob Kelly would not let him become manager. I don't have to tell you it was because Jock was not a Catholic, which was quite disgraceful!

Q Why did Celtic lose to Dunfermline in the 1961 Cup Final?

A Organisation again! We should have beaten them in the first game. In the second match, we were by far the better side. Sometimes we had a little bit of misfortune and had bad goalkeeping but we were not as organised as we should have been. Under Jock, we were organised. I remember they had an outside-left in those days called Harry Melrose and Jock got him to come in and man-mark me. It didn't bother me but it showed that Jock had done his homework, and let's face it, it must have worked – they won the game!

Q At the beginning of 1963, Pat, their occurred an incident at Ibrox which effectively finished your Celtic career.

A Yes, I remember the incident well. The game shouldn't have been played, as the ground was solid with ice and that sort of thing. The advice before the game was 'kick the ball forward and let the forwards chase it'.

Before the match – now Sean Fallon is a friend of mine and I would not say a bad word about him – I asked Sean how he could expect me to kick the ball forward when we had two inside-forwards – Charlie Gallagher and Bobby Murdoch, Bobby was as skinny as a poker at this time – how can you ask them to compete with Harold Davis, Bobby Shearer and people like that. Let's play into their feet, I said. Sean replied we must play it long.

So we went out for the first half, which was a shambles, and as I said the game should not have been played. Then, just about a minute to go, Harry Davis had a shot. I tried to block it but it bounced off me into the net. At half time, Sean started having a go again about playing it long. I took my jersey off and said 'Sean, I can't play like that. If you want us to play like that, then you'd better go and play yourself', and handed him the jersey. I told him I wasn't going out for the second-half, but I had to, as we didn't have any substitutes in those days. I think I would have been substituted today.

Anyway, we were slaughtered in the second-half – and I never played again after that. Mr Kelly happened to be in the dressing room during the argument but then again, what Mr Kelly knew about football was zilch. He just didn't think it was the right thing to do. How can someone say you shouldn't be arguing in a dressing room when things are not going right!

That was 1 January, the next game, I think it was against Aberdeen and we stayed overnight in a hotel up there. Jimmy McGrory came into my bedroom and told me I wasn't playing. When I asked 'Why?' he just repeated that I wasn't playing. I didn't argue with him, I just said, 'well, that's your decision'. The next game was against Falkirk in a Cup tie and I wasn't playing in that, either.

Then, and I can remember this just like it was yesterday, the following Sunday, after 7 o'clock Mass, I was coming back into my Mother's house, with my girlfriend – now my wife Noreen – when I saw sports reporter Jim Rodger standing at the door. After saying hello, he says 'you've been transferred to Manchester United. Matt Busby has been up today to see Bob Kelly'. And that was the finish.

Q Yet the surprising thing for the Celtic fans is that you might not have been first choice for Manchester United because they were looking at another player.

A Yes, they were looking at Jimmy Baxter at that time. But Matt like most football managers – I only found this out afterwards – had spoken to a few people about Jimmy Baxter. He certainly spoke to Denis (Law) about him. Denis is a great friend of mine and has since told me. Matt asked him how we lived, and Denis said that I lived a lot better than Jimmy Baxter. I never really drank at all until I got to Manchester, but that was why he chose me over Baxter.

Pat and Noreen Crerand in 1998.

Q Was it a blow at the time?

A Of course it was, a severe blow! I'm a Celtic supporter. When Jim Rodger told me that I was being transferred, I was in tears. Everyone was totally in shock. My mother was crying.

Q At the same time it had a happy ending.

A Och! It finished up a great move for me. Matt was a tremendous man, we had the makings of a good team down there and I had a great time in Manchester. I enjoyed every minute of it. Unfortunately for me though, not long after I went down, Jock then came back from Dunfermline, a move which was kind of forced on Celtic.

I remember we played Everton in the UEFA Cup match at Old Trafford and Jock came down with Neilly. He was in great form, laughing and joking, as was Neilly, and suddenly it hit me. 'You're going back to Celtic' I said with a smile. He said he couldn't say anything, but he was meeting Bob Kelly the following Sunday at Celtic Park.

Shortly afterwards a *Sunday Express* sports reporter phoned me to ask 'what do you know about big Jock going back to Celtic Park?' I couldn't say anything. He says 'Pat, I know you know'. 'I don't know'. He said 'well I'll let you off the hook and tell you the truth. He is meeting Bob Kelly at Celtic Park on Sunday. So how do you think he would do if he went back?' I just said to him, 'he'll win the League six times in the next seven years!' But I was proved wrong. He won it nine times!

Years of Disappointment

THE CELTIC PLAYERS entered the new dacade with the stern words of their manager ringing in their ears. In his annual report in the *Celtic Football Guide* Jimmy McGrory did not hold back his feelings: 'To say I was disappointed by our performance last season would be a gross understatement.'

Unfortunately, that statement could be applied to several seasons at this time, not only 1959–60. The club had also lost Jock Stein to Dunfermline towards the end of the season, the Pars then prodeeding to win their last six league matehes to hold their place in the first division. Sean Fallon was appointed in Stein's place and ex-player John Higgins came back to help with the reserves. A huge pool of 36 players assembled in July for pre-season training, many of them new names.

Among the squad were some survivors from the early 1950s, like Alec Byrne and Neil Mochan, plus one signed in 1949 – Bertie Peacock. However, it was to the young ones that the club looked for a successful season and manager McGrory reiterated the club's faith in them. In his report he said:

The Celtic squad for season 1960–61 when Sean Fallon was appointed coach. Back row, from left to right: McNamee, Veitch, Carroll, Haffey, Fallon, Rooney, Byrne, Clark. Middle row: Brown, F. Brogan, Parks, O'Neill, Gallacher, Murdoch, Cushley, Jackson, Price. Front row: Fallon (Coach), Chalmers, Hughes, McKay, McNeill, Kennedy, Divers, Crerand, Gribben (Assistant Trainer).

CELTIC PLAYERS 1945–46

NAME	YEAR JOINED	FIRST CLUB
Robert Auld	1955	Maryhill Harp
Alexander Byrne	1954	Port Glasgow
T. Carmichael	1960	St Andrew's United
Robert Carroll	1959	Irvine Meadow
Stephen Chalmers	1959	Ashfield Juniors
John Clark	1958	Larkhall Thistle
John Coltrane	1957	Duntocher Hibs
Francis Connor	1960	Blantyre Celtic
James Conway	1957	Coltness United
Patrick Crerand	1958	Duntocher Hibs
John Curran	1959	Duntocher Hibs
John Divers	1957	Renfrew Juniors
John Donnolly	1956	Armadale Thistle
John Fallon	1958	Fauldhouse United
Charles Gallacher	1959	Yoker Athletic
Francis Haffey	1958	Maryhill Harp
John Hughes	1959	Shotts Bon Accord
Michael Jackson	1957	Benburb
John Kelly	1960	Crewe Alexandra
James Kennedy	1955	Duntocher Hibs
John Kurila	1958	St Francis BG
Ian Lochhead	1959	Schools
Steve Lynch	1959	Schools
Duncan McKay	1956	Maryhill Harp
Donald McMillan	1957	Aberdeen Woodside
John McNamee	1960	Bellshill Athletic
William McNeill	1958	Blantyre Victoria
Thomas Mackie	1959	Johnstone Burgh
Neil Mochan	1954	Middlesborough
Brian Moore	1960	Duntocher Hibs
Daniel O'Hara	1959	Fauldhouse United
William O'Neill	1960	St Anthony's
Robert Paton	1958	Maryhill Harp
Robert Peacock	1949	Coleraine
Ron Sherry	1960	Annbank United
James Upton	1959	St Roch's

'We have confidence in our young players and believe that our policy will pay off in the long run.'

1960–1961 SCOTTISH LEAGUE CUP

Section Games	H	A
Partick Thistle	1-2	1-1
Rangers	1-2	3-2
Third Lanark	2-0	3-1

LEAGUE CUP POSITION

	P	W	D	L	F	A	Points	Position
Celtic	6	3	1	2	11	8	7	2nd

Celtic failed to qualify for next stage

In an all-Glasgow League Club section, Celtic started well with two victories against Third Lanark and Rangers and a draw with Thistle and led the table at the half-way mark. A disastrous second period, though, with successive defeats to Thistle and Rangers, left them out in second place. The scoring was shared between Bobby Carroll (2), Steve Chalmers (1), Neil Mochan (1), John Divers (2), with new man John Hughes top scorer with 5.

1960–1961 SCOTTISH LEAGUE DIVISION I

	P	W	D	L	F	A	Points	Position
Rangers	34	23	5	6	88	46	51	1st
Celtic	34	15	9	10	64	46	39	4th

FIXTURES

	H	A		H	A
Aberdeen	0-0	3-1	Kilmarnock	3-2	2-2
Airdrie	4-0	0-2	Motherwell	1-0	2-2
Ayr United	2-0	3-1	Partick Thistle	0-1	2-1
Clyde	6-1	3-0	Raith Rovers	1-1	2-2
Dundee	2-1	1-0	Rangers	1-5	1-2
Dundee Utd	1-1	1-1	St Johnstone	1-1	1-2
Dunfermline	2-1	2-2	St Mirren	4-2	1-2
Hearts	1-3	1-2	Third Lanark	2-3	0-2
Hibs	2-0	6-0			

A new season and the appearance of a few names stamping their authority in certain positions. Although John Fallon and Frank Conner got occasional runs in goal during this season and the following one, Frank Haffey was the man in charge. In from of him, Dunky McKay and Jim Kennedy were at full-back, behind an established half back line of Pat Crerand, Billy McNeill and Bertie Peacock. The forward line was chosen from many of the same players as the year before, although new names like Charlie Gallagher and John Hughes got their chance. The League season was disappointing, although a fourth place finish was an improvement on the previous year. The defence kept a tighter rein on the goals against but the goal-scoring was also down, to under two per match. Celtic were badly beaten in both Old Firm matches. The 5-1 defeat at Parkhead on 10 September was followed by two further losses (Third Lanark away and Airdrie away) and a home draw with Aberdeen, leaving Celtic, after only five matches near the foot of the table with two points.

From that point on, they were always struggling to catch the leaders. There were good days, like the wins at Airdrie (4-0) and Clyde (6-1) at Celtic Park, and Hibs at Easter Road (6-0). Top scorers in the league were Steve Chalmers (17), Bobby Carroll (6) and Job Divers (9). Bertie Auld lost his place in the team by February, his temper on the pitch supposedly incurring the wrath of the Chairman and in May he was transferred to Birmingham City.

1960–1961 Scottish Cup					
28/01/61		Falkirk	(A)	3-1	18,500
11/02/61		Montrose	(H)	6-0	26,000
25/02/61		Raith Rovers	(A)	4-1	19,359
11/03/61	QF	Hibs	(H)	1-1	56,000
15/03/61	Replay	Hibs	(A)	1-0	39,243
01/04/61	SF	Airdrie	(Hampden)	4-0	72,612
22/04/61	Final	Dunfermline	(Hampden)	0-0	113,618
26/04/61	Replay	Dunfermline	(Hampden)	0-2	87,866

An easy passage through the initial stages was followed by a very tough match against Hibs at Easter Road. Steven Chalmers equalising with only six minutes left. The replay was a typical Celtic-Hibs end-to-end which went into extra-time before John Clark scored the only goal from a corner.

Airdrie were comfortably disposed of in the semi-final and Celtic went through to the final, where they met Dunfermline, now coached by ex-Celtic Jock Stein. Stein had gained a good reputation working with the reserves at Celtic Park; now with Dunfermline in their first ever final, he had them prepared and ready. In front of a fascinated 113,000 fans, Celtic's dashing style was matched by the Pars' more controlled play. The former caught the eye but the latter made the better chances.

On the following Wednesday, under grey skies and a drizzle, only 87,000 turned up. The Celtic support were surprised to see young Willie O'Neill at

The team beaten by Dunfermline in the 1960–61 Scottish Cup final. Back row, left to right: Mackay, Kennedy, Haffey, Crerand, McNeill, Clark. Front row: Gallacher, Fernie, Hughes, Chalmers, Byrne. Inset: Peacock.

Of all these players, Alec Byrne was the least successful in his Celtic career. Yet Alec had speed and control, lacking only the self belief required to join the highest class of forwards – even so, 31 goals in 100 matches is impressive.

left-back, Jim Kennedy having been whisked off to hospital for an operation. Many felt that the experience of Bertie Peacock might have been a more logical choice, but in the end, it did not matter. What did matter was the magnificent display by Pars goalkeeper, Eddie Connachan, who defied the Celtic attack time after time. Dunfermline scored with a break-away goal in 68 minutes then had to endure another period of Celtic pressure before they snatched a second goal after a mistake by Frank Haffey.

1960–1961 Glasgow Cup

	Rangers	(H)	4-2
	Third Lanark	(A)	0-0
Replay	Third Lanark	(H)	3-1
Final	Partick Thistle	(Hampden)	0-2

1960–1961 Charity Cup

Queens Park	(H)	3-3	Celtic won on toss of coin
Clyde	(Hampden)	1-1	Clubs shared Cup

Anglo-Franco – Scottish Friendship Cup

This tournament was made up of eight French teams, four English, and four Scottish. Invitations were based on league position for the 59/60 season and Celtic (9th) only received an invitation because Ayr United (8th) and Kilmarnock (2nd) were in a New York tournament. Hearts, Hibs and Rangers were in the three major European competitions, so Clyde, Dundee, Motherwell and Celtic received their invitation for this tournament.

Anglo-Franco Scottish Friendship Cup Final

06/08/1960	Sedan	(A)	0-3
18/10/1960	Sedan	(H)	3-3

Celtic travelled to France without much knowledge of Sedan, which turned out to be in north-east France, about 100km from Rheims. The match was held on a Saturday evening in front of 3,000 people who saw their local side rather over-run Celtic, scoring all their goals within the first 30 minutes. In the replay, two months later, Celtic played better but Sedan scored in the first minute and got two more before half-time. Late efforts by Steve Chalmers in the 70th and 87th minutes allied to the equaliser in the first half by John Hughes levelled the score on the night, but Sedan earned the points for France over the two legs.

1961–1962 Scottish League Cup

Section Games	H	A
Hibs	2-1	2-2
Partick Thistle	3-2	3-2
St Johnstone	0-1	0-2

	P	W	D	L	F	A	Points	Position
			League Cup Position					
Celtic	6	3	1	2	10	10	7	2nd

Celtic failed to qualify for next stage.

Frank Conner took over in goal for the whole of the League Cup campaign. Too many goals were lost and St. Johnstone proved too strong both home and away. Paddy Crerand missed the start of the season entirely. He had been ordered off while playing for Scotland against Czechoslovakia and the SFA imposed a one-week ban from 12 August. Unfortunately, he was ordered off again in the Falkirk Five-A-Side Tournament in July and the Celtic Chairman increased the ban, without play, to four weeks. Crerand missed the first five matches of the League Cup campaign, including the two defeats by St. Johnstone. His place was shared between Mike Jackson, Billy Price and new boy John Kurila.

1961–1962 SCOTTISH LEAGUE DIVISION 1								
	P	W	D	L	F	A	Points	Position
Dundee	34	25	4	5	80	46	54	1st
Celtic	34	19	8	7	81	37	46	3rd

FIXTURES						
	H	A		H	A	
Aberdeen	2-0	0-0	Motherwell	1-1	4-0	
Airdrie	3-0	0-1	Partick Thistle	5-1	1-1	
Dundee	2-1	1-2	Raith Rovers	0-1	4-0	
Dundee Utd	3-1	5-4	Rangers	1-1	2-2	
Dunfermline	2-1	3-0	St Johnstone	3-1	3-0	
Falkirk	3-0	1-3	St Mirren	7-1	5-0	
Hearts	2-2	1-2	Stirling Albion	5-0	0-1	
Hibs	4-3	1-1	Third Lanark	1-0	1-1	
Kilmarnock	2-2	2-3				

Another of the old school left during the summer of 1961, Bertie Peacock returning to Northern Ireland to become manager of Coleraine. His place at left-half was shared by John Clark and new boy Billy Price. The defence, apart from that position, was invariably Haffey, McKay and Kennedy; Crerand and McNeill, with much more consistency of selection in the forward line as well. Steve Chalmers played most of the matches at outside right with occasional back-ups by Frank Brogan and Bobby Carroll; inside right was invariably Mike Jackson, occasionally Charlie Gallacher, although a young debutant called Bobby Lennox played his first match on 3 March against Dundee; John Hughes held down the centre-forward berth; John Divers was at inside-left and either Alec Byrne or Bobby Carroll at outside-left.

This was a much improved league campaign. The goal-scoring rate increased appreciably while the defence held reasonably firm. Of the seven defeats, only one was at home. Four of these losses came in the first ten matches then the team went another 12 matches unbeaten. Both Old Firm matches were drawn; there were two good victories (plus another two in the League Cup) against the bogey team of recent years Partick Thistle; and the matches against the champions were shared.

A comparison of the respective statistics for this season shows that Celtic matched Dundee in goals for and lost fewer. Their main problem was not winning enough matches or perhaps drawing too many. However, this was a well-deserved win for the men from Dens Park and they went on to be excellent ambassadors for Scotland in the European Cup the following season.

1961–1962 SCOTTISH CUP					
13/12/61		Cowdenbeath	(H)	5-1	19,000
27/01/62		Morton	(A)	3-1	20,600
17/02/62		Hearts	(A)	4-3	35,045
10/03/62	QF	Third Lanark	(H)	4-4	42,500
14/03/62	Replay	Third Lanark	(Ibrox)	4-0	51,000
31/03/62	SF	St Mirren	(Ibrox)	1-3	59,278

Celtic fans had plenty to bite their nails about in this cup run. The Hearts match was as close as the score may suggest; in the Third Lanark tie, Celtic came back from 1-3 down to force a 4-4 draw. In the replay, goals by Chalmers, Hughes (2) and Byrne, all in the second half, took them through to a fourth successive semi-final in this trophy.

Celtic were full of confidence for this tie. The team was playing fairly competently and had trounced St Mirren 5-0 only five days before in a league match. Unfortunately, St Mirren turned on the style in the first half to lead 3-0 at the interval, a lead they maintained until the 70th minute. Then, disastrously for the image for both football and Celtic, there were scenes of hooliganism on the terracings which led to invasions of the pitch by fans and clashes with police. Order was eventually restored and play continued, but the heart had gone out of the game and St Mirren held out comfortably. In the days which followed, Celtic support was all tarred with the same brush as troublemakers.

1961–1962 GLASGOW CUP				
	Queen's Park	(H)	4-1	
	Partick Thistle	(A)	5-1	
Final	Third Lanark		1-1	
Replay	Third Lanark	(Celtic Park)	3-2	12,000

Third Lanark missed a great opportunity in this match to win the Glasgow Cup for the first time since 1909 when they led 2-1 with only 15 minutes left.

The match was played just after a torrential rainstorn had almost flooded the pitch. Indeed, halfway through the first half the referee had to stop the play to allow the ground staff to remove some of the excess water.

Charlie Gallagher gave Celtic the lead in 18 minutes with a low drive from just outside the box and they held this position until half-time, their play much more enthusiastic than Third's. Four minutes later, centre-half Billy

McNeill was taken off after a chest knock and suddenly, Third Lanark were back in the game. In 58 minutes, outside-left Fletcher equalised, and on the 75 minute mark a leader by Matt Gray decived Frank Haffey to put them 2-1 up.

Even with ten-men, however, Celtic's superior power told on the heavy surface and late goals by John Hughes and Charlie Gallacher made it a disappointing night for Third Lanark. At the end, several hundreds of the crowd of just under 12,000 invaded the field just to be near the area where the the presentation of the Cup was to be held.

Team: Haffey, McNeil, Kennedy, McNamara, McNeill, Clark, Lennox, Gallagher, Hughes, Dwas, Chalmers.

1962–1963 SCOTTISH LEAGUE CUP

Section Games	H	A
Dundee	3-0	0-1
Dundee United	4-0	0-0
Hearts	3-1	2-3

LEAGUE CUP POSITION

	P	W	D	L	F	A	Points	Position
Celtic	6	3	1	2	12	5	7	2nd

Celtic failed to qualify for next stage.

This was a tough section to be drawn in, the three teams from the east all very capable. The competition seemed to reflect just what Celtic's problem was in the early 60s – inconsistency. A 3-1 defeat of Hearts was followed by a 1-0 defeat at Dundee; a good 4-0 home win against Dundee United, then a 2-3 loss in Edinburgh. A rollercoaster of a run, one which in the end was not good enough. Hearts went on to take the cup. Top scorers for Celtic were John Hughes (6), Charlie Gallagher (3), Bobby Murdoch (2) and Pat Crerand (1).

1962–1963 SCOTTISH LEAGUE DIVISION I

	P	W	D	L	F	A	Points	Position
Rangers	34	25	7	2	94	28	57	1st
Celtic	34	19	6	9	76	44	44	4th

FIXTURES

	H	A		H	A
Aberdeen	1-2	5-1	Kilmarnock	1-1	0-6
Airdrie	3-1	6-1	Motherwell	6-0	2-0
Clyde	2-0	3-1	Partick Thistle	0-2	5-1
Dundee	4-1	0-0	Queen of South	0-1	5-2
Dundee Utd	1-0	0-3	Raith Rovers	4-1	2-0
Dunfermline	2-1	1-1	Rangers	0-1	0-4
Falkirk	2-1	3-1	St. Mirren	1-1	7-0
Hearts	2-2	3-4	Third Lanark	2-1	0-2
Hibs	2-0	1-1			

In terms of personnel, there was very little difference from the year before. Frank Haffey was the custodian in every league match bar one, when his deputy Dick Madden, just 18 years of age, behind a makeshift defence, picked the ball out of the net six times at Kilmarnock on 27 March. Another debut boy that night was Jimmy Johnstone.

While the idea of a settled team never quite percolated the thinking of those who picked the team in those days, one would have thought that the experience of the year before, when a reasonably settled formation had worked well in the league, would have suggested a continuation of this policy. Unfortunately, this was not the case, the forwards in particular having to get used to playing in different positions. The permutations were ridiculous. seven outside rights; six inside rights; five centre forwards; seven inside lefts; six outside lefts! Nor surprisingly, inconsistency was rife. After an uncertain start losing two of their first four matches, Celtic then went six unbeaten scoring 19 goals, following that with a run of six matches where only three goals were scored. That was the pattern for the season and fourth place, 13 points adrift from the champions, the result.

Bobby Murdoch played his first match against Hearts in August; John Cushley got two games at centre-half; Bobby Craig also played his first match in October; Ian Young made his debut in November; and Tommy Gemmell had his first start against Aberdeen in January; shortly afterwards Pat Crerand left to Manchester United.

1962–1963 SCOTTISH CUP					
28/01/63		Falkirk	(A)	2.0	13,500
06/03/63		Hearts	(H)	3-1	38,000
13/03/63		Gala Fairydean	(H)	6-0	14,000
30/03/63	QF	St Mirren	(A)	1-0	35,644
13/04/63	SF	Raith Rovers	(Ibrox)	5-2	35,681
04/05/63	Final	Rangers	(Hampden)	1-1	129,643
15/05/63	Replay	Rangers	(Hampden)	0-3	120,273

Apart from Gala Fairydean, all the other protagonists on the way to the final gave Celtic a run for their money. In contrast to the disappointing crowd at the semi-final at Ibrox, Hampden was bursting at the seams on the first Saturday in May. Celtic put out a team of Haffey; McKay and Kennedy; McNamee, McNeill and Price; Johnstone, Murdoch; Hughes; Divers and Brogan. On the day, the players rose to the challenge and earned a creditable 1-1 draw with the strong Rangers team. Another huge crowd turned out on the Wednesday evening for the replay. The Celtic fans were hopeful rather than confident but their dreams were shattered when the team was announced. Both wingers had been dropped! Many fans were astonished, as they felt that Jimmy Johnstone on the right-wing had been particularly effective against Davie Provan at left-back for Rangers, while Frank Brogan's long runs had kept Bobby Shearer busy. Even more puzzling was the choice of replacement on the right-wing. Bobby Craig was by then 28, a skilful player but without the pace to prove a success on the wing. The team flopped, was 0-2 down at half-time and lost a third in the second half, as huge gaps appeared in the Celtic end, the disillusioned and even disgusted supporters leaving in droves.

1962–1963 Fairs Cities Cup			
26/09/63	Valencia	(A)	2-4
24/10/63	Valencia	(H)	2-2

This was Celtic's first foray into one of the major European competitions, a difficult baptism, as Valencia were the holders of the trophy. Two goals by Bobby Carroll in Spain kept Celtic in the match but in the return leg at Parkhead, the visitors showed their class and held the Scots comfortably, Alec Byrne and Pat Crerand getting the goals.

The Luis Casanova Stadium in Valencia, site of Celtic's first match in European competition.

1962–1963 Glasgow Cup				
	Rangers	(A)	2-2	
Replay	Rangers	(H)	3-2 (AET)	
	Partick Thistle	(A)	3-1	
Final	Third Lanark		1-2	08/04/63

❁

1963–1964 Scottish League Cup		
Section Games	H	A
Kilmarnock	2-0	0-0
Queen of The South	1-1	3-2
Rangers	0-3	0-3

LEAGUE CUP POSITION

	P	W	D	L	F	A	Points	Position
Celtic	6	2	2	2	6	9	6	2nd

Celtic failed to qualify for next stage.

The Rangers team of this time was just too strong for Celtic and both section match results were entirely predictable. At this point of the season, the team was evolving. Fallon came in for Haffey, Young for McKay. The section had started badly, losing at home to Rangers in the first match, then drawing with Kilmarnock (away) and Queen of the South (home). Then Rangers came up again this time at Ibrox and the fans were astonished to see another surprise choice, 21-year-old Bobby Jeffrey coming in at outside-left. Unfortunately, there was no fairytale ending for Jeffrey as Celtic went down 3-0.

1963–1964 SCOTTISH LEAGUE DIVISION I

	P	W	D	L	F	A	Points	Position
Rangers	34	25	5	4	85	31	55	1st
Celtic	34	19	9	6	89	37	47	3rd

FIXTURES

	H	A		H	A
Aberdeen	3-0	3-0	Kilmarnock	5-0	0-4
Airdrie	9-0	2-0	Motherwell	2-1	4-0
Dundee	2-1	1-1	Partick Thistle	5-3	2-2
Dundee Utd	1-0	3-0	Queen of South	4-0	2-0
Dunfermline	2-2	0-1	Rangers	0-1	1-2
East Stirling	5-2	5-1	St Johnstone	3-1	1-1
Falkirk	7-0	0-1	St Mirren	3-0	1-2
Hearts	1-1	1-1	Third Lanark	4-4	1-1
Hibs	5-0	1-1			

This was a reasonable performance by Celtic, both the goals for and the goals against considerably improved from the year before. After some early changes in the League Cup selections and the first two or three home matches, a fairly settled formation developed. A defence of John Fallon, Ian Young, Tommy Gemmell, John Clark, Billy McNeill and Jim Kennedy with occasional appearances by Frank Haffey, Jim Brogan, John Cushley; while the forward line usually read Johnstone, Murdoch, Chalmers, Divers and Hughes, with Bobby Lennox, Charlie Gallagher, Frank Brogan and Paddy Turner as very infrequent replacements.

While this team was settling down, the League had started. The result was that Celtic lost three of the first five matches, but then went on a fine run of 13 games unbeaten, scoring 42 goals before a strong Rangers team won the New Year's Day fixture. From them on, the team picked up again, losing only to Dunfermline (0-1) on 1 February and Kilmarnock (0-4) on 21 March. However, far too many matches were drawn. Top scorers were Chalmers (26), Murdoch (15), Divers (12) and Hughes (10).

1963–1964 Scottish Cup				
11/01/64	Eyemouth Utd	(H)	3-0	17,000
25/01/64	Morton	(A)	3-1	22,000
15/02/64	Airdrie	(H)	4-1	32,000
07/03/64	Rangers	(A)	0-2	85,000

Once more, the power and strength of the Light Blues were too much for Celtic's more open style, a goal in each half enough to take Rangers through. In the earlier rounds, the goals had come from Johnstone (2), Chalmers (3), Hughes (2), Gallagher (2) and Murdoch (1).

1963–1964 European Cup Winners Cup					
17/09/63		Basle	(A)	5-1	
10/10/63		Basle	(H)	5-0	Agg	10-1
4/12/63		Dinamo Zagreb	(H)	3-0	
11/12/64		Dinamo Zagreb	(A)	1-2	Agg	4-2
26/02/64	QF	Slovan Bratislava	(H)	1-0	
04/03/64		Slovan Bratislava	(A)	1-0	Agg	2-0
15/04/64	SF	M.T.K. Budapest	(H)	3-0	
29/04/64		M.T.K. Budapest	(A)	0-4	Agg	3-4

Celtic were in this competition as a result of being the beaten Cup finalists from the year before, the winners, Rangers, in the European Cup. To the surprise of all their fans, Celtic had an excellent campaign up to the semi-final, playing attractive football which received praise in all quarters and scoring freely.

There was great excitement at Parkhead after the semi-final tie against MTK Budapest. A 3-0 home win surpassed all expectations and it was a confident Celtic party which left for Hungary for the second leg. Unfortunately, more than a touch of naivety was also present. The Chairman, Robert Kelly, believed the club had a duty to entertain as well as win, so the team went out with that attitude in Budapest – and were crushed! MTK were later beaten in the final after a replay by Sporting Lisbon in Antwerp, with Celtic fans everywhere ruing what might have been. In a high-scoring run, the goals came from Johnstone (2), Murdoch (3), Lennox (1), Chalmers (5), Hughes (5) and Divers (3).

1963–1964 Glasgow Cup					
	Partick Thistle	(A)	1-1		
Replay	Partick Thistle	(H)	2-1		
	Third Lanark	(H)	1-1		
Replay	Third Lanark	(A)	3-0		
Final	Clyde	(Hampden)	2-0	13,500	25/03/64

In the first half, Clyde moved the ball round neatly but did not have the strength or ability to get through Celtic's defence. Celtic themselves only threatened occasionally and as a result, the game was goalless by half-time. Two goals in the space of five minutes in the second-half sealed the match.

In 55 minutes, Steve Chalmers rose above the Clyde defence to head a John Hughes corner home; in the 60th minute, Bobby Murdoch hooked the ball into the goal mouth, Clyde keeper McCulloch and centre-half Fraser got themselves into a fankle over the clearance and John Divers came up to push the ball home. This was Celtic's 23rd win in the competition.

Team: Fallon; Young and Gemmell; Clark, McNeill and Kennedy; Johnstone and Murdoch; Chalmers; Divers and Hughes.

1964–1965 SCOTTISH LEAGUE CUP

Section Games	H	A
Hearts	6-1	3-0
Kilmarnock	4-1	0-2
Partick Thistle	0-0	5-1

League Cup Position

	P	W	D	L	F	A	Points	Position
Celtic	6	4	1	1	18	5	9	1st

LEAGUE CUP QUARTER- AND SEMI-FINALS

			H	A		
QF	East Fife		6-0	0-2	Agg	6-2
SF	Morton	(Ibrox)	2-0			
Final	Rangers	(Hampden)	1-2		91,523	

This particular defeat by Rangers was a very galling one for the Celtic fans. The great team which had dominated Scottish football from the late 50s onwards could never be admired by the Celtic support but there was a tacit acknowledgement that it was a good team with talented players. That same support, though, now recognised that the same team was now slightly over the hill and there for the taking, so they were particularly incensed when Celtic once again failed on a major occasion to outdo their chief rivals. The team chosen on the night was Fallon; Young, Gemmell; Clark, Cushley and Kennedy; Johnstone, Murdoch; Chalmers; Divers, and Hughes.

Rangers were out of sorts in the league campaign but rose to the occasion in this match, tactically much more aware than a frankly naïve Celtic. No-one, for instance, seemed delegated to mark Jim Baxter who revelled in the space, and the whole defence pushed forward to help the attack, leaving themselves open to the counter-punch, which naturally came – twice – through Jim Forrest. The match finished with the Celtic end half-empty, and sombre, the opposing one packed and colourful.

1964–1965 SCOTTISH LEAGUE DIVISION I

	P	W	D	L	F	A	Points	Position
Kilmarnock	34	22	6	6	62	33	50	1st
Celtic	34	16	5	13	76	57	37	8th

FIXTURES

	H	A		H	A
Aberdeen	8-0	3-1	Kilmarnock	2-0	2-5
Airdrie	2-1	6-0	Morton	1-0	3-3
Clyde	1-1	1-1	Motherwell	2-0	3-1
Dundee	0-2	3-3	Partick Thistle	1-2	4-2
Dundee Utd	1-1	1-3	Rangers	3-1	0-1
Dunfermline	1-2	1-5	St Johnstone	0-1	0-3
Falkirk	3-0	2-6	St Mirren	4-1	5-1
Hearts	1-2	2-4	Third Lanark	1-0	3-0
Hibs	2-4	4-0			

With the same personnel as the previous season, this was a poor league performance by Celtic. John Fallon's sequence in goal was broken by eight matches for Ronnie Simpson between November and early January. Ian Young and Tommy Gemmell filled the full-back berths, Billy McNeill was at centre-half, apart from injury early in the season when John Cushley took over but there was much chopping and changing elsewhere, with various contenders competing for few positions. At right-half, for instance, John Clark, Jim Brogan and Bobby Murdoch; for the left-half role, Jim Kennedy, Jim Brogan, Willie O'Neill and John Clark; while up front the permutations came from Jimmy Johnstone, Tom Curley, John Hughes, Bobby Murdoch, John Divers, Charlie Gallagher, Steve Chalmers, Hugh Maxwell (signed from Falkirk in November), Bobby Lennox, Joe Haverty, and Bertie Auld (returned from Birmingham in January). Several players had left, Frank Haffey in October 1964 to Swindon, Dunky MacKay to Third Lanark in November 1964 and Frank Brogan in June 1964 to Ipswich.

The problem, from the playing point of view, was the number of goals lost, a very high 57. During the season, there would be a few games where success was achieved only to be followed by a heavy defeat. In the first twelve matches, for instance, 6 were won, two drawn and four lost, to Hearts, (2 4), Kilmarnock (2-5), St. Johnstone (0-30 and Dundee (0-2). Steve Chalmers (11), John Hughes (18) and Bobby Lennox (9) and Bertie Auld (8) were the main scorers, the latter notching five on 10 March when Celtic beat Airdrie 6-0 at Broomfield.

Ironically, although Jock Stein arrived in March 1965, there was no immediate improvement in league form. In fact, four days after beating Dunfermline in the final of the Scottish Cup, Celtic received a 5-1 thrashing at East End Park in the final match of the season.

1964–1965 SCOTTISH CUP

06/02/65		St Mirren	(A)	3-0	28,300
20/02/65		Queen's Park	(A)	1-0	27,443
06/03/65	QF	Kilmarnock	(H)	3-2	47,000
27/03/65	SF	Motherwell	(Hampden)	2-2	52,000
31/03/65	Replay	Motherwell	(Hampden)	3-0	58,959
24/04/65	Final	Dunfermline	(Hampden)	3-2	108,800

Quite an unusual feature in the semi-final, the replay getting a bigger attendance than the first match. This very seldom happens, particularly when the replay is on the Wednesday. Possibly, this was due to Celtic fans who had lost faith returning with confidence in the charisma and application of Jock Stein.

In the Final, Celtic had the first-half advantage of a strong wind but were stunned when Harry Melrose scored in 15 minutes. By the half-hour, though, Celtic equalised when Bertie Auld was first to a Charlie Gallagher shot which hit the bar and rose high into the air. Auld held off the Dunfermline right-back, Willie Callaghan to head the ball home from one yard. Just at the whistle, however, the Pars went ahead again through centre-forward McLaughlin. On the terraces, the Celtic fans were worried, but inside the dressing-room Jock Stein was calm and controlled, telling his team to continue with the system and to keep plugging away, the breaks were sure to come. The first one certainly came quickly, in 51 minutes and again it was Bertie Auld, who after a one-two with Bobby Lennox, steered the ball past Jim Herriott in the Dunfermline goal. Both sides now went all out for victory but, as the game went on, Celtic, even against the wind, were forcing corner after corner, pushing the Dunfermline players back into defence. Another corner, this one over on the left and Charlie Gallagher raced over to take it.

Celtic's first Scottish Cup for 12 years sits before a proud team. Back row, left to right: Young, Gemmell, Fallon, Murdoch, McNeill, Clark. Front row: Chalmers, Gallagher, Hughes, Lennox, Auld. Only seven of this side would play in the European Cup final two years later.

He took an outswinger, at a lovely height, just too far for the keeper to come out but perfectly flighted to be met with a good header. And, on this occasion, it was centre-half Billy McNeill who came running in, his jump carrying him above the opposing defenders and he powered the ball home for the winner.

1964–1965 FAIRS CITIES CUP					
23/09/64	Leixoes	(A)	1-1		
07/10/64	Leixoes	(H)	3-0	Agg	4-1
18/11/64	Barcelona	(A)	1-3		
02/12/64	Barcelona	(H)	0-0	Agg	1-3

Celtic dealt comfortably with the Portuguese opposition of Leixoes in the first round, but the class and experience of Barcelona were too much to handle in the next.

Estadio dei Club de Futbol Barcelona, more commonly known as the Nou Camp today. This photograph was taken in 1963, the year before Celtic played the Catalans in the Fair Cities Cup.

1964–1965 GLASGOW CUP		
Rangers	(H)	2-1
Clyde	(H)	3-0
Queen's Park		5-0

Celtic had little difficulty in winning this Glasgow Cup, after scoring the first goal in only ten minutes. They then gave a fine display of attacking and enterprising football which thoroughly entertained the rather small crowd.

The Big Four planning the morning's work. From left: Neilly Mochan, Jock Stein, Sean Fallon, Bob Rooney (Reproduced by permission of the Herald and Evening Times Picture Library).

Queens Park's defence just could not cope with Celtic's attacks, capably marshalled by Bertie Auld. Their discomfiture started from the first whistle, when Charlie Gallagher intercepted their second pass, pushed. it through to Bobby Lennox, who rounded the keeper to score. By half-time two more had arrived, the first again from Lennox, the second a swerving 20-yard free kick by Auld.

Celtic took the foot off the pedal in the second half, but still scored two more. In 61 minutes, Steve Chalmers headed the ball in from close range and 10 minutes from the end Bobby Murdoch added the fifth from 20 yards.

Team: Fallon, Young, Gemmell, Murdoch, McNeill, Clark, Chalmers, Gallagher, Hughes, Lennox, Auld.

CHAPTER TWENTY
A Surprise Signing –
My Own Story

AT THIS POINT, this history becomes more personal as I joined the Club in January 1965. As will become clear, my background played an important part in my relationship with Jock Stein so a quick review will set the scene in perspective,

At Under-18's schools level in those days, there was only one international match against England on the calendar and I was fortunate enough to play in this match twice, in 1960 and 1961, while at St Gerard's Senior Secondary School in Govan. The trial for the 1960 match was my first big stressful occasion and an incident occurred which has stuck in my mind ever since. The game was only a few minutes old when somebody lobbed a high-ball right over my head into the 18-yard box. As I backed towards my own goal, I glanced at my goalkeeper a couple of times, expecting him to come for the ball. At the very last minute, I realised he was not coming, it was too late to head the ball so I trapped it with the sole of my foot, pulled it backwards, swivelled round my opponent, took the ball out of the penalty area and passed to my wing-half. It must have looked good, although my teacher gave me a rollicking later on for trying something so 'daft' on a wet surface. But I am also quite sure that the selectors on the touch line noticed my name after a manoeuvre like that and in the long run it probably helped. They say you should learn from experience, so whenever any of my sons have been in trials at football or rugby for the various age levels, my last words to them, apart from 'good luck', have always been 'do something to make the selectors remember you'.

The match against England in 1960 was held at Turf Moor, Burnley's ground, although we trained at Deepdale in Preston, where I had the privilege of meeting the great Tom Finney, now, rightly and belatedly, Sir Tom. Unfortunately, we lost that one 2-1, but one year later, at Celtic Park, we got revenge by winning 1-0. I captained the team from centre-half that night, with a future Celtic colleague, Ian Young, at right-back, but the match received little mention in the papers the next day, as they were more interested in the 'Battle of Britain' between Rangers and Wolves, played the same evening.

There were about four of us who played at this Under-18 level two years running. There were some very good players in this team, players with far more talent than I possessed but the only three who lasted any length of time at senior level were Ian Young, Andy Roxburgh and myself. That shows a tremendous drop-out rate from this Under-18 age group level, so it is even more difficult to assess whether boys from younger age groups will make it big time. Talent is only one of the factors which matter. Character, determination, the ability to play under pressure, the ability to ignore the opposition and the crowd, and, of course, hard work, all play an equally large role.

Talking of talent, during this my last year in school, I was in the presence of a really talented performer. At the Scottish Schools Athletics Championships of 1961, I finished second in the triple-jump and was chosen to represent Scotland against England and Wales in a triangular competition held at the Empire Stadium in Cardiff. I was sixth and last in my event which was won by a young man called Lynn Davies who later went on to win the long-jump title at the Olympic Games in Tokyo in 1964.

A good friend of mine and Celtic scout, Joe Conner, was monitoring my progress all this time and he was keen to take me to Parkhead. I, on the other hand, while always Celtic-daft, was not sure that I had the talent to do well there. There was another problem in that I had been accepted by Glasgow University to study dentistry, beginning in October 1961. The course was a long one – 5 years – and arduous, lectures and labs taking up most of the day so any studying had to be done at night. This left me in something of a dilemma. Every boy knew of others who had dropped out of University, generally for lack of work, and I did not want to join that group. At the same time, the call from Parkhead was a flattering one, which any young Celtic fan would feel privileged to receive. In the end, I accepted the invitation but played as an amateur without obligation. That way, I could train whenever I got the chance and played quite a few games in that season of 1961–1962 in Celtic's third team which won the combined Reserve League. It was quite an exciting time to be there because some new players had joined, names like Tommy Gemmell, Bobby Lennox, Jimmy Johnstone and Bobby Jeffrey, so I felt as though I was in the big time.

Second year dentistry was tough, a long trawl through anatomy, physiology and biochemistry, classes all morning, labs in the afternoon plus another on Saturday morning. The workload left little time for any concentrated training and I did not play at all that year – for any official team. I managed to keep training about three or four times a week; this consisted of a four-mile run if I felt in the mood, or a quick two-mile belt around the outside of Bellahouston Park if I felt lazy. To be honest, the latter ones were more frequent. Not very interesting, but the stamina work was to stand me in good stead later on when the role of attacking full-back became more common.

On Saturday afternoons, I tied my laces together, hung my boots over my shoulder and stood beside the dressing rooms in the same park. Some team always had an absentee and I got a game for a variety of teams including Weir's Recreation and Rancel, the combined Celtic and Rangers outfit. It was good fun and extremely good for my ego as I was often asked to sign forms with the team for which I played. I started playing properly again at the beginning of season 1964–1965 and made the first team at Glasgow University. The standard was pretty good, the training was well thought out and our old pitch at Garscadden was one of the best I ever played on! In recent years, Glasgow University, like other educational institutions, has seen the need to raise more money, so these pitches are now a fine housing estate.

For some years after Sunday mass, it had become the norm for Joe Conner, my dad and I to chew over the football scene with Joe particularly pleased that I was playing again. What I didn't know, though, was that the dear old guy had been watching me, not from the touch-line but from behind walls or trees or cars all over central Scotland. Just after New Year 1965, he arrived unexpectedly at our house in Cardonald with some surprising news. Apparently, he had been giving some glowing reports about me to Sean Fallon back at Celtic Park. Sean had also come to see me without my being aware of it and Celtic now wanted me to sign a contract.

I was stunned but secretly pleased, as I though I had missed my chance at senior level. By then I was half-way through my fourth year and felt that I could cope with whatever was thrown at me *and* spare some time for training. Mum wasn't too keen but dad was quite blunt; 'there are a lot of dentists, son, but not everyone gets a chance to play for Celtic!' That was exactly my own feelings, so, a few days later, I arrived in the early evening at Celtic Park to sign professional forms. This should have been one of those special occasions in my life, but, in reality, while the outcome was good, the event itself was disappointing. Celtic Park in those days was rather drab, the office area small and uninspiring, the surroundings fairly musty. Sean Fallon handled the proceedings, with Joe Conner also present and I had the privilege of meeting the great Jimmy McGrory, the manager of Celtic.

I had read much about this man's achievements as a free-scoring centre-forward, many of them unsurpassed to the present day. The squat figure with a huge neck still gave testimony to the strength and power he must have got brought to his game. More surprising was the diffident, almost laid-back approach to the job of manager, which contrasted sharply with the heads of various departments within the Dental Hospital, my only means of comparison at the time. Once the papers were all signed, I was taken in to meet the various members of the Board. First, I was introduced to the Chairman, Robert Kelly, who held out his left hand – upside down – for me to shake. Later, I discovered that he had had a withered right arm since birth and always shook hands in that way, but on that January evening, it totally confused me and I gripped his hand with both of mine, just to be on the safe side.

Next up was Desmond White, the Treasurer, who also put his left hand out in exactly the same manner. To say I was astonished is putting it mildly; I was beginning to think it was some sort of Club custom. Later I discovered that Mr White had walked into an aircraft propeller during the war hence his use of the left hand as well. Whatever the reason, my bewilderment must have shown on my face. When I was introduced to the third Director present, a very jovial man called Tom Devlin, he started to put his left hand out then burst out laughing as he extended his right. The other Director present, Jimmy Farrell, also found my reaction amusing and he congratulated me on my joining the Club. He seemed very interested in my welfare and I was to have a good relationship with him, as did many of the other players in the years which lay ahead, even more so after 1969 when he became my father-in-law.

So that was it; and this by now fully-signed player returned the next evening for my first training session and a real surprise! Our sessions with the University team had been held at Westerlands near Anniesland Cross – nowadays also a housing estate – and were handled by coaches with a background from Jordanhill College, the PE Training Establishment. They were well-structured, we got plenty of ball-work and I thoroughly enjoyed them. Imagine my shock then, when I arrived at Parkhead for my first training session and found that all we did was track work. This seldom varied. We started with a quick lap of 440 yards then walked a lap; a two-lap run (880 yards) then walked another lap; 4 x 220 yard sprints, walk the next 220; 8 x 100 yard sprints down the straight, walk the bends; four laps of 50 yards sprint then 50 yards walk and that was it. Requests to the coach for a ball were always met with the same reply, 'Oh, you'll get enough of that on a Saturday!'. Since the coach stood at the bottom of the tunnel and the only lights put on were the ones underneath the main stand, quite a few unwilling trainers went down the home straight a damn sight quicker than they went down the back straight. However, there were a number of good trainers at the evening sessions which made them very competitive.

Good trainers many of these lads might have been but not all of them made the grade at Celtic Park for one reason or another. Frank McCarron, who captained Scottish Under-18 schoolboys the year after me only played one match for Celtic before moving to Carlisle where a badly broken leg affected his career adversely. There was Gerry Sweeney, wing-half, who went on to have a very good run with Bristol City, or Tony Taylor, a very quick left-winger, later to play with Crystal Palace and even manage the Canadian National Team. At a time when very few young players had cars, Tony bought himself a little runabout but he was rather embarrassed by the fact that it was a three-wheeler. Worried about receiving some stick from the senior players, he used to park it across London Road behind the flats. None of the part-timers gave him any abuse; after every training session we broke the record for the number of people in a three-wheel car and got a run into town! Some players in our group at night had already played for the first team, players like Jim Brogan and John Cushley.

My rival for the right-back berth in the reserves – and already the incumbent – was a laddie from Lanarkshire, John Halpin, a nice guy who never showed any reaction to another right-back joining the Club. Initially, he and I shared the full-back slot, or I played centre-half, but as the season drew to a close I seemed to be first choice at full-back. In those days, Celtic had both a reserve team and a combined reserve team, so between the two the young players had many matches to play, especially in the last few weeks of the season. Before then, of course, a most significant event in the history of Celtic Football Club had occurred, when Jock Stein returned as manager in March 1965. Even at evening training, where he only occasionally put in an appearance, there was an extra 'buzz' after that and the full-timers told me that training for them had changed out of all recognition.

Before long, our paths crossed, with the boss letting me know in no uncertain terms who was in charge. It was a night match, in chilly conditions, so I decided on extra coverage. My physique was of the slim variety back then, only 11st 6lbs at 6ft 1in, and I took some time to get warm on the field even though a lot of effort was being put in. My answer was a tee-shirt under the strip, which not only kept me warm initially but seemed to 'even out' the body heat generated during the match. Without realising it, I was imitating the Continentals, most of whose players wear one, even in the warmest of weather. Anyway, on this particular night, I was pulling on the tee-shirt when I heard a voice behind me say 'hey, hey, hey!' I turned round; it was Jock Stein. 'What's that?', he said. 'A tee-shirt'. 'Aye, but what are you going to do with it?' he asked. 'Wear it under my strip' I replied. His answer was unequivocal. 'Not in this damn team you won't' and the tee-shirt was handed to the trainer. This was my first experience of Jock Stein's authority and his occasional intransigence which, at the beginning, was used to supplement his authority. Nobody else among the reserves wore a tee-shirt, so I couldn't either, even if that might have helped me to play more comfortably or more efficiently. The manager was the Boss, the players obeyed or else. That was the system of the time and Jock Stein had come up through the system. This trifling incident was merely a flick of managerial power, to show not only me, but the others as well, who was in charge. It succeeded in doing so.

As the season drew to a close, there was great excitement around the Club as the first-team headed towards the Scottish Cup Final. For the reserve squad, however, there were other considerations. The papers were full of stories that Jock Stein was going to cut the number of players at the Club and we all pondered our future. In those days if the Club wished to retain a player, they had to be informed by 30 April. When I arrived home on 29 April that year there had been no communication from Celtic Park, so to say I was nervous was putting it mildly. What made it ever more galling was that I had just played for the Combined Reserve League team against Rangers and nobody said anything. There were various comments among the players about the frees list, but no communication from those in charge was forthcoming. We all left for home still unsure of our position. The following day, I left the house before the post arrived and spent all day at the Dental Hospital but with my mind elsewhere. I arrived home to find that no letter had arrived and with a sinking heart I raced out to buy the evening paper, nothing there either. There was a Glasgow Cup First Round tie between Celtic and Rangers at Parkhead but I needed the time to study, so I sat all night looking at my books without really concentrating. Eventually I couldn't wait any longer so dad and I set out from the house. There was a pub not far away in Paisley Road West outside which I had seen a news vendor selling the morning papers at the dead of night. I had never bought one so I had no idea of when he appeared, or even if he did so every night. My dad and I walked up and down Paisley Road West across the road from that pub for what seemed like an eternity before the guy appeared, followed a few minutes later by a man bearing the papers.

I was across the road in a flash, bought a paper and found a street light to illuminate the pages. There it was; 'Celtic have freed 20 players', was the headline. I quickly checked the list. My name was not there! I then checked the list of 31 retained players and there it was, although not in the most prominent place. The first 20-odd names were in alphabetical order in one paragraph; then followed another section, with some seven or eight names in any order. Mine was the second last, with Gerry Sweeney behind me! Still, I had been retained, that was the important news and suddenly I felt ten feet tall. It had been a good finish to the season for Celtic, the first team had won the Scottish Cup; the Reserves their League; and the Combined Reserve team their League as well. Twenty players had been freed and the Combined Reserve team scrapped for the following season but there was much to look forward to in 1965–1966 and I wanted very much to be part of it.

1965–1966

We had the month of July off from Dental School, so I was able to join the full-timers for the start of pre-season training, around the third week in July. Parts of it were very impressive, other aspects less so. The training itself was nearly always done with a ball, apart from the essential sprint work and circuit exercises. Celtic Park or Barrowfield were the choices of venue, although if the weather was inclement the pitch load was shared further afield, like Mount Vernon dog-track beside the Zoo, the pitches beside Colvilles at Cambuslang, or occasionally the beach at Seamill.

There were loads of balls for the work, much more than required, plus plenty of bibs, cones, benches, weights etc. The training outfit was a different matter. Every day we each received a new short-sleeved tee-shirt and jockstrap but the shorts, socks and heavy jersey were merely dried and aired from the day before. Both the jersey and the shorts were numbered individually so every player received the same one, but the socks were a different matter. These had been dried from the day before and were merely dropped in a pile on the treatment table in the dressing room, when there was a rush to get a decent – or fairly clean – pair. If the previous day had been wet and muddy, the socks, now dry but with mud marks all over them, would stand up stiff as a board and the players had to pummel and twist them into the proper shape. Not very comfortable. Still, the training was interesting and there were always some relevant powders in the chemist to treat the athlete's foot!

I started the season in the Reserve team, gradually taking over the right-back position for my exclusive use, enjoying the chance to come forward whenever an opportunity presented itself. The mid-week matches were the important ones; that was when the Boss came along to watch and everyone raised their game accordingly. Praise is not something dished out generously at Football Clubs, but I got the impression I was doing all right. Joe Conner, the scout, and old Jimmy Gribben, a retired trainer then in charge of the boot room, were particularly supportive and I will always be grateful to them for their help. Then came my big break. Celtic had been drawn against Go-Ahead Deventer of Holland in the first-round of the Cup-Winners Cup, with the first leg away from home. There was no suggestion that I was required to travel with the party, although, even if chosen, my final year studies would have precluded that. The result was a comfortable 6-0 win for Celtic which made the return leg something of a formality. Much to my surprise I was chosen to play, taking over from Ian Young on the night, and, for the first time in my life, I received some coverage in the press. Celtic lost 1-0 and received some stick in the papers the following day for failing to put the Dutch team to the sword, although my own performance was well received.

The team that night is worth listing: Simpson; Craig, Gemmell; Murdoch, McNeill, Clark; Johnstone, Chalmers; McBride; Lennox, Hughes. Yes, it was the first outing of the defence which took the field in Lisbon two years later, with three of the forwards on that night in Portugal – Johnstone, Lennox and Chalmers – also playing.

Two days later, though, I was back in the Reserves and stayed there for two weeks, a very frustrating period after tasting the glamour of the European side. During this time, Celtic won the League Cup for the first time since 1957, thanks to two penalties by John Hughes.

On 13 November I came back into the team and for the rest of the season competed with Ian Young for the right-back berth, although Billy McNeill also had some matches there for reasons I will explain later. On 3 January I was told that I was in the team to play Rangers, my first Old Firm match. It is hard to relate to those who have never been to one just what an atmosphere surrounds this match. Every player is reminded about it for weeks beforehand, in fact since the last one, with the fans desperate for success in this particular fixture, which makes the winning supporters feel superior in their work-places.

I was almost overwhelmed with good wishes from perfect strangers, much more so than for any other match, quickly realising just how important they are to many fans. This one proved rather special, as Celtic won 5-1 on a hard and frosty Celtic Park, with goals by Bobby Murdoch, Charlie Gallagher and a hat-trick by Steve Chalmers. In spite of all the aggro and bitterness surrounding the occasion, I was much impressed by the style, and, more importantly, the sportsmanship of my immediate opponent, Davie Wilson, a lesson for all young players.

After beating Aarhus of Denmark (1-0 (A), 2-0 (H)) in the second round of the Cup-Winners Cup, where again I played the home leg, Celtic were drawn against Dynamo Kiev in the quarter-finals, a really tough draw, with the home leg first, a situation disliked by most players and managers. It was one of thoses special nights at Parkhead and for the first time I felt the inspirational atmosphere of an almost full house. Whereas good crowds were present for the Go Ahead match and also for Aarhus, over 60,000 were crammed in to Celtic Park to see the cream of Ukranian talent. And talented they certainly were, strong as well. It took two excellent goals by Bobby Murdoch and a magnificent strike by Tommy Gemmell to send us to the Soviet Union three up. I received special permission from the Dean of the Dental Hospital to travel and was really looking forward to the trip.

As well as the players and management staff, Directors and Club doctor, about a dozen supporters were on our chartered plane from Aer Lingus as we left from Abbotsinch. Initially, the flight was uneventful, but suddenly the pilot announced over the intercom that we would be landing at

Copenhagen, although we would be circling for a while to burn off fuel. I was in the usual trio who were to travel together for a few years. Me at the window; Murdoch in the middle, although he spent most of the time leaning across me to look out the window; and Chalmers on the aisle seat, frequently asking me if I could see anything out the window, but preferring the outside from where he once told me in all seriousness that he could 'make a bolt for it' if there was any trouble! I often wondered where he was going to bolt to! As we eventually came down towards the runway, Murdoch, leaning across as usual, said in a very matter-of-fact tone 'look at that, there are some fire engines and tenders lined up along the runway. There must be a plane in trouble?' One second later the truth dawned on him and he sat back in his seat and tightened his seatbelt. Quite apprehensive, but relieved to be rid of his weight, I did the same while Chalmers, obviously oblivious to Murdoch's comments said 'can you see anything interesting out that window, Cairney?' He never received a reply because I had my eyes closed at the time, but we landed safely without any further trouble.

At this point, I had better explain the 'Cairney' bit. I have always said that this was the way in which I most resembled a Brazilian player; I took another name, a single one at that! Others, less generous, said it was the right way for me to play my football — under an assumed name! In either case, the pseudonym was first used by the late Neilly Mochan during a reserve match at Parkhead, during the autumn of 1965. I had received a slight ankle cut which kept me out of the team for a couple of weeks or so and when I came back into action, Jock Stein, much to my astonishment, said he was ready to give me a run at centre-forward, where I would get more to do. I scored a couple of goals and was generally running round like a mad thing when one of the scouts, newly arrived at the match, came to sit beside Neilly Mochan and asked 'who's is that at centre-forward?' 'That's Cairney' said 'Smiler', 'This Man Craig!' There was a series on TV at the same time where the part of Ian Craig, a very earnest young schoolmaster, was played by the actor John Cairney. And that's how I received my nickname, probably the most used amongst the team. Nobody every called me by my christian name again. Some years later 'Cairney' and 'Cairney' were team mates — at quizball!

The rest of the flight to the Soviet Union was uneventful. We landed first in Moscow, where we spent a few hours in freezing conditions, long enough for a walk round Red Square before setting off again for more pleasant conditions in Tbilisi, in Georgia, where the sun shone and the temperature for football was just perfect. After all these years, I have three recollections of life in Tbilisi. Firstly, every male seemed to be not only a smoker, but a chain smoker, and most seemed to roll their own; secondly, all the adult males wore the most enormous flat caps, designed, I suppose, to keep the sun off their heads; and thirdly, a fair amount of manual work, like road-sweeping, was done by women. Some things have never caught on in this country!

The return leg was played in the early evening, I recall, in very hot and humid conditions. Three up we may have been, but there was no attempt to sit on our lead; we were told to play the match as though we were still level. Certainly, there was no cavalier attitude on the part of our players. We kept a disciplined defence, I seldom overlapped, nor did Tommy Gemmell on the other side, mainly we sat in and protected the defence. My immediate opponent, Khmelnitsky, was a very powerful man, had kept me very busy in Glasgow and was no less talented in Tbilisi. At one point in the second half he ran back towards a pass from his own full-back, then tried to sell me a dummy by letting it run through his legs. It almost worked, but I read it right and moved across to block his path. We collided heavily and fell away from each other, then he came towards me and shouted into my face, obviously displeased with my manoeuvre, for which the referee had not whistled up.

I was rather rudely making gestures back that he was all mouth. It was really one of those flashpoints where much noise is made but physical violence usually absent. Suddenly, though, I received a blow from the side which caught me on the cheekbone and lower jaw, forcing my cheek against my teeth, leaving the inside of my mouth cut and bleeding. The blow also knocked me sideways for a second. On turning back, I realised that Khmelnitsky had not struck me, but out of the corner of my eye I saw a figure running away and I turned to give chase. Quickly, my team-mates held me back and the referee stepped in, eventually ordering Khmelnitsky and myself off, while the guilty party got off scot-free. The thrower of the punch – and the runner away – was Joseph Szabo, a Soviet Union International who has recently been manager of one of the emerging new Soviet States.

To say I was incensed was an understatement and I flatly refused to go, a situation easily rectified by the referee, who merely ordered a couple of the Red Army soldiers, hundreds of whom were seated in the first two rows of the stadium, to escort Mr Khmelnitsky and myself to the dressing room. We went.

I was accompanied down by Jimmy Steel, that great guy who worked so hard for Celtic, massaging the players each and every day we were away. He had come with me into the dressing room obviously to make sure I was alright. When I told him shortly after I got there that I was fine, I told him to go back up and watch the game again. He insisted on staying but I equally insisted that he go back up to the bench. Just as I had got my kit off and wrapped a towel round me prior to going in for a shower, the dressing room door opened and three supporters of the team came in the door obviously intent on some form of discussion with me or possibly there was more than that on their mind. Anyway, I turned round and moved towards them and shouted really angrily at them. This was quite easy for me as I was still flaming mad over having been sent off. Anyway, much to my surprise. the three bolted out the door, so perhaps Craig in full flight was a frightening experience for them. The game finished 1-1 so we were through to the semi-final of the Cup-Winners Cup. The whole travelling party were delighted, although both my face and pride were sore. My mood was not improved later that night when the boss informed me that I would have to apologise to the Chairman. When I asked him the obvious question – why? – I was told bluntly that it was Club policy for any player to do so in such circumstances. Through a swollen jaw, in the foyer of our hotel, I was equally forthright – pointing out that I had been on the receiving end of an assault, had done nothing to merit dismissal, and therefore there was nothing to apologise for. We parted on less than amicable terms.

The journey back from Tbilisi proved a nightmare. Problems with the plane caused us to climb aboard and disembark on several occasions. There was one moment which had always stuck in my memory. We were all seated on the plane, baggage safely stored away but with the steps still attached. The pilot started the engines and slowly built them up to high revs. We were not expecting to take off because this was the third or fourth time we had all been in this position. At that point, the co-pilot came through the doors from the cockpit and started down the steps, which were on my side of the plane. Outside, the area was lit up by arc lamps so I could see him talking to someone at the foot of the steps before ducking under the edge of the wing and looking up towards the engine. Taking a pocket torch from inside his jacket, he used it to inspect the under-side of the wing! A pocket torch? What the hell would he be able to see with that? I would have found it farcical if I hadn't been so worried! In fact, I refrained from mentioning it to Chalmers in case he 'made a bolt for it!' Eventually we took off, but due to further problems diverted to Stockholm, where we spent a lovely evening in the very luxurious Grand Hotel and the following morning and afternoon out in the snow-bound countryside. Twice during this period Jock Stein asked me if I had apologised yet and twice I repeated my refusal.

Arriving back in Glasgow late on Friday night we were whisked to Celtic Park where a training-session was hurriedly organised to shake off the stiffness of travel. Even so, it was a fairly bleary-eyed and tired group of players which reported back at Parkhead the following day to travel to Edinburgh for the League match against Hearts at Tynecastle. The Directors had made efforts to persuade the SFA to re-arrange the fixture due to our travelling problems, but to no avail.

Arriving at Tynecastle we went out to inspect the pitch, then came back into the dressing room, where, when the team was announced, I received an unwelcome surprise. I was dropped! I could see some of the players looking at me in a questioning manner but I said nothing, collected my complimentary ticket and left the changing room. Outside, I met the Treasurer, Desmond White. 'You'd better hurry up' he said, 'its 2.35'. 'I'm not playing', I replied. He was obviously taken aback, barely managing an 'Oh' and a raised eyebrow as we went our separate ways. In the match itself Celtic looked, not unnaturally, a bit jaded, whereas Hearts were really up for it. My replacement at the right-back was one Billy McNeill, who had been injured some weeks before and lost his centre-half slot to John Cushley. 'Wilbur' (Cushley's nickname – after the Irish player Wilbur Cush) was playing well, although that day he was given a hard time by the Hearts centre-forward Willie Wallace. The match ended in a 3-2 defeat for Celtic.

At this point I must journey a few years hence to 1970. The squad had just travelled to Seamill for a few days' rest although I had not been feeling great when I reported at Parkhead. By the time we reached Seamill, all the symptoms of flu' were evident. The coach – Neilly Mochan – telephoned my wife and arranged for her to meet me at the McDonald Hotel in Giffnock, to which I would be transported by the boss himself. Jock Stein was in great form as we travelled up in the Club Mercedes talking about various aspects of the game. Then, out of the blue, he made an astonishing statement. 'You know, Cairney, you're responsible for me getting a free hand at Celtic Park'. I was truly amazed. I asked 'how come', and he explained the sequel to the incidents in the Soviet Union – my ordering-off, refusal to apologise, being dropped and so on. Apparently, as I surmised at the time, I had been dropped for disciplinary reasons according to Club custom. After the match, however, and the unwelcome defeat, Desmond White had been incensed that a team which had done so well abroad had been changed for such an illogical reason. He had gone on to back me up, saying I was quite right not to apologise, as I had no reason for doing so.

The outcome, Jock Stein went on, was that from that point on the occasional interventions by the Chairman, Robert Kelly, ceased. He explained that the Chairman never quite told him what to do but frequently queried his team selections, comments like 'I wouldn't play him', or 'he's much better further forward'. From then on, he made all the decisions.

There was another sequel from that night in Tbilisi. That date was also the one chosen for the Final Year Dinner of my fellow students at the Dental Hospital and, of course, I missed it. On my return I was approached by one of the older lecturers. 'Did you hear what the Dean said about you at the dinner?' he asked. I replied that I hadn't, whereupon he informed me that his exact words were that I had 'disgraced myself in Georgia' that night. He went on quickly to say that, from the newspaper reports, the statement was untrue and that I should go to see the Dean and complain. I pointed out, reasonably enough, that I was about to sit my Finals and, as the Dean was overseeing the whole affair, I did not want to rock the boat. 'Nonsense!' he replied, 'never let anyone say things about you that are untrue' and he pushed me in towards the Dean's secretary's office to make an appointment.

A few days later, I nervously knocked at his door and went in. 'Yes, Mr Craig', Professor White said in precise tones, looking up from the papers on his desk. 'Well, at the Final Year Dinner, you apparently said that I had disgraced myself in Georgia and that was just not true', I replied. His next comment rather floored me 'so I understand – and I would hope that you would accept my apology'. I was too perplexed to do anything other than agree and we shook hands before I left. The lecturer's advice was quite right, and I was pleased with the Dean's apology; later though, I realised that an approach from him to me when he had learnt the circumstances might have been more appropriate!

For the remainder of that season, there were some high points – and low ones. I played my first Scottish Cup tie in February, against Stranraer, leaving me in the very unusual position, at that time anyway, of having played four Cup ties in Europe before playing one in the Scottish Cup. March was a bad month. I was sitting the first part of my Finals at the time and finding that there were not enough hours in the day to cope with everything that was happening. The boss spoke to me about it, and, as a result, I took some time off – an opportunity which Ian Young grabbed with both hands, getting a six-game run in the League and both legs of the Cup-Winners Cup semi-final against Liverpool.

Celtic should have had this tie wrapped up at Celtic Park. We were well in control, got a solitary goal through Bobby Lennox, but missed a number of chances which were to prove costly. I didn't think that either full-back, Ian Young or Tommy Gemmell, looked comfortable against their immediate opponents, so when we travelled to Liverpool for the second leg I was quite hopeful of a place. The Reds' outside-left, Peter Thomson, was a talented player, quick with good control, very effective when in the mood. Ian Young and I used different approaches to wingers, he having a liking for the quick tackle, my own style preferring to run the winger into non-effective areas before stepping in. At the same time, I was much more likely to get forward and support the attack, although I was fairly inexperienced at this level. It was, then, a difficult decision for the boss, and, in the end, he gave Ian Young the nod, much to my intense disappointment. My mood was hardly improved on receiving my complimentary ticket, which, as all the non-playing group discovered when we went out of the dressing room only seconds before the kick-off, was for the other side of the ground!

Unfortunately for Celtic, the night was wet, the pitch very slippery, which seemed to inhibit some of our flowing moves. Liverpool won 2-0, although Bobby Lennox scored what looked like a good goal, only to see it chopped off for a very dubious off-side decision. Ian Young was given a very difficult night by Peter Thomson, as he was again only a few days later in the Scottish Cup Final by Rangers' Davie Wilson, this match finishing goalless. Four days later, I was brought in again for the replay where I had a hard time facing the skill and control of Davie Wilson as well as experiencing the first of many tussles against Willie Johnstone, 'Bud', as he was known. In spite of reports to the contrary, we always got on fine off the park and I would put him very near the top of the list of good wingers that I met. For that reason, I am particularly pleased with my record against him in Old Firm matches, as I feel I never did any worse than 50/50 against him, and frequently did better than that.

That may seem a rather selfish way of looking at a match but I believe that football, like many team sports, is a whole series of one-to-one confrontations all over the pitch. If six or seven players in one team overshadow their immediate opponents, then enough possession is generated to do well and possibly win the match. In this particular game, my first Old Firm Final, I felt I kept both Johnstone and Wilson fairly quiet and even managed one or two sorties forward myself. Unfortunately, my efforts were to no avail, as Kai Johannsen, Rangers' Danish international, strode forward and fired a fine shot past Ronnie Simpson for the winning goal. Incidentally, this was a perfect example of my analysis of a match in the paragraph above. Kai won the ball from John Hughes, who was so annoyed at losing it that he forgot to chase back, with the result the Dane had all the time in the world to shoot.

Defeat in a situation like that was a shattering blow to us all, but we had to put it behind us quickly, because with only ten days of the season left we had three vital League matches to play. We won the first two against Morton at Cappielow 2-0, and Dunfermline at East End Park 2-1, with Jimmy Johnstone and Bobby Lennox on the score sheet each time.

The scene was all set, then, for one of Celtic's most important League matches ever, or at least since the title was last won, in season 1953–1954. The final match was against Motherwell at Fir Park, and all during the week the papers were full of comments, interviews, statistics and advice. If Celtic won the title would be theirs, a draw would also be sufficient but the boss soon put us right on that one. His attitude was that we wanted to go out with a flourish. We had won 26 of our games so far out of 33, and he wanted to finish with a good performance at Fir Park. It was a really tough match. Motherwell, always difficult to beat at home, rose to the occasion. Each and every one of their players treated the match as though it was a Cup Final, and the defence had its hands full with a very eager set of Motherwell forwards. Because of the nature of the match, I had seldom managed to get forward with any effect. With minutes to go, however, I saw my opportunity, won the ball from my opponent in the middle of the park and went on a good run right down to the by-line before hammering the ball across the face of the goal where it was met by Bobby Lennox and flashed into the net giving us a 1-0 victory. The recollections of Lennox and myself on this particular moment differ slightly. He says he met my shot with the side of his foot, having made his choice to place it in the corner of the net and executed the move perfectly. My own recollection is that my hard drive across the face of the goal hit his shins and ricochetted straight into the net! Either way, we were happy it happened, and the Celtic players were delighted.

As a finale to the season, it could not have been better, yet I always remember Jock Stein saying he was disappointed at missing out on the Cup-Winners Cup, the final of which was held in Glasgow, with the strong favourites – Liverpool – beaten by Borussia Munchen-Gladbach. It was, perhaps, an example of Stein's vision for Celtic – not content with them being the best in Scotland but wanting them up with the top guns in Europe as well. A difficult target to achieve, yet a tribute to the man was the way he modelled his team to perform such a task along the lines of the Real Madrid team which had so impressed him in 1960. At a time when many European coaches tended to a defensive attitude, Jock Stein's team entertained and thrilled the crowd.

It had been a great season for me personally. I had got my place in the team, had some wonderful European moments, experienced the thrill – and disappointment – of losing an Old Firm Scottish Cup Final and then played my part in the final day of the championship. However, while the players, the manager and the Directors jetted off across the Atlantic for a tour of the USA, Canada and Mexico, I got my head down to concentrate on my final exams.

1965–1966 Scottish League Division 1

	P	W	D	L	F	A	Points	Position
Celtic	34	27	3	4	106	30	57	1st

Fixtures

	H	A		H	A
Aberdeen	7-1	1-3	Kilmarnock	2-1	2-0
Clyde	2-1	3-1	Morton	8-1	2-0
Dundee	5-0	2-1	Motherwell	1-0	1-0
Dundee Utd	1-0	4-0	Partick Thistle	1-1	2-2
Dunfermline	2-1	2-0	Rangers	5-1	1-2
Falkirk	6-0	4-3	St Johnstone	3-2	4-1
Hamilton	5-0	7-1	St Mirren	5-0	3-0
Hearts	5-2	2-3	Stirling Albion	6-1	0-1
Hibs	2-0	0-0			

1965–1966 EUROPEAN CUP WINNERS CUP

	Go Ahead Deventer	(A)	6-0		
	(Holland)	(H)	1-0	Agg	7-0
	A.G.F. Aarhus	(A)	1-0		
	(Denmark)	(H)	2-0	Agg	3-0
QF	Dynamo Kiev	(H)	3-0		
	(USSR)	(A)	1-1	Agg	4-1
SF	Liverpool	(H)	1-0		
		(A)	0-2	Agg	1-2

1965–1966 SCOTTISH LEAGUE CUP

Section Games	H	A
Dundee	0-2	3-1
Dundee United	3-0	1-2
Motherwell	1-0	3-2

LEAGUE CUP POSITION

	P	W	D	L	F	A	Points	Position
Celtic	6	4	0	2	11	7	8	1st

LEAGUE CUP QUARTER- AND SEMI-FINALS

QF	Raith Rovers	(A)	8-1		
	Raith Rovers	(H)	4-0	Agg	12-1
SF	Hibs	(Ibrox)	2-2 (AET)		
Replay	Hibs	(Ibrox)	4-0		
Final	Rangers	(Hampden)	2-1		107,609

1965–1966 SCOTTISH CUP

	05/02/66	Stranraer	(H)	4-0	15,500
	21/02/66	Dundee	(A)	2-0	29,000
QF	05/03/66	Hearts	(A)	3-3	45,965
Replay	09/03/66	Hearts	(H)	3-1	72,000
SF	26/03/66	Dunfermline	(Ibrox	2-0	53,900
Final	23/04/66	Rangers	(Hampden)	0-0	126,522
Replay	27/04/66	Rangers	(Hampden)	0-1	98,202

In — and Out!

1966–1967

The summer of 1966 was a most frustrating time for me in the football sense.
While I was at home sitting my Finals, Celtic were having a most successful
tour of North America and Mexico, by some way the most successful of such
tours ever undertaken by the Club.

1966 NORTH AMERICAN AND MEXICAN TOUR RECORD					
P	W	D	L	F	A
11	8	3	0	47	6

Every time I picked up the papers, some journalist was going into raptures
over this performance, or that display, and I did notice that the full-back
pairing of Tommy Gemmell and Willie O'Neill seemed to have official
approval. This was confirmed once the season started and I spent an
unhappy few months in the Reserves waiting for a chance. This is a difficult
time for any player, one which he can only accept for a while before starting

*Celtic 1966–67. Back row, left to right: Brogan, O'Neill, Young, Cushley, Gemmell, Craig, Cattenach,
Gallacher. Middle Row: Neil Mochan, Goodwin, Quinn, John Clark, Hughes, Martin, Fallow, Simpson,
Kennedy, McCarron, Halpin, Henderson, Hay, Bob Rooney. Front row: Jock Stein, Taggart, Johnstone,
Chalmers, McBride, McNeill, Murdoch, Lennox, Auld, Macari, Gorman, Sean Fallon.*

to ask questions. I was no different from anyone else in this situation and regularly knocked on the Boss's door for a chat. These conversations were all along the same lines and finished similarly. My argument was that I was playing well in the Reserves, had been the man in charge at the end of the previous season, and, although realising that the team was playing well, with the full-backs doing OK (you never give too much praise to a rival!), I deserved the chance to regain my place.

The Boss, calmly and infuriatingly, would agree with most of the above but felt he couldn't change a winning team. Naturally, he would then stress what a valuable player I was to the Club and that, even if there was the slightest drop in form by either of the incumbents, I was in! That usually pacified me, but, from speaking to many other players involved in similar discussions, I have since discovered that their bosses all said exactly the same words to them! Perhaps there is some manual lying around – *The Manager's Guide to Double-Speak*. Apart from the annoyance of being in the Reserves, everything else was good, the place having a real 'buzz' about it. The early matches of the League were going well, the League Cup campaign was equally effective and the first tie in the European Cup was just around the corner.

Behind the Scenes

The backroom personnel at this time were all pals of the players. In fact, the whole show was run by surprisingly few people. Jock Stein, Sean Fallon and Neilly Mochan ran the football side; Bobby Rooney attended to the injuries; Jim Kennedy was the Supporters' Liaison man; the 'Old Boss' – Jimmy McGrory – was the Public Relations Officer; Johnny Bonnar and another couple of guys ran the Pools operation; and there was a secretary in the main office. Nowadays, the inside of Celtic Park reminds me of a Cecil B. Demille film epic – there is a cast list of thousands!

The role of Assistant Manager could not have been an easy one for Sean Fallon. Jock Stein was a very restless individual, wanting to be involved in everything and I would think that working in close proximity to him must have been hard on the nerves. Sean was also the 'ticket' man, in charge of both complimentary and bought ones for the big matches. The players officially received a fairly small allocation for European matches and other all-ticket games – 10 or 12, I seem to remember plus two complimentary tickets – whereas each of us had at least three times that many asking us to get them one. Before every major match, the players were all scrounging round asking Coaches and Directors if they had any spare briefs. Times like that must have been a nightmare for Sean. Players would go in to see him with comments like 'great to see you, Sean', and come out several minutes later muttering something decidedly uncomplimentary.

I only once saw him stuck for words. At the Hindu Club, just outside Buenos Aires, where we were preparing for the World Club Championship in 1967, Sean and Jock were having a game of golf and a few of the players, not allowed to play ('keep your mind on the game lads') were watching. Sean was not playing very well and after taking three shots round a dog-leg, found himself about 100 yards from the green, with a lake occupying the space in between. Turning to his caddy, he asked, in his soft Irish brogue, 'what should I do here?' The young boy's answer, even in broken English, was perfectly clear: 'Pick up ball and walk in!'

Neilly Mochan was a great football enthusiast who loved to talk about the game and its characters. Mention has been made earlier in this book about the power of his shooting at the height of his career. Well, in the late 60s, he could still thump a ball around, and take part in our training matches every day. When we arrived in a 'foreign' city on our European travels — always on a Monday afternoon back then — we would check into our hotel then set out for a walk to loosen up the legs. These were always led by Neilly, sometimes with unusual consequences. In Amsterdam, for instance, where there was a threat by the South Moluccan terrorists to shoot Jimmy Johnstone, a large posse of police surrounded the players as they set out. Neilly chose the route at random and took us down the Kanalstrasse, the main avenue in the red-light district of the city, where the prostitutes in their (lack of?) working clothes, sit at the windows to entice the customers in. Talk about keeping the players' minds focused on the game!

In Prague he took us through what looked like an alley to get back to the hotel. Unfortunately, the alley led into the large square of an army barracks, where as the troops were being put through their manoeuvres complete with rifles on shoulder, twenty or so Celtic players and officials cut through their ranks to get to the other side. Chaos was the word!

Bob Rooney, who always referred to us as 'his boys' had a very dry sense of humour. Before one of my initial matches for the first team, Jock Stein gave the final instructions then said 'OK everyone'. Immediately, Bob, who was acting as trainer that night, piped up before anyone else. 'Just remember, guys, it's me that's on tonight, so if any of you get injured, make sure that you're near the dug-out!' The remark broke the tension but I was not sure if he meant it!

A few weeks before the European Cup Final I went in to see him, not for treatment, but in connection with one of his other duties — the provision of boots. 'Bob, I burst one of my boots'. 'What foot?', says he. I was quite taken aback. 'My left foot'. 'Well, that's all right then, we'll just tape it. You don't use that one very often!' However, when he saw the boot in question even he realised that it was beyond repair. 'I'd better get you a new pair' he grumbled, 'and take care of them this time!'. I must point out that we had just won the Scottish Cup, were trying to win the Scottish League, and I was just about to play in the European Cup Final.

After the latter match, fans raced onto the pitch and I was stripped of jersey, boots and socks, arriving back in the dressing room holding on firmly to my shorts and jock strap. A few days later, it was announced that Celtic would play Real Madrid on 7 June in Alfredo Di Stefano's benefit match, so I went in again to see Mr Rooney. 'Bob, I need a new pair of boots'. 'You're joking, you got a bloody pair only a few days ago! What the hell did you do with them?' I explained the details and he shook his head before very grumpily giving me a new pair. He could not resist a parting shot, 'now make sure you keep these for a few years!' Unfortunately, in packing my gear in our hotel after the match in Madrid, I must have omitted or forgotten to include the boots because when I got back to to Glasgow they were nowhere to be found. I didn't have to report back to Celtic Park until pre-season training, but as I did not fancy asking Bob for another pair, I resolved the predicament in a sensible manner. I bought myself boots in a sports shop!

There were other unusual features at Celtic Park back then. The Supporters' Liaison man, Jim Kennedy, or 'Presi' as he was known to us all, was efficient at his job but never displayed many of what are known as the 'social graces' in dealing with the fans. Older supporters will remember the little window to the right of the entrance behind which 'Presi' did his work. 'I see you're back, it must be a big game!' he would ask one fan. 'Are you sure you're not counting the dead ones as well?' he queried of another, obviously suspicious of the number of supporters in that club. A thick skin was a necessary prerequisite for the envoys of clubs sent to collect the tickets. Even the far-travelled were not immune to the treatment. I was speaking to some fans from Thurso one day when one of them walked across and knocked at the window to collect his club's allocation. The slide window crashed open and 'Presi' shouted, through a mouthful of food, 'can ye no see I'm at my dinner?'

There are always fans milling around the doors of footballs clubs trying to brass their way in. In the late 1960s at Celtic Park this problem was exacerbated by the number of 'big' matches we played in for the various trophies. The man delegated to stop anyone entering without a ticket – a very nice guy if you produced the necessary documents, a holy terror if you didn't – was Bill Peacock. Bill's instructions were obviously quite clear: 'unless someone has a ticket, they do not get in'. That was the brief he was given, and my goodness did he obey that instruction. The list of people left out was extensive, even the famous were not immune. Don Revie and Bill Nicholson, for instance, the night of the Fiorentina match; or Bobby Lennox, who, arriving at Parkhead to play for the Scottish League against the League of Ireland, was stopped by Bill's upraised arm. 'Where's your ticket, Bobby?' 'Bill, I come here every day to train' replied the astonished Lennox. 'But that's with Celtic', countered Peacock, completed unfazed, 'this is with the Scottish League and you'll need a ticket to get in!'

My own favourite moment with Bill Peacock, however, was at one European tie. As I approached the front door at Celtic Park he had halted a guy wearing a huge parka jacket, with a camera slung over each shoulder and a light meter hanging down round his neck. Between his legs he had a bag on which were stamped the big words *Daily Record/Sunday Mail* – and he was harassed, frantically searching through the many pockets in the jacket for his entry pass. Bill recognised me, waved me past with a nod and a smile, then turned back to the prospective intruder; 'so tell me, son, how am I supposed to know you are a photographer?'

The training was hard – and very competitive – as there was a number of quality players all vying for 11 places. The toughest match of any week was the one which rounded off the training session, the 'bibs' versus the 'non-bibs'. These matches were fiercely contested, neither side willing to give any quarter. Sometimes one side would be a few players short through injury but the rest just fought on. Once you were allocated to one of the teams, it would never cross your mind to play for the other lot. Neilly Mochan used to switch between the sides, as occasionally did Jock Stein, although he had a pronounced limp from that ankle injury. If his particular team that day was being beaten he would referee as well and it might be some time before the scores were 'levelled' and he could blow the whistle. The Boss's favourite moments at training were when he took the goalkeepers for a warm-up session. While we loosened up and did some light running around the periphery of Barrowfield, the Boss would hit balls to the goalkeepers, his left peg strikes starting gently then increasing in power until all the goalkeepers were working quite hard.

On a personal level, I was expecting some problems when I joined in 1965. Few professional footballers in this country come from a university background and I was unsure how that would work out. In the mid-1960s there was still an aura of mystique about university life. There was only one in Glasgow, for instance, (Strathclyde had not been awarded university status by that time and was known as the Royal College of Science and Technology) and there were no TV programmes, as now, to show life behind the scenes. There were two under-graduates with Celtic at that time – John Cushley and I – but, frankly, we were never regarded as different in any way. Once the other guys realised that we could misbehave like the rest on a night out, we were in!

There are many facets which make up a football club; the manager, the players, the back room boys, the support and even the stadium with its staff and surroundings all play their part. Contrary to that old cliché about the fans being the most important factor, it is the players who matter most. Without them, there is no match. With good players, success can be achieved. If very good players are present, then the chances of success are even greater. When performers like these are directed by a top quality coach, then the sky is the limit. This was the scenario when I joined up at Celtic Park. There was a pool of high-class but under-achieving players already there and with the addition of only two more, plus the astute direction of Jock Stein, the team improved rapidly.

The record for the following nine years is incredibly consistent (see Chapter 22) and I was very lucky to be there for seven of them. The merits of the team and the individual players have been discussed and dissected many times, so there is no need for me to do that here. What I do give in the following lines is a personal review of each player and a favourite memory or anecdote of each one.

Left: the author, who played 231 times for Celtic and scored 6 goals, in 1965. I'm quite impressed with the way that right foot of mine is at the correct angle to strike the ball, so the picture was obviously taken before ligament damage to the same ankle caused some variation in position!

Right: the author in 1997, now tinting his hair?

Ronnie Simpson — 188 appearances, 91 shut-outs (48 per cent).

Ronnie Simpson

'Faither' was an unprepossessing figure on the pitch, the long stride for his height making him look a little ungainly. The old Glasgow expression 'nae twa pun o' him hinging the gether' always springs to my mind. Ronnie was excellent at spreading himself on his line, making his figure appear much bigger than it really was, and he was very brave as well. He used his experience to shout instructions throughout the match, mainly at me, but since he played without his dentures in place, I could never understand a single word!

Favourite memory: The back-heel just outside the penalty area in Lisbon may have delighted the fans but, I can assure you, the defence nearly had a heart attack.

Just before a charity match in Ashington, Northumberland, Jock Stein told us he was going to watch the match from the Directors' Box instead of the dug-out but he wanted us to show these people how we could play. In the first minute, Ronnie ran across his line to shepherd a header from the opposing centre-forward past the post. Unfortunately, it slipped just inside for the first goal. One minute later, he fumbled a high cross and John Gorman, now Assistant-Manager of England, mis-kicked the ball into the roof of our own net. Two down. Thirty seconds later, Jock Stein was on the bench. 'Cairney' he yells at me, 'what does that old bugger think he's doing?'

Ronnie heard it too and his face was like fizz. At the next corner for the opposition I couldn't resist teasing him. 'I hope you don't mind my asking, Ronald', I started in my best upper-class accent, but he soon broke in and told me where to go in no unmistakable terms. For once, on the pitch, I understood him perfectly.

Tommy Gemmell

T.G. was confidence personified. If he had any doubts about either his own play or the opposition, then in four years of rooming with him, I never saw any signs of it. On the pitch he had an arrogance in his play which stood him in good stead. With a fine touch on the ball and good stamina, the attacking full-back role suited him down to the ground. Rooming with him was an experience. Waiters would arrive with some drinks shortly after lights out. His contempt for time meant we were always in trouble for being late, or perhaps I should re-phrase that and say that I got a row for not getting him there on time. Yet the same guy once woke me early one Holiday of Obligation to tell me to go Mass!

Favourite memory: I have many but most are libellous. Two I can tell you. The first showed the confidence in the man. He was woefully short with a

Tommy Gemmell — 428 appearances, 64 goals.

pass-back in Novisad against Vojvodina in the quarter-final of the European Cup in 1967 which led to their only goal. At the reception after the match he was sitting by himself looking down and I went over to try and cheer him up. 'Don't worry Cairney' he said with conviction, 'there's another leg to go and I'll make it up to you all then'. He did.

One moment Tam would want to forget was before the League Cup Final at Hampden in 1969 when we played St Johnstone. Coming into the dressing room just after 2.30 pm, Tam started to take his jacket off only to find that, while he had been outside chatting to fans, the Boss had announced the team and Davie Hay was playing in his place!

Bobby Murdoch

'Chopper's' career was very much in the balance before Jock Stein arrived. A grafter but not really mobile enough for the inside-forward role of the old W/M formation, Bobby found his forte further back in mid-field, where he could dominate the play in front of him yet still come forward to score the occasional goal. He was the ideal player to play with. No matter how hard a time he was having, he would always be there for a pass or to help out. That does not always happen, and I would like to think that I did the same for him.

Bobby Murdoch — 484 appearances, 105 goals.

343

At a reception in his honour recently, I was asked to say a few words. I was happy to do so, while pointing out that it would be the first time in over 30 years that I had said anything nice about him! Bobby was equally uncomplimentary, remarking that the hump on his back came from playing in front of me! Both remarks were very typical of our relationship.

Favourite memory: I found him sitting, still dressed in his strip, under a shower in Lisbon after the match against Benfica. The forwards had been poor that night and couldn't hold the ball, with the result that the defence was vastly over-worked and lost a three-goal lead in the clammy heat of a Portuguese evening. I told Bobby that we had won the toss to go through to the next round, but, with his face up to the cool running water, he was quite blunt, 'at this moment, Cairney, I don't give a —!'

That was at least different from his normal reaction after a match. Bobby was always 'greeting'. He cried when we won, he bubbled when we lost, he even had tears in his eyes when we drew! The hard man image was very much a veneer. Underneath was a big softie.

Billy McNeill

One feature of the Lisbon team often overlooked is that the back three were all over six feet and good in the air. That puts me in perfect position to state that Billy, or 'Caesar', was among the best headers of a ball, in timing, direction and power, that I have ever seen. Even when tightly marked he

Billy McNeill — 790 appearances, 34 goals.

would manage to get his head to a ball at corners or free-kicks, and he scored some memorable goals. That same talent also served him well in defence. I've never been convinced that 'Captains' are very important in most team sports (apart from cricket), but Billy handled that role with aplomb and he was an impressive spokesman for the squad.

A great asset, from our point of view, was his relative freedom from injury. A Celtic team of those years announced without Billy's name at centre-half didn't seem right and that, perhaps, was the best tribute we could pay him. I have asked him several times, without ever receiving a satisfactory answer, why someone who played over 700 times for Celtic should only have been ordered off against East Stirling and the Bermuda National team?

Favourite memory: Firstly, the rather haunted look in his eyes when he realised, from the safety of the dressing room in Lisbon, that he would have to go back out through the throng of Celtic supporters to receive the famous trophy.

And secondly: coming onto the bus the morning after the Benfica match in Lisbon when we lost a three-goal lead and won by the toss of a coin, Billy stopped beside the Chairman, Sir Robert Kelly, and apologised for any noise coming from the players' rooms the previous night. Sir Robert simply stared ahead and grunted 'I don't know what you were all bloody celebrating, anyway!'

John Clark

'Luggy' was quite a quiet bloke, probably more wrapped up in football than any of the others, so it is good to see him back at Parkhead in a new role. His style was extremely unflamboyant, but very effective. He seldom seemed to rush but was always hard to get past in training matches. Celtic's opponents obviously found that difficult as well. You could tell from John's demeanour when a big occasion was looming. He constantly re-arranged the fit of his jacket, particularly round the lapels, then straightened or adjusted one of his seemingly unending supply of ties. Just before any match he was a real nuisance to the rest of us. He was a frequent visitor to one of only two toilets in the dressing room, almost hogging it in fact, leaving the rest of the nervous ones to share the other.

Favourite memory: His child-like query when penalised, standing slightly hunched, with his hands open and up-turned, for all the world an innocent abroad. Yet, John was always a competitor, sometimes impatient with other players' problems.

This was reflected a few years ago, in 1995 to be exact, when Celtic were asked to field an 'old-crocks' team to play the Feyenoord one which won the European Cup in 1970. I was part of the team which was winning 5-0 when the Dutch got a free-kick. As it was to be taken by Wim Van Hanagem, we

John Clark – 318 appearances, three goals.

organised a ten-man wall leaving only a small space up in the postage-stamp corner uncovered. True-to-form, Van Hanagem bent the ball round the wall right into the small area. Even though it was impossible for the goalkeeper – Evan Williams – to get there and we all knew that, John could not let it go without comment; 'Oh! For God's sake Evan, you must have known he was gonna put it up there!'

Jimmy Johnstone

Jimmy was an amazing player. In all the years I have spent playing or watching football, nobody – and I mean nobody – has ever played like him. There were, in the last World Cup, some players with great close control – Suker, Ortega, Veron, Bergkamp, Ilie, Ronaldo – but none of them terrified their opponents quite like Jimmy Johnstone, who just drove at them and used his wonderful skill and balance to make many look flat-footed.

On a personal level, he was, and always is, the friendliest guy you could possibly meet. (I would say Lennox would be a match for him), yet he was also a strange paradox. Letters sent to him from all over the world would go unanswered, mainly because he was too busy doing something else. However, if he heard of anyone ill in hospital, particularly a Celtic fan, then he was off like a shot to visit them. When I came into the first team I was a little in awe of his talent and reputation. I discovered later that he thought I would

Jimmy Johnstone – 515 appearances, 129 goals.

be rather stuck up and superior. By the third match we were giving each other a fair bit of abuse, and we have remained great pals ever since.

Favourite memory: One of the advantages of my career at Celtic was that I could see Jimmy's performances from a closer position than anyone else. One sticks out above all the others. When we played Real Madrid in Alfredo Di Stefano's benefit match Jimmy gave their left-back the biggest roasting I have ever seen a player receive. He beat him in every possible way plus one or two I had not thought of. A wonderful player – I often wonder how much he would be worth in today's inflated transfer market.

Jimmy was terrified of flying because of a bad experience on a trip back from the USA. A few years ago, the Lions agreed to play a charity match in Iceland. At Glasgow Airport, very early one Sunday morning, a bleary-eyed group gathered for the flight, Jimmy's nervousness very evident. A pilot walked over to us and asked; 'are you the gentlemen for Iceland'. The Wee Man was blunt. 'Aye, what sort of plane have you got?' The pilot smiled, 'Oh! We have one big plane and one small plane'. Jimmy grabbed his bags and headed off. 'Right, guys' he declared, 'who's coming on the big plane?' as confidently as he could. It was a brave effort on his part, but I will never forget the look on his face when he realised that the 'big plane' was an eight-seater!

Willie Wallace

As a Hearts player, Willie had been a thorn in Celtic's flesh for a few years, always raising his game to suit the occasion. So when the Boss paid Hearts a considerable transfer fee for his signature, we were not surprised. Of our strikers, three – Johnstone, Lennox and Chalmers – were the mobile type, pulling defenders all over the place then arrowing-in on goal. Willie, like Joe McBride before him, was comfortable in and around the penalty area, using his strength to hold defenders off and his powerful shot, which needed very little backswing, to score. Willie was a goal-scoring success right from the start, but his two goals in the first leg of the semi-final against Dukla Prague in 1967 almost repaid the transfer fee and also stamped his credentials with the support, who, naturally, are a little apprehensive about any new signing.

Favourite memory; he always called me 'son' and seemed to think I needed some protection! When I scored an own goal against Rangers in the Scottish Cup at Ibrox in 1970, Willie Johnstone ruffled my hair as he went past. The referee was only yards away looking at me for a reaction, so I did nothing. Out of the corner of my eye, though, I saw Willie punch Johnstone obviously on my behalf. At half-time, he came over in the dressing room. 'Are you

Willie Wallace – 234 appearances, 135 goals.

alright, son?' he asked. 'I'm fine, Willie' I replied, 'But Bud's going to have a hard time in the second half.' 'Good for you Cairney', he approved, slapping me on the shoulder. 'By the way, son, you can fight your own battles in future. I nearly broke my bloody hand!'

Our relationship got off to an embarrassing start, at least in my case. When we first met, after a few minutes chat, I asked him if he had a sore throat? 'Wispy' replied, to my horror, that he always spoke that way!

Steve Chalmers

Steve had been at Celtic Park for a number of years, scored a good number of goals but he had won very little in the way of medals. He, therefore, like some of the other 'older hands' – McNeill, Clark, Auld – was desperate for success and more than played his part. A laid-back character normally, he became highly nervous before a match. The bigger the occasion, the worse he became. He liked routine. He would eat the same meal down at Seamill before a European tie, he had to sit in the same seat on the bus, with me beside him (I don't know why; he was monosyllabic to a fault at a time like that); always got changed for the match in the same order, left boot before

Steve Chalmers – 405 appearances, 228 goals.

right-boot etc, shorts last. I always felt that there was something 'right' about his scoring the winning goal in Lisbon. In a better-paid era, that should have been perhaps his last match for the club – what a way that would have been to go out.

Favourite memory: two in particular from my early days. After training and showering, he always put his shoes and socks on first then stood up on the bench to put the rest of his clothes on! Before a match, he used to go into the showers, unscrew the lid of a little bottle on the window-ledge and take a swig from it. I later found out that it contained brandy – to settle the nerves! Simpson, Auld and Wallace were other imbibers in this custom.

One incident I would like to have seen, but missed, occurred in San Francisco, when Celtic played Bayern Munich in 1966. Stevie went up for a high ball, and as he came down he was punched on the side of the face. Recovering his balance, he looked round to see who it was, recognised the assailant and gave chase. The spectators present then had the wonderful spectacle of watching Steve Chalmers, one year later the scorer of the winning goal in the European Cup Final, chasing Gerd Muller, who eight years later scored the winning goal in the 1974 World Cup Final. Big legs against wee legs, but the little ones escaped retribution.

Bertie Auld

Bertie was very calm before a European Cup Final, assuring us that everything would be okay. 'Don't forget, guys, I've played in one already.' So he had, for Birmingham City against Roma in the Fairs' Cities Cup Final (the forerunner of the UEFA Cup), in 1961. This was his second spell at Parkhead and he received a new lease of life under Jock Stein. Very sharp over the first few yards and a fine passer of the ball, he also scored a few important goals at vital times. Another strength was his confidence. With Bertie in the dressing room it was likely to be noisy and full of laughter, a very essential ambience for success.

Favourite memory: as we assembled under the stairs leading to the pitch in Lisbon, with the Italians, all bronzed and oiled alongside us, I was thinking what an unprepossessing bunch we must look. We all had very short haircuts, few of which suited us; we were quite white in colour, overlaid with a touch of red from the heat; Ronnie Simpson, who looked 40 normally, was more like 60 without the teeth; wee Jimmy was asking Giacinto Faccetti – the future Italian captain – if he would like to swap his jersey afterwards (Faccetti's expression was a mixture of confusion and bewilderment); while Bertie walked with a decided limp, even when fit. Suddenly, though, he raised his voice and launched into the words of 'The Celtic Song', quickly, we all joined in, and it did make us all feel better straight away. For that act alone, he deserved our thanks.

Bertie Auld — 279 appearances, 85 goals..

On tour to the USA in 1970, we played Eintracht Frankfurt, in New York, I think. Early in the match, Bertie hit me with an awful pass, the ball arriving at the same time as my opponent, who rightly took the opportunity to flatten me. Picking myself up, I shouted angrily at Bertie, cursing him for the pass. He held up his hands in apology, but I also noticed the half-smile was there as well. From that time on, every time he got the ball he hit me with it. In the second-half I was trying to hide behind other players, but still the passes arrived, accompanied by the cheery shout 'Is that one alright Cairney!'

Bobby Lennox

In all the years that I have known the little guy, he has never changed, ever bright and cheery, always affable. His mere presence in the dressing room always made it a brighter place and he was everyone's pal. At the same time, he was a great player, quite superb at running onto a ball at pace and putting it away without changing either feet or direction. That is a very difficult skill, most players preferring to pull it onto their favourite side before shooting. Bobby was often pulled up for off-side when he wasn't, a victim of the linesman's dilemma. A player is either on-side or off-side at the moment

Bobby Lennox – 571 appearances, 273 goals.

that the ball is played to him, and if a linesman watches the pass being struck, then looks towards the forward's position, very often the forward looks off-side at that moment. At the time of playing the pass, though, he was on-side. Bobby was very quick off his mark and was often caught like this. This problem is much more recognised today than it was in the 1960s, particularly since the advent of slow-motion replay. If 'Lemon', as he was known, was playing today, he might have been whistled up less often.

Favourite memories: firstly, his bout of hand-waving and side-slapping in the second-half at Lisbon, when arguing with the referee over a possible penalty. I thought he was doing a speeded-up impersonation of the big children's star of the time, Andy Pandy.

Secondly, his look of horror when he was ordered off in South America in the World Club Championship. He could not believe it. His fellow players were astonished. We thought he must have shouted 'boo' too loudly, because Bobby was courtesy personified on the pitch.

Thirdly: a few years ago, we arrived in Dublin for a Testimonial Dinner and booked into Jury's Hotel. Bobby and I were paired up as room-mates and he said 'I've got the key here, Cairney', and we set off to find our room. 'What number?' I asked. '107', he replied, so we just took the stairs up to the first floor. Unfortunately, all those rooms ran from 200 onwards, so back down stairs we went. 'Let's try the basement' he says, so down we go this time, only to find cupboards and lockers but no rooms. Up we went again. 'Could I see that key, please?' I asked and he handed it over. I could see the problem straight away. The 'key' turned out to be a plastic card, on which was stamped the information that Messrs Lennox and Craig had booked into Jury's Hotel at 1.07 pm!

Joe McBride

I have mentioned all the players who took the field at Lisbon that evening. But I can't finish without naming one, who, but for injury, would certainly have been there. In the first half of the 1966–67 season, Joe was in great form, scoring 35 goals in 24 matches. Then, against Aberdeen on Christmas Eve, he damaged a knee – the injury turned out to be more complicated than expected and he missed the rest of the season, although he still finished as Celtic's – and Scotland's – top scorer.

Joe McBride – 94 appearances, 86 goals.

Joe has never let any bitterness show at missing what turned out to be a wonderful day, and the rest of the guys admired him for that. He had his knee operation in Killearn Hospital some 20-odd miles from Parkhead, yet each and every player went out there to see him. An excellent player, and a nice guy.

Favourite memory: In June 1997 a group of ex-Celts were invited by the Celtic Supporters' Association of America for a week's stay in the Flamingo Hotel, Las Vegas. Joe was up early the first morning to examine the inside and outside of the hotel. To the left of the swimming-pool, are two other pools, where flamingoes and penguins are the star attraction. Now, Joe has obviously never watched any nature programmes on TV, because he was fascinated by the fact that two of the flamingoes were standing on one leg. After walking round them a couple of times to review the situation, he decided help was required and approached a gardener weeding one of the flower-beds. 'Excuse me,' he asked in his most polite manner, 'Where is the other leg of that flamingo over there?' The gardener did not even raise his head, as he replied, 'Usually, up it's arse!'

Good fun, our guys, but there was a very healthy competition for places, with John Fallon, Willie O'Neill, Ian Young, John Hughes and Charlie Gallagher jousting with those already mentioned for those precious first-team jerseys.

As I mentioned before, if there is a nucleus of good players in a team, then the chances of success are reasonable. If they are coached by a good manager, then those chances are increased. All of us were lucky at that time to be under the guidance of one of the best-ever managers, so before I review Celtic's most successful-ever season, let's take a look at the driving force behind that success.

CHAPTER TWENTY TWO
The Boss — Jock Stein

THERE WAS NEVER any doubt who was in charge of football matters at Celtic Park in those glory days. Jock Stein had a 'presence' which dominated proceedings; in fact he was charismatic at a time when the word was seldom heard or little understood.

Undoubtedly, the ups and downs of his own playing career, allied to a tough start in life as a miner, forged a specific attitude to the game. Football had few fun moments at Albion Rovers and Llanelli, clubs at the wrong end of the soccer scale, whose very existence was often threatened. Even worse, his Welsh tenure was on a solo basis, wife Jean and young daughter Ray remaining in their council house in Hamilton while 'John' Stein, as he was known on arrival in Llanelli, found digs in Mansel Street.

No doubt the 'Jock' appellation started in these days. At least he was on a full-time contract of £12 per week, doubling his previous wage at Cliftonhill, but that part of Wales was, is and forever will be rugby country, the faithful gathering every Saturday to watch their beloved Scarlets at Straddy Park. It must have been a difficult time for the whole family. Travel from Llanelli to Hamilton — by train — was a long tedious journey, yet the trip would have been undertaken on a fairly regular basis, using up valuable money. Giving up the house and moving to Wales was unthinkable. In those days contracts were only for one season, a precarious existence, especially in a non-league outfit with poor crowds. A much more likely scenario was an eventual return to the pits, hence the importance of maintaining the house in Hamilton.

Jock Stein must then have been astonished — and delighted — when Celtic came in for his services in December 1951, Parkhead Reserve Team coach Jimmy Gribben receiving the credit for recommending him. To judge from Stein's actions when the European Cup arrived back with him at Parkhead on Friday 26 May 1967, there was a close link between the two men. Pushing his way past the crowd in the foyer, Stein immediately visited the boot room to show Gribben the trophy. His move back to Celtic was a much unheralded affair. Frankly, he was not well enough known as a player on the return to make any headlines. Among his family circle, though, more than one eyebrow was raised in disapproval. Almost to a man, they supported the 'other' side and were not pleased that Stein had moved over to the opposition.

From a playing point of view, his career at Celtic Park was at first surprising and latterly successful. Purchased initially as very much a stop-gap measure, he quickly made the centre-half berth his own, using guile and experience to compensate for a lack of pace. In a team of strong characters, he was appointed captain and led Celtic to the Coronation Cup win of 1953 and the League and Cup 'double' of 1953-1954. Unfortunately, a bad injury to his ankle, received against Rangers in August 1955, meant months of pain and constant treatment. After a final match in 1956 – a friendly against Coleraine – Stein realised that his ankle would no longer take the rigours of professional football and retired.

Whilst still a player, though, several incidents occurred which were to influence his coaching and managerial style. In discussions with me over the years, Jock Stein often stressed how impressed he had been, not only by the great Hungarian team which comfortably beat England and Scotland in 1953 and 1954, but also the various formations and tactics used in the World Cup of 1954 in Switzerland, where the Celtic team had travelled as an award for winning the 'double' in the same year. The teams at this time, certainly in Scotland anyway, still played a fairly rigid W/M formation devised after the deployment of the stopper centre-half in the late 1920s. This was the theory. In practice, however, it meant two full-backs and a centre-half forming a defensive line which pivoted around the latter; two wing-halves, one attack-minded, one more defensive; two inside-forwards, one slightly deep, one attacking; and three forwards, or as we would say today, 'strike' players: one on each wing and one through the middle. You can imagine the surprise, then, a thinking player like Jock Stein must have felt on seeing the Hungarians, with their centre-forward, Nandor Hidbgkuti, playing deep and roaming all over the pitch, or watching the Brazilians, in the throes of developing the 4-2-4 system, triumphant four years later.

Captain of that Celtic team he certainly was, and probably one of the boys, but even then, I would imagine a distance would have appeared between himself and those who lacked the work ethic. All during my time with Jock Stein, he abhorred players who 'cheated'. In his view, that meant players unwilling to give 100 per cent effort to their own game, or ones reluctant to work as a team or those who debased opponents. In that Celtic squad of the early 1950s, like most eras, there were a few in these categories and Stein seldom mentioned them. Oh, he would acknowledge their talent, of course, but rather grudgingly, then enthuse over the skills and efforts of men like Neilly Mochan and Bertie Peacock.

In my own era, one incident left him particularly furious. The Lisbon Lions took the field as an eleven for the last time against Clyde on 1 May 1971 at Celtic Park. Ronnie Simpson did not play, but led the side out, which in front of a 35,000 crowd romped to a 6-1 win. At one stage, Bertie Auld, in

THE BOSS – JOCK STEIN

his last match, sat on the ball and waved the Clyde players towards him. It was a typical piece of cheek by Bertie but Jock was disgusted and let him know that in no uncertain manner afterwards. It was an insult to fellow-professionals to belittle them like that, he said, adding that as far as he was concerned the incident spoiled the whole day for him.

On his retirement from the game Jock Stein was appointed coach to the Reserve Team in the summer of 1957, in which capacity he soon won the praises of some young stars (see Chapter 18).

Then followed what must have been some difficult years. From the comments of various players in this book alone there seems little doubt that the Chairman, Robert Kelly, picked the team and the manager, Jimmy McGrory, read it out. Very little though was given to training sessions, tactics, team balance, coaching etc. Yet, under Jock Stein in the Reserves, all these factors were being discussed, explained and put into practice! Consequently the Reserve Team blossomed. So why was he not promoted to a first team position and given the chance to succeed at a higher level?

The accepted version is that the Celtic Board, or rather the Chairman, wanted Stein to gain some managerial experience before being brought back as manager. Unfortunately, this scenario only surfaced years later when Jock Stein was already established and is probably fictional, as were some other stories of the time. During the 1950s, for instance, the Celtic Chairman tended to suggest, and perhaps later believe, that he had recommended Jock Stein to the Club, whereas most others reckoned that Jimmy Gribben was the instigator.

Jock Stein once told me that he felt he could go no further at Celtic Park, but when I asked him why he merely smiled and changed the subject. In retrospect, my naivety was probably showing. The Chairman in the late 1950s was still the Chairman in the late 1960s! There are three possible reasons why Celtic allowed Stein to go. Firstly, he had no talent for the post! From the comments of the players involved, and subsequent results, this can be dismissed. Secondly, he was too strong a personality for the Board to handle. This theory has definite possibilities. After the autocracy of Willie Maley ended in 1940, the Celtic Board, first under the Chairmanship of Tom White (until 1947) and then Robert Kelly, went in for mild-mannered managers whom they could control easily (Jimmy McStay; Jimmy McGrory). Certainly the Jock Stein I knew was not in the same mould. He would have wanted control; perhaps this was not to the liking of the Directorate. The third possibility is one I would like to dismiss as easily as the first, yet it must be fully considered. Though ecumenical in their employment of players, the Celtic Board and management had always been nominally Catholic. The crowds at this period in Celtic's history were dropping due to the lack of success, with only the die-hards, who were probably of Irish and Catholic backgrounds, consistent in their attendance. Was the Board worried that the appointment of a non-Catholic manager might affect attendances further, or did it just not fancy the idea? Either option would be distasteful and my fervent hope would be that the second theory, that the Board was worried about controlling Stein, is the correct one.

Jock Stein's move from Celtic's Reserves to the hot seat at East End Park seemed to surprise a few at the time, but from Dunfermline's point of view it was a fortuitous appointment. Stein saved the club from relegation in his first season, won the Scottish Cup in the second, and had a good run in Europe in the third. He was always eager to learn from other teams and formations, so the European Cup final between Real Madrid and Eintracht Frankfurt at Hampden Park in May 1960 was essential viewing for him. These are his thoughts from an interview I conducted with him in May 1980:

Q This match was eagerly anticipated but how did you assess the teams beforehand?

A Well, the fact that Eintracht had played so well against Rangers was the important thing. They had scored a lot of goals in the two games and we all knew about Real Madrid. They had some great players. We were told repeatedly about Di Stefano, we knew about Puskas and Gento, Del Sol and people like that. The difference then was that we were always talking about forwards. Nowadays we tend to talk more about defenders. The important thing was that both teams had players who could score goals.

Q What was your abiding memory of the game?

A I had just moved to Dunfermline and got two tickets for the Stand and was really looking forward to the game. We were all wanting to see the deep-lying centre-forward. We knew that Di Stefano was a great player, and he could score goals, but we wondered how it all happened and we saw it unfurl before our own eyes.

He was a player, that was the important thing. He wasn't a centre-forward or a mid-field player, he was just a player who played where his team wanted him to be and set up the play. He could take the ball from the back men and give it to the front men or he could score goals himself. I think that was the thing we found impressive in a player of his standard. An outstanding feature of his game was that he left the impression that we would never see a better player than him and I think that still holds true for many of us.

Q What lessons did you take from the game?

A I think we realised then that to be a team as they were, we ought to have players coming into scoring positions from outwith the forwards. I think their backs came forward and were an important part of the team. I think another important factor was that the centre-half was purely just a defender, who when in trouble just kicked the ball anywhere. He was very safe and that allowed the people round him to get on with the game and get forward.

Q And how do you look back on the match?

A Oh! As a marvellous exhibition of football. I think that we were all privileged to see a game like that at Hampden Park.

One year later, in the spring of 1964, Jock Stein joined Hibs and within months the team won the Summer Cup. By that time, Celtic had been trophy-less since the League Cup win of 1957. The fans were in despair – and rebellious. Displays of anger directed at the Directors' Box became commonplace, particularly after defeats in the Cup competitions. Eventually even an intransigent Chairman like Bob Kelly realised that the existing policies were not going to work and made the decision which secured Celtic's future – and gained him a knighthood!

Jock Stein arrived in March 1965, and from that point on success followed. The record for the next nine years was quite astonishing, especially when laid out as seen below. No wonder the fans of these years have such happy memories! At the beginning of his Celtic managerial career Jock Stein was under the same interfering pressure from the Chairman as his predecessors. He told me himself in most unusual circumstances (see page 330).

CELTIC'S RECORD IN MAJOR COMPETITIONS 1964–1975

Year	League Championship	Scottish Cup	League Cup	European Cup	European Cup-Winners' Cup
1964–65	—	Celtic	F	—	—
1965–66	Celtic	F	Celtic	—	SF
1966–67	Celtic	Celtic	Celtic	Celtic	—
1967–68	Celtic	—	Celtic	—	—
1968–69	Celtic	Celtic	Celtic	QF	—
1969–70	Celtic	F	Celtic	F	
1970–71	Celtic	Celtic	F	QF	—
1971–72	Celtic	Celtic	F	SF	—
1972–73	Celtic	F	F	—	—
1973–74	Celtic	Celtic	F	SF	—
1974–75	—	Celtic	Celtic	—	—

Like most managers of that period, Jock Stein preferred a master/servant relationship with his players. This may seem antiquated to today's minds but was quite normal back then. The discipline of National Service had only ceased some five years earlier, and even in the Swinging Sixties the attitude of 'obeying' was still more prevalent than today. The players had another reason for accepting Stein's wishes. Most had been at Celtic Park for some years, played in teams capable of good football, yet had never won a major trophy. Now, this very confident manager had appeared preaching a different gospel, assuring them that success could be theirs for the taking. Who wanted to rock the boat? As time went on, though, and success became commonplace, many players found the dictatorial approach unsettling and challenged it, with a transfer the almost inevitable outcome! I would say the period during the years 1965–1968/69 were the Halcyon Days, with every player reluctant to say or do anything to spoil his chances of selection.

During this time, for players used to the interminable trackwork of the former regime, training was a revelation. Nearly always done with a ball, it involved all the skills required in the game and their deployment in match situations. It was hard, but enjoyable, with those in charge, Jock Stein and Neilly Mochan, really good at the difficult art of mixing the strenuous drills with the fun moments. Stein himself was a real contrast, one minute gruff and grumpy, the next full of charm. When my wife had two miscarriages in the early 1970s he was the first to send flowers and cards to her; at the same time he wasn't talking to me!

Every player had their moments when managerial disfavour was their lot and I was no different! I must be strictly honest and say that I was probably as much to blame as he was. I found it difficult to be treated like a schoolboy in my mid-twenties so occasionally it rankled and my only come-back was to be a fairly constant challenger of authority. I never did this in a nasty way, but the expression which would most describe the situation was, I kept needling the boss and boy, did I know how to needle! Because of this our relationship was a volatile one, although he always had my respect. Two separate incidents spring readily to mind. The first came fairly early in my Celtic career. The Boss had explained a specific system to be used against a Continental side, and after he had discussed it in detail I raised my hand to ask a question. Angrily he waved it away. 'Just do what I've said', he growled, 'and everything will work out'.

A few minutes later, as I left the room down at Seamill Hydro, he came up alongside. 'You always want to ask bloody questions', he said, with feeling. I was rather reckless and replied, 'It might be nice sometimes if you wondered why I wanted to ask them', before walking away. He was up after me quickly. 'What do you mean', he demanded. At that point he suggested that we went back into the room where the blackboard was laid out. 'Okay, ask your questions'. I pointed out, trying to be humble, that I thought his plan was a good one, but that there were certain problems on my side of the pitch. The first was that Murdoch, whilst a great player, had periods when his fitness rather let him down, and I sometimes had to do a bit of covering for him. I also pointed out that in front of him, played a genius – Jimmy Johnstone; but while he, the Boss, was going into detail about the team plan, Jimmy was either looking at the ceiling or picking his nails, so he was not paying the slightest attention and very often I had his man to mark as well! At this point I could see that I had him and he started to laugh. From then on, after any team talk, he would wait behind and I would be allowed to ask my questions!

The second incident occurred at Celtic Park. I had been a substitute in this particular match, I suspect a Cup tie, and the rest of the boys, playing against 'lower' opposition, were not trying too hard in the first half, or perhaps taking the mickey, with the result that at half-time the match was level. In the dug-out in the first-half Jock Stein was not a happy man, and as

I walked up the tunnel on hearing the referee's whistle I thought that this could prove to be quite an entertaining interval. I went into the dressing room, collected my cup of tea from the table and went and sat down behind the door. First one in was Jock Stein; the second man in was John Fitzsimmons, the Club doctor. Stein immediately turned to him and said 'What do you want'? The doc was very surprised and looked to me for support. Frankly he wasn't getting any! 'I'm just in to see if there are any injuries', he said. Jock Stein turned on him and replied, 'The only injury in that team in the first half is heart trouble and I'll soon fix that for them. So you can get out!'. The wee doc made his exit looking very downcast. The players came in and Stein started. Firstly the goalkeeper, then the right-back and so on and so forth, right along the line – each one getting his full share of his displeasure. He then walked up and down the dressing room for a few minutes shouting and letting everybody know just what he thought of the first-half performance. By this time I was sitting in the corner with a cup of tea in my hands and gazed intently at the surface of the cup. Suddenly, Stein's voice tapered off, and I could see out of the corner of my eye that the feet were pointing in my direction. That is a very difficult position to be in. You can only not look up for a certain length of time and eventually I had to raise my eyes to meet his. 'And as for you', he said with feeling, 'what a bloody player you must be if you cannae get your place amongst this shower of idiots!'.

All very normal! People involved in high-pressure situations must occasionally expect to have blow-outs. None of us thought of stress in those days, yet stress certainly existed. Naturally, it was easier for the player to cope with all this. For the manager, sitting in the dug-out during a match, handling the calls from the press and TV for comments and interviews and meeting the expectations of the support, the strain must have been enormous. But, naively, few players gave that a thought. Even when his first squad of players had all left, he was still there trying to maintain the same standards with another group of players, the expectations probably even higher than in previous years. Few other managers could have matched his instant success, especially with so few changes in personnel. He had a wonderful ability to assess the opposition, anticipate how they would play on the night, then arrange his own team to best advantage. Without his sure touch at the helm, none of that first squad would have achieved their potential.

As a group, we were quite well aware of how fortunate we were to be at Celtic Park at that time, with Jock Stein in charge. Considering that we came from all over the West of Scotland, the players 'gelled' as a group and have remained close to this day. The analogy of a 'family atmosphere' is not quite a true picture, I suspect, but friendships, which were made and cemented in battle conditions, have stood the test of time. We had great help from Neilly Mochan, Sean Fallon and Bob Rooney, of course, but without Jock Stein's leadership, none of it would have been possible. Before we went to Lisbon, he made it quite clear that he wanted Celtic to win the Cup *and*, at the same time entertain the viewing public. To the puzzlement of some players he immediately put our new status as Champions of Europe to a tough test by taking on Real Madrid in Alfredo Di Stefano's Benefit match.

He was Mr Celtic at the time, yet his immediate reward was a disappointing CBE. It was an anachronistic piece of thinking by the British Establishment. The man at the helm – doing all the work, taking all the decisions – receives a CBE; the figurehead at the top, with no input into the victory, gets the knighthood! I did once ask if he felt hard done by, considering that Alf Ramsay and Matt Busby had received their knighthoods, but he merely shrugged his shoulders and said 'Och, these things happen!'

The horrendous car crash in 1975 took a lot of his fire away. When he became manager of Scotland I interviewed him a few times at the SFA offices in Park Gardens, where he received me with great courtesy. The huge panorama of football knowledge was still there, but I sensed the all-pervasive drive of former years was not. We discussed a whole range of football issues, including his time at Celtic Park and the personalities involved. I expected some bitterness over his treatment at the end but found none expressed. In fact, he was more interested in expressing good wishes for his successors to do well.

Jock Stein's death in 1985 was a tragedy, not only for his family, but for Scottish football, yet there was something appropriate about the circumstances as well. This was a man who lived for the game, who loved to watch it and discuss it. He might have moaned about his problems, or complained about his pressures, but it was his life, his work and his hobby. For him to leave us at such an emotive moment, when we had just qualified for the second successive World Cup under his charge was shocking, but somehow fitting.

At his funeral his 'boys' all gathered in sorrow, to a man declaring their gratitude for his help and encouragement. Many of these had been on the verge of leaving Celtic Park just before he arrived in 1965. Within two years they would be European Champions and set the standard for the following decade. Many were involved in the process, both on the pitch and behind the scenes, but one man – Jock Stein – was the instigator and controller. He truly does deserve to be numbered among the top rank of the best ever managers.

My own gratitude to him was enormous, but in the way that these things happen there was never an occasion when I expressed it to him. Perhaps the

Jock Stein and my wife Elisabeth on our wedding day, 14 June 1969.

best tribute I could, and indeed ever did pay him, was an unconscious one. When I reflected back on those meetings at the SFA offices I realised that, even as a by then 40-year-old cynic, I had unhesitatingly referred to him as 'Boss' all through the proceedings!

CHAPTER TWENTY THREE (1967)
We Scale New Heights

As Christmas 1966 approached, the Celtic support had every reason to be happy. On a personal level though, I was becoming more and more frustrated. Certainly the team was winning – the League Cup was already in the bag – but I was not truly convinced either by the full-back partnership or the job the whole defence was doing. Frankly, Willie O'Neill was playing better than Tommy Gemmell, who I thought never looked comfortable at right-back. Some statistics may help in the overall assessment. For the first 17 matches of the League campaign, with Gemmell and O'Neill as the full-back pairing, Celtic scored 58 goals and lost 22. For the final 17 matches, with myself and Gemmell in the roles, we scored only 53 but lost a miserly 11. Incidentally, Tam scored only twice in the league from the right-back slot but got five from left-back.

After a 2-3 defeat to Dundee United at Tannadice on Hogmanay, Jock Stein obviously decided that a change was required and I was brought in, holding down the position for the rest of the season. In the next two months, we played seven league matches and two Scottish Cup ties, scoring 36 goals with the loss of only three. It was heady stuff and I enjoyed the overlapping role, although it was extremely hard work.

We had been drawn against Vojvodina Novisad in the quarter-final of the European Cup, with the first leg in Yugoslavia. Novisad is about 150 miles north-west of Belgrade, and was then a very unsophisticated town, only the main roads were tarmacadammed, the side roads were just packed earth. By comparison, the pitch was in great condition, the floodlights ranked among the best I have ever played under, and the team was a very strong one. Yugoslav sides have always been noted for their pace and power and this one was no different. We played a very disciplined match in Novisad, and only a defensive mistake allowed them to score.

In the return leg at Celtic Park, Jock Stein decided to go for the same approach, a controlled possession game with, naturally, a little more emphasis on attack. It took quite some time but eventually we levelled it at 1-1, and increased our tempo, trying to snatch a winner. To be honest, I felt that we were in control of the play at that point and would not lose another goal; at the same time, their defence was very competent in handling our attacks, the goalkeeper Pantelic in particularly good form. In the midst of the hard work and tension, I was beginning to anticipate a third match and was trying to remember the venue, when we won that fateful corner which led to Billy McNeill's superb winner.

A semi-final draw against the Czech Army Team, Dukla Prague, was another hard tie, but a good team performance at Celtic Park, with Willie Wallace in very sharp form, left us with a 3-1 lead to take to Czechoslovakia. Everyone, including the management, was apprehensive about this return leg. Only a few years before, in the Cup-Winners Cup, Celtic had taken a 3-0 lead to Budapest where, thanks to a very open style of play, they were beaten 4-0. This time round, Jock Stein decided to protect a lead and defend in depth, the only time in my years with him that such an attitude was countenanced.

He wasn't happy with the choice. None of us were too keen either. Our back four marked in zones and this style was perhaps more in tune with Italian man-for-man marking. There did not seem to be any lights at Dukla Prague's ground, a fairly basic affair set in a hollow, so the match was played in the afternoon. It was a tough time for us and on the day there were some difficult moments. When we won possession, most team-mates were either in a square position or just marginally further forward, so the choice of options was limited. Up front, Steve Chalmers plied a lonely furrow, chasing everything. The aim was achieved – a 0-0 draw – but frankly, the game would never be remembered as a classic. Still, one of Europe's best-known teams had been vanquished and after the match, as soon as we had changed, a happy group of players, manager and directors headed for the airport for the flight home.

Dukla Stadium. When Celtic played there in 1967, there were certainly no floodlights, as the match started in the early afternoon.

'*A job well done*'. *The author leaving the field after Aberdeen had been beaten 2 - 0 in the 1967 Scottish Cup Final (Reproduced by permission of the Herald and Evening Times Picture Library).*

By then, I knew I was in trouble. I had not been feeling great all day, although I was able to play without any great problem. Soon after though, my temperature started to fluctuate – cold one minute, hot the next – and by the time I was seated on the plane, all my joints were sore. I was kept away from the rest of the players as much as possible, and, on arrival in Glasgow, was whisked home and went straight to bed. To say I was worried was an understatement. The Scottish Cup Final against Aberdeen was coming up in four days' time and I was desperate to play. However, after a bad time from Tuesday night until Wednesday evening, I felt much better and reported back to training on the Thursday morning as right as rain.

The general public are sometimes surprised by the speed with which a footballer, or any athlete in general, can develop the symptoms of 'flu and just as quickly shrug them off, but that happens to fit people all the time. Certainly, I felt fine and on the Saturday took my place at right-back in the final. Aberdeen were a good side at that time and were expected to give us a hard match but, in truth, from the very beginning we were always in control, although the final score – 2-0 – was not a true reflection of the play.

I knew myself that I had played well and the press coverage on the following days tended to agree with that. I even got a rare 'well done' from Jock Stein after the match because he was quite aware of how hellish I had felt on the way back from Prague.

However, while that was two trophies already in the cupboard, the more important two were still up for grabs, and the pressure was on. The tension was not helped when, four days after the Cup Final, we went down badly at Tannadice by 2-3. We only had two defeats during this season, both of them by Dundee United and each by 2-3. It was one of those nights when we played reasonably well, but the opposition were determined to put up a good show against the Cup winners, and they surpassed themselves.

The crucial match was the next one, at Ibrox. Victory here would clinch the Championship; a defeat would prolong the competition to the last day. The heavens opened that Saturday and made the surface of the pitch very heavy, slippery and treacherous. The Celtic fans must have had their hearts in their mouths, particularly when we went behind to a Sandy Jardine special. Thanks to wee Jimmy, though, who got two for us, with only a few minutes to go we were 2-1 up and heading for victory. Then, Roger Hynd came powering through to the bye-line and tried to hook the ball back to an incoming forward. I moved out to anticipate the cut-back but Roger, on the muddy surface, mis-kicked the ball which went between me and the goal and it was scrabbled home for the equaliser. It was a sickening moment, but we held out to the end, thus clinching our second successive championship and keeping alive our hopes of a Grand Slam. There was one final match against Kilmarnock on 15 May which we won 2-0 to finish the season, and then we got down to preparing for the big one. By this time, I was becoming more confident and I was quite sure that I would be part of the defence in the match in Lisbon. That seemed to pick itself, but up front there were quite a few chasing the five places.

The team later known as the Lisbon Lions had played together for the first time against St Johnstone at Muirton Park, in Perth, on 14 January, and had two further league outings, on 19 April against Aberdeen, and on 6 May against Rangers. There were two similar appearances in the Scottish Cup, against Queen's Park in the quarter-final and the final against Aberdeen; while in Europe, they played in that non-event, the away match in Prague. So, for Jock Stein, there was a choice of five players from Johnstone, Wallace, Chalmers, Lennox, Auld, Gallacher and Hughes – always assuming, of course, that he was happy with his defence. I had three areas of concern at this time. The first was probably the least troublesome. Every player in a talented squad worries about his place in the team, but I was pretty happy that I would retain my place for the final. Another fear was injury, but I decided just to give everything 100 per cent and hope for the best, rather than pull out of any challenges to protect myself etc. The third problem was turning out to be the most difficult one to assuage, and surprisingly enough it concerned my Dad.

Almost a shrine nowadays in the eyes of Celtic fans, the Estadio Nacional was, in truth, an unlikely setting for a European final, with stands on only three sides.

Dad, at that time, was a manager in the furniture department of Glasgow South's Co-op. As a result of this, he worked on a Saturday and could only get to mid-week matches. Now, he really floored me by saying that he did not want to go to Lisbon. I couldn't believe my ears and asked him why. He was quite honest about it. He said he thought that Inter-Milan would be too strong for us and he did not want to go over there and see us beaten. I accepted that, but just in case he changed his mind I held a ticket for him and booked a seat on a plane. This had been organised for me by a man called John McCabe from Bishopbriggs, later to cross my path in another way when he became head-teacher of my kids' primary school. (Talk about the naivety of children. One day, my oldest son came in and asked me 'Dad, Mr McCabe says I'm a Lisbon Cub. What does that mean?') As the days passed, I worked hard on Dad but he only changed his mind at the last minute. However, I had the ticket and seat all ready so off he went on the great adventure.

Our base was the Palacio Hotel in Estoril, just west of Lisbon, a fairly busy place full of holiday-makers. Our visit was a business one, of course, so we were kept busy with some light training sessions. The night before the game we walked about 200 yards along the promenade, then turned left to head out into the country. A friend of Jock Stein's, called Lennox (I think?), had a house there, where we watched some international match on television. The Boss was worried about the number of fans coming to the hotel and just wanted us to be out of the way for a while. As we came back down the road, by this time in semi-darkness, Neilly Mochan pointed to his right. 'Look, there's the hotel over there. Let's take a short cut down here.' So, on the night before the biggest match of their lives, the entire squad climbed a fence and headed down a hill in the dusk, climbing another fence at the bottom to get into the grounds of the hotel. It was sheer lunacy, but a perfect example of our naïve attitude.

Of the day itself, I have clear memories of some parts, none at all of others. I remember going to Mass in the morning, and the throng of supporters in and around the hotel. I can clearly recall Neilly Mochan coming into my room in the early afternoon, when I was trying to get some rest, and telling me I was a bloody nuisance! 'What have I done now?' I asked. 'We've just signed a deal with Adidas for the match and you are the only one who wears Puma. I've got to take your boots, paint out the white flash with black paint, then put in three white stripes!' As the match went on, I could see the white strips slowly disappearing and the white flash showing through.

The bus trip to the Stadium was another highlight as we seemed to have the only driver in and around the Lisbon area unsure where the National Stadium was. Eventually, we pointed out that all the other buses and cars seemed to be going the opposite direction, so he turned the bus round to head along with them. I think this helped us in the end as there was less time to dawdle in the dressing-room. We had to get changed quickly.

I have dealt with the singing in the tunnel on another page (see Bertie Auld page 350) but must touch on it again as a surreal moment, rather gallus Glaswegians on one side, bronzed, smooth but startled Italians on the other. No sooner had the game started, though, when I was involved in giving away a penalty-kick. Now, let me immediately protest my innocence. I had been assured that my opponent Capellini was all left-foot, so when he ran in on goal from the right-hand side, I assumed that at some point, he would want to pull the ball to his left. I decided that I would block any attempt to do so, but when the challenge came, he went down rather like an ageing actor and I believe the referee was completely conned by it

When I see some of the things that are not given as penalties today, I think I was quite unlucky. A question I am often asked is, 'What does a player think about at a time like that?'. Well, in my case, I can assure you that my thoughts were with my Dad up in his seat watching all that. I had spent time persuading him to come over against his better judgement, and now he had to sit through it all.

Meanwhile, up in the Stand, Dad's reaction was mixed. 'Well, I didn't think it was a penalty to be quite honest, because the Italian player wasn't going towards goal and I think he had over-run the ball. Probably, the referee was as nervous as the players and over-reacted. What worried me more was that that might be the only goal of the whole match and Jim would get the blame for the defeat. In retrospect, it probably helped a lot because the Italians just fell back on defence and Celtic were allowed to take control.'

A signed programme from the 1967 European Cup final.

On the pitch, one or two players were uncomplimentary about my tackle (their names I will ever remember) while others told me to forget it. At half-time, Jock Stein came over with instructions to put the incident behind me and do something to redeem myself. (At full-time, incidentally, he told me what a stupid bloody tackle that had been!) Fortunately, everything turned out fine. This match has been shown on television and discussed so often,

370

Having made the journey from the dressing room on the other side of the stadium by a very circuitous route, Billy McNeill holds up the European Cup.

that there is no reason for me to go into any detail here. Let's just say that everyone played their part, and, from a personal viewpoint, my laying on of the equalising goal probably made up for my indiscretion in the seventh minute.

After the match it was pandemonium – and disappointing! The fans' fervour boiled over at the end and thousands jumped onto the pitch to applaud their heroes. I lost shirt, boots and socks to supporters, eventually reaching the dressing-room, firmly holding on to my shorts and jock strap. Those Celtic fans were always there when needed. They got behind the team whenever they were down and were often regarded as our 'extra man'. Yet, on that day, their actions took a little of the gloss off the proceedings for me. It would have been wonderful for the players to receive their Cup and medals on the pitch and be allowed to take a lap of honour, not just for the fans present in Lisbon but for the many thousands of others watching on television. The presentation of our medals was anti-climactic to say the least. After being kept waiting for a long time by the Italians at the ensuing banquet, an official came up and placed two containers of medals on our table. We more or less helped ourselves to them. It was a rather disappointing end to a wonderful day – and a superb season.

❖

1966–1967 Scottish League Division I								
	P	W	D	L	F	A	Points	Position
Celtic	34	26	6	2	111	33	58	1st

FIXTURES

	H	A		H	A
Aberdeen	0-0	1-1	Hibs	2-0	5-3
Airdrie	3-0	3-0	Kilmarnock	2-0	0-0
Ayr United	5-1	5-0	Motherwell	4-2	2-0
Clyde	5-1	3-0	Partick Thistle	6-2	4-1
Dundee	5-1	2-1	Rangers	2-0	2-2
Dundee Utd	2-3	2-3	St Johnstone	6-1	4-0
Dunfermline	3-2	5-4	St Mirren	1-1	5-0
Falkirk	5-0	3-0	Stirling Albion	7-3	1-1
Hearts	3-0	3-0			

1966–1967 SCOTTISH LEAGUE CUP

Section Games	H	A
Clyde	6-0	3-1
Hearts	3-0	2-0
St Mirren	8-2	1-0

League Cup Position

	P	W	D	L	F	A	Points	Position
Celtic	6	6	0	0	23	3	12	1st

LEAGUE CUP QUARTER- AND SEMI-FINALS

QF	Dunfermline	(H)	6-3		
	Dunfermline	(A)	3-1	Agg	9-4
SF	Airdrie	(Hampden)	2-0		
Final	Rangers	(Hampden)	1-0	94,532	

1966–1967 SCOTTISH CUP

	28/01/67	Arbroath	(H)	4-0	31,000
	18/02/67	Elgin City	(H)	7-0	34,000
QF	11/03/67	Queen's Park	(H)	5-3	34,000
SF	01/04/67	Clyde	(Hampden)	0-0	56,704
Replay	05/04/67	Clyde	(Hampden)	2-0	55,138
Final	29/04/67	Aberdeen	(Hampden)	2-0	126,102

1966–1967 EUROPEAN CUP

	Zurich	(H)	2-0		
	(Switzerland)	(A)	3-0	Agg	5-0
	Nantes	(A)	3-1		
	(France)	(H)	3-1	Agg	6-2
QF	Vojvodina Novisad	(A)	0-1		
	(Yugoslavia)	(H)	2-0	Agg	2-1
SF	Dukla Prague	(H)	3-1		
	(Czechoslovakia)	(A)	0-0	Agg	3-1
Final	Inter Milan		2-1		
	(Italy)				
	Estadio Nacional, Lisbon		55,000		

1966–1967 GLASGOW CUP

	Rangers	(A)	4-0	
	Queen's Park	(H)	4-0	
Final	Partick Thistle	(Celtic Park)	4-0	07/11/66

The European Cup back at Celtic Park. At front: Gemmell, Johnstone, Craig, McNeill, Lennox, Hughes, Auld, Wallace (Reproduced by permission of the Herald and Evening Times Picture Library).

At the end of the match, after the Stadium had emptied, my Dad, my Uncle Philip, and a pal of mine called Pat Roper, now a singer in New York, were reluctant to leave the scene. Dad was a happy man. 'I was delighted that Celtic had won, but I was even more happy that Jim was not going to take the blame for any mishap. He more than redeemed himself with his performance after the penalty and when he laid on the equaliser, I was even more pleased. What a day! I was with Pat Roper and Jim's Uncle Philip, my brother-in-law. He had been to the Olympics in 1936 in Berlin where he saw Jesse Owens win his medals in front of Adolph Hitler and he had gone to London in 1948. Now, he was sitting there in Lisbon, with tears streaming down his face, saying that this was the greatest day of his life.'

The following day, a very happy Celtic party left for the trip back to Glasgow, the huge European Cup Trophy taking pride of place on the plane. At the airport, on our return, we were greeted and congratulated by John Lawrence, the Chairman of Rangers. I never thought he received enough praise for this very magnanimous gesture. Indeed, he was castigated for doing so by a section of the Rangers support, but I thought his actions transcended the bitter rivalry between the clubs.

While the ensuing bus trip through Glasgow was just amazing with cheering crowds everywhere, the reception at Celtic Park exceeded all our expectations. Officially, it was said that about 40,000 or so packed into the

The last picture taken before the big event. This shows the team, in training strips, the day before the final. In retrospect, the tension was showing on more than one face.

The Lisbon Lions with the European Cup. In total, few photographs were taken. In fact, for at least four, if not five of the eleven players, the first time we had an individual photograph taken with a replica of the trophy was in May 1998. Jock Stein's attitude was: 'Now we have won it, let's put it behind us and do it again.' We got close several times, but no other Celtic side has managed to repeat the achievement.

ground that night, but I have since seen photographs of the terracing and suspect that more than that were present.

The players piled onto a lorry and, preceded by pipers, made trip after trip round the track, everyone desperate to show off the European Cup to the fans. We could have gone on all night but eventually, Jock Stein stopped the lorry, we took one final bow and went back into the Pavilion. It was a memory that will live with me for the rest of my life.

Inside, a buffet had been laid on for the team and we tucked in happily never tiring of the constant congratulations from Directors, officials and friends. We described play time and time again as we circulated around the groups, everyone caught up by the euphoria of the occasion.

I met many people that night, but as the evening went on I was attracted more and more to a red-haired student called Elisabeth, whom I eventually asked out to dinner. But that's another story!